Ancient Views on Music and Religion

Books by David Whitwell

The Sousa Oral History Project
The Art of Musical Conducting
The Longy Club: 1900–1917
La Téléphonie and the Universal Musical Language
Extraordinary Women
A Concise History of the Wind Band
Essays on the Modern Wind Band
Essays on Performance Practice
A New History of Wind Music
The College and University Band
The Early Symphonies of Mozart
Music of the French Revolution
Stories from the Podium

On Composers
Wagner on Bands
Berlioz on Bands
Chopin: A Self-Portrait
Liszt: A Self-Portrait
Schumann: A Self-Portrait in His Own Words
Mendelssohn: A Self-Portrait in His Own Words

On Education
Philosophic Foundations of Education
Foundations of Music Education
Music Education of the Future

Aesthetics of Music
Aesthetics of Music in Ancient Civilizations
Aesthetics of Music in the Middle Ages
Aesthetics of Music in the Early Renaissance
Aesthetics of Music in Sixteenth-Century Italy, France and Spain
Aesthetics of Music in Sixteenth-Century Germany, the Low Countries and England
Aesthetics of Baroque Music in Italy, Spain, the German-Speaking Countries and the Low Countries
Aesthetics of Baroque Music in France
Aesthetics of Baroque Music in England

The History and Literature of the Wind Band and Wind Ensemble Series

Volume 1 The Wind Band and Wind Ensemble Before 1500
Volume 2 The Renaissance Wind Band and Wind Ensemble
Volume 3 The Baroque Wind Band and Wind Ensemble
Volume 4 The Wind Band and Wind Ensemble of the Classical Period (1750–1800)
Volume 5 The Nineteenth-Century Wind Band and Wind Ensemble
Volume 6 A Catalog of Multi-Part Repertoire for Wind Instruments or for Undesignated Instrumentation before 1600
Volume 7 Baroque Wind Band and Wind Ensemble Repertoire
Volume 8 Classical Period Wind Band and Wind Ensemble Repertoire
Volume 9 Nineteenth-Century Wind Band and Wind Ensemble Repertoire
Volume 10 A Supplementary Catalog of Wind Band and Wind Ensemble Repertoire
Volume 11 A Catalog of Wind Repertoire before the Twentieth Century for One to Five Players
Volume 12 A Second Supplementary Catalog of Early Wind Band and Wind Ensemble Repertoire
Volume 13 Name Index, Volumes 1–12, The History and Literature of the Wind Band and Wind Ensemble

Ancient Voices

Ancient Views on Music and Religion
Ancient Views on the Natural World
Ancient Views on What Is Music
Contemporary Descriptions of Early Musicians
Early Thoughts on Performance Practice
Early Views on Music and Ethics
Music Performance in Ancient Societies

Renaissance Voices

Essays on Renaissance Philosophies of Music
Renaissance Men on Music

www.whitwellbooks.com

David Whitwell

Ancient Voices
Views on Music by Ancient and
Medieval Writers

Ancient Views on Music and Religion

Edited by Craig Dabelstein

WHITWELL PUBLISHING • AUSTIN, TEXAS, USA

Ancient Voices: Views on Music by Ancient and Medieval Writers
Ancient Views on Music and Religion
Dr. David Whitwell

WHITWELL PUBLISHING
AUSTIN, TX 78701
WWW.WHITWELLPUBLISHING.COM

© 2013 by David Whitwell
All rights reserved. First edition 2013

Composed in Bembo Book.
Published in the United States of America.
All images used in this book are in the public domain except where otherwise noted.

ISBN-13: 978-1-936512-72-0
ISBN-10: 1936512726

Cover design by Daniel Ferla.

Contents

	Acknowledgement	vii
1	Ancient Views on Music and Religion	1
2	Ancient Views on Music and Prophesy	21
3	Ancient Hebrew Views on Music and Religion	29
4	Ancient Views on Music and Religion among the Romans And Early Christians	37
5	Ancient Views on Music in Heaven	59
6	St. Augustine's Views on Music	69
7	Ancient Views on Roman Church Music during the Dark Ages	89
8	Ancient Views on Roman Church Music during the Pre-Renaissance	113
9	St. Thomas Aquinas' Views on Music	131
10	Ancient Views on Roman Church during the 14th Century	139
11	Ancient Views on Roman Church during the 15th Century	153
12	Ancient Views on Music during the 16th Century	163
13	Martin Luther on Music	183
14	Praetorius on 16th-Century Performance Practice	195
15	Ancient Views on Church Music in the Baroque	217
	Bibliography	237
	About the Author	253
	About the Editor	255

Acknowledgments

I am indebted to my friend and colleague, Craig Dabelstein, for his help in preparing this book for publication.

David Whitwell
Austin, Texas

Ancient Views on Music and Religion

O temple, thy skilled master is not present; thy fate who decrees?
The psalmist, who knows the song, is not present; thy fate to the ... drum he chants not!
He that knows how to touch the drum is not present, thy fate he ... sings not!

Sumerian stela, 2,400 BC

THIS ANCIENT SUMERIAN SONG OF LAMENTATION reveals that even in the most ancient extant written accounts by man we already see vocal and instrumental music playing an important role in religious ceremonies. And this passage, written 4,500 years ago, seems to be describing something already long accepted. Indeed, Roger Bacon pointed out that while the ancients knew of the various sciences, they only actually used two: astronomy for the calendar, and music for worship.[1] What made music so indispensable to religious celebrations so long ago?

Part of the power and mystery of music, judging by some early comments, was found in the fact that music is the only art you cannot see. In both the musical and religious performance one can see the performer or priest as well as the impact on the listener or worshiper; but you cannot see the thing itself (music or religion). This similarity must have been part of the reason why music had such a powerful functional role in the celebration of religion by the ancients. Even as late as the third century AD writer, Lactantiuis, we find this same comparison.

> His offering is innocence of soul; His sacrifice praise and a hymn. For if God is not seen, He ought therefore to be worshiped with things which are not seen.[2]

In addition to not being able to see music itself, there was no notation of music which one could see, which left musician and listener with only the ear to experience music. This no doubt helped musician and listener focus on the emotions of the music, a characteristic of music well documented in the oldest extant literature.

Having to associate music with the ear, but cannot see, has led to a long tradition of finding analogy in other things which cannot be seen, such as angels' voices in this seventeenth-century play:

> Here sounds a music whose melodious touch
> Like angels' voices ravishes the sense.[3]

---

[1] *Opus Majus*, 'Causes of Error,' XIV, in *The Opus Majus of Roger Bacon*, trans. Robert Burke (New York: Russell & Russell, 1962).

[2] Lactantius, 'The Divine Institutes,' in *The Works of Lactantius*, trans. William Fletcher (Edinburgh: T. & T. Clark, 1886), I, 420.

[3] Cyril Tourneur (d. 1626), *The Atheist's Tragedy*, V, i.

2 Ancient Views on Music and Religion

All these above mentioned characteristics of music resulted, in performer and listener as well, in the essential goal of concentrating on what is behind the notes. Among fine musicians, this is the goal even today.

The focus on what is behind the notes, and not the notes themselves, was another strong tie between music and the religious experience, for the clear implication is that what is 'behind the notes' is a direct communication of divine origin. It is for this reason that we find so many references in ancient literature to the musician himself (including poets, as poetry was sung) being divine. Homer is quoted as having said, 'God inspired me with melodies.'[4] Indeed, one scholar reminds us that the best musicians in ancient Greece were called *theioi*, 'divine.'[5] Ovid also made such a comment:

> We bards are classed as holy, heaven's care;
> Divinity, they say, flows in our veins.[6]

The poet Tibullus tried to turn this reputation into a more secular advantage:

> But you, my girl, watch out; the gods love poets;
> I warn you, have respect for a sacred bard.[7]

It follows that there are a number of references to poet–musicians addressing a plea to one or another god to communicate the necessary divine inspiration. Ovid, for example, describes a singer begging Jove to 'inspire my song!'[8] Horace addresses a similar plea to the god, Mercury:

> Grant me music, Mercury, as you did when
> Stones moved inot place for Amphion singing;
> Bear my song, O tortoise-shell deftly strung with
> Seven strings sounding.[9]

And, indeed, Ovid reports the gods did supply the needed inspiration.

> Be kind, ye fair, to the poetic choir
> Whom Muses love and deities inspire.[10]

---

4   Quoted in Saint Justin Martyr, *The Monarch or The Rule of God*, trans. Thomas B. Falls (New York: Christian Heritage, Inc.), 455.

5   Apostolos N. Athanassakis, *The Homeric Hymns* (Baltimore: Johns Hopkins University Press, 1976), 474ff.

6   Ovid, *Amores*, III, 9.

7   Tibullus, *Poems*, II, v.

8   Ovid, *Metamorphoses*, X, 143.

9   Horace, *Odes*, I, 12.

10 Ovid, *The Art of Love*, III, 539.

There is even some interesting discussion in the ancient literature which speculates on exactly how the gods transmit this divine communication to the singer. Plato believed there had to be some form of genetic knowledge, evidence for which he saw in otherwise uneducated boys;[11] in the actions of animals, which were clearly not rational beings and as an explanation for dreams, where one acts in a dream in ways he would never act if awake.[12] But such examples, he says, are quite different from the case of the musician. His inspiration comes from somewhere else, from the 'Muse.' To explain how the gods communicate through the poet–singer to the audience, Plato uses an analogy with the magnet through which the listener receives the inspiration directly from the god.

> SOCRATES. The gift which you possess of speaking excellently about Homer is not an art, but, an inspiration; there is a divinity moving you, like that contained in the stone which Euripides calls a magnet, but which is commonly known as the stone of Heraclea. This stone not only attracts iron rings, but also imparts to them a similar power of attracting other rings; and sometimes you may see a number of pieces of iron and rings suspended from one another so as to form quite a long chain: and all of them derive their power of suspension from the original stone. In like manner the Muse first of all inspires men herself; and from these inspired persons a chain of other persons is suspended, who take the inspiration.
>
> ......
>
> Do you know that the spectator is the last of the rings which, as I am saying, receive the power of the original magnet from one another? Yourself, and the actor, are intermediate links, and the poet himself is the first of them.[13]

The early Roman Christian Church reclothed this idea in order to make God the central feature in Art. Thus we read in the ninth-century Irishman, Joannes Scotus Eriugena, that God passes the inspiration to the artist who then expresses it in an art object, which in turn is viewed by the observer. Once again in this case the observer has a direct path to God.

> As the understanding [*intellectus*] of the artist precedes the understanding of the art, and the understanding of the art precedes the understanding of what is in it and made by it, so the understanding of the Father, the Artificer, precedes the understanding of His Art, i.e., His Wisdom, in which He created all things. Next the knowledge of everything made in and by that Art follows the understanding of the Art itself. Whatever true reasoning finds prior in any sense must precede according to natural sequence.[14]

---

[11] *Meno*, 85e.

[12] *Republic*, IX, 571c; also see III, 411e.

[13] *Ion*, 533d, 535e.

[14] Joannes Scotus Eriugena, *Periphyseon on the Division of Nature*, trans. Myra Uhlfelder (Indianapolis: Bobbs-Merrill, 1976), III, 3.

It is in this respect that a number of early writers describe the artist when under this divine inspiration as being in a 'divine frenzy' or 'out of his head,' the point being, we suppose, that the mere mortal cannot contain the power of this direct communication with God.[15] The third-century Church philosopher, Origen, mentions what he calls 'madness' in discussing the nature of the direct communication between God and the artist.

> There are besides ... certain special energies of this world, spiritual powers, which bring about certain effects ... there being, for example, a peculiar energy and power, which is the inspirer of poetry; another, of geometry; and so a separate power, to remind us of each of the arts and professions of this kind. Many Greek writers have been of opinion that the art of poetry cannot exist without madness; whence also it is several times related in their histories, that those whom they call poets were suddenly filled with a kind of spirit of madness ... Now these effects we are to suppose are brought about in the following manner: As holy and immaculate souls, after devoting themselves to God with all affection and purity, and after preserving themselves free from all contagion of evil spirits, and after being purified by lengthened abstinence, and imbued with holy and religious training, assume by this means a portion of divinity, and earn the grace of prophecy, and other divine gifts ... And the result of this is, that they are filled with the working of those spirits to whose service they have subjected themselves.[16]

There were exceptions. In the songs of the twelfth century wandering students for some student–poets the inspiration now was wine. One says he drinks not for thirst, but for better thinking ability.[17] Another is somewhat more specific, contending that the quality of his poetry is dependent on the quality of the wine!

> Special gifts for every man
> Nature will produce,
> I, when I compose my verse,
> Vintage wine must use,
> All the best the cellar's casks
> Hold of these libations.
> Such a wine calls forth from me
> Copious conversations.
>
> My verse has the quality
> Of the wine I sip,
> I can not do much until
> Food has passed my lip,
> What I write when starved and parched
> Is of the lowest class,

---

15 The early Church father, Tertullian (160–225 AD), describes dreams as 'ecstasy,' translating Genesis 2:21 as 'And God sent an ecstasy upon Adam and he slept.' This power we call ecstasy, in which the sensuous soul stands out of itself, in a way which even resembles madness. Tertullian, *De Anima*, trans. Alexander Roberts in *Ante-Nicene Christian Library* (Edinburgh: T. & T. Clark, 1884), XLV.

16 Origen, *De Principiis*, trans. Frederick Crombie, in *The Writings of Origen* (Edinburgh: T. & T. Clark, 1871), III, iii.

17 *Bacchic Frenzy*, in John Symonds, *Wine Women and Song; Mediaeval Latin Students' Songs* (New York: Cooper Square Publishers, 1966), 173.

> When I'm tight, with verse I make
> Ovid I surpass.
>
> As a poet n'er can I
> Be appreciated
> Till my stomach has been well
> Filled with food and sated,
> When god Bacchus gains my brain's
> Lofty citadel
> Phoebus rushes in to voice
> Many a miracle.[18]

Another wandering poet of the late Middle Ages found the source of his inspiration in a place more familiar to artists of our own time. The Archpoet of Cologne frankly promises us,

> And poems more sweet than tongue can tell
> I'll write you—if you pay me well.[19]

But, as we said, these were exceptions. For a very long time the special ties between music and religious ceremonies, the association of the musician in communicating the divine inspiration, instead of popular entertainment, and the serious purpose on the part of so many poet–musicians resulted in a long period in which the art of music stood at the highest levels of society.

There is a surprising amount of description which has come down to us regarding the use of music in ancient societies. Following are some examples which we found quite interesting.

Based on the surviving evidence, Sumeria (3,000 BC) is one of the oldest civilizations in which we can document a sophisticated tradition of music. Since they believed music was of divine origin, they created temples for a number of gods, all of whom they believed had to be entertained, to keep them in good spirits, by singing and playing of instruments.[20] Among these gods was one called *Enlil*, the father of humanity, who governed with a musical instrument called *al*. Sundrey, following a study of music and religion in this society, arrived at the following description:

> The earliest orders of the sacred service were simple. They consisted of sacrifices, in which supplications to the gods were supported by musical ceremonies. The songs were accompanied by flutes, aulos, and lyres. Certain ceremonies required accompaniment of sacred drums. Later, this simple religious service developed into a complicated pattern of liturgical actions. It contained four or more

---

[18] In *Estuans intrinsecus*, in *Vagabond Verse*, trans. Edwin H. Zeydel (Detroit: Wayne State University Press, 1966), 67.

[19] In *Fama tuba dante sonum*, in George Whicher, *The Goliard Poets* (George Whicher, 1949), 123.

[20] Alfred Sendrey, in *Music in the Social and Religious Life of Antiquity* (Rutherford: Fairleigh Dickinson University Press, 1974), 31. He points out that among the most ancient civilizations, only China and the Hebrews did not ascribe music to divine origin. This book is the finest book on the subject.

> hymns, performed with choir singing and instrumental accompaniment. In coeval records we find a minute description of the liturgical ceremony, as it was performed during the full bloom of Sumerian culture.
>
> First of all, a chosen priest applied the magic formula necessary for the purification and consecration of the participants. Then the psalmists had to sustain the opening supplication with their singing; a professional musician (*nar*) furnished the required instrumental accompaniment. The principal psalmist (a sort of 'high priest') chanted a hymn to the gods Ea, Shamash and Marduk, to the accompaniment of the aulos. Sacred services ended with the singing of an epic poem, which must have been well known to everyone, since the entire congregation took part in it.[21]

There is an account which lists the names of 164 liturgical singers for a single year. Another document lists 64 female temple slaves for the temple at Lagash.[22] The titles of some of these musicians indicate one was in charge of supervising the choir and another responsible for the rehearsal of the choir. Farmer mentions a similar document from Akkad, also 3,000 BC, in which some temple musicians are described as those who 'know the melodies' and are 'masters of the musical movements.'[23] The former no doubt expressing the fact that there was as yet no notated form of music and the 'musical movements' some ancient root of what would become the movements of the Greek choral singers and in time, perhaps, some movements of the modern conductor (or visa versa?).

In Babylonia (2,000–562 BC), named for the former Sumerian capital, Babylon, we still find the same god mentioned above, *Ea*, who is now called the god of the mysteries and arts and was especially associated with the flutist–psalmist. Toward the end of this Babylonian period is where we find Nebuchadnezzar and his court music ensemble, which is described in detail in the Book of Daniel, 3:5 and 15, of the Old Testament.[24]

From such ancient practices comes the Egyptian combination of the mystery of music and the worship of gods. First there was the god, *Hesu*, who created music. The goddess, *Hathor*, was both the goddess of love and of music. There is a painting depicting the worship of this goddess in a later Graeco-Roman temple at Medamund, north of Thebes. We see a group of female musicians, with harp, drum, and lute, beneath a hieroglyph description:

> The members of the choir take up their instruments and play them. The songstresses in full number adore the Golden Goddess and make music to the Golden Goddess: they never cease their chanting.

---

[21] Ibid., 33.

[22] Ibid., 32.

[23] Henry G. Farmer, 'The Music of Ancient Mesopotamia,' in *The New Oxford History of Music* (London: Oxford University Press, 1966), 235.

[24] This account demonstrates the problem one encounters in attempting to consider the older parts of the Old Testament as literal history. The Book of Daniel was written four hundred years after the events it describes and so is prone to all the mistakes and exaggerations of oral tradition. Furthermore, the actual instruments mentioned in Daniel, karna, mashrokita, kathros, sambyke, pesanterin, and sumponyah, are expressed in several languages, including Greek, and at least two of them have no agreed upon modern meaning. In view of these difficulties, the modern translator has tended to simply make up names of instruments which might be familiar to his readers. Thus the *King James Version* gives us a typical Renaissance band, consisting of cornett, flute, harp, sackbut, psaltery, and dulcimer! The *Revised Standard Version* (1952) invents an improbable ensemble of horn, pipe, lyre, trigon, harp, and bagpipe.

The text of the hymn is written behind the lutanist and a singer. We take notice especially of the aim of this music, 'nourishment for the heart.'

> Come, O Golden Goddess, the singers chant
> for it is nourishment for the heart to dance the *iba*,
> to shine over the feast at the hour of retiring
> and to enjoy dance at night ...
>
> The royal children satisfy you with what you love
> and the officials give offerings to you.
> The lector priest exalts you singing a hymn,
> and the wise men read the rituals.[25]

In yet another painting celebrating Hathor, no fewer than twenty-nine female musicians are pictured with percussion instruments.

Another goddess, *Merit*, was considered to be the personification of music. And then there was the strange dwarf god *Bes*, usually associated with childbirth but who, nevertheless, is usually pictured playing a variety of musical instruments.

In the oldest tomb paintings of the Old Kingdom (2686–2181 BC), we can see musicians included in scenes associated with the worship of the gods. During this period we can see a testimonial to the importance of individual musicians simply from the fact that they were allowed to have their tombs in the vicinity of the royal ones. Also, the hieroglyphic texts which accompany the tomb paintings speak of the importance of these musicians in their very titles: 'royal music director,' 'leader of ritual music,' and 'inspector of vocal music.'

In later periods we also learn the names of some of the musicians are also identified as having positions related to the worship of these gods. One of these, Amenemhab, who appears several times in the Eighteenth Dynasty is described in a stela as having 'followed the king's footsteps in foreign lands.' He is identified as holding a very high office, 'overseer of the singers of the North and South,' and he describes his role as a performer in the temple:

> I purify my mouth. I adore the gods. I exalt Horus who is in the sky. I adore him. The Ennead listens, the inhabitants of the Underworld rejoice. They appear at my voice.

In a tomb painting he is called, 'chief of singers of Amun,' and appears singing to the sun god the following song.

> Praise to you millions and millions of times!
> I have come to you, adoring your beauty.
> Your mother Nut [the sky] embraces you.
> You are joyful as you traverse the sky and the earth.
> May the gods of the Underworld [as the sun passes underneath the earth] worship you and sing your
> praise when you hear my words which worship you every day,

---

[25] Lise Manniche, *Music and Musicians in Ancient Egypt* (London: British Museum Press, 1991), 61.

> So that you endow me with a burial in peace after enduring old age and my *ba* being among my ancestors, following the king.[26]

Reading such texts, we are not surprised that in Egypt music went under the name, 'hy,' which also meant 'joy' or 'gladness.' We might add that a hieroglyph picturing a simple lute was the symbol for 'good.'

When female musicians appear in the New Kingdom (1567–1085 BC) some of them also have apparent positions in the temple with titles such as 'Chief of the Singers.' The tomb paintings tells us of music in the temple by both solo and choral singers, dances accompanied by instruments, and processions around the altar. Athenaeus,[27] speaking of the period of Ptolemy (285–246 BC), quotes a reference to a 'choral band of 600 men,' with 300 harp players participating in the music for a festival.

During the most recent period, that is toward the end of ancient Egyptian era, we continue to find the association of music with the religious festivals but the festivals now seem to have fallen to very low and crude forms. They are much more similar to the Roman cult festivals than they are to those of their own forbearers. The early historian, Herodotus, for example, provides two such descriptions.

> When they travel to Bubastis, this is what they do. They sail thither, men and women together, and a great number of each in each boat. Some of the women have rattles and rattle them, others play the aulos through the entire trip, and the remainder of the women and men sing and clap their hands. As they travel on toward Bubastis and come near some other city, they edge the boat near the bank, and some of the women do as I have described. But others of them scream obscenities in derision of the women who live in that city, and others of them set to dancing, and others still, standing up, throw their clothes open to show their nakedness. This they do at every city along the riverbank. When they come to Bubastis, they celebrate the festival with great sacrifices, and more wine is drunk at that single festival than in all the rest of the year besides. There they throng together, man and woman (but no children), up to the number of seven hundred thousand, as the natives say.[28]
>
> ......
>
> On the eve of the festival of Dionysus, each one of them cuts the throat of his pig in front of the doorway and then gives it, to take away, to the swineherd who has sold it to him. For the rest of the festival in honor of Dionysus, except for the dance choruses, the Egyptians celebrate it almost in everything like the Greeks. But instead of phalluses they have another invention, which are eighteen-inch-high images, controlled by strings, which the women carry round the villages; these images have a penis that nods and in size is not much less than all the rest of the body. Ahead there goes an aulos player, and the women follow, singing in honor of Dionysus.[29]

---

[26] Quoted in Ibid., 59.

[27] Athenaeus, in *Deipnosophistae*, V, 201.

[28] *The History of Herodotus*, trans. David Grene (Chicago: University of Chicago Press, 1987), 157.

[29] Ibid., 152.

It seems clear that much of the culture of early Greece was based on earlier Egyptian models. Plato confirms that the traditions of religious celebration in Greece originally came from Egypt,[30] but in his view the real origin was older, with the gods themselves, who gave them an ideal purpose.

> The Gods, pitying the toils which our race is born to undergo, have appointed holy festivals, wherein men alternate rest with labor; and have given them the Muses and Apollo, the leader of the Muses, and Dionysus, to be companions in their revels, that these may be saved from degeneration, and men partake in spiritual nourishment in company with the Gods.[31]

This last thought, that 'men partake in spiritual nourishment in company with the Gods,' we find particularly interesting, for in our view the idea of learning from and communicating with great minds (great composers) is one of the most important values in the study of music. Strabo, the first century AD Greek geographer, made a similar observation:

> Music, which includes dancing as well as rhythm and melody, at the same time, by the delight it affords and by its artistic beauty brings us in touch with the divine.[32]

Plato, in the passage quoted above, singles out Apollo, who was one of the most discussed gods in ancient Greece. Interestingly enough, in view of the discoveries about music by the medical profession during our generation, Apollo was both the god of music and medicine.

Tibullus, a Roman poet, attributes to Apollo not only the usual association with music, but also emphasizes his powers of prophesy—a power Apollo has but not the muses or Bacchus.

> His long robes hid the hallowed form from sight,
>   and the hem seemed to ripple round his feet.
> At his left side a lyre hung, worked with skill
>   that made it gleam with gold and tortoise-shell,
>   and while he sang, he plucked it with a quill.
> But O the warning sung at that song's end!
> 'Gods love all poets,' he said, 'and such men find
>   Bacchus, Apollo, and each Muse a friend.'
> Yet those wise sisters and the god of wine—
>   they lack the power to see the future plain.
> Jove's gift of foresight is not theirs but mine.
> To me, inevitable fate is clear.[33]

Tibullus mentions prophesy in association with Apollo in another poem, although here he goes under the name Phoebus.[34]

---

[30] Plato, *Laws*, 799.

[31] Ibid., 653d.

[32] *The Geography of Strabo*, trans. H.L. Jones (Cambridge: Harvard University Press, 1960), X.3.9.

[33] Tibullus, *Poems*, III, iv.

[34] Phoebus and Apollo are one and the same.

> Your blessing, Phoebus; a new priest enters your temple.
> Be gracious, greet his coming with voice and lyre,
> and when your fingers set the strings to sounding,
> let it be loyalty that they inspire.
> Come, be among us while we heap the altars,
> your brow encircled with a wreath of bay—
> comb your long hair, put on your treasured raiment,
> O come, god bright and beautiful as the day!
> Be as you were when you sang of Jove's triumph
> with Saturn finally driven from the throne.
> Prophet, the priest who serves you learns the meaning
> of the notes of that bard to which the future is known ...[35]

Some of the older Egyptian gods are still found in Greece, especially Hermes, who is now called Mercury. Ovid, in his *Metamorphoses*, has the god, Mercury, tell the story of the invention of the panpipe, the instrument always associated with the Greek god, Pan, and known to the ancient Greeks as the *Syrinx*.

> And Mercury came flying
> On winged sandals, wearing the magic helmet,
> Bearing the sleep-producing wand, and lighted
> On earth, and put aside the wings and helmet
> Keeping the wand. With this he plays the shepherd
> Across the pathless countryside, a driver
> Of goats, collected somewhere, and he goes
> Playing a little tune on a pipe of reeds,
> And this new sound is wonderful to Argus.
> 'Whoever you are, come here and sit beside me,'
> He says, 'This rock is in the shade; the grass
> Is nowhere any better.' And Mercury joins him,
> Whiling the time away with conversation
> And soothing little melodies, and Argus
> Has a hard fight with drowsiness; his eyes,
> Some of them, close, but some of them stay open.
> To keep himself awake by listening,
> He asks about the pipe of reeds, how was it
> This new invention came about?
>   The god
> Began the story: 'On the mountain slopes
> Of cool Arcadia, a woodland nymph
> Once lived, with many suitors, and her name
> Was Syrinx. More than once the satyrs chased her,
> And so did other gods of field or woodland,
> But always she escaped them, virgin always
> As she aspired to be, one like Diana,

---

35 Tibullus, *Poems*, II, v. Propertius, in Poem II, 31, tells of visiting a temple built to honor Apollo by Caesar Augustus. He describes seeing a marble statue of Apollo, posed as singing with his lyre.

> Like her in dress and calling, though her bow
> Was made of horn, not gold, but even so,
> She might, sometimes, be taken for the goddess.
> Pan, with a wreath of pine around his temples,
> Once saw her coming back from Mount Lycaeus,
> And said ...' and Mercury broke off the story
> And then went on to tell what Pan had told her,
> How she said *No*, and fled, through pathless places,
> Until she came to Ladon's river, flowing
> Peaceful along the sandy banks, whose water
> Halted her flight, and she implored her sisters
> To change her form, and so, when Pan had caught her
> And thought he held a nymph, it was only reeds
> That yielded in his arms, and while he sighed,
> The soft air stirring in the reeds made also
> The echo of a sigh. Touched by this marvel,
> Charmed by the sweetness of the tone, he murmured
> *This much I have!* and took the reeds, and bound them
> With wax, a tall and shorter one together,
> And called them Syrinx, still.[36]

The early Greek poet, Bion, wrote that the god Athena invented the flute, by which we assume he meant the transverse flute. For Horace, one of the muses, Calliope, also played the flute.

> Calliope, descend from the skies, O queen,
> And sing your flute a lingering melody,
> Or lift your lovely voice alone, or
> Sing to the lyre or the harp of Phoebus.
>
> Hark! Is illusion sweetly deceiving me?
> I seem to hear those strains, as I seem myself
> A stroller in the scared groves where
> Waters and breezes are softly stirring.[37]

And, of course, for modern day musicians the best-known of the Greek gods was Orpheus, whose 'music calms the savage breast.' There is no better account of the story of Orpheus than that found in Ovid.

> While with such songs the bard of Thrace drew the trees, held beasts enthralled and constrained stones to follow him, behold, the crazed women of the Cicones, with skins flung over their breasts, saw Orpheus from a hill top, fitting songs to the music of his lyre. Then one of these, her tresses streaming in the gentle breeze, cried out: 'See, see the man who scorns us!' and hurled her spear straight at the tuneful mouth of Apollo's bard; but this, wreathed in leaves, marked without harm-

---

36 Ovid, *Metamorphoses*, I, 671ff.

37 Horace, *Epistles*, III, 4.

ing him. Another threw a stone, which, even as it flew through the air, was overcome by the sweet sound of voice and lyre, and fell at his feet as if it would ask forgiveness for its mad attempt. But still the assault waxed reckless: their passion knew no bounds; mad fury reigned. And all their weapons would have been harmless under the spell of song; but the huge noise of the Berecyntian flutes, mixed with discordant horns, the drums, and the breast-beatings and howlings of the Bacchanals, drowned the lyre's sound; and then at last the stone's were reddened with the blood of the bard whose voice they could not hear. First away went the multitudinous birds still spellbound by the singer's voice, with the snakes and the train of beasts, the glory of Orpheus' audience, harried by the Maenads; then these turned bloody hands against Orpheus and flocked around like birds when in the day they see the bird of night wandering in the daylight; and as when in the amphitheater in the early morning of the spectacle the doomed stag in the arena is the prey of dogs. They rushed upon the bard and hurled at him their wands wreathed with green vines, not made for such use as this. Some threw clods, some branches torn from trees, and some threw stones. And, that real weapons might not be wanting to their madness, it chanced that oxen, toiling beneath the yoke, were plowing up the soil; and not far from these, stout peasants were digging the hard earth and sweating at their work. When these beheld the advancing horde, they fled away and left behind the implements of their toil. Scattered through the deserted fields lay hoes, long mattocks and heavy grubbing tools. These the savage women caught up and, first tearing in pieces the oxen who threatened them with their horns, they rushed back to slay the bard; and, as he stretched out his suppliant hands, uttering words then, but never before, unheeded, and moving them not a whit by his voice, the impious women struck him down. And (oh, the pity of it!) through those lips, to which rocks listened, and to which the hearts of savage beasts responded, the soul, breathed out, went faring forth in air.

The mourning birds wept for thee, Orpheus, the throng of beasts, the flinty rocks, and the trees which had so often gathered to thy songs; yes, the trees shed their leaves as if so tearing their hair in grief for thee. They say that the rivers also were swollen with their own tears, and the naiads and dryads alike mourned with disheveled hair and with dark bordered garments. The poet's limbs lay scattered all around; but his head and lyre, O Hebrus, thou didst receive, and (a marvel!) while they floated in mid-stream the lyre gave forth some mournful notes, mournfully the lifeless tongue murmured, mournfully the banks replied. And now, borne onward to the sea, they left their native stream and gained the shore of Lesbos near the city of Methymna. Here, as the head lay exposed upon a foreign beach, a savage serpent attacked it and its streaming locks still dripping with the spray. But Phoebus at last appeared, drove off the snake just in the act to bite, and hardened and froze to stone, just as they were, the serpent's widespread, yawning jaws.

The poet's shade fled beneath the earth, and recognized all the places he had seen before; and, seeking through the blessed fields, found Eurydice and caught her in his eager arms.[38]

Whereas our knowledge of the use of music in the cult-religious celebrations of Egypt is limited to what we can see and read in the pictures on the walls of the tombs, in the case of Greece we have actual contemporary literature, especially from the fifth century BC on. There are some very vivid descriptions of cult-religious celebrations in the plays of Euripides. Probably we must allow for theatrical embellishment, but the elements here, the participation of women, of dancing and the role of music, are found in many early writers. One example, from *Helen*, is set in the time of the gods.

---

[38] Ovid, *Metamorphoses*, XI, 1ff.

Loudly rattled the Bacchic castanets in shrill accord, what time those maidens, swift as whirlwinds, sped forth with the goddess on her chariot yoked to wild creatures, in quest of her that was ravished from the circling choir of virgins …

But when for gods and tribes of men alike she made an end to festal cheer, Zeus spoke out, seeking to soothe the mother's moody soul, 'Ye stately Graces, go banish from Demeter's angry heart the grief her wanderings bring upon her for her child, and go, ye Muses too, with tuneful choir.' Thereon did Cypris, fairest of the blessed gods, first catch up the crashing cymbals, native to that land, and the drum with tight-stretched skin, and then Demeter smiled, and in her hand did take the deep-toned flute, well pleased with its loud note …

Oh! mighty is the virtue in a dress of dappled fawn-skin, in ivy green that twineth round a sacred thyrsus, in whirling tambourines struck as they revolve in the air, in tresses wildly streaming for the revelry.[39]

And in *The Bacchae* we are given a somewhat more secular description set in the present time.

> Uplift the dark divine wand,
> The oak-wand and the pine-wand,
> And don thy fawn-skin, fringed in purity
> With fleecy white,[40] like ours …
>
> For thee of old some crested Corybant
> First woke in Cretan air
> The wild orb of our orgies,
> Our Timbrel; and thy gorges
> Rang with this strain; and blended Phrygian song
> And sweet keen pipes were there.
>
> But the Timbrel, the Timbrel was another's,
> And away to Mother Rhea it must wend;
> And to our holy singing from the Mother's
> The mad Satyrs carried it, to blend
> In the dancing and the cheer
> Of our third and perfect Year;
> And it serves Dionysus in the end! …
>
> Hither, O fragrant of Tmolus the Golden,
> Come with the voice of timbrel and drum;
> Let the cry of your joyance uplift and embolden
> The God of the joy-cry; O Bacchanals, come!
> With pealing of pipes and with Phrygian clamor,
> On where the vision of holiness thrills,
> And the music climbs and the maddening glamour …[41]

---

[39] 1302ff.

[40] This reminds one of the Mormons, who change into white clothes for some ceremonies.

[41] 109ff.

The mention of Dionysus here may surprise the reader as we usually identify the celebration of this god with ancient Rome. But it may have had remote roots in Greece as well, as suggested by Euripides:

> For I sing this day to Dionysus
> The song that is appointed from of old.[42]

Just before these lines there is a stage note which describes a Greek stage chorus.

> There comes stealing in from the left a band of fifteen Eastern Women, the light of the sunrise streaming upon their long white robes and ivy-bound hair. They wear fawn-skins over the robes, and carry some of them timbrels, some pipes and other instruments. Many bear the thyrsus, or sacred Wand, made of reed ringed with ivy.

There is an interesting reference to Dionysus by Plato in his discussion of Absolute Beauty. He seems to suggest that the music lovers miss the beauty of these festivals as they are only interested in the music.

> Musical amateurs, too, are a folk strangely out of place among philosophers, for they are the last persons in the world who would come to anything like a philosophical discussion if they could help it; while they run about at the Dionysian festivals as if they had let out their ears for the season to hear every chorus, and miss no performance either in town or country. Now are we to maintain that all these and any who have similar tastes, as well as the professors of quite minor arts, are philosophers? ...[43]

One passage in Euripides mentions regular cult celebrations which were held at night.

> For thy worship is aye performed with many a sacrifice, and never art thou forgotten as each month draweth to its close, when young voices sing and dancers' music is heard abroad, while on our wind-swept hill goes up the cry of joy to the beat of the maidens' feet by night.[44]

The dancing was not always sedate, and hence a reflection of the character of the accompanying music, as we see in another comment by Euripides, 'lift high the nimble foot.'[45] In yet another place, Euripides also mentions that dancing was also done around the altar.[46]

Thucydides, the fifth-century historian of the Peloponnesian Wars reminds us that the Delian games also included religious rites of purification and he quotes some lines from Homer which speak of dancing and singing in these festivals.

---

[42] *The Bacchae*, 70. Arrian, the second century AD historian in *The Campaigns of Alexander* (New York: Penguin, 1978), 130, writes of the Athenians worship of Dionysus and the older Egyptian tradition.

[43] *Republic*, 476c.

[44] *The Heracleidae*, 777ff.

[45] *Electra*, 868.

[46] *Iphigenia in Aulis*, 675.

> Phoebus, where'er thou strayest, far or near,
> Delos was still of all thy haunts most dear.
> Thither the robed Ionians take their way
> With wife and child to keep thy holiday,
> Invoke thy favor on each manly game,
> And dance and sing in honor of thy name.[47]

Herodotus also mentions in passing the hymns sung by the women of Delos.[48]

The sense we have here of the power of the music is emphasized in a Chorus from *The Eumenides* by Aeschylus, where music is described as completely possessing the participant.

> But our sacrifice to bind,
> Lo, the music that we wind,
> How it dazeth and amazeth
> And the will it maketh blind,
> As it moves without a lyre
> To the throb of my desire;
> 'Tis a chain about the brain,
> 'Tis a wasting of mankind.[49]

In the next generation, in the writings of Plato, we discover much detail about these cult-religious ceremonies. In his *Laws*[50] we learn the festivals were based on the calendar, with twelve festivals for twelve gods, that they included sacrifices, that some were for women only and that there were music contests attached to them.

Here we also read that there had been a general decay in the traditions of musical practice which had been taken from Egypt. Accordingly, Plato proposes a number of laws to correct the violations he finds. His extensive discussion of the practice of music in the cult-religious festivals is quite interesting.

> AN ATHENIAN STRANGER. No one in singing or dancing shall offend against public and consecrated models, and the general fashion among the youth, any more then he would offend against any other law. And he who observes this law shall be blameless; but he who is disobedient shall be punished by the guardians of the laws, and by the priests and priestesses. Suppose that we imagine this to be our law.
> CLEINIAS. Very good.
> AN ATHENIAN STRANGER. Can anyone who makes such laws escape ridicule? Let us see. I think that our only safety will be in first framing certain models for composers. One of these modes shall be as follows:—If a sacrifice has been offered, and the victims burnt according to law,—if, I say, anyone who may be a son or brother, standing by another at the altar and over the victims, horribly blasphemes, will not his words inspire despondency and evil omens and foreboding in the mind of his father and of his other kinsmen?
> CLEINIAS. Of course.

---

47 Thucydides, *The Peloponnesian War* (New York: Modern Library, 1951), 201.
48 Herodotus, *The Histories*, IV, 34.
49 Gilbert Murray, *The Complete Plays of Aeschylus* (London: George Allen, 1952), lines 326.
50 Lines 828ff.

> AN ATHENIAN STRANGER. And this is just what takes place in almost all our cities. A magistrate offers a public sacrifice, and there come in not one but many choruses, who take up a position a little way from the altar, and from time to time pour forth all sorts of horrible blasphemies on the sacred rites, exciting the souls of the audience with words and rhythms and melodies most sorrowful to hear; and he who at the moment when the city has offered sacrifice makes the citizens weep most, carries away the palm of victory. Now, ought we not to forbid such strains as these? And if ever our citizens must hear such lamentations, then on some unblest and inauspicious day let there be choruses of foreign and hired musicians with barbarous Carian chants. That is the sort of thing which will be appropriate if we have such strains at all; and let the apparel of the singers of the funeral dirge be, not circlets and ornaments of gold, but the reverse.
>
> Enough of all this. I will simply ask once more whether we shall lay down as one of our principles of song—
>
> CLEINIAS. What?
>
> AN ATHENIAN STRANGER. That we should avoid every word of evil omen; let that kind of song which is of good omen be heard everywhere and always in our state. I need hardly ask again, but shall assume that you agree with me …
>
> And our third law will be to the effect that our poets, understanding prayers to be requests which we make to the Gods, will take special heed that they do not by mistake ask for evil instead of good. To make such a prayer would surely be too ridiculous …
>
> Shall we make a law that the poet shall compose nothing contrary to the ideas of the lawful, or just, or beautiful, or good, which are allowed in the state? …
>
> It will be proper to have hymns and praises of the Gods, intermingled with prayers; and after the Gods prayers and praises should be offered in like manner to demigods and heroes, suitable to their several characters.
>
> CLEINIAS. Certainly.
>
> AN ATHENIAN STRANGER. In the next place there will be no objection to a law, that citizens who are departed and have done good and energetic deeds, either with their souls or with their bodies, and have been obedient to the laws, should receive eulogies; this will be very fitting.
>
> CLEINIAS. Quite true.
>
> AN ATHENIAN STRANGER. But to honor with hymns and panegyrics those who are still alive is not safe; a man should run his course, and make a fair ending, and then we will praise him; and let praise be given equally to women as well as men who have been distinguished in virtue.[51]

In order to make certain these laws of composition are observed, Plato recommends the necessity of censors.

> Nor shall the composer be permitted to communicate his compositions to any private individuals, until he shall have shown them to the appointed judges and the guardians of the law, and they are satisfied with them.[52]
>
> ……
>
> O ye sons and scions of the softer Muses, first of all show your songs to the magistrates, and let them compare them with our own, and if they are the same or better we will give you a chorus; but if not, my friends, we cannot.[53]

---

[51] *Laws*, 800.

[52] Ibid., 801d.

[53] Ibid., 817d.

After the discussion of the laws which the composers must not break, Plato now offers his recommendations regarding the character of music which might be acceptable.

> There are many ancient musical compositions and dances which are excellent, and from these it is fair to select what is proper and suitable to the newly-founded city; and they shall choose judges of not less than fifty years of age, who shall make the selection, and any of the old poems which they deem sufficient they shall include; any that are deficient or altogether unsuitable, they shall either utterly throw aside, or examine and amend, taking into their counsel poets and musicians, and making use of their poetical genius; but explaining to them the wishes of the legislator in order that they may regulate dancing, music and all choral strains, according to the mind of the judges; and not allowing them to indulge, except in some few matters, their individual pleasures and fancies. Now the irregular strain of music is always made ten thousand times better by attaining to law and order, and rejecting the honeyed Muse—not however that we mean wholly to exclude pleasure, which is characteristic of all music. And if a man be brought up from childhood to the age of discretion and maturity in the use of the orderly and severe music, when he hears the opposite he detests it, and calls it illiberal; but if trained in the sweet and vulgar music, he deems the severer kind cold and displeasing. So that while he who hears them gains no more pleasure from the one than from the other, the one has the advantage of making those who are trained in it better men, whereas the other makes them worse ...
>
> We must distinguish and determine on some general principle what songs are suitable to women, and what to men, and must assign to them their proper melodies and rhythms. It is shocking for a whole harmony to be inharmonical, or for a rhythm to be unrhythmical, and this will happen when the melody is inappropriate to them. And therefore the legislator must assign to these also their forms. Now both sexes have melodies and rhythms which of necessity belong to them; and those of women are clearly enough indicated by their natural difference. The grand, and that which tends to courage, may be fairly called manly; but that which inclines to moderation and temperance, may be declared both in law and in ordinary speech to be the more womanly quality.[54]

Regarding the musical contests associated with the religious festivals, Plato seemed to have little interest. Here he only concludes that they are not difficult to organize and do neither much good nor much harm to the public.

> As to rhapsodists[55] and the like, and the contests of choruses which are to perform at feasts, all this shall be arranged when the months and days and years have been appointed for gods and demigods, whether every third year, or again every fifth year, or in whatever way or manner the gods may put into men's minds the distribution and order of them. At the same time, we may expect that the musical contests will be celebrated in their turn by the command of the judges and the director of education and the guardians of the law meeting together for this purpose, and themselves becoming legislators of the times and nature and conditions of the choral contests and of dancing in general. What they ought severally to be in language and song, and in the admixture of harmony with rhythm and the dance, has been often declared by the original legislator; and his successors ought to

---

[54] Ibid., 802.

[55] An extremely interesting performer who presented, in public, works of literature in a kind of sung-speech. They alone kept alive the works of Homer for perhaps two centuries until there was developed a written form of the Greek language in which they could be written down. They sang the *Iliad* and the *Odyssey* from memory!

> follow him, making the games and sacrifices duly to correspond at fitting times, and appointing public festivals. It is not difficult to determine how these and the like matters may have a regular order; nor, again, will the alteration of them do any great good or harm to the state.[56]

The decay in the ancient traditions which so worried Plato seemed to have continued until the end of the ancient Greek era. A brief description from the last chapter of this practice, the so-called Roman Period of Ancient Greece, is found in Athenaeus.

> But the men of today, who pretend to sacrifice to the gods and call together their friends and intimates, curse their children, quarrel with their wives, drive their slaves to tears, threaten the crowd ...[57]

Our principal source of information on the ancient Hebrews is the Old Testament. We have mentioned above one problem with the Old Testament, the case of words whose meaning is no longer known, an example of which we have mentioned above with respect to the ensemble of Nebuchadnezzar (fn. 24, p. 6). There is also the problem of centuries of oral tradition before the stories were written down, which led to problems in exaggeration. An example of this can be seen in Josephus's account of Solomon's dedication of the Temple. Josephus assures us that the ceremony included a performance by 200,000 trumpets![58] This would surely have exceeded all the trumpets of antiquity.

The Old Testament must also be understood as a redaction of much older materials by a variety of anonymous authors. As a result, here and there one suddenly finds a passage which seems very much 'out of place' with regard to the character of the rest of the Old Testament. Such an example is the strange cult-religious celebration found in Psalm 81, a ceremony which one might expect to find in ancient Roman literature but not in the Old Testament.

> Raise a song, sound the timbrel,
> the sweet lyre with the harp.
> Blow the trumpet at the new moon,
> at the full moon, on our feast day.

A similar passage, for example, is found in Tacitus and it describes a military ritual associated with a lunar eclipse.

---

56 Plato, *Laws*, 835.

57 Athenaeus, *Deipnosophistae*, VIII, 364.

58 Josephus, *Jewish Antiquities*, VIII, 95.

> Suddenly in a clear sky the moon's radiance seemed to die away ... And so they raised a din with brazen instruments and the combined notes of trumpets and horns.[59]

In general, however, the Old Testament is filled with detail about the use of music in religious celebrations. It tells us of the actual organization of the music of the Temple and several times mentions surprisingly large numbers.[60] Indeed, in one place we are told that 'those who offer praises to the Lord with instruments' numbered 4,000![61] We are given actual names for players of trumpet, harps, lyres, and cymbals,[62] the fact that they must be 30 years of age to fully participate in the service,[63] and even such details as the name of the wood the string instruments were constructed of.[64] And Numbers 10 is an extraordinary essay on the trumpet, its manufacture and its use.

Missing here, of course, are all the old gods of Mesopotamia and Egypt. But what about the Hebrew God? Was he a musician also, like some of those pagan gods of Egypt and Greece? Zechariah 9:14 tells us God was a trumpet player, but Psalm 105 describes him as a choral conductor.[65] Plutarch, in his 'Concerning Music,' reports that 'some have thought that the God himself played upon the aulos.'

---

[59] Tacitus, *Annals*, I, 28. References to this particular cult ceremony can be found in two works of Restoration England: Swift's poem, 'A Simile on our Want of Silver,' and in the; play, *Oedipus* (II, i) by Nathaniel Lee,

> A vast Eclipse darkens the laboring Planet:
> Sound there, sound all our instruments of war;
> Clarions, and Trumpets, Silver, Brass, and Iron,
> And beat a thousand drums to help her labor.

Tacitus, in *The History*, V, 5, mentions that some thought the religious music of the Jews was based on secular cult traditions:

> From the fact, however, that their priests used to chant to the music of auloi and cymbals, and to wear garlands of ivy, and that a golden vine was found in the temple, some have thought that they worshiped Father Liber ... though their institutions do not by any means harmonize with the theory; for Liber established a festive and cheerful worship, while the Jewish religion is tasteless and mean.

[60] 1 Chronicles 15:16ff; 25:5ff; Ezra 2:40, 65; and Nehemiah 7:43. 1 Ezra 7:22 says the Temple musicians paid no taxes!

[61] 1 Chronicles 23:5.

[62] 1 Chronicles 15:16ff; 16:5ff, 42; Nehemiah 12:34ff.

[63] 1 Chronicles 23:3. Sendrey, *Music in the Social and Religious Life of Antiquity*, 104ff discusses the relationship of children to this musical environment, including a quotation from the Mishnah which suggests children could stand with their elders and sing, but not play instruments.

[64] Almug wood is specified in 1 Kings 10:12 and Algum wood in 2 Chronicles 9:11 [*Revised Standard Version*, 1952]. Can we find a hint of the sound of the lyre in two passages which read, 'my soul moans like a lyre' [Isaiah 17:11 and Jeremiah 48:36]?

[65] The early Church father, Clement of Alexandria, also referred to 'the Choir-master, the Lord,' in *The Miscellanies*, trans. William Wilson (Edinburgh: T & T Clark, 1884), VI, xi.

Ancient Views on Music and Prophesy

… for the inspired prophet of the violet-eyed Muses is ready to sing …

THE ABOVE FRAGMENT by the sixth century BC poet, Bacchylides, is the only example we know from the repertoire of the ancient Greek lyric poets which suggests the use of music for prophesy. But that may only be because so little of the poetry of the Greek lyric poets is extant, for we find more examples among the Roman lyric poets whose work was based on the Greeks. And as for the civilization before, upon which the Greek civilization was based, we know of the significance of prophesy among the Egyptians from the story of Joseph.[1]

Both the literature of the ancient Greeks and the Romans contain references to the special relationship with the gods which inspired their poetry. One can imagine that it is then only a very short step to bring the message of the gods forward in the form of prophesy.

The Roman lyric poets were singers.[2] Probably this relationship of poetry and music had little changed from the time of the Greek lyric poets, as seems documented by Horace (66–8 BC).

> I am in love, as Anacreon, poet of Teos, is said to
> Have been with his Bathyllus once,
> He who lamented his love to his lyre in the simplest of meters
> And unelaborated forms.[3]

And like the Greeks before them,[4] the Roman lyric poets gave credit to the gods for their inspiration. This example by Horace is especially germane as Phoebus was synonymous with Apollo, who was, among other things, the god of music and prophesy.

> Phoebus has inspired me, and Phoebus gave me
> Technical skill in song and the name of poet.[5]

---

[1] Genesis 40:14.

[2] Documented as singers by their own words were Ovid (*Letters in Exile*, 1, 1), Propertius (*Poems*, 1, 3) and Virgil (*Georgics*, IV, 564).

[3] Horace, *Epodes*, 14.

[4] An interesting example from the Greek lyric poets is by Pindar (sixth century BC),

> Sing, O Muse, sing high and clear
> O polytonal many-voiced Muse,
> Make a new song for girls to sing.
> About the towered temple of Therapne.

[5] *Odes*, IV, 6.

Similarly, to Mercury, Horace addresses a plea for musical inspiration,

> Grant me music, Mercury, as you did when
> Stones moved into place for Amphion singing;
> Bear my song, O tortoise-shell deftly strung with
> Seven strings sounding.[6]

and in another place to the Muse, Calliope ('beautiful voiced').

> Calliope, descend from the skies, O queen,
> And sing your flute a lingering melody,
> Or lift your lovely voice alone, or
> Sing to the lyre or the harp of Phoebus.[7]

Strabo, the first century AD Greek geographer, also reminds his listeners of this connection with the divine.

> Music, which includes dancing as well as rhythm and melody, at the same time, by the delight it affords and by its artistic beauty brings us in touch with the divine.[8]

Ovid, in his plea to the gods for inspiration, includes a rare early description of a professional singer tuning up, with a specific indication of some kind of harmony.

> And when he had tried the chords by touching them with his thumb, and his ears told him that the notes were in harmony although they were of different pitch, he raised his voice in this song: 'From Jove, O Muse, my mother—for all things yield to the sway of Jove—inspire my song!'[9]

At the same time, these Roman lyric poets make a point to remind their listeners that they themselves are favored by the gods. They are taking advantage of the ancient assumption of a connection between music and the divine, a topic we have mentioned in the previous chapter. Thus, a poem of Tibullus warns the ladies to have respect for the poets who are favored by the gods.

> But you, my girl, watch out; the gods love poets;
> I warn you, have respect for a sacred bard.[10]

Ovid, as well, mentions that the poets are favored by the gods.

> We bards are classed as holy, heaven's care;
> Divinity, they say, flows in our veins.[11]

---

[6] Horace, *Odes*, III, 11.

[7] Ibid.

[8] *The Geography of Strabo*, trans. H. L. Jones (Cambridge: Harvard University Press, 1960), X.3.9.

[9] Ovid, *Metamorphoses*, X, 143.

[10] Tibullus, *Poems*, II, v. In the Poem III, iv, Apollo says, 'Gods love all poets.'

[11] Ovid, *Amores*, III, 9.

As we have suggested, one would expect to find more than just occasional references to music and prophesy among the ancient Egyptians and Greeks. For whatever reason, it is only among the Roman lyric poets of the first century BC that we begin to find this topic as a familiar theme. There are two poems by Tibullus which speak of music and prophesy with respect to Apollo, a true Greek god adopted by the Romans. It is interesting to us, in view of the wide-spread modern clinical research as it relates to music, that Apollo was also the god of medicine, as well as music and prophesy.

> His long robes hid the hallowed form from sight,
>   and the hem seemed to ripple round his feet.
> At his left side a lyre hung, worked with skill
>   that made it gleam with gold and tortoise-shell,
>   and while he sang, he plucked it with a quill.
> But O the warning sung at that song's end!
> 'Gods love all poets,' he said, 'and such men find
>   Bacchus, Apollo, and each Muse a friend.'
> Yet those wise sisters and the god of wine—
>   they lack the power to see the future plain.
> Jove's gift of foresight is not theirs but mine.
>   To me, inevitable fate is clear.[12]

Tibullus mentions prophesy in association with Apollo in another poem, although here he goes under his alternate name, Phoebus.

> Your blessing, Phoebus; a new priest enters your temple.
>   Be gracious, greet his coming with voice and lyre,
>   and when your fingers set the strings to sounding,
>   let it be loyalty that they inspire.
> Come, be among us while we heap the altars,
>   your brow encircled with a wreath of bay—
>   comb your long hair, put on your treasured raiment,
>   O come, god bright and beautiful as the day!
> Be as you were when you sang of Jove's triumph
>   with Saturn finally driven from the throne.
> Prophet, the priest who serves you learns the meaning
>   of the notes of that bard to which the future is known.
> You guide the lots as they fall; you show the augur
>   what marks of the god to read in the entrails;
> with you as master, the Sibyl's six-metered strophes
>   have given us counsel whose wisdom never fails.[13]

---

[12] Tibullus, *Poems*, III, iv.

[13] Tibullus, *Poems*, II, v. Propertius, in Poem II, 31, tells of visiting a temple built to honor Apollo by Caesar Augustus. He describes seeing a marble statue of Apollo, depicted as singing with his lyre.

Another poem from the same century, Poem 64 by Catullus (84–54 BC), is the earliest extant example we know in which women are also associated with the use of music for prophesy. Here we are told that elder ladies ('their snow white heads') sang a song of prophesy while working spindles and making thread from wool.

> Then as they worked, their song
> Of fate arose in voices, clear and strong,
> And all of time will never prove it wrong.

We find from this century additional examples by Cicero (106–43 BC), who mentions the 'sing-song ritual of augury'[14] and Virgil (70–19 BC), in whom we read,

> The prophets sang that she would have a glorious
> Fame and fate, but bring great war upon
> Her people.[15]

The second century Church father, St. Justin Martyr, wrote of the divine connection enjoyed by poets when he recalls a comment by a poet–musician in Homer, 'God inspired me with melodies.'[16] In the third century Church father, Origen, we find a particularly interesting passage as it gives a kind of curriculum for reaching the status of prophecy.

> There are besides ... certain special energies of this world, spiritual powers, which bring about certain effects ... there being, for example, a peculiar energy and power, which is the inspirer of poetry; another, of geometry; and so a separate power, to remind us of each of the arts and professions of this kind. Many Greek writers have been of opinion that the art of poetry cannot exist without madness; whence also it is several times related in their histories, that those whom they call poets were suddenly filled with a kind of spirit of madness ... Now these effects we are to suppose are brought about in the following manner: As holy and immaculate souls, after devoting themselves to God with all affection and purity, and after preserving themselves free from all contagion of evil spirits, and after being purified by lengthened abstinence, and imbued with holy and religious training, assume by this means a portion of divinity, and earn the grace of prophesy, and other divine gifts ... And the result of this is, that they are filled with the working of those spirits to whose service they have subjected themselves.[17]

The most familiar early accounts of the association of music and prophesy are those found in the Old Testament. Perhaps the best known among these is found in 2 Kings 3:15 when the prophet Elisha says,

> Now bring me a minstrel, And when the minstrel played, the power of the Lord came upon him.[18]

---

14 Cicero, *De Divinatione*, I, xlvii.

15 Virgil, *Aeneid*, trans. L. R. Lind (Bloomington: Indiana University Press, 1958), VII, 83.

16 Saint Justin Martyr, *The Monarchy or The Rule of God*, trans. Thomas B. Falls (New York: Christian Heritage, Inc.), 455.

17 Origen, *De Principiis*, trans. Frederick Crombie, in *The Writings of Origen* (Edinburgh: T. & T. Clark, 1871), III, iii.

18 All Old Testament references are from the *Revised Standard Edition*. In another well-known instance when a musician is called for, in 1 Samuel 16:23, the musician turns out to be David and the purpose is to drive out an evil spirit. This is more like music therapy than music prophesy.

Whereupon, Elisha makes his prophesies. Interestingly, in 2 Kings 9:11 Elisha is called a madman. But this may only be the use of 'mad' as in 'frenzy,' a common description of poets in the full absorption of their work. Another reference to the 'madman' is found in Jeremiah 29:26.

> The Lord has made you priest instead of Jehoiada the priest, to have charge in the house of the Lord over every madman who prophesies, to put him in the stocks and collar.

Another well-known reference to music and prophesy is found in 1 Samuel 10:5, where an entire group of prophet–musicians is mentioned.

> … you will meet a band of prophets coming down from the high place with harp, tambourine, flute [aulos] and lyre before them, prophesing.

Yet another ensemble of prophet–musicians are listed in 1 Chronicles 25:1.

> David and the chiefs of the service also set apart for the service certain of the sons of Asaph and of Heman, and of Jeduthun, who should prophesy with lyres, with harps, and with cymbals.

This passage then lists the names of four men 'who prophesied under the direction of the king' and six men who prophesied 'under the direction of their father, Jeduthun, who prophesied with the lyre.' Another fourteen men and three women, children of Heman, who were 'under the direction of their father in the music in the house of the Lord with cymbals, harps, and lyres.' Aside from the large number of participants here, perhaps the most interesting information is that these people were designated 'for the service,' implying that prophesy with music was part of the actual church service.

An Old Testament reference to women, with respect to prophesy and music, is found in Exodus 15. Here, after Moses leads his people in a song of thanksgiving for having crossed the Red Sea,

> Then Miriam, the prophetess, the sister of Aaron, took a timbrel in her hand; and all the women went out after her with timbrels and dancing.

In terms of music the New Testament stands in strong contrast to the rich descriptions of the use of music in the Old Testament. In the New Testament there is not a single reference to instrumental music in the service. Angels play trumpet, but there is not a single reference to a living man playing one. We have speculated that much of this prejudice toward instrumental music must lie in the fact that the Christian church was for some time an outlaw organization which had to hold its services in secrecy and therefore could not afford to have loud instruments of music which might give away their location.

As instrumental music is omitted in references to the religious service in the New Testament, so is music omitted from references to prophesy. In Acts 21:9 there are 'four unmarried daughters, who prophesied,' daughters to Philip, but they do not do so with music. When, in 1 Corinthians 14:26, the church service is defined as a hymn, a lesson, a revelation and an interpretation,[19] we take the latter to be prophesy, but again without mention of music. In Luke 1:67 Zechariah was filled with the Holy Spirit and prophesied, but not with music. Ephesians 5:18ff and Colossians 3:16 speak of three kinds of church music: psalms, hymns and spiritual songs. But there is no reference to prophesy with respect to any of them.

After the Middle Ages there are few references to music and prophesy. Roger Bacon (b. ca. 1214) cites the use of music for prophesy in the Old Testament citing the example of Elijah who requested that a string instrument be brought to him,

> in order that his soul, stirred by the delight of physical harmony, might be caught up to contemplate divine things.[20]

We know of only one specific reference to music and prophesy during the Renaissance and it is in a play by Lope de Vega (1562–1635). In his *The Knight from Olmedo* a musician is heard, and we first note here the reference to the state of the listener with respect to the affect of music:

> There is someone singing. Who can it be? It sounds far off. A peasant going early to the fields and singing as he goes. It is nearer now. That is no rustic accent—he has an instrument, and the song is sweet and sonorous. How melancholy music sounds when one's own thoughts are sad!

The musician is identified as a peasant and he sings a song of warning, prophetizing the death of Alonso. When the singer is questioned further about the meaning of his song, he replies,

> I cannot tell you more about the song or its history than that I learned it from one Fabia. If it concerns you, I can do no more for you; you have heard me sing it. Go back. Do not pass this stream.[21]

During the seventeenth century, the only references to music and prophesy are again heard on the stage. The deep spiritual roots of Spanish society are evidenced in two instances in these plays where the purpose of music is for prophesy. In Calderon's *The Surgeon of Honor* (Act III) there is a group of musicians who sing songs of prophesy, and in Molina's *The Trickster of Seville* (III) songs of prophesy are sung by off-stage singers from the spirit world who accompany the 'Stone Guest.'[22]

There is also a reference to the use of music for prophesy found in one of the few Racine plays which mentions music. *Athaliah*, not only has a singing chorus, but the appearance of unidentified 'music' on stage to enhance the religious atmosphere. Referring to this scene in the Preface, Racine reflects on the use of music for prophesy in the Old Testament.

---

[19] Older English dictionaries give 'interpretation' as one of the meanings of 'prophesy.' Also see 1 Corinthians 14:6, 'I bring you some revelation or knowledge or prophesy or teaching.'

[20] 'Moral Philosophy,' *Opus Majus*, in *The Opus Majus of Roger Bacon*, trans. Robert Burke (New York: Russell & Russell, 1962), the concluding lines of Part Three.

[21] *The Knight from Olmedo*, in Jill Booty, in *Lope de Vega, Five Plays* (New York: Hill and Wang, 1961), 199, 221ff.

[22] This play is one of the sources for Mozart's *Don Giovanni*.

> This scene, which is a kind of episode, brings in music very naturally, by the custom which several prophets had of entering into their holy trances to the sound of instruments: witness that troop of prophets who came before Saul with the harps and lyres which were borne before them …

During the eighteenth century there appears a curious tract, 'The Age of Reason,' by the famous Thomas Paine. He has noticed that nowhere in the bible does there appear the word, 'poet,' or 'poetry.'[23] From this he makes a considerable leap by contending that all the references to prophesy are really just references to poetry. This, in turn, leads him to such extraordinary observations as the following:

> We are told of Saul being among the prophets, and also that he prophesied; but we are not told what they prophesied, nor what he prophesied. The case is, there was nothing to tell; for these prophets were a company of musicians and poets, and Saul joined in the concert, and this was called prophesying.

So what are we to make of three thousand years of reference to the use of music and prophesy? It seems reasonable to suppose that the ancients assumed relationship between music and religion must have led to this idea, but, on the other hand, perhaps it has something to do with the nature of music itself. We are thinking here of the fact that the experience of music lies in a different part of the brain than that which is concerned with rational thought. Something like this, we believe, was on the mind of the great nineteenth century philosopher, Herbert Spencer, when he observed,

> And thus we may in some measure understand how it happens that music not only so strongly excites our more familiar feelings, but also produces feelings we never had before—arouses dormant sentiments of which we had not conceived the possibility and do not know the meaning; or as Richter says—tells us of things we have not seen and shall not see.[24]

After centuries of little comment on music and prophesy, during the late twentieth century there has been a revival of sorts in this practice. A flutist named Bob Quaderer has written the following:

> When I play—sometimes it seems it is more than just myself. I feel that my playing somehow reflects the beauty of heaven. I preach with Celtic Flute and prophesy with my music. I play at conferences, coffee houses, churches and bookstores. I describe myself as a Celtic 'New Age' artist.

Another new exponent is Durga Ma. We found the following at www.drterrypreston.com.

> While searching for her spiritual master, an endeavor that took her nearly three years, Durga Ma encountered a prophesy involving her music. The wise old woman who spoke this prophesy had no prior knowledge of Durga Ma or of her previous musical experience.

---

[23] Part First, Section 5.

[24] Herbert Spencer, *Essays on Education and Kindred Subjects* (London: J. M. Dent & Sons, 1966), 323.

> The prophesy said that she would find her path soon, and that after several years of spiritual practice and meditation, she would return to her music and create a 'new music' that had the power to move the listener into deep meditative states …
>
> In the process of answering a request to tell the story of her spiritual journey, Durga Ma recalled this prophesy and suddenly realized that she was in the middle of its fulfillment. The prophesy was coming true. When asked 'How do you create this music?' she answers, 'I don't. It's not created by me, but through me.'

Another who makes an identical comment is Pastor Loren Sandford, who describes his experience as follows:[25]

> When I'm leading worship and I sense a song of the Lord coming, I take a little time to listen. The sense is often something like 'hearing' a song in my heart that I can't quite actually hear, but can only feel. It can also come as a sense of pressure welling up from inside of me that isn't really me. I know then that it's the Holy Spirit.
>
> Most often I'll allow the instruments to run through a series of chords derived from the song we've been doing just prior. That gives us a track to run on while we wait on the Lord so that we lose neither our own concentration, nor that of the congregation. I might sing awhile in tongues as I listen. I listen until I receive a sense of what the Spirit of Jesus is saying, and until I pick up at least a fragment of melody that can form a basis for what comes after. I also listen for the beginning of a word. 'Lord, what is the content of this I'm sensing?' When I get at least the beginning of that inspiration, I open my mouth and begin. After that, it just flows.

For Pastor Sandford there is also a political goal here; he complains of the 'closed system of Christian marketing that so effectively locks out what is different, innovative and revolutionary.' 'Locked out' apparently includes his brand of 'prophetic music,' which he clearly believes might be the means for religion to recapture its broad base.

> Prophetic music wins souls because [it] works as well with the unbeliever as with the believer. If Bob Dylan could inspire a generation in the world with songs people called prophetic, how much more should we be able to inspire the unbelieving by means of the Holy Spirit? We'll never be able to do it with songs filled with Christian cliché and insider language that the outside world cannot understand. If we want to reach the world again, we're going to have to learn to be human again, to sing comprehendible lyrics with a level and form of passion the world can feel with us.

We can never know exactly what those musician–prophets of the ancient world were doing, but some spark of their fire appears to have leaped twenty centuries to ignite a 'New Age.'

---

[25] www.newsongfellowship.org

Ancient Hebrew Views on Music and Religion

ONE OF OUR PRIMARY SOURCE OF KNOWLEDGE of the early Hebrew people is, of course, one of man's great works of literature, the Old Testament. But the value of the Old Testament as an historical document is limited by the fact that it is evidently a compilation of earlier works written centuries later than the events described, not to mention considerable linguistic problems.[1]

As history, the Old Testament is a particular problem with respect to the years before the Egyptian period of these peoples. As Sendrey points out, 'The Bible condenses 800 years of the early history of the Jews in a few short sentences.'[2] Sendrey also makes the interesting observation that much of Genesis may have originally existed as sung epic poetry, perhaps in the tradition of the epics of Homer, before it was set down in the form of prose.[3] In this regard we might add that literature which is passed down over long periods of time in an oral form is also subject to the natural tendency to improve the story by exaggeration. A typical example of this can be seen in Josephus's account of Solomon's dedication of the first Temple. Josephus assures us that the ceremony included a performance by 200,000 trumpets![4] This would surely have exceeded all the trumpets of antiquity.

While we know these people were originally wandering desert tribes, we are told very little of their culture during these years, and certainly very few hints of their musical practice. Since water is of paramount importance to desert life, perhaps we can assume the 'Well Song' in Numbers at least reflects on those nomadic years.

> Spring up, O well!—Sing to it!—
> the well which the princes dug,
> which the nobles of the people delved,
> with the scepter and with their staves.[5]

Perhaps another reflection of the earliest times is found in Psalm 81, which sings of a truly pagan festival—something uniquely 'out of place' in the Old Testament.

> Raise a song, sound the timbrel,
> the sweet lyre with the harp.

---

[1] For example the various superscriptions before the Psalms. See Alfred Sendrey, *Music in the Social and Religious Life of Antiquity* (Rutherford: Fairleigh Dickinson University Press, 1974), 108–137, for a wonderful summary of these terms in their original language, together with their attempted solution by a wide selection of scholars. We also recommend Sendrey's book as the best general discussion of music and instruments found in the Old Testament.

[2] Ibid., 77. As Sendrey also points out, the 'invention' of musical instruments given in Genesis 4:21 refers to instruments which are actually already of a rather advanced stage of development.

[3] Ibid., 138.

[4] Josephus, *Jewish Antiquities*, VIII, 95.

[5] Numbers 21:17. All references are taken from the *Revised Standard Version* (New York: Nelson, 1952).

> Blow the trumpet at the new moon,
> at the full moon, on our feast day.

While the years the Hebrews spent in Egypt form a critical role in the drama of the Old Testament story, few actual details of this 430-year period are supplied. It is clear that most of this time the Hebrews lived freely in Egypt and were 'captives' in only the final eighty years of this period. During the first 350 years they were apparently free enough to conduct their own 'border wars,'[6] independent of the Egyptians, enjoyed the economic freedom to maintain their own large herds of cattle,[7] and enjoyed sufficient cultural respect that one of them actually married the daughter of a Pharaoh.[8] We can assume therefore that during this long period they were free to absorb much from the older Egyptian culture, including musical practices. In the case of Moses, we are told he 'was instructed in all the wisdom of the Egyptians.'[9]

In a famous instance of the absorption of Egyptian culture which Moses distinctly did not approve of, the singing and dancing around the statue of the golden calf, the singing and general celebration was so loud that Joshua, hearing them from the distance, thought a war had broken out in the camp![10]

The Old Testament also fails to give us much information about the period of captivity in Babylonia, after the destruction of Solomon's Temple in 537 BC. Again, it appears they were not 'captives' in the modern sense of the word, for when the 42,000 of them were allowed to return they brought back with them 7,337 slaves of their own, in addition to 245 male and female [slave] singers![11] One of the apocryphal books also mentions that they returned with all their musical instruments.[12]

It is evident, in any case, that the Hebrews preserved their musical heritage during this period, as we can read in some of the most beautiful lines of the Old Testament.

> By the waters of Babylon,
> there we sat down and wept,
> when we remembered Zion.
> On the willows there
> we hung up our lyres.
> For there our captors
> required of us songs …[13]

---

6 1 Chronicles 7:21.

7 Exodus 9:6, 7; 10:9.

8 1 Chronicles 4:18.

9 Acts 7:22.

10 Exodus 32:17.

11 Nehemiah 7:67 and 1 Esdras 5:42. Ezra 2:65 gives 200 singers.

12 1 Esdras 5:2. The apocryphal books appear in the early Septuagint and Vulgate versions of the Old Testament, but are considered spurious by the modern Jewish and Protestant faiths.

13 Psalm 137.

The Old Testament does not discuss at length festivals comparable to the ones Plato discussed in ancient Greece. There are two references to festivals with singing, but whether they are true religious festivals or more of a cult-type worship of Spring one cannot say on the basis of the information given.

> He will exult over you with loud singing as on a day of festival.[14]

> The flowers appear on the earth,
> the time of singing has come ...[15]

We can assume that the early Hebrews maintained schools for the training of those who performed the music in the Temple, as did other peoples of this time, including the Egyptians.[16] Further, the constant references in the Old Testament to the importance of the performance of musical instruments in the Temple by the Temple officials presupposes some ongoing discipline of instruction. Sendrey believes there must have been organized 'schools' of music, carrying on musical traditions many of which the Hebrews may have first learned in Egypt.

> One cannot help assuming the existence of one or several such 'schools' when one finds in the biblical text a sudden and unexplained upsurge of large choirs and orchestras, consisting of thoroughly organized and trained musical groups, which would be virtually inconceivable without lengthy, methodical preparation. Similar schools of music are known to have existed among other nations of Antiquity, far back in times of Sumeria.[17]

This seems especially evident in passages such as the following, from Psalm 33, where we read of *skillful* performance on a rather sophisticated instrument, not to mention the suggestion of ability in composition.

> Praise the Lord with the lyre,
>   make melody to him with the harp of ten strings!
> Sing to him a new song,
>   play skillfully on the strings, with loud shouts.

The Old Testament itself does not discuss the actual educational process, but does seem to suggest the heads of the major families were in charge of at least the administrative aspects. In such a reference to the family of Heman we also encounter the word 'skillful' once again.

---

[14] Zephaniah 3:18

[15] Song of Solomon 2:12.

[16] Carl Engel, *The Music of the Most Ancient Nations* (London: Reeves, 1909), 323, finds Old Testament references to music schools at Bethel, Naioth, Jericho, Gilgal, and Jerusalem.

[17] Sendrey, *Music in the Social and Religious Life of Antiquity*, 94–95 and 86. Sendrey speculates on the nature of this music education on pp. 95–97.

> God had given Heman fourteen sons and three daughters. They were all under the direction of their father in the music in the house of the Lord with cymbals, harps, and lyres ... The number of them who were trained in singing to the Lord, all who were skillful, was two hundred and eighty-eight.[18]

A similar passage[19] mentions, 'Chenaniah, leader of the Levites in music, should direct the music, for he understood it.' An apocryphal book says specifically that these leaders instructed the people in both music and writing.

> Leaders of the people by their counsels, and by their knowledge of learning meet for the people, wise and eloquent in their instructions:
> Such as found out musical tunes, and recited verses in writing.[20]

In only one place in the modern versions of the Old Testament is there a clear reference to teaching music to people other than the professional musicians of the Temple. Moses is told, 'write this song, and teach it to the people of Israel.' And indeed we are told he did this in the same day![21] A similar command in Jeremiah,[22] 'teach to your daughters a lament, and each to her neighbor a dirge,' is probably meant rhetorically.

There are also two references in the Psalms which make us wonder of perhaps the early Hebrews went beyond merely contending, as did the Greeks, that music forms character in the young, to actually teaching specific moral principles, and even laws, through music.

> I will sing of loyalty and of justice.[23]
> ...
> ... thy statutes have been my songs.[24]

The Old Testament is rich in its detail of the music of the Temple. The apocryphal book of Ecclesiasticus gives credit to David for the formal establishment of this tradition.

> In all his works he praised the Holy One most high with words of glory; with his whole heart he sang songs, and loved him that made him.
> He set singers also before the altar, that by their voices they might make sweet melody, and daily sing praises in their songs.[25]

---

[18] 1 Chronicles 25:5ff.
[19] 1 Chronicles 15:16ff.
[20] Ecclesiasticus 44:4ff.
[21] Deuteronomy 31:19, 22.
[22] Jeremiah 9:20.
[23] Psalm 101.
[24] Psalm 119.
[25] Ecclesiasticus 47:8ff.

Regarding the actual organization of the music of the Temple, the Old Testament several times mentions surprisingly large numbers.[26] Indeed, in one place we are told that 'those who offer praises to the Lord with instruments' numbered four thousand![27] We are given actual names for players of trumpet, harps, lyres, and cymbals,[28] the fact that they must be thirty years of age to fully participate in the service,[29] and even such details as the name of the wood the string instruments were constructed of.[30]

One would assume some rotation of these forces took place, but we have no specific information regarding this. Indeed, there is only an occasional reference, such as the two priests who were 'to blow continually before the ark of the covenant,'[31] to any specific role performed by these musicians.

The general role of these musicians is clear, however, and that was to lead in the praise of the Lord. This is nowhere more evident than in Psalm 150:

> Praise him with the [shofar] sound;
> Praise him with lute and harp!
> Praise him with strings and pipe!
> Praise him with sounding cymbals;
> Praise him with loud clashing cymbals!

That these large forces sometimes performed together is evident in an extraordinary description of praise associated with thanksgiving.

> ... and all the Levitical singers, Asaph, Heman, and Jeduthun, their sons and kinsmen, arrayed in fine linen, with cymbals, harps, and lyres ... with a hundred and twenty priests who were trumpeters; and it was the duty of the trumpeters and singers to make themselves heard in unison in praise and thanksgiving ... and when the song was raised, with trumpets and cymbals and other musical instruments, in praise to the Lord ...[32]

By 'unison' here we believe is meant rather 'together,' for it is unlikely the great numbers of singers and instruments were always heard in unison. This supposition seems confirmed by the reference to a 'great variety *of sounds*' in the following description of the Temple music:

---

[26] 1 Chronicles 15:16ff; 25:5ff; Ezra 2:40, 65; and Nehemiah 7:43. 1 Esdras 7:22 says the Temple musicians paid no taxes!

[27] 1 Chronicles 23:5.

[28] 1 Chronicles 15:16ff; 16:5ff, 42; Nehemiah 12:34ff.

[29] 1 Chronicles 23:3. Sendrey, *Music in the Social and Religious Life of Antiquity*, 104ff discusses the relationship of children to this musical environment, including a quotation from the Mishnah which suggests children could stand with their elders and sing, but not play instruments.

[30] Almug wood is specified in 1 Kings 10:12 and Algum wood in 2 Chronicles 9:11. Can we find a hint of the sound of the lyre in two passages which read, 'my soul moans like a lyre' [Isaiah 17:11 and Jeremiah 48:36]?

[31] 1 Chronicles 16:5ff.

[32] 2 Chronicles 5:12ff. Other references to songs of thanksgiving are found in 1 Chronicles 16:7, Nehemiah 12:27ff ('with singing, with cymbals, harps and lyres'), Psalm 26:7, Psalm 95, Psalm 107, Isaiah 51:3ff, which gives the complete text of a thanksgiving song, 1 Maccabees 13:51 and 1 Esdras 5:59ff.

> The singers also sang praises with their voices, with great variety of sounds was there made sweet melody.[33]

Another passage[34] speaks of cymbals, harps, lyres, trumpets, and singing altogether in the service. Perhaps these large forces are also intended by several references to 'Make a joyful *noise.*'[35]

But what are we to make of the form of praise represented by the following?

> And David and all the house of Israel were making merry before the Lord with all their might, with songs and lyres and harps and tambourines and castanets and cymbals.[36]

We assume 'making merry ... with all their might' must have included dancing, which probably would not have been unusual even in the Temple at this time. On the other hand, there are certainly references to praising the Lord outside the Temple. A notable example is the song sung by Moses as the waters came together killing all the Egyptians.

> I will sing to the Lord, for he has triumphed gloriously;
> the horse and his rider he has thrown into the sea.[37]

The richest body of songs of praise are, of course, found in the Book of Psalms. While one hundred and fifty-one[38] have come down to us, it is evident that this is but a very small portion of what must have been a great literature unto itself. In the case of King Solomon, for example, who is represented by no more than two psalms in the Old Testament, we are told elsewhere that he alone composed a thousand and five psalms.[39]

Another specific kind of music mentioned in the Old Testament in regard to the practice of religion is processional music. Once again, with regard to the ark of the covenant, we read of a procession 'to the sound of the horn, trumpets, and cymbals, and made loud music on harps and lyres.'[40] Psalm 68 even gives us the order of the procession: singers in front, then 'maidens playing timbrels,' and finally the instrumentalists. These processions may have also been rather joyous affairs, for once we read of David 'dancing' to the sound of the [ram's] horn.[41]

---

33 Ecclesiasticus 50:18.

34 2 Chronicles 29:25ff.

35 Psalm 95 and Psalm 100.

36 2 Samuel 6:5. An almost identical passage is found in 1 Chronicles 13:8, which adds the trumpet.

37 Exodus 15.

38 All modern scholars consider the Book of Habakkuk to be a 'misplaced' Psalm.

39 1 Kings 4:32. We refer the reader once again to Sendrey's outstanding discussion, *Music in the Social and Religious Life of Antiquity*, 108–137, of the superscripts which contain information relative to the singing of these psalms, as well as the term Selah which appears throughout them.

40 1 Chronicles 15:28.

41 2 Samuel 6:13.

There was also music of the bridal processions.[42] In a description of one of these we read,

> The bridegroom came forth, and his friends and brethren, to meet them with drums, and instruments of music ...

only to be slaughtered by Jonathan.

> Thus was the marriage turned into mourning, and the noise of their melody into lamentation.[43]

There were also funeral processions, the latter no doubt implied in various references to the singing of laments and dirges.[44] One such passage suggests that there were also professionals in 'wailing,' for we read this was left to 'those who are skilled in lamentation.'[45]

Certainly the most unusual musical practice in the service of their religion is the Old Testament's mention of the Hebrew's use of music for prophesy. Twice we read of the request for a musician for this purpose. Saul said, 'seek out a man who is skillful in playing the lyre,' in this case it turns out to be David, who 'took the lyre and played it with his hand.'[46] And again, Jehoshaphat, King of Israel, says,

> Now bring me a minstrel. And when the minstrel played, the power of the Lord came upon him.[47]

In a few instances we are told the names of those who specialize in this art. For example in one place we are told that it is the sons of Asaph, Heman and Jeduthun, 'who should prophesy with lyres, with harps, and with cymbals.'[48] It may seem odd to read of cymbals associated with prophesy, but then Miriam, the sister of Aaron is identified as 'the prophetess,' as well as a percussionist.[49]

A very extensive discussion can be found in the Old Testament regarding the use of the trumpet by the ancient Hebrews, although these accounts are not directly for religious functions. Numbers 10:1ff even contains information on the making of trumpets. First of all, we see here the silver trumpet, not the ram's horn instrument. Although the dating of all the material in the Old Testament is problematic, one can generally assume that the silver trumpets were carried away from Egypt, for these would be impossible to make in the desert. Over time, of course, these instruments would become worn out and the ram's horn became their surrogate.

---

[42] Jeremiah 7: 34, in 'the streets of Jerusalem.'

[43] 1 Maccabees 9:39ff.

[44] 2 Chronicles 35:25 and Amos 8:3 and 10.

[45] Amos 5:16.

[46] 1 Samuel 16:16. In 1 Samuel 18:10 we are told David practiced everyday on his lyre. In Amos 6:5 we are told he also invented musical instruments.

[47] 2 Kings 3:15.

[48] 1 Chronicles 25.

[49] Exodus 15:20.

With the trumpet signals being so influential as to cause great masses of people to move, it is easy to understand why we are told here that only the high priests can play them.[50] And what a variety of signals we have here, with even the implication of two-part signals, for two trumpets playing in unison would be indistinguishable from one trumpet heard from a distance.

These instruments must have produced enough sound to be heard for a considerable distance. In one place we read of a very impressive progression of trumpet volume, 'a long blast,' followed by 'a very loud blast,' and then 'the sound of the trumpet grew louder and louder.'[51] Perhaps an additional clue to the potential volume of sound capable of being produced by these early trumpets can be found in several symbolic references to the instrument. When, for example, all the scattered people will be called back from the various nations, how is this to be done?—'In that day a great trumpet will be blown.'[52] Or again, 'Cry aloud, spare not, lift up your voice like a trumpet.'[53]

The best known references to trumpet signals in the Old Testament are those used in military circumstances, among which are two familiar stories, the blowing down the walls of Jericho[54] and the story of Gideon's famous surprise attack when, at night, he surrounded the enemy and gave them the impression that a much greater army was accompanying him. As it was, he had three hundred trumpet players.[55]

Perhaps we should mention in passing that one finds in the Old Testament a number of examples of the use of music common to later medieval civic life, in the civic watchman, occupational music and even music played to accompany civic punishment.

> And every stroke of the staff of punishment which the Lord lays upon them will be to the sound of timbrels and lyres.[56]

---

[50] A rare exception is found in 2 Samuel 20:1, where we read, 'Now there happened to be there a worthless fellow, whose name was Sheba, the son of Bichri, a Benjaminite; and he blew the trumpet.'

[51] Exodus 19:13ff.

[52] Isaiah 27:12.

[53] Isaiah 58. In another symbolic trumpet reference, in Zechariah 9:14, 'the Lord God will sound the trumpet.' In Psalm 105, however, he is described as a leader of singing.

[54] Joshua 6:4ff.

[55] Judges 6:34ff. Other examples of the use of military trumpet signals can be found in Numbers 31:6, 2 Samuel 2:28, 2 Chronicles 13:12, Jeremiah 4: 19ff, Jeremiah 6, Jeremiah 42:14, Hosea 8, Joel 2:1 and 15, Amos 3:6, and Zephanian 1:16.

[56] Isaiah 30:32.

Ancient Views on Music and Religion among the Romans and Early Christians

> *At Pergamum in the secret and concealed parts of the temple,*
> *whither no one but the priests is allowed to approach ...*
> *there was a sound of drums.*[1]
>
> Julius Caesar

THE ORIGIN OF THE USE OF MUSIC in the religious-cult celebrations in ancient Rome is assigned, by tradition, to the time of Numa Pompilius (seventh or eighth centuries BC) when singers and dancers performed rites in honor of the god Mars.

The Idaean Mother was the mythical mother of the founders of Rome and the music of her festival is mentioned by Virgil.

> To speak truly, not men, rush out on the heights of Mount Dindymus,
> Where the aulos gives out a tune to its devotees.
> The kettle-drum calls you, the Berecyntian flute of the Mother
> Of Ida; yield arms to he-men and give up your swords.[2]

Ovid refers to another festival with ancient roots, the religious rite for the Egyptian god, Ibis, and offers interesting detail.

> The procession is ready? Good! Let it begin.
> The priest does not delay but turns to face the assembled congregation, bows three times to the altar,
> signals the chorus master for the pious hymn to commence,
> takes a breath, and intones: 'Offer thy throat,
> O terrified victim, freely to me.' He raises
> the shining knife and holds it high, as the rite,
> awesome, dreadful, but beautiful too, is re-enacted.[3]

This ceremony was based on a much older one and in one poem Ovid clearly questions the value of continuing these Epyptian rituals.

> What use is that Egyptian ritual,
> Those timbrels, these long nights of chastity?
> When evil fate dooms good men, may I be
> Forgiven if I've no faith in gods at all![4]

---

[1] Civil Wars, Book III, 105.

[2] Virgil, *Aeneid*, trans. L. R. Lind (Bloomington: Indiana University Press, 1958), IX, 642.

[3] Ovid, *Amores*, 94ff.

[4] Ibid., III. 9.

On one famous occasion in the fourth century BC, the aulos players who performed for the religious festivals went on strike when the city could not pay their full wages for participating in the Feast of Jupiter. The aulos players actually left town and took up residence in Tibur, leaving Rome without the whole range of services usually rendered by these players, as noted by Ovid.

> The aulos was missed in the theater, missed at the altars; no dirge accompanied the bier on the last march.[5]

After negotiations failed to secure the return of these players, citizens of Tibur proposed to trick them into returning, thoughtfully helping them save face by providing masks and long gowns. The earliest account of this often retold incident is by Livy, who added that this story 'would scarcely be worth mentioning, were it not connected to religion.'

> The aulos players were angry at having been forbidden by the last censors to hold their feast in the temple of Jupiter, according to ancient custom, and marched off to Tibur in a body, with the result that there was no one in the City to play the auloi at sacrifices. The Senate was seized with pious misgivings about the incident, and sent delegates to Tibur to request the citizens to do their best to return the men to Rome. The Tiburtines courteously promised to do so, and first summoned the aulos players to their senate house and urged them to go back to Rome. Then, when they found that persuasion achieved nothing they dealt with the men by a ruse nicely in tune with their nature. On a public holiday various citizens invited parties of aulos players to their homes on the pretext of celebrating the feast with music, and sent them to sleep by plying them with wine, for which men of their kind are generally greedy. In that condition they dumped them, heavily asleep, in carts and carried them off to Rome. The carts were left in the Forum and the aulos players knew nothing until daylight surprised them there, still very drunk. The people quickly gathered round them and prevailed on them to stay. They were given permission on three days a year to roam the City in fancy dress, making music and enjoying the license which is now customary, and those of them who played auloi at sacrifices had their right to hold a feast in the temple restored.[6]

Ancient Rome was a society which had numerous gods for every aspect of public and private life. So many gods that Varro estimated their number at 30,000 and Petronius (7–66 AD) said some towns had more gods than inhabitants.[7] Lucretius offers this explanation for the people's need for gods as he discusses the origin of Pan.

> I have sometimes heard
> As many as six or seven echoes cry
> In answer to one voice. So hills to hills
> Redound and bounce reiteration back
> Each to the other till the nearby folk
> Invent the presences of goatfoot gods,

---

5   Ovid, *Fasti*, VI, 666ff.

6   Livy, *History of Rome*, IX, 30.

7   Quoted in Alfred Sendrey, in *Music in the Social and Religious Life of Antiquity* (Rutherford: Fairleigh Dickinson University Press, 1974), 383ff.

> Satyrs and nymphs and fauns, night-wandering,
> Whose rumpuses and rowdy pranks, they swear
> To the last man, disturb the peace at night;
> And they go on to talk about the sound
> Of music, sweet and sad, the twang of strings
> The pipes, the singing voices. Far away,
> If you believe their stories, farmer-folk
> Listen while Pan, nodding his shaggy head
> with the pine needles hanging over his ears,
> Keeps time, lips up and down the open reeds
> So that the woodland melodies pour out
> With never a silence. No man likes to think
> His home is some forgotten wilderness
> Abandoned even by gods, and this is why
> They toss around these marvels in their talk,
> These stories of the weird and wonderful.[8]

A cult-religious festival in honor of Cybele is described in a poem by Catullus (84–54 BC).

> To the Phrygian forests, to the fame of Cybele,
> Where the cymbals sing loud and the smitten drums
> Resound and on rounded reed and the double-pipe
> Breathe out a booming bass, where the maenads,
> Ivy-wreathed and wanded and wagging their heads,
> Shriek shrilly and shake the emblems;
> Take the way of the wandering worshipers thither
> Devotion directs us to dance and adore.[9]

The cult of Isis had its origin in Greece and began to be celebrated in Rome in the second century BC. These festivals also included music and the accompanying shrines dedicated to this god were built by the Romans in places as distant as London. Another festival transported from Greece was that of Ceres, the goddess of agriculture. Cicero reports that these observances were conducted in Greek and led by a Greek priestess.[10] Virgil describes one of these festivals:

> See that your country folk adore the goddess:
> For her let milk and honey flow, and wine,
> And lead the sacrificial victims round the crops
> Three times, to bring good fortune, let a chorus
> Follow the procession, singing hymns
> To Ceres, ask her blessing on their homes;
> Let no one lay his sickle to the grain

---

[8] *The Way Things Are*, Book IV, 577.
[9] Catullus, Poem 63.
[10] Cicero, *Pro Balbo*, xxiv, 55.

> Until, with festive oak wreath on his brow,
> He honors Ceres' name in dance and song.[11]

Another festival with rural origins was that of Bacchus, in celebration of grapes and wine. In one reference to this festival, Ovid speaks of this hidden ritual continuing for ten days[12] and with a large participation of musical instruments.

> When suddenly timbrels sounded, unseen timbrels
> Harsh in their ears, flutes piped, and horns resounded
> And cymbals clashed, and all the air was full
> Of the smell of myrrh and saffron, and their weaving
> Turned green, and the hanging cloth resembled ivy
> Or grape-vines, and the threads were tendrils clinging.[13]

An additional reference by Ovid seems to point not to the rural character but to the later secret ceremonies of women. Ovid gives us a vivid picture of the ritual dress of the women in this episode when Procne invades this female ceremony looking for her sister.

> It was the time when all the Thracian mothers
> Held festival for Bacchus, and the night
> Shared in their secrets; Rhodope by night
> Resounded as the brazen cymbals clashed,
> And so by night the queen went from her palace,
> Armed for the rites of Bacchus, in all the dress
> Of frenzy, trailing vines for head-dress, deer-skin
> Down the left side, and a spear over the shoulder.
> So, swiftly through the forest with attendants,
> Comrades and worshipers in throngs, and driven
> By madness, terrible in rage and anger,
> Went Procne, went the Bacchanal, and came
> At last to the hidden cottage, came there shrieking,
> 'Hail, Bacchus!' broke the doors in, found her sister,
> Dressed her like all the others, hid her face
> With ivy-leaves, and dragged her out, and brought her
> Home to the palace.[14]

This festival of *Bacchanalia,* for the Roman god Bacchus, in time developed into one characterized by music, drinking, and sexual depravity. Representatives from all levels of Roman society seem to have participated eagerly in this celebration, which now adopted the name of the Greek god, Dionysus. The historian Livy suggests that the purpose of the music seems to have been in part to drown out the cries of the victims.

---

[11] Virgil, *Georgics*, I, 344ff.
[12] Ibid., XI, 96.
[13] *Metamorphoses*, IV, 391ff.
[14] Ibid, VI, 585ff.

There were initiatory rites which at first were imparted to a few, then began to be generally known among men and women. To the religious element in them were added the delights of wine and feasts, that the minds of a larger number might be attracted. When wine had inflamed their minds, and night and the mingling of males with females, youth with age, had destroyed every sentiment of modesty, all varieties of corruption first began to be practiced, since each one had at hand the pleasure answering to that to which his nature was more inclined. There was not one form of vice alone, the promiscuous matings of free men and women, but perjured witnesses, forged seals and wills and evidence, all issued from this same workshop; likewise poisonings and secret murders, so that at times not even the bodies were found for burial. Much was ventured by craft, more by violence. This violence was concealed because amid the howlings and the crash of drums and cymbals no cry of the sufferers could be heard as the debauchery and murders proceeded.[15]

In 186 BC the testimony of a woman came to the attention of one of the consuls and led to an investigation of this cult. Her testimony confirms the picture drawn by Livy, but adds that a choir participated.

It was common knowledge that for the past two years no one had been initiated who was over the age of twenty. As each one was introduced, he became a kind of sacrificial victim for the priests. They led the initiate to a place which resounded with shrieks, with the chanting of a choir, the clashing of cymbals and the beating of drums, so that the victim's cries for help, when violence was offered to his chastity, might not be heard.

Whenever bad omens seemed to occur, a special rite was held to appease the apparent displeasure of the gods. Livy assures us that during a period of days in 201 BC, the sun appeared red for an entire day, a lamb was born with a pig's head, a pig was born with a human head, and several children were born whose 'sex was doubtful.' During the subsequent panic this caused, the infants in question were 'immediately thrown into the sea' and a rite was organized in which the twenty-seven virgins again marched through the streets of Rome singing a hymn, composed on this occasion by Publius Licinius Tegula.[16]

In 17 BC, Augustus instituted a three-day festival in honor of Saturn, called *Saturnalia*, featuring theatrical plays, called *ludi*, and competitions. Percussion instruments were a feature of this festival, reflecting an ancient myth about the god Saturn. An oracle having told that he would be deposed by his son, Saturn sought to prevent this by eating all of his offspring. Finally his wife, Rhea, tricked him after giving birth by concealing a stone in infant garments, which Saturn swallowed. To keep the baby secret, Rhea's servants beat on helmets and shields to create noise to cover its cries. An account of this festival by Ovid also mentions a parade and the fact that even the law courts closed in its observance.

Let the sky revolve thrice on its never-resting axis; let Titan thrice yoke and thrice unyoke his steeds, straightaway the Berecyntian pipe will blow a blast on its bent horn, and the festival of the Idaean Mother will have come. Eunuchs will march and thump their hollow drums, and cymbals clashed on

---

[15] Livy, *History of Rome*, XXXIX, viii, 5–14.
[16] Livy, Ibid., XXXI, 12.

cymbals will give out their tinkling notes; seated on the unmanly necks of her attendants, the goddess herself will be borne with howls through the streets in the city's midst. The stage is clattering, the games are calling. To your places, Quirites! and in the empty law courts let the war of suitors cease![17]

There was also a festival of Juno, who was the mythical daughter to Saturn and wife to Jupiter. Ovid describes some of the music used.

> Here, to the sound of auloi and solemn chanting,
> The long procession passes every year
> Through streets bedecked, with white Falerian heifers
> From their own fields, while all the people cheer ...[18]

Finally, in view of the important role music played in these early Roman cult-religious celebrations, we should perhaps not be surprised that some festivals were held in honor of musical instruments. There was a festival day in honor of the aulos, held each June 13, and called 'lesser Quinquatrus,' during which,

> the aulos players take a holiday, and after roaming through the City, assemble at the Temple of Minerva.[19]

Another festival, held March 23 and May 23, called 'Tibulustrium' [*lustrum*, 'purificatory offering'[20]] celebrated the trumpet. Ovid says the ceremony involved a blessing of the instruments, 'to purify the melodious trumpets,' a ceremony Varro said took place in the Shoemaker's Hall.[21]

THE EARLY CHRISTIANS

It was in opposition to the wealth and extravagance of the Romans that we must try to understand the views of the early Christians. In particular, it is clear that the ancient Roman practice of music in their cult-religious ceremonies had a direct relationship with the subsequent views of church music formed by the early Christian Church fathers. Here we shall focus on the Christian Church during the four centuries between the time of Jesus and the creation of

---

[17] *Fasti*, IV, 179ff.

[18] *Amores*, III, 13.

[19] Marcus Varro, in *On the Latin Language*, VI, 17.

[20] Ibid., V, 153.

[21] Ibid., VI, 14.

the New Testament in the year 367 AD.[22] One should begin by pointing out that at first there not one Christian Church, but many. In the year 187 AD one writer counted twenty and in the year 384 AD a writer found eighty variants. And in this early period the young Christian Church beliefs were not far removed from the practice of the Jews, indeed the principal difference being dietary.[23] The Roman official writing at the end of the first century AD, Pliny the Younger, in a report to the Emperor Trajan, has left a very rare first-hand description of these early Christians and he seems to imply that they are beginning to use the old deserted temples and even carrying on the old Jewish practice of animal sacrifice.

> It is my custom to refer all my difficulties to you, Sir, for no one is better able to resolve any doubts and to inform my ignorance.
>
> I have never been present at an examination of Christians. Consequently, I do not know the nature of the extent of the punishment usually meted out to them, nor the grounds for starting an investigation and how far it should be pressed. Nor am I at all sure whether any distinction should be made between them on the grounds of age, or if young people and adults should be treated alike; whether a pardon ought to be granted to anyone retracting his beliefs, or if he has once professed Christianity, he shall gain nothing by renouncing it; and whether it is the mere name of Christian which is punishable, even if innocent of crime, or rather the crimes associated with the name.
>
> For the moment this is the line I have taken with all persons brought before me on the charge of being Christians. I have asked them in person if they are Christians, and if they admit it, I repeat the question a second and third time, with a warning of the punishment awaiting them. If they persist, I order them to be led away for execution; for, whatever the nature of their admission, I am convinced that their stubbornness and unshakeable obstinacy ought not to go unpunished. There have been others similarly fanatical who are Roman citizens. I have entered them on the list of persons to be sent to Rome for trial.
>
> Now that I have begun to deal with this problem, as so often happens, the charges are becoming more widespread and increasing in variety. An anonymous pamphlet has been circulated which contains the names of a number of accused persons. Amongst these I considered that I should dismiss any who denied that they were or ever had been Christians when they had repeated after me a formula of invocation to the gods and had made offerings of wine and incense to your statue (which I had ordered to be brought into court for this purpose along with the images of the gods), and furthermore had reviled the name of Christ: none of which things, I understand, any genuine Christian can be induced to do.

---

[22] In 367 AD Bishop Athanasius of Alexandria selected the books to be included and this was ratified by the Church Council of Hippo in 393 and by the Council of Carthage in 397. Because the New Testament was thus assembled, rather than being rewritten by a redactor as much of the Old Testament was, we have the much written about problems of left-out books, misplaced books and a number of curious inconsistencies which exist among the various books. For example, in the first four books, books supposedly written by men who knew Jesus, the Jesus of Luke was from a poor family and was born in a manger where he was visited by shepherds. But the Jesus of Matthew was an aristocrat who came to claim the throne, was born in a house where he was visited by other kings. Luke describes Jesus as the gentle shepherd who says, 'turn the other cheek,' while Matthew pictures a Jesus who says, 'Do not think that I have come to bring peace on earth; I have not come to bring peace, but a sword!'

[23] For the reader who might be interested in studying the differences between the Jewish, Christian and Moslem churches in the first several centuries of the Christian Era, we highly recommend an excellent study by an important scholar of this period, Robert Eisenman, *James the Brother of Jesus* (New York: Viking, 1996).

> Others, whose names were given to me by an informer, first admitted the charge and then denied it; they said that they had ceased to be Christians two or more years previously, and some of them even twenty years ago. They also declared that the sum total of their guilt or error amounted to no more than this: they had met regularly before dawn on a fixed day to chant verses alternately amongst themselves in honor of Christ as if to a god, and also to bind themselves by oath, or for any criminal purpose, but to abstain from theft, robbery, and adultery, to commit no breach of trust and not to deny a deposit when called upon to restore it. After this ceremony it had been their custom to disperse and reassemble later to take food of an ordinary, harmless kind; but they had in fact given up this practice since my edict, issued on your instructions, which banned all political societies. This made me decide it was all the more necessary to extract the truth by torture from two slave-women, whom they call deaconesses. I found nothing but a degenerate sort of cult carried to extravagant lengths.
>
> I have therefore postponed any further examination and hastened to consult you. The question seems to me to be worthy of your consideration, especially in view of the number of persons endangered; for a great many individuals of every age and class, both men and women, are being brought to trial, and this is likely to continue. It is not only the towns, but villages and rural districts too which are infected through contact with this wretched cult. I think though that it is still possible for it to be checked and directed to better ends, for there is no doubt that people have begun to throng the temples which had been almost entirely deserted for a long time; the sacred rites, which had been allowed to lapse are being performed again, and flesh of sacrificial victims is on sale everywhere, though up till recently scarcely anyone could be found to buy it. It is easy to infer from this that a great many people could be reformed if they were given the opportunity to repent.[24]

It does seem clear that the leaders of what would become the new Roman Christian Church had a general goal of creating a new kind of Roman citizen, one who would stand in sharp contrast to the excesses of the Roman citizens during the Empire. We have some indication of how severe the contrast was in an anonymous poem of the early second century, 'The Shepherd of Hermas,' which complains that one is beginning to see among Christians the re-emergence of pagan customs, including rouge, dyed hair, painted eyelids, drunkenness, avarice, and adultery.[25] At about the same time we find some insights in the lives the early Christians were expected to live in a passage by Minucius Felix in which he suggests how a 'pagan,' a Roman citizen who is non-Christian, might address the Christian.

> Look: you Christians are menaced with threats, torments and tortures ... And where is that god of yours who can help those who come to life again, but cannot help those who are alive? ...
>
> But in the meantime, in your anxious state of expectation, you refrain from honest pleasures: you do not go to our shows, you take no part in our processions, you are not present at our public banquets, you shrink in horror from our sacred games, from food ritually dedicated by our priests, from drink hallowed by libation poured upon our altars. Such is your dread of the very gods you deny.

---

[24] *The Letters of the Younger Pliny* (New York: Penguin Books, 1985), 293.

[25] Quoted in Will Durant, *Caesar and Christ* (New York: Simon and Schuster, 1944), 599. Durant attributes the falling standards to failing discipline following the failure of Jesus to reappear, as expected, in the year 100 AD.

> You do not bind your head with flowers, you do not honor your body with perfumes; ointments you reserve for funerals, but even to your tombs you deny garlands; you anemic, neurotic creatures, you indeed deserve to be pitied—but by our gods. The result is, you pitiable fools, that you have no enjoyment of life while you wait for the new life which you will never have.[26]

St. Basil, in the fourth century, was still arguing for a rather plain and pale new Christian Roman.

> As plumpness and a healthy color betoken the athlete, so leanness of body and the pallor produced by the exercise of continence mark the Christian.[27]

The Church took a strong position against the exhibition of emotion, in particular in numerous warnings about the dangers of emotions found in the theater, calling it the first step toward sin.[28] As one example, taken from a great many, consider this warning by Lactantius:

> For a too great eagerness for pleasure both produces danger and generates disgrace, and that which is especially to be avoided, leads to eternal death. Nothing is so hateful to God as an unchaste mind and an impure soul. Nor let any one think that he must abstain from this pleasure [sex] only, but also the other pleasures which arise from the rest of the senses, because they also are of themselves vicious, and it is the part of the same virtue to despise them. The pleasure of the eyes is derived from the beauty of objects, that of the ears from harmonious and pleasant sounds, that of the nostrils from pleasant odor, that of taste from sweet food,—all of which virtue ought strongly to resist, lest, ensnared by these attractions, the soul should be depressed from heavenly to earthly things, from things eternal to things temporal, from life immortal to perpetual punishment.[29]

St. Basil advised the Christian against even laughing, for laughter is also a form of emotion.

> Indulging in unrestrained and immoderate laughter is a sign of intemperance, of a want of control over one's emotions, and of failure to repress the soul's frivolity by a stern use of reason … Moreover, Jesus appears to have experienced those emotions which are of necessity associated with the body … but, so far as we know from the story of the Gospel, He never laughed.[30] From this apparently follows the New Testament's admonition, 'Let there be no … silly talk, nor levity.'[31]

---

[26] Marcus Minucius Felix, *Octavius*, trans. G. W. Clarke (New York: Newman Press, 1974), XII, 4.

[27] St. Basil, 'The Long Rules,' trans. Sister Monica Wagner, in *Saint Basil Ascetical Works* (New York: Fathers of the Church, Inc.., 1950), 273.

[28] This position would have dramatic ramifications for the notation and study of music for the next 2,000 years.

[29] Lactantius, 'Epitome of the Divine Institutes,' trans. William Fletcher in *The Works of Lactantius* (Edinburgh: T. & T. Clark, 1871), II, lxii.

[30] Ibid., 271. Basil further cites Luke 6:25, 'Woe to you that laugh now, for you shall mourn and weep.' Clement of Alexandria, 'The Instructor,' trans. William Wilson (Edinburgh: T. & T. Clark, 1884), 219ff, makes a similar injunction against laughter.

[31] Ephesians 5:4.

Such warnings by the early Church fathers extend even to the activities of the private home. St. John Chrysostom condemns music and dance in the celebration of private occasions. He tells of Herod who had his wife dance as part of his celebration of his birthday. But this was wrong!

> He ought to have honored the day with hymns and thankfulness to the Master, but he honored it with dishonor. For what is more dishonorable than dancing?
>
> Listen, you men and women who celebrate your own greatest days with such dances and songs. There are no small evils, even though they seem to be neither good nor bad; it is because they seem to be neither good nor bad that they are great evils … Does someone have the boldness to bring dancing into the house of one of the faithful, and is he not afraid that a thunderbolt will sweep down from above to consume all things with its flames? I say this also to the women, that they may also correct the men and lead them away from such pleasure.[32]

What are the entertainments of the Devil, this writer asks?

> Every form of sin, spectacles of indecency, horse racing, gatherings filled with laughter and abusive language.[33]

Having in mind the evils associated with music at festive banquets, St. John Chrysostom recommends that the Christian teach his family to sing sacred music instead at the table.

> This I say, not only that you may yourselves sing praises, but also that you may teach your wives and children to do so … especially at the table. For since Satan, seeking to ensnare us at feasts, for the most part employs as allies drunkenness, gluttony, immoderate laughter, and an inactive mind; at this time, both before and after table, it is especially necessary to fortify oneself with the protection of the psalms and, rising from the feast together with one's wife and children, to sing sacred hymns to God …
>
> What if drunkenness or gluttony does make our minds dull and foolish? Where psalmody has entered, all these evil and depraved counsels retreat.
>
> And just as not as a few wealthy persons wipe off their tables with a sponge filled with balsam, so that if any stain remain from the food, they may remove it and show a clean table; so should we also, filling our mouths with spiritual melody instead of balsam, so that if any stain remain in our mind from the abundance, we may thereby wipe it away …
>
> And as those who bring comedians, dancers, and harlots into their feasts call in demons and Satan himself and fill their homes with innumerable contentions (among them jealousy, adultery, debauchery, and countless evils); so those who invoke David with his lyre call inwardly on Christ.[34]

Needless to say, anything touching on carnal love was discouraged in the Christian. For example, the second century Church Father, Saint Cyprian, admonishes,

---

32 St. John Chrysostom, *Baptismal Instructions*, 157.
33 Ibid., 168.
34 St. John Chrysostom, 'Exposition of Psalm XLI,' quoted in Oliver Strunk, *Source Readings in Music History* (New York: Norton, 1950), 68ff.

> For God has indeed given man a voice, and yet he should not sing love songs and songs that are coarse.[35]

Another Church writer of this same century criticizes women for singing love songs.

> You are rejecting the law when you wish to please the world. You dance in your houses; instead of psalms, you sing love songs.[36]

The Church also took a position against the Christian developing a love for art. First, their position was that one must not love art or the artist, but rather God who made the artist. Second, to love art represented a love for the present life, which was in direct conflict with the Church's strongest position of appeal to the broad citizenry of Rome—that it was only the *next* life that mattered.

The Church burned all the pagan books it could find, including those of the Greek philosophers Plato and Aristotle. The Church closed the schools, taking the position that a Christian does not need to think; we will tell him what to think. Once you believe, the second century Church father Tertullian says, search no further. You should accept the Church's answers and curiosity ought not to range beyond it. Such restless curiosity, the feature of heresy, is never gratified.[37] Basil is more to the point: Don't question the Church authorities!

> No one is to concern himself with the superior's method of administration or make curious inquiries about what is being done.[38]

Thus it followed that Clement gave a new Christian interpretation of the most famous phrase of Greek antiquity, 'Know thyself.'

> And the maxim 'Know thyself' means here to know for what we are born. And we are born to obey the commandments.[39]

With this brief picture of the early Church during the four centuries before the creation of the New Testament, it will be no surprise to the reader to encounter the sense of contempt held by the early Christian philosophers toward music in the earlier religious practices. Minucius Felix mentions the drums which were a frequent participant in cult-religious celebrations.

---

[35] Saint Cyprian, 'On the Dress of Virgins,' trans. Sister Angela E. Keenan (New York, Fathers of the Church, Inc., 1958), 11.

[36] Commodianus, 'In Favor of Christian Discipline,' quoted in *The Writings of Tertullianus* (Edinburgh: T. & T. Clark, 1895), 464.

[37] Tertullian, 'On Prescription Against Heretics,' trans. Alexander Roberts in *Ante-Nicene Christian Library* (Edinburgh: T. & T. Clark, 1884), XIff.

[38] St. Basil, *Saint Basil Ascetical Works*, 326.

[39] Clement of Alexandria, *The Miscellanies*, trans. Alexander Roberts (Edinburgh: T. & T. Clark, 1869), XII, Book VII, Pg. 420.

> In a survey of Roman rituals you would find so many practices that are laughable if not pitiable. Some devotees run about naked in the depths of winter; others move in procession wearing felt caps and parading old shields; or they beat drums of hides and go begging from quarter to quarter, dragging their gods with them.[40]

The second-century writer, Clement of Alexandria, also mentions music in the course of his attack on the Greeks and their cult-religions.

> How in the world is it that you have given credence to worthless legends, imagining brute beasts to be enchanted by music, while the bright face of truth seems alone to strike you as deceptive, and is regarded with unbelieving eyes?
>
> ……
>
> If I go on further to quote the symbols of initiation into this mystery (those of Attis, Cybele and Corybantes) they will, I know, move you to laughter, even though you are in no laughing humor when your rites are being exposed. 'I ate from the drum; I drank from the cymbal …' Are not these symbols an outrage?[41]

In another place he provides a very rare description of the role of music in the Egyptian religious service.

> We shall find another testimony in confirmation … of certain of the tenets which pertain to each sect being culled from other Barbarians, chiefly from the Egyptians … For the Egyptians pursue a philosophy of their own. This is principally shown by their sacred ceremonial. For first advances the Singer, bearing some one of the symbols of music. For they say that he must learn two of the books of Hermes, the one of which contains the hymns of the gods, the second the regulations for the king's life. And after the Singer advances the Astrologer, with a horologe in his hand and a palm, the symbols of astrology.[42]

Later he also castigates the Roman cult-religions, and those of Cyprus, several times mentioning the music associated with them.

> Yes, and let the sanctuaries of Egypt and the Tuscan oracles of the dead be delivered over to darkness. Homes of hallucination in very truth they are, these schools of sophistry for unbelieving men, these gambling-dens of sheer delusions. Partners in this business of trickery are goats, trained for divination; and ravens, taught by men to give oracular responses to men …
>
> The raving Dionysus is worshiped by Bacchants with orgies, in which they celebrate their sacred frenzy by a feast of raw flesh. Wreathed with snakes, they perform the distribution of portions of their victims, shouting the name of Eve, that Eve through whom error entered into the world; and a consecrated snake is the emblem of the Bacchic orgies.[43]

---

40 Marcus Minucius, *Octavius*, trans. G. W. Clarke (New York: Newman Press, 1974), XXV, 11.

41 Clement of Alexandria, *Exhortation to the Greeks*, trans. G. W. Butterworth (Cambridge: Harvard University Press, 1939), 35.

42 Clement of Alexandria, *The Miscellanies*, trans. Alexander Roberts (Edinburgh: T. & T. Clark, 1869), XII, Book V, iv.

43 Ibid., 29ff.

Clement's personal feelings are clearly evident in his unkind description of the pagan priests.

> Let any of you look at those who minister in the idol temples. He will find them ruffians with filthy hair, in squalid and tattered garments, complete strangers to baths, with claws for nails like wild beasts; many are also deprived of their virility.[44]

The most striking difference between the Old and New Testaments is the treatment of instrumental music. Following the extensive descriptions of the use of music in the Temple which one finds in the Old Testament, it is somewhat astounding to discover that there is not a single reference to a musical instrument being used in a religious service anywhere in the New Testament. The nearest New Testament correspondence to those exhortations of the Psalms, 'Praise the Lord with Trumpets, Praise the Lord with Cymbals,' is a passage where instruments are not actually named, but a phrase is used which is often a surrogate for instrumental music in early literature. This, as we have mentioned above, is the phrase, 'making melody' to the Lord.[45]

There is not a single reference in the New Testament to a live person playing the trumpet. Nevertheless, it seems odd that an instrument like the trumpet, an instrument so much a part of every ancient culture, should be entirely absent in this book. Actually, the word appears, but there is no description of a person actually playing the trumpet. It is played by angels (once a septet of angels!),[46] once by God,[47] once as the 'last trumpet' of Judgment Day,[48] once

---

[44] Ibid., 201.

[45] Ephesians 5:19. This same passage appears also in Colossians 3:16, but without the mention of the instrumental music. All quotations are from the *Revised Standard Version* (1952).

[46] Matthew 24:31 and Revelation 8:02. The early Church writers had a particular fascination with the number seven. Clement, in *The Miscellanies*, trans. Alexander Roberts (Edinburgh: T. & T. Clark, 1869), XII, bk. VI, p. 389, says, 'the whole world revolves in sevens,' pointing to the seven known planets, seven stars in several constellations, seven phases of the moon, seven lyre strings, and seven (!) senses: two eyes, two ears, two nostrils, and the mouth. Victorinus, Bishop of Petau, in *The Writings of Tertullianus* (Edinburgh: T. & T. Clark, 1895), III, 392, makes an interesting observation on the frequency of the number seven in the bible, including seven horns of the Lamb [Revelation 5:6], seven eyes of God [Zechariah 4:10], seven eyes are the seven spirits of the Lamb [Revelation 4:5], seven torches burning before the throne of God [Revelation 4:5], seven golden candlesticks [Revelation 1:13], seven young sheep [Leviticus 23:18], seven women in Isaiah [Isaiah 4:1], seven churches in Paul [Acts 6:3], seven deacons [Acts 6:3], seven angels [Revelation], seven trumpets [Joshua 6, Revelation 8], seven seals to the book, seven periods of seven days and seven weeks in Daniel [Daniel 9:25], seven of all clean things in the ark [Genesis 7:2], seven revenges of Cain [Genesis 4:15], seven years for a debt to be acquitted [Deuteronomy 15:1], the lamp with seven orifices [Zechariah 4:2], and the seven pillars of wisdom in the house of Solomon [Proverbs 9:1].

[47] 1 Thessalonians 4:16.

[48] 1 Corinthians 15:52.

it is heard from the City of God,[49] once as a symbol of God's loud voice,[50] and when God will destroy Babylon—then we will finally be rid of all these trumpeters, harp players, flute players, and 'minstrels.'[51]

Apart from this meager list, there are no further references to brass players which are not metaphors or symbols. There are two remaining references to woodwind instruments, and one of these is used only in a metaphoric expression complaining that the people are not paying attention to what their religion's leaders are saying, 'We piped and you did not dance.'[52]

The remaining woodwind reference is found in the Book of Matthew,[53] where, before he could perform one of his miracles of raising a girl from the dead, Jesus had to first chase the aulos players out of a ruler's house, saying, 'Depart, for the girl is not dead but sleeping.'[54] This is actually a rare example of 'paganism' which escaped the editorial eye of the Church, referring as it does to one of the Greek myths. Philetaerus, in the fourth century BC, cites a myth that if one goes to Hades, but is a recognized lover of good music, one is permitted 'to revel in love affairs,' whereas 'those whose manners are sordid, having no knowledge of music,' are condemned to spend eternity carrying water in a fruitless effort to fill 'the leaky jar.'[55] Thus Philetaerus exclaims, 'Zeus, it is indeed a fine thing to die to the music of the aulos!' By this he meant arranging to have these musicians playing as one dies so as to demonstrate to the gods that one truly appreciated music.

It is in the context of this myth that we understand a line in Menander's play, *Old Cantankerous*. The character, Getas, enters the stage from a shrine as an aulos player begins to play for him. Getas tells the aulos player to stop playing, 'I'm not ready for you yet!' This is precisely the meaning of the comment by Jesus.

The only reference to percussion instruments in the New Testament does them little credit.

> If I speak in the tongues of men and of angels, but have not love, I am a noisy gong or a clanging cymbal.[56]

It is easy to understand the objections to many of the pagan rituals, but musical instruments posed a special problem for the new Church fathers. How were they to deal with the numerous references to musical instruments in the Old Testament? Moreover, the general role of these musicians is clear, and that was to lead in the praise of the Lord. What, therefore, were they going to say about a passage such as Psalm 150:

---

49 Hebrews 12:19.

50 Revelation 10:10.

51 Revelation 18:22. 'Flute' players here, of course, mean auloi.

52 Matthew 11:17.

53 Matthew 9:23.

54 Matthew 9, 24. Again, 'flute' should read aulos.

55 Philetaerus, *The Aulos Lover*, quoted in Athenaeus, *Deipnosophistae*, XIV, 633.

56 1 Corinthians 13:1.

Praise him with the trumpet sound;
Praise him with lute and harp!
Praise him with strings and pipe!
Praise him with sounding cymbals;
Praise him with loud clashing cymbals!

The only possible recourse the fathers of the new Church had, if they wished to eliminate the pagan musical instruments, was to take the position that those passages in the Old Testament were not referring to *real* musical instruments—they were only metaphors! A typical example of this official 'spin' can be seen in the following passage by Clement of Alexandria.

> The Spirit ... sings, 'Praise Him with sound of trumpet;' for with sound of trumpet He shall raise the dead. 'Praise Him on the psaltery;' for the tongue is the psaltery of the Lord. 'And praise Him on the lyre.' By the lyre is meant the mouth struck by the Spirit, as it were by a plectrum. 'Praise with the timbrel and the dance,' refers to the church meditating on the resurrection of the dead in the resounding skin. 'Praise Him on the chords and organ.' Our body He calls an organ, and its nerves are the strings, by which it has received harmonious tension, and when struck by the Spirit, it gives forth human voices. 'Praise Him on the clashing cymbals.' He calls the tongue the cymbal of the mouth, which resounds with the pulsation of the lips.[57]

Even the trumpet, which the Old Testament had always associated with the high priest, is transformed by the new Church writers into a metaphor. Clement of Alexandria, for example, declares, 'The trumpet of Christ is His gospel.'[58] And, indeed, one notices that in the New Testament, while there are many references to trumpets being played by seven angels, or treated metaphorically, there is not a single instance of a trumpet being played by a real man!

The most extensive discussion of music by Clement is found in a chapter entitled, 'The Mystical Meanings in the Proportions of Numbers, Geometrical Ratios, and Music.' Once again he implies that the instruments of the Old Testament were only used metaphorically.

> The lyre, according to its primary signification, may by the psalmist be used figuratively for the Lord; according to its secondary, for those who continually strike the chords of their souls under the direction of the Choir-master, the Lord. And if the people saved be called the lyre, it will be understood to be in consequence of their giving glory musically, through the inspiration of the Word ... You may take music in another way, as the ecclesiastical symphony at once of the law and the prophets, and the apostles along with the gospel, and the harmony which obtained in each prophet, in the transitions of the persons.[59]

The third-century Christian was apparently beginning to ask, 'But if instrumental music is mentioned in the Old Testament, why may we not enjoy it?' The error the Christian makes, Novatian explains, is in taking these passages literally, and not in their context of religious purpose.

---

57 Clement of Alexandria, *The Instructor*, trans. William Wilson (Edinburgh: T. & T. Clark, 1884), 216.
58 Clement of Alexandria, *Exhortation to the Greeks*, 249.
59 Clement of Alexandria, *The Miscellanies*, Book VI, xi.

> In Scripture, we also read of nablas, kinnors, timbrels, flutes, citharas, and dancing troupes ... Why, then, should a faithful Christian not be at liberty to be a spectator of things that the divine Writings are at liberty to mention? I can, with reason, state here that it would have been far better for such people to lack knowledge of the Scriptures, than to read them in such a manner. Words and noble deeds which have been put down in writing to stimulate us in the practice of evangelical virtue are misinterpreted by them as so many incentives for the practice of vice. These things were written not to make spectators of us, but to incite our minds to greater enthusiasm for salutary things, given that the pagans show great enthusiasm for things far from salutary ...
>
> And that David danced before the Lord does in no way encourage faithful Christians to take seats in the theater. He did not distort his body in obscene movements and dance out the drama of Grecian libido. The nablas, kinnors, flutes, timbrels, and citharas played to the Lord—not an idol. Therefore, no approval whatever is given for spectators of illicit things. Through the devil's artifice, things that were holy are changed into illicit things.[60]

In the fourth century we find St. Augustine trying to assert that the Old Testament references to cymbals were only in fact references to good neighbors! He says, for example, of the above quoted 'Praise him with sounding cymbals,' in Psalm 150,

> Cymbals touch each other in order to play and therefore some people compare them to our lips. But I think it better to think of God as being praised on the cymbals when someone is honored by his neighbor rather than by himself.[61]

Apart from these circuitous and metaphorical apologies for the appearance of instrumental music in the Old Testament services, some early Christian fathers also argued from an anti-Semitic perspective. Theodore of Cyrus (d. ca. 460), for example portrays the Jews as almost childlike.

> If old Levities used those instruments in the Temple of God to praise Him, not because it pleased Him ... Once it happened, however, He tolerated it, wishing to take them from the error of idolatry. Since they were fond of play and laughter, and since all this sort of thing took place in the temples of the idols, He allowed it, thus to lead them, and by the smaller evil to avoid the greater.[62]

The origin of Church music, according to St. John Chrysostom, was to lessen the toil of religious contemplation. Here, again, there is a certain anti-Semitic tone, as John seems to suggest that God only gave the Jews music because they were basically lazy and could not otherwise concentrate.

---

[60] Novatian, 'The Spectacles,' trans. Russell J. DeSimone, in *The Fathers of the Church* (Washington, D.C.: The Catholic University of America Press), II 3ff. The third-century Greek Church father, Origen (185–254 AD) pointed to the potentially embarrassing phrase in Song of Solomon 1:2, 'That he would kiss me with the kisses of his mouth,' and declared this is also a metaphor for 'that he would pour his words into my mouth and I would hear him speaking and see him teaching.' See, Origen, 'Word as Flesh,' in Hans Urs von Balthasar, *Spirit and Fire*, trans. Robert J. Daly (Washington, D.C.: The Catholic University of America Press, 1984), 150.

[61] Translated by James W. McKinnon, 'Musical Instruments in Medieval Psalm Commentaries and Psalters,' *Journal of the American Musicological Society* 21 (1968): 7.

[62] Ibid.

> When God saw that many men were rather indolent, that they came unwillingly to Scriptural readings and did not endure the labor this involves, wishing to make the labor more grateful and to take away the sensation of it, He blended melody with prophecy in order that, delighted by the modulation of the chant, all might with great eagerness give forth sacred hymns to Him. For nothing so uplifts the mind, giving it wings and freeing it from the earth, releasing it from the chains of the body, affecting it with love of wisdom, and causing it to scorn all things pertaining to this life, as modulated melody and the divine chant composed of number [rhythm].[63]

In another place, we find St. John Chrysostom attacking the contemporary Jews based on the passage in Old Testament, Numbers 10, in which God specifically instructs the high priests on the construction and use of trumpets. He criticizes them for giving preference to the trumpet over other traditional articles of worship, such as the golden altar of incense, the holy of holies, etc.

> Did you lose all those and keep only the trumpets? Do you Christians not see that what the Jews are doing is mockery rather than worship.[64]

Even as late as the thirteenth century, in Thomas Aquinas, we find this anti-Semitic excuse for the instrumental music of the Old Testament.

> Old Testament [musical] instruments were used both because the people were more coarse and carnal, so that they needed to be aroused by such instruments as well as with promises of temporal wealth, and because these instruments presaged the future.[65]

One is almost tempted to believe that if they could, the early Church fathers would have created a new church without music at all. Certainly they felt that the musical instruments themselves were too strongly associated with the pagan past. And they had another problem, the early Church was an outlaw organization which met in secret and you cannot have trumpets blowing and cymbals crashing during a religious service for fear of giving away their location.[66]

Indeed it is probably fair to say that some Church fathers had objections to music in general and in particular its role in school. A cautious few could see value in music, as for example Clement of Alexandria, who says traditional learning, including music, may be useful, so long as we pick and choose.

> I call him truly learned who brings everything to bear on the truth; so that, from geometry, and music, and grammar, and philosophy itself, culling what is useful, he guards the faith against assault.[67]

---

[63] St. John Chrysostom, 'Exposition of Psalm XLI,' quoted in Oliver Strunk, *Source Readings in Music History* (New York: Norton, 1950), 67.

[64] St. John Chrysostom, 'Against Judaizing Christians,' 93.

[65] Thomas Aquinas, *Disputations*, XXXIX, 249ff.

[66] Nowhere is this more evident than in Salzburg where one can still visit a church carved out inside a mountain by early Christians as a means of achieving secrecy.

[67] Clement, *The Miscellanies*, I, ix.

The third-century Church philosopher, Origen, was another who recognized that there is an important value to some subjects, including music, which stood apart from spiritual association. In his discussion, he sarcastically used the term, 'princes of this world,' to mean the famous Greek philosophers.

> I am of the opinion ... that there is another wisdom of this world besides those ... which belong to the princes of this world, by which wisdom those things seem to be understood and comprehended which belong to the world. This wisdom, however, possesses in itself no fitness for forming any opinion either respecting divine things, or the plan of the world's government,[68] or any other subjects of importance, or regarding the training for a good or happy life; but is such as deals wholly with the art of poetry, or grammar, or rhetoric, or geometry, or music, with which also, perhaps medicine should be classed. In all these subjects we are to suppose that the wisdom of this world is included.[69]

The third-century writer, Lactantius, was no doubt not alone in expressing his concerns over the 'dangers' in listening to music. In one place, he presumes 'pleasure of the ears' has the capacity of leading one to vice, he seems to regard music as not terribly dangerous because what we hear in music does not remain with us, as compared to the words of poetry.

> Pleasure of the ears is received from the sweetness of voices and melodies, which indeed is as productive of vice as that delight of the eyes of which we have spoken. For who would not deem him luxurious and worthless who should have scenic arts at his houses? But it makes no difference whether you practice luxury alone at home, or with the people in the theater. But we have already spoken of spectacles: there remains one thing which is to be overcome by us, that we be not captivated by those things which penetrate to the innermost perception. For all those things which are unconnected with words, that is, pleasant sounds of the air and of strings, may be easily disregarded, because they do not adhere to us, and cannot be written.[70]

It is also worthy of note that he acknowledges, in the above quotation, the power of music to 'penetrate to the innermost' part of us. He mentions this in another place, where he is discussing the tendency of the senses to lead man to vice. One gets the distinct impression that, while he would never speak in favor of music generally, he had observed, and was perhaps disturbed by, the powerful impact of music on the listener.

> But he who is carried away by hearing, to say nothing respecting songs, which often so charm the inmost senses that they even disturb with madness a settled state of the mind ...[71]

---

68 A reference to Plato's *Republic*.

69 Origen, 'De Principiis,' trans. Frederick Crombie, in *The Writings of Origen* (Edinburgh: T. & T. Clark, 1871), III, iii.

70 Lactantius, 'The Divine Institutes,' trans. William Fletcher in *The Works of Lactantius* (Edinburgh: T. & T. Clark, 1886), I, Book VI, xxi.

71 Lactantius, 'Epitome of the Divine Institutes,' trans. William Fletcher in *The Works of Lactantius* (Edinburgh: T. & T. Clark, 1871), II, lxii.

However, he concludes, if we are going to listen to music, it should be music which has two aesthetic characteristics, that which nourishes the soul and that which improves you as a person. The only type of music which does this, of course, is music which praises God.

> Let nothing be agreeable to the hearing but that which nourishes the soul and makes you a better man. And especially this sense ought not to be distorted to vice, since it is given to us for this purpose, that we might gain the knowledge of God. Therefore, if it be a pleasure to hear melodies and songs, let it be pleasant to sing and hear the praises of God. This is true pleasure, which is the attendant and companion of virtue.[72]

But, the early Church fathers were blocked from entirely eliminating music for two reasons. First, there was the account of angels singing at the birth of Christ—that could neither be overlooked nor explained away. Second, in Matthew 26:30 in the New Testament, there is a reference to Jesus singing!

So, vocal music was in and the most frequently mentioned form of music in the new Church is the singing of hymns, although musically we know little about these early forms. The Old Testament has numerous references to the role of singers in the Jewish service, but the vocal form, 'Hymn,' appears only in the New Testament. While there are only two instances in the New Testament of persons singing hymns in the present tense,[73] there are a number of recommendations that hymn singing should be a part of the future observances of the Christians.[74] In one of these cases, singing is specifically recommended when the singer himself *feels cheerful*.[75]

Undoubtedly Hymns were first sung in unison, as indeed St. Gregory Nazianzus, a fourth-century writer implies, 'while they harmonize many mouths into a single voice.'[76] This would make plausible the resultant effect when St. Paulinus of Nola speaks of the congregation of the faithful engaging in 'lusty rendering of holy hymns.'[77]

It has long been recognized that some of the Psalms seem to indicate antiphonal or responsorial form of singing, and Basil mentions such two-part antiphonal singing in the fourth century. This account is unusually interesting in suggesting that some of the original musical traditions may have come from older religious practice, the Church's protestations against the 'pagans' notwithstanding.

> As to the charge regarding psalmody, by which especially our slanderers terrify the more simple, I have this to say, that the customs now prevalent are in accord and harmony with those of all the churches of God. Among us the people come early after nightfall to the house of prayer, and in labor

---

[72] Lactantius, 'The Divine Institutes.'
[73] Matthew 26:30, which includes Jesus singing, and Acts 16:25, which describes Paul singing in prison.
[74] Romans 15:9, I Corinthians 14:15, 26, Ephesians 5:19, and Colossians 3:16 and James 5:13.
[75] James 5:13.
[76] Saint Gregory of Nazianzus, 'Concerning his own Affairs,' trans. Denis Meehan (Washington, D.C.: The Catholic University of America Press), 34.
[77] *The Poems of St. Paulinus of Nola*, trans. P. G. Walsh (New York: Newman Press, 1975), Poem 27, 542ff.

and affliction and continual tears confess to God. Finally, rising up from their prayers, they begin the chanting of psalms. And now, divided into two parts, they chant antiphonally, becoming master of the text of the Scriptural passages, and at the same time directing their attention and the recollectedness of their hearts. Then, again, leaving it to one to intone the melody, the rest chant in response; thus, having spent the night in a variety of psalmody and intervening prayers, when day at length begins to dawn, all in common, as with one voice and one heart, offer up the psalm of confession to the Lord, each one making His own the words of repentance. If, then, you shun us on this account, you will shun the Egyptians, and also those of both Libyas, the Thebans, Palestinians, Arabians, Phoenicians, Syrians, and those dwelling beside the Euphrates—in one word, all those among whom night watches and prayers and psalmody in common have been held in esteem.[78]

......

A psalm implies serenity of soul; it is the author of peace, which calms bewildering and seething thoughts. For, it softens the wrath of the soul, and what is unbridled it chastens. A psalm forms friendships, unties those separated, conciliates those at enmity ... So that psalmody, bringing about choral singing, a bond, as it were, toward unity, and joining the people into a harmonious union of one choir, produces also the greatest of blessings, charity.[79]

The chief value of singing psalms, according to Basil, is 'to calm and soften the wicked spirits which trouble souls.'[80] But he makes an interesting distinction here in saying that a 'bad' person cannot properly sing the psalms.

Not if someone utters the words of the psalm with his mouth, does that one sing to the Lord; but, all who send up the psalmody from a clean heart, and who are holy, maintaining righteousness toward God, these are able to sing to God, harmoniously guided by the spiritual rhythms. How many stand there, coming from fornication? How many from theft? How many concealing in their hearts deceit? How many lying? They think they are singing, although in truth they are not singing. For, the Scripture invites the saint to the singing of psalms. 'A bad tree cannot bear good fruit,' nor a bad heart utter words of life.[81]

We have another detailed description of the new Church music from St. Jerome, in his 'Commentary on the Epistle of Paul to the Ephesians.' Interestingly enough, he takes as his point of departure the only passage in the New Testament which even hints at the use of instrumental music in the service,

Be filled with the Spirit, addressing one another in psalms and hymns and spiritual songs, singing and *making melody* to the Lord with all your heart.[82]

---

78 St. Basil, 'Letter to the Clergy of Neo-Caesarea,' in *Letters of Saint Basil*, trans. Sister Agnes Way (New York: Fathers of the Church, 1955), II, 83.

79 St. Basil, 'Homily 14,' in *Exegetic Homilies*, trans. Sister Agnes Way (Washington, D.C.: The Catholic University of America Press), 213.

80 Ibid., 214. In Homily 21, Ibid., 341, Basil says the purpose of psalm singing is to 'correct the passions of the soul.' He then quotes, without comment, references to many musical instruments in Psalm 61.

81 Ibid., 217.

82 Ephesians 5:19. This same passage appears also in Colossians 3:16, but without the reference to 'making melody.'

'Making melody' is a phrase found in the Old Testament and in late medieval and Renaissance literature which is used as a synonym for some form of instrumental music. We believe this phrase simply slipped by unnoticed by the committee which assembled the New Testament, as we know it, in the fourth century. Jerome neatly sidesteps any implicit approval of instrumental music by mistranslating the final part as 'in your heart,' instead of 'with all your heart,' rendering the phrase 'making melody' a metaphor.

It is of further interest that St. Jerome, while recognizing here three basic kinds of Church music, psalms, hymns, and songs, returns to the ancient Greek concept of *ethos*.

> How the psalm, the hymn, and the song differ one from another we learn most fully in the Psalter. Here let us say briefly that hymns declare the power and majesty of the Lord and continually praise his works and favors, something which all those psalms contain to which the word 'Alleluia' is prefixed or appended. Psalms, moreover, properly affect the seat of the *ethos* in order that by means of this organ of the body we may know what ought to be done and what ought not to be done. The subtle moralist, however, who inquires into these things and examines the harmony of the world and the order and concord of all creatures, sings a spiritual song. To express our opinion more clearly to the simple-minded, the psalm is directed toward the body, the song toward the mind. We ought, then, to sing and to make melody and to praise the Lord more with the heart than with the voice.[83]

By this last sentence, Jerome means that it is not music itself, but the person, which praises God. Further, it is not the music which is important, but the *words* of the music which one sings.

> Let the servant of Christ sing so that he pleases, not through his voice, but through the words which he pronounces … [so that one does not] make of the house of God a popular theater.

St. John Chrysostom makes this same point: it is the words of church music which are most important, adding that one must not be inattentive when singing, 'but so the mind may hear the tongue.'[84] Even if you don't understand the words, they are still the most important thing!

> Even though the meaning of the words be unknown to you, teach your mouth to utter them meanwhile. For the tongue is made holy by the words when they are uttered with a ready and eager mind.[85]

Regarding the emphasis on the words, rather than the music, in church music, we have that remarkable passage by St. Augustine in which, after stating that the main reason for music is to help weaker minds rise to the feeling of devotion, he admits that on occasion he, too, began to listen to the *music* rather than the words. When he caught himself doing so, he considered that he had sinned.

---

[83] Quoted in Oliver Strunk, *Source Readings in Music History* (New York: Norton, 1950), 72.

[84] St. John Chrysostom, 'Exposition of Psalm XLI,' quoted in Oliver Strunk, *Source Readings in Music History* (New York: Norton, 1950), 68.

[85] Ibid., 69.

> Yet when it befalls me to be more moved with the voice than the words sung, I confess to have sinned penally, and then had rather not hear music.[86]

In any case, this kind of vocal church music was sufficient for Augustine, who saw no need for additional instruments.

> We sing praises to God, we chant our 'Alleluias' with hearts attuned to harmony far better than with the chords of the lyre.[87]

Augustine here was only expressing the view of the majority of early church writers, identical with the opinion of St. John Chrysostom that there was simply no need for instrumental music in the Church; no need for the long-practiced skill of these players.

> Here there is no need for the cithara, or for stretched strings, or for the plectrum, or for art, or for any instrument; but, if you like, you may yourself become a cithara, mortifying the members of the flesh and making a full harmony of mind and body ...
>
> Here there is no need for art which is slowly perfected; there is need only for lofty purpose, and we become skilled in a brief decisive moment.[88]

Finally, another of these early references to Church music is particularly interesting in its unconscious reflection of the function of the twin hemispheres of the brain, 'I will sing with the spirit and I will sing with the mind also.'[89] Ten verses earlier in this same chapter there is another reference to the spirit of the music. Here, in a famous passage, it is suggested that it is this quality which makes music itself comprehensible.

> If lifeless instruments, such as the flute or the harp, do not give distinct notes, how will anyone know what is played? And if the bugle gives an indistinct sound, who will get ready for battle?

---

[86] *The Confessions*, Book X.

[87] 'Sermon 243,' in Ibid., 278.

[88] Ibid., 70.

[89] I Corinthians 14:15.

Ancient Views on Music in Heaven

ONE OF THE MOST INTERESTING and curious points of agreement among the religions of all cultures is the assumption of a future life, as is documented by the ancient pyramids of Egypt and today's suicidal bombers in the Near East. According to Gibbon, the promise of a new and better life was one of the most important selling points for the new Christian Church and one of the most important explanations for its rapid growth.

> When the promise of eternal happiness was proposed to mankind on condition of adopting the faith, and of observing the precepts, of the gospel, it is no wonder that so advantageous an offer should have been accepted by great numbers of every religion, of every rank, and of every province n the Roman empire.
>
> The ancient Christians were animated by a contempt for their present existence, and by a just confidence in immortality, of which the doubtful and imperfect faith of modern ages cannot give us any adequate notion.[1]

The belief in this promise continues to be strongly held by Protestant and Catholic churches everywhere. Given its promise, it is more than a little curious that church philosophers have been so reluctant to tell us what Heaven will be like, aside from the popular notion of people wearing wings and sitting on clouds playing harps.

> Although I do not think anyone ever supposed there were sculptures or plays in heaven, it came to be taken for granted that there was music.[2]

When you think about it, it is rather interesting to consider all the things which are never spoken of as existing in heaven by theological and philosophical books. No one ever speaks of paintings, sculpture or books, not to mention houses, dogs and cats,[3] food and drink, golf or tennis. How *do* the people there spend their time—for eternity, after all? They must perform and listen to a lot of music, for music seems to be the only agreed upon activity assumed to exist there.

One must assume that the origin of this idea lies in the association of music with the divine assumed by many ancient writers as the reader has seen in the first chapter. At least one spiritual philosopher, the fifteenth-century Spanish rabbi, Meir ibn Gabbai, believed that in a proper performance of music, a 'magical resonance' occurs between earth and heaven, 'Because just as I am arousing here below, so the arousal will also be on high.'[4]

---

[1] Edward Gibbon, *The History of the Decline and Fall of the Roman Empire* (Philadelphia: Henry T. Coates & Co., 1845),I, XVI.

[2] Bryan Magee, *The Philosophy of Schopenhauer* (Oxford: Clarendon Press, 1983), 181.

[3] Will Rogers once famously pointed out that there do not seem to be dogs in Heaven, so when he died he would like to go to wherever they went.

[4] Avocat ha-Qodesh, quoted in Stuart Isacoff, *Temperament* (New York: Random House, 2003), 112.

For most writers of the Christian era, interest in this subject begins with the account in the New Testament where we are told that a choir of angels appeared and sang to shepherds, announcing the birth of Jesus.[5] By the way, in the fifteenth-century anonymous play, *The Shepherds*, one of the Chester mystery plays, there is a humorous scene in which the shepherds do not understand what the choir of angels is trying to tell them, because the choir was singing in Latin! The shepherds argue at length trying to decide what the words were which they heard in this music. 'Gloria' was heard by one as 'grorus glorus.' No, says another, it was 'glorus, glarus, glorius,' etc. Finally, they give up and decide that they should sing something to bring them solace and a passing Trowle teaches them to sing a popular song, 'Trolly, lolly, lolly, lo.'[6]

Another who reportedly actually heard this chorus of heavenly singers, according to Gregory of Tours (538–594 AD), was Severinus, the bishop of Cologne.

> The blessed Severinus, bishop of Cologne, lived an honorable life and was praiseworthy in all respects. One Sunday, while he and his clerics were as usual visiting the holy shrines, he heard a chorus of singers on high at the hour when the blessed man died. He summoned his archdeacon and asked whether the voices that he heard so attentively were also striking his ears. The archdeacon replied: 'Certainly not.' Then Severinus said: 'Listen carefully.' The archdeacon began to stretch his neck up, pricked up his ears, and with the assistance of a staff stood on his tiptoes. But I believe that this man who did not deserve to hear these songs was not of equal merit. Then the archdeacon and the blessed bishop together knelt on the ground and prayed to the Lord that divine mercy might allow this man to hear the singing. They stood up, and again the old bishop asked: 'What do you hear?' The archdeacon replied: 'I hear the voices of men chanting Psalms, as if in heaven; but I do not know at all what it is.' Severinus said to him: 'I will tell you what this is. My lord bishop Martin has migrated from this world, and now the angels are escorting him on high with their singing.'[7]

While nearly every writer attributes the music of heaven to angels, this passage is one of few we know where the angels are specifically called male. Also, it is quite rare when anyone on earth claims to have heard this music. According to Johannes de Grocheo, in *De Musica* (ca. 1300 AD), only someone such as this bishop is able to hear this music.

> Nor is it pertinent for a musician to treat of the song of angels, unless he has been at the same time a theologian and a prophet; no one can have any experience of such song except by divine inspiration.[8]

In a play by Molina (seventeenth century)[9], *Damned for Despair* (III, iii), which was one of the sources for Mozart's *Don Giovanni*, the character, Paulo, hears 'Heavenly music filling the air!' This performance was by two angels who are bearing the soul of a criminal, Enrico, up

---

5   Some modern editions say simply 'praise' rather than 'sing.'

6   *The Shepherds*, 386ff., quoted in David Mills, *The Chester Mystery Cycle* (East Lansing: Colleagues Press, 1992), 140ff.

7   Gregory of Tours, 'The Suffering and Miracles of the Martyr St. Julian,' V, xxxvi, trans. Raymond Van Dam, in *Saints and their Miracles in late Antique Gaul* (Princeton: Princeton University Press, 1993), 206.

8   Johannes de Grocheo, *De Musica*, trans. Albert Seay (Colorado Springs: Colorado College Music Press, 1967), 10.

9   Fray Gabriel Tellez (ca. 1581–1648) wrote under the name of Tirso de Molina.

to heaven. Another seventeenth-century play, by the English playwright, Thomas Dekker, in *The Virgin Martyr* (V, i) has two references to music of the spirit world, one of which reads, 'tis in the Ayre, or from some better place, a power divine.'[10]

Then there is that curious remark by Aristotle that he had heard that on the Ionian island of Lipara, there was a tomb where at night one could distinctly hear, 'the sound of drums and cymbals, and laughter, along with uproar and the rattle of castanets.'[11] The German composer and critic, Johann Mattheson (1681–1764), believed that while in the Garden of Eden man could hear the music of heaven, but once expelled this knowledge was lost.[12] Mattheson also believed that the music of heaven existed before the creation of the earth, a conclusion he apparently based on Job 38:7.

> when the morning stars sang together,
> and all the sons of God shouted for joy.

Some of the most interesting commentary on the music of heaven is by philosophers who find that even if we cannot hear this music, it nevertheless has some specific purpose on earth. The fourteenth-century English writer, Richard Rolle, for example, finds the first purpose of music sung by angels is to comfort the soul.

> Also oure Lorde comforthes a saule by Aungells sange. Bot what that sange es, it may noghte [be] dyscryuded be no bodyly lyknes, for it es [spiritual], and abown all manere of ymagynacyone and mans reson.[13]

Only those with a pure soul can hear this song, but if they can, then they can sing a new song, of heavenly bliss, without deceit or pretending.

> Than [truly] may he synge a newe sange, and [truly] may be here a blysfull heuenly sown and Aungells sange, with-owtten dessayte or feynynge.[14]

And finally, Rolle considers the singing by the angels as being almost a kind of insurance policy, protecting the listener against sin. Accordingly, he warns that if you see a man spiritually occupied fall into sin, deceits or 'frensyes,' you will know he has never heard angel's song or heavenly sound. For truly, hearing the angel's song makes one so wise he cannot succumb to the sins of fantasy, indiscretion or tricks of the devil.

---

[10] His contemporaries, Beaumont and Fletcher, in *The Pilgrim* (V, iv) have a stage note calling for the music of Fairies.

[11] 'De Mirabilibus,' 839a.

[12] Johann Mattheson, *Der vollkommene Capellmeister* (1739), trans. Ernest Harriss (Ann Arbor: UMI Research Press, 1981), Foreword III. In his book, *Behauptung der Himmlischen Musik ...* (1747), Mattheson elaborates on his belief in the existence of music in Heaven and the origin of music in angels worshiping God.

[13] Richard Rolle, 'Of the Vertu,' in *English Writings of Richard Rolle*, ed. Hope Allen (Oxford: Clarendon Press, 1963), 17.

[14] Ibid., 18.

> For [truly], he that verreyly heres Aungels sange, he es made so wyse that he sall never erre by fantasye, ne by indiscrecyon, ne by no sleghte of the deuelle.[15]

Zarlino, the famous sixteenth-century Italian theorist, found one purpose of the music in heaven to be a genetically implanted aid for the support of man in manual labor.

> Many were of the opinion that in this life every soul is won by music, and, although the soul is imprisoned by the body, it still remembers and is conscious of the music of the heavens, forgetting every hard and annoying labor.[16]

John Milton apparently thought that the music of heaven played a role in helping singers learn to connect with the divine. In his poem, 'To Leonora, as She Sings at Rome,' music is referred to as a 'Third Intelligence' which comes from Heaven which enters the throat of the singer and 'graciously teaches mortal hearts the power to grow accustomed insensibly to sounds immortal.'[17]

Regarding the function of music in heaven, Thomas Mace (1613–1709) offers his interesting belief that normal languages will not be used and that we will all communicate through music there.

> And I am subject to believe (if in Eternity we shall make use of any languages, or shall not understand one another, by some more spiritual conveyances, or infusions of perceptions, than by verbal language) that music itself may be that eternal and celestial language.[18]

A typical example is found in the fourteenth-century English 'Merceres' play when of course the most familiar image of functional music in heaven is the trumpet which announces the Day of Judgment. God says,

> Therefore mine angels will I send
> To blow their trumpets, that all may hear
> The time is come when I make end.
> Angels, blow your trumpets high,
> Every creature for to call.[19]

---

[15] Ibid., 19.

[16] 'Le Istitutioni harmoniche,' quoted in Claude V. Palisca, *Humanism in Italian Renaissance Musical Thought* (New Haven: Yale University Press, 1985), 179.

[17] 'To Leonora, as She Sings at Rome,' in *The Works of John Milton*, ed. Frank Patterson (New York: Columbia University Press, 1931–1938), I, 229.

[18] Thomas Mace, *Musick's Monument* [1676] (Paris: Editions du Centre National de la Recherche Scientifique, 1966), 272. The use of music as a literate language had many supporters, including Voltaire. It was finally achieved, apparently, by François Sudre in the nineteenth century although no one else was ever able to duplicate his amazing public demonstrations. See www.whitwellbooks.com

[19] J.S. Purvis, *The York Cycle* (London: S.P.C.K, 1957), 374.

The use of the plural here, when God says he will send his angels to blow their trumpets, reminds us of the terrible tales of destruction told in the Book of Revelations, 8:2ff, when seven angels,[20] one by one, blow their trumpets. The passage begins,

> Now the seven angels who had the seven trumpets made ready to blow them. The first angel blew his trumpet and there followed hail and fire, mixed with blood, which fell on the earth; and a third of the earth was burnt up, and a third of the trees were burnt up, and all the green grass was burnt up.

Chaucer creates an interesting variation on the use of the trumpet on the Day of Judgment in his poem, 'The House of Fame.'[21] In this allegorical dream, we come upon the goddess of Fame who sits in judgment of various groups of people making their pleas for lasting fame. To help dispense her judgments, she calls upon Aeolus, the god of the winds, to bring his trumpets [*clarioun*]. One of these is a trumpet of gold, called 'Clear Praise' [*Clere Laude*], and the other is black, made of brass by the devil, and is called 'Slander.' When this black trumpet is blown, the sound, coming out as fast as a ball from a gun, is described as a foul noise, a kind of black, blue, red, greenish smoke, such as comes from the chimney where men melt lead.

For a group of people who have done good works, but never received credit, the golden trumpet is blown. Presumably the golden trumpet was also blown for the next group, those who don't want credit, their good works having been done for goodness and for no other reason. 'I grant your wish,' says the goddess of Fame, 'let your works die!'

The following group also wanted no fame, for their works were done for God. 'What! are you mad?,' the goddess responds, 'You think you will do good and have no glory for it?' She has the golden trumpet 'ring out in music' their deeds for all the world to hear.

The next group is surely troubadours, for their 'good works' have all been done for women, for which 'women loved us madly,' but often rewarded only with brooches or rings. For all this hard work, they felt they deserved renown and the goddess agreed and had the golden trumpet play again.

Another group, though they were 'gluttonous swine and idle wretches full of the rotten vice of sloth,' thought they deserved fame on the same basis as the previous group, but the goddess had them condemned by the black trumpet. The following group of 'treacherous' people received the same reward.

John Milton, in 'Paradise Lost,' mentions the heavenly trumpet when the angels Michael and Gabriel are at war against Satan.

> Nor with less dread the loud
> Ethereal Trumpet from on high began to blow ...
> In silence their bright Legions, to the sound
> Of instrumental Harmonie that breathed
> Heroic Ardor to adventurous deeds ...[22]

---

[20] In Joshua 6:8 there are also seven trumpets, who play a role in the fall of the walls of Jericho.

[21] This poem also contains, we believe, a rare fictional description of one of the medieval minstrel schools.

[22] 'Paradise Lost,' in VI, 60ff, *The Works of John Milton*, ed. Frank Patterson (New York: Columbia University Press, 1931–1938), II, 180.

Speaking of Satan, we might digress briefly to observe that the nature of the music of hell has never been of much interest to early writers. The sole example we are familiar with is by Voltaire. In his, 'The Maid of Orleans,' he offers a description of Hell which includes, 'songs in praise of drinking loudly roar.'[23] A resident of Hell observes,

> Cursed and tormented here, why care a jot
> For psalms and praises sung where we are not?

We find interesting some of the specific things the various early writers looked forward to on the day when they would at last hear the music in heaven. The first century BC, Roman poet, Tibullus, looked forward not only to hearing the singing, but to his belief that 'Venus herself will lead me along the way.'[24] The great sixteenth-century French poet, Pierre de Ronsard, looked forward to hearing in heaven, in person, the singing by the great lyric poets of ancient Greece.

> Ah, God! to think, mine ear
> Alcaeus' lyre shall hear,
> And Sappho's, over all
> Most musical![25]

It was hearing 'Spirits immortal sing' that Milton looked forward to.[26] The seventeenth-century English poet, Edward Young, declared that when he got there he would not sing with the heavenly choir at all unless it was conducted by Raphael!

> But sing no more—no more I sing,
> Or reassume the lyre,
> Unless vouchsafed an humble part
> Where Raphael leads the choir.[27]

And Alexander Pope upon imagining that he hears the music of heaven, utters some of the most famous lines in English literature,

> The world recedes; it disappears!
> Heaven opens on my eyes! my ears
> With sounds seraphim ring:
> Lend, lend your winds! I mount! I fly!
> O Grave! where is thy Victory?
> O Death! where is thy Sting?[28]

---

[23] 'The Maid of Orleans,' in *The Works of Voltaire* (New York: St. Hubert Guild, 1901), XL, Canto V.
[24] Tibullus, *Poems*, I, iii.
[25] *Songs and Sonnets of Pierre de Ronsard*, trans. Curtis Page (Westport: Hyperion Press, 1924), 113.
[26] 'Paradise Lost,' II, 552 in *The Works of John Milton*, II, 57.
[27] Edward Young, 'Resignation,' in *Edward Young: The Complete Works* (Hildesheim: Olms, 1968), II, 123.
[28] 'The Dying Christian to his Soul' (1712), in *The Works of Alexander Pope* (New York: Gordian Press, 1967), IV, 409.

So what do the early writers and philosophers think the music in heaven will sound like? In early literature some form of the word 'sweet' was often associated with the most beautiful music. The use of this word appears to have evolved from the expression, 'honeyed' music in ancient Greek literature. And so in the fourteenth-century English poet, Richard Rolle, we find 'all kinds of sweet tones of music, as any man's heart might like.'

> And of alkyn swet tones of musyke,
> That til any mans hert mught like.[29]

In the fifteenth century we find the English poet, John Lydgate, varies the idea by writing of 'sugared' music.

> Herd of angelis, with sugrid notis cleer,
> Celestial song in ther melodie …[30]

Again we find 'Sweet harmony' in the sixteenth-century Italian poet, Guarini,[31] and 'Sweet, charming symphonie,' in Milton in describing the music of the angels. Happy or gay music in heaven, imagined the seventeenth-century Dutch poet, Joost van den Vondel.

> O choristers of love,
> Whose choral hymns and harmony
> Amid the flow of radiant ray
> Make heaven's hall with music gay,
> And fill our hearts with melody,
> And steep our hearts in bliss untold.[32]

Most descriptions of the music of heaven involves choirs. The seventeenth-century English poet, James Thomson, thinks he already hears them.

> Methinks I hear the full celestial choir,
> Through Heaven's high dome their awful anthem raise;
> Now chanting clear, and now they all conspire
> To swell the lofty hymn from praise to praise.[33]

---

[29] Richard Rolle, 'The Pricke of Conscience,' (Berlin: A. Asher, 1863), 9252.

[30] John Lydgate, *The Life of Saint Alban and Saint Amphibal*, ed. J. E. Van Der Westhuizen (Leiden: Brill, 1974), 4127.

[31] Giambattista Guarini, *The Faithful Shepherd* [Il Pastor Fido], in *Five Italian Renaissance Comedies* (New York: Penguin Books, 1978). Guarini (1538–1612) served the courts of Florence and Urbino both as a courtier and in diplomatic and literary duties.

[32] 'Lucifer,' II, lines 500ff. Joost van den Vondel (1587–1679), after inheriting a hosiery shop from his father, engaged in a program of self-education through which he studied Latin, Greek, Italian, French and German. Considered one of the most important Dutch poets of this period, he wrote some twenty-eight plays.

[33] 'An Ode on Aeolus's Harp,' in *The Poetical Works of James Thomson* (London: Bell and Daldy, c. 1860), II, 228. James Thomson (1700–1748) was highly respected by both Voltaire and Lessing, but has never been esteemed by his own countrymen.

His contemporary, John Milton, says a *thousand* choirs,

> Their loud up-lifted Angel trumpets blow,
> And the Cherubick host in thousand choirs
> Touch their immortal Harps of golden wires …[34]

and sound symphonious of ten thousand Harps that tuned Angelic harmonies.[35]

The twelfth-century mystic, Hildegard von Bingen, agrees, saying there will be more singers than sands of the sea or fruit of the earth! She describes their voices with great enthusiasm.

> For most of the good angels look up to God. They acknowledge God with all the melodious sound of their hymns of praise, and laud in wonderful harmony the mysteries that have always been with God and are still with God today. The angels can never stop praising God because they are unencumbered by earthly bodies. They bear witness to the Godhead through the living resonance of their splendid voices, which are more numerous than the sands of the sea and which outnumber all the fruits that the Earth might ever produce. Their voices have a richer harmony than all the sounds living creatures have ever produced, and their voices are brighter than all the splendor of the sun, moon, and stars sparkling in the waters. More wonderful is this sound than the music of the spheres that arises from the blowing of the winds that sustain the four elements and are well adjusted to them.[36]

Beyond the choirs of angels, early writers anticipate a variety of other instruments will be heard in heaven. John Milton mentions the instrumental sounds made by the angels in a passage where he also describes the angels as 'millions of spiritual Creatures' who 'walk the Earth Unseen, both when we wake, and when we sleep.'

> Celestial voices to the midnight air,
> Sole, or responsive each to others note
> Singing their great Creator: oft in bands
> While they keep watch, or nightly rounding walk
> With Heavenly touch of instrumental sounds
> In full harmonic number joined, their songs
> Divide the night, and lift our thoughts to Heaven.[37]

In 'Paradise Lost' he contemplates hearing 'songs and choral symphonies.'[38]

Some seventeenth-century writers expect to find the still popular Renaissance instruments in heaven, as we see, for example, in a poem by Matthaus Apelles von Lowenstern.

> Great bands of angels round him soar,
> Psalter and harp make His glory more.[39]

---

[34] 'At a solemn Musick.'

[35] 'Paradise Lost,' VII, 557.

[36] 'Vision Six: 4,' in *The Book of Divine Works*, ed. Matthew Fox (Santa Fe: Bear & Company, 1987), 181ff.

[37] 'Paradise Lost,' in *The Works of John Milton*, IV, 682ff, II, 130ff. Celestial Choirs are mentioned again in Book VII, 254.

[38] 'Paradise Lost,' V, 160ff, in Ibid., II, 149.

[39] Matthaus Apelles von Lowenstern (1594–1648), 'Alcaic Ode,' in Ibid., 215. Lowenstern began his career as a lowly teacher and then became Kapellmeister in Bernstadt. He had the good fortune to marry an aristocratic young lady, which, in time, led to his becoming an imperial counselor to Ferdinand III, who also raised him to nobility.

Another seventeenth-century poet, Thomas Traherne, adds a lute to the instruments he expects to hear in heaven, in a Christmas poem which begins, 'Shall Dumpish Melancholy spoil my Joys.'

> Shake off thy Sloth, my drowsy Soul, awake;
> With Angels sing
> Unto thy King,
> And pleasant Musick make;
> Thy Lute, thy Harp, or else thy Heart-strings take,
> And with thy Musick let thy Sense awake.[40]

His contemporary, Richard Crashaw, anticipates that as angels are invisible, so will be their instruments when he writes, 'Angels with crystal viols come.'[41]

Richard Rolle expects to find a complete wind band, as is suggested by his use of a phrase exclusively associated with them in early English literature.

> Alle other manere of melody,
> Of the delytable noys of mynstralsy.[42]

When the Puritan, John Bunyan, uses the term 'noise' with regard to the music in heaven he appears to mean only trumpets. In his *Pilgrim's Progress*, he gives an extended description of the music he foresees will meet those who arrive in heaven.

> There came out also at this time to meet them, several of the king's trumpeters, clothed in white and shining raiment, who, with melodious noises, and loud, made even the heavens to echo with their sound ...
>
> This done, they compassed them round on every side; some went before, some behind, and some on the right hand, some on the left ..., continually sounding as they went, with melodious noise, in notes on high ... Thus, they walked on together; and as they walked, ever and anon these trumpeters, even with joyful sound, would, by mixing their music with looks and gestures, still signify to Christian and his brother, how welcome they were into their company.[43]

---

[40] 'On Christmas-Day,' in Thomas Traherne, *Centuries, Poems and Thanksgivings* (Oxford: Clarendon Press, 1958), 110. Thomas Traherne (1634–1674) published no poetry during his life and his name was not known until the discovery of a manuscript in 1910.

[41] 'The Weeper,' in *The Complete Poetry of Richard Crashaw*, ed. George Williams (New York: New York University Press, 1972), 129.

[42] Rolle, *English Writings of Richard Rolle*, 9252.

[43] 'Pilgrim's Progress,' in *The Works of John Bunyan*, ed. George Offor (London: Blackie and Son, 1853), III, 165. John Bunyan (1628–1688) is considered the greatest prose writer among the Puritans of the seventeenth century. Only the Bible was so widely read in English homes for the subsequent three centuries. Bunyan was also the epitome of the 'hell and brimstone' preacher.

Later in the Celestial City, 'the trumpets continually sound so melodiously,' that people could not sleep yet they woke as refreshed as if they had.[44] Finally, in his poem, 'One Thing is Needful,' we wonder if he was anticipating better intonation from the string instruments in heaven.

> The strings of music here are tuned
> For heavenly harmony.[45]

Since, of course, no one can know what the music of heaven will really be like, we have seen many centuries of writers and philosophers taking the music they know on earth and supposing that that is what they will hear in heaven. But the English writer, Joseph Addison (1672–1719), says no, it's the other way around. The music we have on earth reflects that of heaven.[46]

> Music—the greatest good that mortals know,
> and all of Heaven we have below.

We think perhaps that's the best way to think of it and it reminds us of something Schubert once said about the first movement of Mozart's *G minor Symphony*:

> If you listen very carefully, you can hear the wings of angels.

---

44 Ibid., 240. A similar musical welcome is described in 'The Holy War,' in Ibid., III, 359.

45 'One Thing is Needful,' in Ibid., III, 733.

46 Martin Peerson (1572–1650) made a similar comment in the dedication for his *Mottets or Grave Chamber Music* of 1630. He wrote, 'that heaven upon earth, which it found here, in Musicke and Harmonicall proportions.' Which in turn recalls the line in the 'Lord's Prayer,' Matthew 6:10, 'Thy will be done, on earth as it is in heaven.'

St. Augustine on Music

IN AUGUSTINE (354–430 AD) we come to the most important Christian philosopher of the first five hundred years of the Christian Era. No one else was so influential in the future development of the Church and even today his impact can still be measured in the Roman Catholic Church. For our subject he offers a rare and extensive view of music in society before the onset of the 'Dark Ages.'

He had a broad education in the liberal arts, including music, and enough study of 'pagan' philosophy, the philosophy of the ancient Greeks, to make him believe in Reason almost as much as he believed in God. His intelligence is evident in his ability to form some very important questions, and for this we join in his standing ovation. But it is when we read his answers that we must take our seat and offer only polite applause, for his answers on our subject are too often simply wrong.

His powerful, rational mind did not seem to be accompanied by any genuine appreciation of the irrational, the arts, or the contribution made to life by the emotions. Since he describes having had a very full range of normal life experiences before he joined the Church, we are astonished that his writings suggest that he completely failed to understand the point and purpose of music. We prefer to believe that the views he left were restricted by his role as a Church leader and that we are not seeing the true scope of his thought.

Regarding his own education in the liberal arts, including music, Augustine maintains that in his youth he studied and understood them all without the benefit of a teacher.

> Whatever was written, either on rhetoric, or logic, geometry, music, and arithmetic, by myself without much difficulty or any instructor, I understood.[1]

Understanding the liberal arts was, for the fourth-century Church fathers, somewhat of an irrelevant concept. Faith was what mattered. Only later did some Church philosophers come to believe that the liberal arts might have a value in helping the Christian understand this message. For Augustine, education had one central purpose: to help man understand the difference between himself and God!

> All instruction in wisdom, the purpose of which is the education of men, is for distinguishing the creator and the creature, and worshiping the one as Lord and confessing the other as subject.[2]

---

[1] *The Confessions*, trans. Edward B. Pusey (New York: Collier), Book IV.
[2] *Eighty-Three Different Questions*, trans. David L. Mosher (Washington, D.C.: The Catholic University of America Press), 81.

In another place, speaking to a poet, he takes a broader view.

> You must return to those verses, for instruction in the liberal arts, if only it is moderate and concise, produces devotees more alert and steadfast and better equipped for embracing truth.[3]

Perhaps because he sensed that the mysteries of music lay outside the realm of Reason, Augustine unfortunately fails to accept that the study of music can make any positive contribution to the mind.

> Studies that are taken up with things that are more curious than solidly worthwhile—granted even that on occasion they are not entirely useless—dissipate the mind and hence must be put in our second category. Just because one aulos player so delighted the ears of the populace, according to Varro, that they made him a king is no reason for supposing that we can effect enlargement of the mind by aulos playing.[4]

The only value he can recommend in the study of music is a secondary one, for learning 'order.' And even in this case only moderate study is recommended.

> Now in music, in geometry, in the movements of the stars, in the fixed ratios of numbers, order reigns in such manner that if one desires to see its source and its very shrine, so to speak, he either finds it in these, or he is unerringly led to it through them. Indeed, such learning, if one uses it with moderation—and in this matter, nothing is to be feared more than excess—rears for philosophy a soldier ... so competent that he sallies forth wherever he wishes and leads others as well, and reaches that ultimate goal, beyond which he desires nothing else, beyond which he neither ought nor can seek anything.[5]

Augustine reveals in his *Confessions* that he, when young, had had some experience in acting and in the composition of poetry. But what little he tells us of this experience only reflects his later lack of sympathy, reflecting the Church position, with the arts and his subsequent feelings of emptiness.

> [From my 19th year to my 28th] hunting after the emptiness of popular praise, down even to theatrical applause, and poetic prizes, and strife for grassy garlands, and the follies of shows, and the intemperance of desires.[6]

Neither were these feelings of emptiness filled by music, books or entertainment.

> For I bore about a shattered and bleeding soul, impatient of being borne by me, yet where to repose it, I found not. Not in calm groves, not in games and music, nor in fragrant spots, nor in curious banquetings, nor in the pleasures of the bed; nor in books or poetry, found it repose.[7]

---

3   *Divine Providence and the Problem of Evil*, trans. Ludwig Schopp (New York: CIMA Publishing Co.), 261.

4   *The Magnitude of the Soul*, trans. Ludwig Schopp in *Writings of Saint Augustine* (New York: CIMA), II, xx.

5   *Divine Providence*, 289.

6   *The Confessions*. This last reference included, in his youth, a lusty appreciation of the female sex, which resulted in one of the most memorable prayers of the Middle Ages, 'Give me chastity—but not yet!'

7   *The Confessions*, Book IV.

The man should have left us a much more vivid description of early medieval aesthetics than he did. But if the perspective he left is a limited one, it is nevertheless one of the most interesting discussions of its kind extant from the fourth century.

From a passing admission by Augustine, we know there were listeners who appreciated music purely for music's sake in the fourth century. He is speaking of various things which make men happy, when he contributes the following illustration of knowledgeable listeners of good music.

> Many decide that for them the happy life is found in vocal music and in the sounds of string instruments and auloi. Whenever these are absent, they account themselves unhappy, whereas when they are at hand, they are thrilled with joy.[8]

But Augustine does not include himself among those who enjoy such enthusiasm for secular music. In his *Confessions*, he mentions only that as a youth he found some poetry which he sang and it became part of him, while in other cases it did not stay with him.

> For verses and poems I can turn to true food, and 'Medea flying,' though I did sing, I maintained not; though I heard it sung, I believed not ...[9]

Augustine has left an account of an artist-composer, no doubt a friend of his youth, which perhaps reveals some of his own concerns about art music. Augustine admits here that he has sufficient knowledge of music to judge this artist as being quite musical, but he was bothered that this artist preferred to withdraw from his friends to work and did not want to be disturbed when composing. Augustine worries that his friend will thus lose his ability for *intellectual* communication, so his basic advice is for him to stop working and go have a drink!

> When we had returned, we found Licentius eagerly striving to compose verses. But Helicon would never have relieved him of his thirst, for—although only one course was served at our lunch—he had quietly withdrawn when we had reached about the middle, and he had drunk nothing.
>
> I said to him: 'I wish that some day or other you would master poetry, since you have become so ardently attached to it: not that this kind of perfection would afford me any great pleasure, but because I see you have become so eager for it that you can be alienated from it only by disgust, and this readily happens after perfection has been reached. Furthermore, since you are quite musical, I should prefer to have you inflict your own verses on our ears, rather than have you—like the little birds we see enclosed in cages—singing words you do not understand in those Greek tragedies. But I advise you to go for a drink, if you have any regard for Hortensius and philosophy. In fact, in that disputation between yourself and Trygetius, you have already offered her your first fruits as a most pleasing libation, and she, far more than poetry, has enkindled in you a glowing desire for the knowledge of great and truly profitable things. But, while I wish to invite both of you back to the arena of those intellectual exercises that impart refinement to the mind, I fear lest it become a labyrinth for both of you.'[10]

---

[8]   *The Free Choice of the Will*, trans. Robert P. Russell (Washington, D.C.: The Catholic University of America Press), xiii i.

[9]   *The Confessions*, Book III.

[10] *Answer to Skeptics*, trans. Ludwig Schopp (New York: CIMA Publishing Co.), IV, 7.

The reader will notice the reference in the above to the fact that most poetry was sung. In another treatise, Augustine mentions this poet and his singing again, now expressing even more concern that his poetry might separate him from reality.

> Here, fearing that his running to extremes on poetry might take him away from philosophy, I said: 'I am vexed somewhat because, singing and crooning in all kinds of meter, you pursue that verse-making of yours which may be erecting between yourself and reality a wall more impenetrable than they are trying to rear between your lovers (Pyramus and Thisbe), for they used to sigh to each other through a tiny natural crevice.'[11]

Regarding the theater, Augustine particularly objected to the use of plot and song to glorify the pagan gods, many of whom, in their very myths, were guilty of a variety of crimes.

> I must confess that the better educated pagans [Greeks] reject such stories about their gods ...
> [But], however much they may protest, they cannot wholly clear their gods of crime if they have to stage for them, on demand, shows in which they basely depict the very stories they so loftily deny. For, so long as the gods are so greatly appeased by these false and filthy goings-on, even if the burden of the legendary song is a divine sin which never happened, it is still a real sin for the gods to be delighted with it.[12]

In another place, Augustine blames the pagan gods themselves for the introduction of theater.

> The stage plays, those exhibitions of depravity and unbounded license, were not introduced in Rome by men's vices, but by the command of your gods ... If your mind retains enough sense to esteem the soul more than the body, then choose whom you should worship.[13]

For fourth-century Romans the ancient cult-religious ceremonies were now more of a ritual than theology to govern their lives. Augustine focuses on one of the more ancient and popular, the 'obscene rites of the Phrygian goddess Cybele,' in his *The City of God*, where he criticizes the Roman citizen who participates in this festival.

> Why, then, now that disaster has laid a heavy hand on you, do you complain about Christian civilization, if it be not that you desire to wallow securely in voluptuousness and, free from all restraint, give free rein to your profligate conduct? For, you do not desire to have peace and abundance of all things, in order to use these goods like decent men, that is, with measure, sobriety, temperance, and piety. No, your purpose is rather to pursue every kind of pleasure with insane extravagance; thus, out of your prosperity, you conjure up that corruption of morals which is more deadly than the fury of your enemies.[14]

Now Augustine provides a first-hand description of the cult-religious celebrations as he knew them in the fourth century.

---

[11] *Divine Providence and the Problem of Evil*, 247.

[12] *The City of God*, XVIII, xii.

[13] Ibid., I, xxxii.

[14] Ibid., I, xxx.

> I myself, in my younger days, used to frequent the sacrilegious stage plays and comedies. I used to watch the demoniacal fanatics and listen to the choruses, and take delight in the obscene shows in honor of their gods and goddesses, of the virgin Caelestis and the Berecynthian Cybele, mother of the gods. Before the latter's couch on the day of her solemn bathing, ribald refrains were publicly sung about her by lewd actors that were unfit for the ear of the mother of the gods, and of the mother of any Senator or decent man—so unspeakably bestial, in fact, that even the mothers of the players themselves would have been ashamed to listen …
>
> Surely, the comedians themselves would have blushed to rehearse at home before their mothers the obscene words and actions which they uttered and performed in public before the mother of the gods and in the presence of a vast assemblage of both sexes. If curiosity could entice such numbers to come, a shocked sense of decency surely should have hurried them home. If these enormities are religious service, what can sacrilege be? If that bathing is purification, what is pollution?[15]

From his later perspective as a very Reason-centered Church philosopher, Augustine suggests that a temple dedicated to Plato would be better than what he had witnessed in the celebration of Cybele.

> How much more sensible and proper would it be to have Plato's writings read in a temple dedicated to him than to have the mutilation of the priests of Cybele, the consecration of eunuchs, the slashing of insane men, in the temples of the demons, the perpetration of every cruel and foul, or foully cruel and cruelly foul, abomination that is wont to pass for a religious rite.[16]

Although Augustine freely admits his participation in performing music in his youth, again speaking later as a Church philosopher the reader has noticed that in the foregoing discussion of music and the arts he has chosen to portray himself as a somewhat disinterested observer. In a later book, however, he gives himself away through demonstrating a thorough personal knowledge of both the physical and psychological nature of music.

In a separate book, *On Music*, Augustine defines music as the science of modulating [*modulandi*] well.[17] Augustine apparently used this word as a synonym for 'movement,' as indeed one finds in a modern English dictionary which gives the alternate definition, 'to adjust to or keep in proper measure or proportion.'[18] From this it followed, as the reader will find below, that for Augustine the science of composition had to do with the organization of conceptual materials and not with the communication of emotional ideas. Augustine uses this word again when he points out that similar organizational structures are found in oratory and dance, although he was hesitant to associate them with music.

> Many things in singing and dancing are reprehensible, and that, if we take the word *modulatio* from them, the almost divine art [of music] becomes degraded.

---

[15] Ibid., II, iv.

[16] Ibid., II, vii.

[17] Saint Augustine, *On Music*, trans. William Francis Jackson Knight (London: Orthological Institute, 1949), I, ii.

[18] *Webster's Ninth New Collegiate Dictionary*.

The element of music which was most susceptible to rational discussion, under the definition given above, is rhythm. For Augustine, the rhythm of music was closely tied to mathematics and the rhythms of poetry. Indeed, he says what grammarians teach is 'the difference between long and short syllables.'[19] He contends that it is at this level that the listener is delighted by the rhythmic organization of music, that it is these 'short interval lengths which delight us in singing and dancing.' Here he also makes the interesting observation that we can not retain the perception of music which lasts an hour or more.

> All well measured movements admittedly belong to the rationale of this discipline, if indeed it is the science of mensurating well ... keeping within themselves their end of ornament and delight, yet even in proper ratios these movements ... cannot be suited to our senses when accomplished in a long space of time, an hour or more.[20]

Augustine also notes that when historical poetry is set to music these long and short syllables are sometimes altered according to the 'rationale of the measure,' the music having precedence. The grammarian objects to this, he says, but 'the science of music is not outraged in the least.'[21] He provides an interesting example of this kind of alteration in the lengthening of a final syllable with music, when followed by a rest. He suggests there is a natural desire for the ear to hear a longer note in such a circumstance, even as long as twice its indicated length.

> Why, too, is a short syllable taken for a long one when followed by a rest—and not by convention, but by natural consideration directing the ears ... The nature of hearing and passing over in silence allows the lengthening of a syllable beyond two times: so what is also filled with rest can be filled with sound.[22]

The phrase, 'rationale of the measure,' suggests that the old system of rhythm based on syllabic modes was developing into the modern practice of meter organized on pulse. Augustine, in the following, seems to define this in a way which appears to the modern reader very much like music with and without bar lines.

> Since it is not the same thing to roll forward, although in legitimate feet [the 'longs' and 'shorts'], yet without any definite end, and to progress likewise in legitimate feet, but to be bounded by a fixed end, these kinds, therefore, had to be distinguished by names. So the first was called only by the name proper to it, rhythm, but the other by meter as well as rhythm.[23]

---

[19] *On Music*, II, i.

[20] Ibid., I, xiii.

[21] Ibid., II, i and II, ii.

[22] Ibid., VI, x. We see this principle in the Baroque long appoggiatura, where a following space is filled with the resolution. In music of the Classical Period there was a preference for the reverse: notes followed by rests were played one-half their notated value.

[23] Ibid., V, i.

An even stronger suggestion of a modern concept of meter can be seen in his implication that a conductor was responsible for the control of this aspect of time.

> Now, fix your ears on the sound and your eyes on the beats. For the hand beating time is not to be heard but seen, and note must be taken of the amount of time given to the arsis and to the thesis.[24]

Finally, Augustine suggests that this delight which one takes in organized time has its origin in the innate organization of the 'laws of equality, unity, and order,' of the universe, which in turn are created by God.[25] Augustine follows this thought immediately by observing that God has also given man an innate ability to perceive form. In a poem, for example, our pleasure derives from the whole, not the individual rhythms alone as they are heard.

> In a poem, if syllables should live and perceive only so long as they sound, the harmony and beauty of the connected work would in no way please [the listeners]. For they could not see or approve the whole, since it would be fashioned and perfected by the very passing away of these singulars.[26]

The first five books of Augustine's *On Music* consist of lengthy discussions of the old rhythmic modes of poetry, a discourse he understands most readers will find rather dull.

> Let's hope a dutiful labor will readily excuse our triviality in the eyes of benevolent men.[27]

In Book Six he proceeds to a more philosophic level, which he presumes those 'with tumultuous tongues taking vulgar delight in the noise of rhythm-dancers' will probably not read.

It is here, in Book Six, that we find the most extraordinary discussion on the essence of music to be found in the first six centuries of the Christian Era. This thoughtful passage, which reveals the true depth of Augustine's interest in music, begins with his asking, 'Where is music?' Is it [1] in the sound itself, [2] in the perception of the listener, [3] in the performer, or [4] in the memory?

Regarding the first, he suggests that everyone would accept the possibility of a sound, such as a drop of liquid, existing where there is no listener to hear it. The second, of necessity, requires the first.

Number three, the performance, Augustine does not consider as fundamental as the first two, for we can hear music in our minds where there is no sound or performance at all. This kind of listening is, of course, closely related to the fourth, memory.

---

[24] Ibid., II, xiii.
[25] Ibid., VI, xi.
[26] Ibid.
[27] Ibid., VI, i.

> Consider, too, the fourth class, that is, the class of those numbers[28] in the memory. For, if we draw them out by recollection, and, when we are carried away to other thoughts, we again leave them as if hidden in their own hiding places, I don't think it is difficult to see they can exist without the others.[29]

Before proceeding, Augustine now brings up a fifth possibility, regarding the perception of music, one he mentions in several other places, a kind of innate, genetic template for judging music.

> I believe, while we were discussing these things, a fifth kind appeared from somewhere, a kind in the natural judgment of perceiving when we are delighted by the equality of numbers or offended at a flaw in them.[30]

Augustine concludes that of the four forms of music mentioned above, the fourth, memory, is to be preferred. This is because it not only can exist without sound or performance, but it also lasts indefinitely, whereas 'live' music quickly disappears.[31]

Now he asks, of the remaining three, which is the most important? Augustine, in words assigned to his student, says that performance must be the most important, 'according to the rule that things making are to be preferred to those made.' But, for a Christian philosopher, there is a problem in admitting this, for it implies that the corporeal is more important than the incorporeal (soul).[32] At the same time, this is the essential question for Augustine: Should one value music, or art in general, so highly in view of the fact that it is *man* made?

Augustine's solution to this problem is again based on his concept of a kind of innate, genetic template, a God given music, against which man-made music is to be judged. He quotes from the Scriptures[33] a passage which he says refers to this God given template and not to earthly music.

> So it is truly said in the Holy Scriptures, 'I have gone the rounds, to know and consider and seek wisdom and number.' And you are in no way to think this was said about those numbers shameful theaters resound with, but about those, I believe, the soul does not receive from the body [the ears], but receiving from God on high it rather impresses on the body.[34]

But, if music is in the soul, implanted by God, can we say we hear the music outside the soul at all?

---

[28] Among the writers of this period, this is a frequently used synonym for music.

[29] Ibid., VI, iii.

[30] Ibid., VI, iv.

[31] Ibid.

[32] Ibid.

[33] A passage we cannot find.

[34] *On Music*, VI, iv.

> It must be carefully considered if there is really nothing called hearing unless something is produced in the soul by the body. But it is very absurd to subordinate the soul like a matter to the body as an artisan. For the soul is never inferior to the body, and all matter is inferior to the artisan. The soul, then, is in no way a matter subordinated to the body as an artisan. But it would be, if the body worked numbers in it. Therefore, when we hear, [music is] not made in the soul by [music] we know in sounds.

His student asks, 'What happens, then, when a person hears?' Before attempting to answer, Augustine admits doubt and suggests it might be better to answer it some other time.

> Whatever it is—and perhaps we cannot find or explain it—it won't result, will it, in our denying the soul's being better than the body? ... But if, because of the infirmity of either or both of us, the [answer] should be less than we wish, either we ourselves shall investigate it at another time when we are less agitated, or we shall leave it to more intelligent people to examine, or, unworried, we shall leave it unsolved.

Nevertheless, Augustine says, 'I shall say right away what I think.' His essential point seems to be his belief that when we hear music, the soul hears the sensory input, but without emotion. Upon the sensory perception, it is the soul which produces the emotions in the body.

> I think the soul, then, when it senses, produces these actions on the passions of the body, but does not receive these passions.[35]

Augustine concludes this discussion by observing that of these, now five, possible definitions of music only the God-given template form, which he now names 'the judicial,' is undying. The others 'either pass away when they are made or are stricken out of the memory by forgetfulness.'[36]

In a later book called *The Retractions*, Augustine mentions his book, *On Music*, and concludes that the value of music to the Christian is to see God. It was this fortunate thought, that secular knowledge can lead one to understanding the Christian message, which saved the liberal arts from extinction during the coming Dark Ages.

> I wrote six books *On Music*. The sixth of these became especially well known because in it a subject worthy of investigation was considered, namely, how, from corporeal and spiritual but changeable numbers, one comes to the knowledge of unchangeable numbers which are already in unchangeable truth itself, and how, in this way, 'the invisible attributes' of God, 'being understood through the things that are made, are clearly seen.'[37]

---

35 Ibid., VI, iv, 10.

36 Ibid., VI, vii.

37 *The Retractions*, trans. Sister Mary Bogan (Washington, D.C.: The Catholic University of America Press), X. Augustine quotes here, Romans 1:20.

The foregoing discussion, no matter how interesting it is for its time and place, is really only a discussion of the physical mechanism of hearing music. But the importance of music to man does not lie in the physiological nature of hearing, no matter how fascinating that is, but its role as a special language to communicate feelings. Augustine surely understood this on some level but his role in the church made it impossible for him to discuss this openly. From the beginning of the Christian Era the Roman Church, as part of its goal of creating a 'new' Roman citizen, attempted in every possible way to remove emotions from the life of the new Christian. For the Church, the emotions were the first step on the road to sin.

This unnatural position made it necessary for the Church and its spokesmen to create a number of explanations which have no basis in fact. One basic explanation held that the emotions associated with the senses have no true reality in themselves but are actually constructs of the rational mind.

> Now, whatever can be so imagined in the mind's eye is certainly not a body but only the likeness of a body, and that power of the mind which can perceive this likeness is itself neither a body nor an image of a body. Moreover, that faculty which perceives and judges whether this likeness is beautiful or ugly is certainly superior to the object judged.
> Now, this faculty is a man's reason, the essence of his rational soul.[38]

And this line of thought was often connected to the Church's concern that we not worship works of art, or the artist, but rather God who made the artist.

> Music, that is the science or perception of rhythm, is granted by the liberality of God to mortals having rational souls, to teach a great truth. Hence, if a man who is skilled in composing a song knows what lengths to assign to what tones, so that the melody flows and progresses with beauty by a succession of slow and rapid tones, how much more true it is that God permits no periods of time in the birth and death of His creatures—periods which are like the words and syllables in the measure of this temporal life—to proceed either more quickly or more slowly than the recognized and well-defined law of rhythm requires, in this wonderful song of succeeding events, for the wisdom through which He made all things is to be esteemed far above all the arts.[39]

Rarely therefore does Augustine admit the relationship of music and emotions. In the following passage, and here it may only be a figure of speech, he refers to the ability of music to soothe the feelings, a virtue enumerated by almost all earlier philosophers.

---

[38] *The City of God*, trans. Gerald G. Walsh (New York: Fathers of the Church, 1952), VIII, 31.

[39] 'Letter to Jerome,' in *Letters of Saint Augustine*, trans. Sister Wilfrid Parsons (New York: Fathers of the Church, 1955), Nr. 166. In a letter (Nr. 26) to the poet, Licentius, Augustine, using music as a metaphor for good speech, says music can have charm, but not excite one to action.

> If I sing and you dance to another tune, it will not bother me, for my song has its own charm, even if it does not stir feet to the dance.

Thereupon, this recollection brought to my mind a way in which I could soothe your feelings, in case I had irritated you, namely, to summon you to the Lord, the Creator of every sort of harmony, by the music of poetry.[40]

In his book, *On Music*, Augustine is attempting to define good composition, when he rather inadvertently uses an example which reflects the emotional nature of music and has nothing to do with Reason. It is possible, he says, for music to be pleasing when it shouldn't.

For example, if one should sing sweetly and dance gracefully, wishing thereby to be gay when the occasion demanded gravity....[41]

In all other discussions of music, however, Augustine's emphasis is on the rational or conceptual qualities he finds in music. It is from this same perspective that Augustine gives us a glimpse into his views of the aesthetic purpose of music, in a passage in which he is discussing the association of Reason and the arts. First, he says, Reason is innate, planted by God. In infancy it appears to be asleep, but is awakened with education. He then remarks on the 'astonishing achievements' which Reason has made possible, including those in the arts.

Or think of the originality and range of what has been done by experts in ceramics, by sculptors and by painters; of the dramas and theatrical spectacles so stupendous that those who have not seen them simply refuse to believe the accounts of those who have.[42]

It is interesting that he does not include music in this listing of the arts, but rather includes it in the category of human communication.

It was human ingenuity, too, that devised the multitude of signs we use to express and communicate our thoughts—and, especially, speech and writing. The arts of rhetoric and poetry have brought delight to men's spirits by their ornaments of style and variety of verse; musicians have solaced human ears by their instruments and songs....

In yet another place he suggests that the appreciation of music is one of rational reflection of its beauty, not a response to its emotional content.

Consideration of beauty, even corporeal beauty, whether visible as in colors and shapes, or audible as in songs and melodies, a consideration proper only to a rational mind, is not the same as the stirring of lust, which must be restrained by reason.[43]

---

[40] 'Letter to Paulinus and Therasia,' trans. Sister Wilfrid Parsons in *Letters of Saint Augustine* (New York: Fathers of the Church, 1951) Nr. 32.

[41] *On Music*, I, iii.

[42] *The City of God*, XXII, 484.

[43] *Against Julian*, trans. Matthew A. Schumacher (New York: Fathers of the Church, 1957), XIV, 73.

One can see a clear pattern here, the highest aesthetic in music is that in which Reason participates. In the following passage he makes the distinction that pleasure in music is music which is reasonably organized. A mere beautiful chord is not 'reasonable.' We should also remind the reader how important it is that Augustine mentions harmony here. This is five hundred years before our traditional music history texts find the first evidence of even two-part writing!

> I see, therefore, two things wherein the faculty and power of reason can even be brought before the senses: namely, the works of man which are seen and his words which are heard. In each case the mind uses a twin messenger, the eye and the ear, according to the needs of the body. Thus, when we behold something formed with well-fitting parts, not absurdly do we say that it appears reasonable [fashioned]. In like manner, when we hear a melody harmonized well, we do not hesitate to say that it sounds reasonably [harmonized] …
>
> In so far as we have been able to investigate, we now detect certain traces of reason in the senses, and, with regard to sight and hearing, we find it in pleasure itself … With regard to the eyes, that is usually called *beautiful* in which the harmony of parts is wont to be called reasonable; with regard to the ears, when we say that a harmony is reasonable and that a rhythmic poem is reasonably composed, we properly call it *sweet*. But, we are not wont to pronounce it reasonable when the color in beautiful objects allures us or when a vibrant chord sounds pure and liquid, so to speak. We must therefore acknowledge that, in the pleasure of those senses, what pertains to reason is that in which there is a certain rhythmic measure.[44]

Augustine continues this thought by explaining where he finds reason with respect to three classes of music. He classifies vocal music the highest since it is made by the body, 'God made instruments,' so to speak. Next highest is the music of wind instruments, because, as we presume the point to be, they use at least the breath from inside the body. The final, and lowest, category is percussion, which includes string instruments—anything you play upon. He then provides a virtual history of the development of mind and sound, seen through the eyes of a rational Christian philosopher. Sound itself has little value, he says, unless it is organized by reason.

> Reason, being endowed with the keenest powers of discernment, quickly saw what difference there was between sound itself and that of which it was a symbol. It saw that to the jurisdiction of the ears pertained nothing more than sound, and that this was threefold: sound in the utterance of an animate being, or sound in what breath produces in musical instruments, or sound in what is given forth by percussion. It saw that to the first class pertained actors of tragedy and comedy or stage players of this kind, and in fact all who give vocal renditions; the second class was restricted to auloi and similar instruments; and that to the third class were attributed the cithara, the lyre, cymbals, and everything that would be tonal on being struck.
>
> Reason saw, however, that this material was of very little value, unless the sounds were arranged in a fixed measure of time and in modulated variation of high and low pitch. It realized that it was from this source that those elements came which it had called *feet* and *accents*, when, in grammar, it was treating of syllables with diligent consideration. And, because in words themselves it was easy to notice the syllabic *longs* and *shorts*, interspersed with almost equal frequency in a discourse, reason

---
44 *Divine Providence*, 309ff.

endeavored to arrange and conjoin them into definite series. At first it followed the sense of hearing itself in this, and superimposed measured link-units, which it called *segments* and *members*. Then, lest the series of feet be carried further than its discernment could continue, it set a limit at which *reversion* to the beginning should be made, and, precisely on this account, called it *verse*. But, whatever was not restricted by a definite limit, and yet ran according to methodically arranged feet—that, it designated by the term *rhythm*. In Latin this can be called nothing other than *number*. Thus, poets were begotten of reason. And, when it saw in them great achievements, not in sound alone, but in words also and realities, it honored them to the utmost, and gave them license for whatever reasonable fictions they might desire. And yet, because they took origin from the first of the liberal disciplines, it permitted grammarians to be their critics.

Reason understood, therefore, that in this fourth step of ascent—whether in particular rhythm or in modulation in general—numeric proportions held sway and produced the finished product. With the utmost diligence it investigated as to what their nature might be, and, chiefly because by their aid it had elaborated all the aforesaid developments, it concluded that they were divine and eternal. From then onwards, it most reluctantly endured their splendor and serenity to be clouded by the material stuff of vocal utterances. And, because whatever the mind is able to see is always present and is acknowledged to be immortal, numeric proportions seemed to be of this nature. But, because sound is something sensible, it flows away into the past and is imprinted on the memory. By a reasonable fiction it was fabled that the Muses were the daughters of Jupiter and Memory. Now, with reason bestowing its favor on the poets, need it be asked what the offspring likewise contained? Since this branch of learning partakes as well of sense as of the intellect, it received the name of *music*.[45]

In another book, *The Teacher*,[46] Augustine gives yet another example of his personal belief that reason is at the heart of music appreciation. He states that the act of speaking words is a form of teaching. His pupil, Adeodatus, answers, 'But what about singing, which also uses words?' Augustine says, 'There is a form of teaching by way of recalling,' and this is what music does. Adeodatus responds, 'No, I don't sing to recall something, I sing only for pleasure.' Augustine's response once again suggests he fails to understand the pleasure of music for music's sake. Pleasure for him must be something rational, here in the ordering of sound.

> I see what you mean. But you notice, do you not, that what pleases you in singing is a certain melodious ordering of the sound?

Augustine maintains that to some degree the rational understanding which lies behind musical performance is innate. He first gives the example of birds, which although lacking reason, nevertheless give forth music which is 'most accurately and aptly proportioned.'[47] A singer untrained in music is genetically analogous to the bird.

> What good singer, even though he be unskilled in the art of music, would not, by the same natural sense, keep in his singing both the rhythm and the melody known by memory? And what can become more subject to measure than this? The uninstructed man has no knowledge of it. Nevertheless, he does it by nature's doing.

---

45 Ibid., 316ff.

46 *The Teacher*, trans. Robert Russell (Washington, D.C.: The Catholic University of America Press), i.

47 *Divine Providence*, 326.

It follows, therefore, that music itself is of a lesser category of importance than Reason. What man understands through Reason, he says, can never be taken away from him. Music, however, is fleeting and disappears. The listener cannot keep music!

> Even if the beautiful singing of a vocalist were to last forever, his admirers would vie with one another to come to hear him; they would press about each other, and, as the crowd became larger, would fight over seats so that each might be closer to the singer. And as they listened, they could not take any of the sound to keep for themselves but could only be caressed by all the fleeting sounds.[48]

In the dialogue which follows, the reader can see the difficulties which the early philosophers had due to their inaccurate understanding of the brain. It is very clear to us today, thanks to clinical brain research, that we are basically bicameral persons. We have an intellectual side of ourselves, whose domain is language, math and rational knowledge of all kinds. But we also have an experiential side of ourselves, in which our brain records and validates the knowledge and understanding which results from pure personal experience. What we have learned from love is real, but not rational.

The early philosopher knew only one side, so to speak. This placed the early philosopher in the very difficult position of trying to explain all sorts of human activity which is not rational, including the emotions and music above all. Today it is very easy for us to understand that we can have a rational understanding of music (theory) and at the same time an experiential understanding of music. But Augustine did not understand this and his basic struggle in what follows was in attempting to explain experiential leaning by musicians, which he calls imitation, in view of the fact that he knew it was not rational learning. And not being rational, it was therefore a lesser human activity.

In the following he makes two points. First, he who listens to music without understanding the theory of it (the rational) is nothing but a beast. Second, it is fine to listen to music for relaxation, but to be absorbed by it would be disgraceful.

> AUGUSTINE. Now tell me, then, don't [singers] all seem to be similar to the nightingale, all those which sing well under the guidance of a certain sense, that is, do it harmoniously and sweetly, although if they were questioned about the numbers or intervals of high and low notes they could not reply?
> STUDENT. I think they are very much alike.
> AUGUSTINE. And what's more, aren't those who like to listen to them without this science to be compared to beasts? For we see elephants, bears, and many other kinds of beasts are moved by singing, and birds themselves are charmed by their own voices. For, with no further proper purpose, they would not do this with such effort without some pleasure.
> STUDENT. I judge so, but this reproach extends to nearly the whole of human kind.
> AUGUSTINE. Not as much as you think. For great men, even if they know nothing about music, either wish to be one with the common people who are not very different from beasts and whose number is great; and they do this very properly and prudently. But this is not the place to discuss that. Or after

---

48 *The Free Choice of the Will*, xiv.

great cares in order to relax and restore the mind they very moderately partake of some pleasure. And it is very proper to take it in from time to time. But to be taken in by it, even at times, is improper and disgraceful.[49]

Instrumental musicians offered an additional problem to Augustine, because it was obvious that their technique had to be based on something other than just moving their fingers. But is this 'something other' the product of Reason (or we would say, theory or left-brain)? No, he concludes, it is only imitation of the teacher and because it is mere imitation it cannot be art. We remind the reader, again, he could arrive at this conclusion only because his perspective did not admit the acknowledgement of experiential learning as something co-equal with rational learning.

> AUGUSTINE. Those who play on auloi or lyres or any other instrument of this kind, they can't be compared to the nightingale, can they?
> STUDENT. No.
> AUGUSTINE. How, then do they differ?
> STUDENT. In that I find a certain art in these instrument players, but only nature in the nightingale.
> AUGUSTINE. That's true. But do you think it ought to be called an art even if they do it by a sort of imitation?
> STUDENT. Why not? For imitation seems to be to be so much a part of the arts that, if it is removed, nearly all of them are destroyed. For masters exhibit themselves to be imitated, and this is what they call teaching.
> AUGUSTINE. But don't you think art is a sort of reason, and those who use art use reason?
> STUDENT. It seems so.
> AUGUSTINE. Therefore, whoever cannot use reason does not use art.
> STUDENT. I grant that, too ...
> AUGUSTINE. I have asked you whether you would say lyre players and aulos players or any other men of this sort had an art, even if what they do in singing they do by imitation. You have said it is an art, and you have affirmed this so true it seems to you that, if imitation were done away with, nearly all the arts would be destroyed. And from this it can be concluded that anyone who does something by imitating uses an art, although, perhaps not everyone who uses an art acquired it by imitating. But if all imitation is art, and all art reason, all imitation is reason. But an irrational animal does not use reason; therefore, it does not posses an art. But it is capable of imitation; therefore, art is not imitation.[50]

It follows, he concludes, that if the musicians' 'imitation' (experiential knowledge) is not rational, then it cannot be called knowledge at all.

> Nor do I affirm that all those who handle such instruments lack science, but I say they do not all have science. For we are considering this question for the following purpose: to understand, if we can, how correct it is to include science in the definition of music. And if all pipers, aulos players, and others of this kind have science, then I think there is no more degraded and abject discipline than this one.[51]

---

49   *On Music*, I, iv.

50   Ibid.

51   Ibid.

Today we would probably call the acquisition of technique by the instrumental player a form of knowledge attained by experience, and furthermore neurologists can cite the precise part of the brain in which this experiential learning takes place. Augustine, however, not being aware of the independent and co-equal existence of experiential learning, was forced to deny that the acquisition of technique had anything to do with the mind. In the following the student gives the correct answer, but then Augustine contradicts him with the nonsense that if we could somehow understand the science of music better, better technique would follow. For anyone who does not understand how silly this is, we propose they read ten books on 'The Science of Dancing the Tango' and then step out onto the dance floor and see if they can tango.

> AUGUSTINE. I believe you attribute the greater or less mobility of the fingers not to science but to practice, don't you?
> STUDENT. Why do you believe so?
> AUGUSTINE. Because just now you attributed science to the mind alone. But, although in this case the mind commands, you see the act belongs to the body.
> STUDENT. But, since the knowing mind commands this of the body, I think the act ought to be attributed to the mind rather than the servile members.
> AUGUSTINE. But, don't you think it is possible for one person to surpass another in science, even though the other person move his fingers much more easily and readily?
> STUDENT. I do.
> AUGUSTINE. But, if the rapid and readier motion of the fingers were to be attributed to science, the more science anyone had the more he would excel in the rapidity of the motion.
> STUDENT. I concede that.[52]

Having denied that rational knowledge is involved in learning to play an instrument, how then does Augustine account for the process of learning? His answer is that it is a kind of rote repetition committed to memory, made possible by a very interesting premise that a kind of innate understanding, shared by both players and listeners.

> AUGUSTINE. How do you explain the fact that an ignorant crowd hisses off an aulos player letting out futile sounds, and on the other hand applauds one who sings well, and finally that the more agreeably one sings the more fully and intensely it is moved? For it isn't possible to believe the crowd does all this by the art of music, is it?
> STUDENT. No.
> AUGUSTINE. How then?
> STUDENT. I think it is done by nature giving everyone a sense of hearing by which such things are judged.
> AUGUSTINE. You are right. But now consider this, too, whether the aulos player himself is also endowed with this sense. And if it is so, he can, by following his own judgment, move his fingers when he blows on the aulos, and can note and commit to memory what he decides sounds well enough; and by repeating it he can accustom his fingers to being carried about without hesitation or error, whether he gets from another what he plays or whether he finds it himself, led and abetted as he is by the nature we spoke of. And so, when memory follows sense, and the joints, already subdued

---

[52] Ibid.

and prepared by practice, follow memory, the player sings as he wishes, the better and more easily the more he excels in all those things which reason just now taught us we have in common with the beasts: that is, the desire of imitating, sense, and memory.[53]

Augustine now questions whether it isn't the case that most artists performed for money and not in the service of their art. But, he concedes, in the voice of his student, that it must be possible to do both.

> When he accepts applause or when money is given him, he doesn't give up his science, if he chanced to have any, to please the people with. But, heavier with pennies and happier with the praise of men, he returns home with the same discipline entire and intact. But he would be a fool if he despised these advantages. For, if he hadn't gotten them, he would be much poorer and more obscure; having gotten them, he is no less skilled.[54]

Augustine also observes that some musicians value applause higher than their music itself. He then seconds the advice given by nearly all earlier philosophers: the artist must not concern himself with the public. The highest art, he concludes, is found in the artist who learns and exhibits his art without respect to applause or money, but 'who loves his art for itself'—although he expresses doubt that such an artist exists.[55]

It is only the foregoing, together with the Church's attempt to rid emotions from the life of the faithful, that the modern reader can make sense of Augustine's few comments on Church music. Even so, the reader will find some of his statements remarkable indeed.

It was the pleasure associated with the senses which troubled this Christian philosopher, for according to the Church the pure pleasure of the senses was inevitably associated with evil. Thus, with regard to hearing church music, the danger lay in being caught up in the beauty of the music, rather than the conceptual message of the words of the hymns. When he does this, Augustine says, he feels he has sinned.

> The delights of the ear had more firmly entangled and subdued me; but Thou didst loosen and free me. Now, in those melodies which Thy words breathe soul into, when sung with a sweet and attuned voice, I do little repose; yet not so to be held thereby, but that I can disengage myself when I will …
>
> Yet again, when I remember the tears I shed at the Psalmody of Thy Church … and how at this time I am moved not with the singing, but with the things sung, when they are sung with a clear voice and modulation most suitable, I acknowledge the great use of this institution. Thus I fluctuate between peril of pleasure and approved wholesomeness; inclined the rather (though not as pronouncing an irrevocable opinion) to approve of the usage of singing in the church that so by the delight of the ears the weaker minds may rise to the feeling of devotion. Yet when it befalls me to be more moved with the voice than the words sung, I confess to have sinned penally, and then had rather not hear music.[56]

---

53 Ibid., I, v.
54 Ibid., I, vi.
55 Ibid.
56 Ibid., Book X.

Augustine commends the Church of Milan for its effective employment of congregational singing of hymns for the purpose of 'consolation and exhortation,' and adds the very interesting comment that the tradition had begun in the Eastern Churches.

> Then it was first instituted that after the manner of the Eastern Churches, Hymns and Psalms should be sung, lest the people should wax faint through the tediousness of sorrow: and from that day to this the custom is retained, divers (yea, almost all) congregations, throughout other parts of the world, following herein.[57]

In hearing such singing, Augustine experienced the catharsis he was unable to experience in art music.

> How did I weep, in Thy Hymns and Canticles, touched to the quick by the voices of Thy sweet-attuned Church! The voices flowed into mine ears, and the Truth distilled into my heart, whence the affections of my devotion overflowed, and tears ran down, and happy was I therein.[58]

This is a rather remarkable reaction, if he was listening to the *words* of the hymn, and not the music. In an Easter sermon, Augustine seems to suggest that any sense of emotion in such music is found in the Christian's heart-felt concentration on the meaning of the words.

> What is expressed in the Hebrew language by 'Alleluia' is, in Latin, *Laudate Dominum*, or 'Praise the Lord.' So, let us praise the Lord our God, not only with our voice, but also with our heart, since he who praises from the heart praises with the voice of the inner man.[59]

Augustine immediately follows this with an extraordinary conclusion, in view of our understanding of the bicameral nature of the brain. While man is thinking left-brained [language] as he sings, God is hearing it right-brained!

> As far as men are concerned, the voice is a sound; as far as God is concerned, it expresses an emotion.

In any case, this kind of vocal church music was sufficient for Augustine, who saw no need for additional instruments.

> We sing praises to God, we chant our 'Alleluias' with hearts attuned to harmony far better than with the chords of the lyre.[60]

---

57 *The Confessions*, Book IX.
58 Ibid.
59 'Sermon 257,' trans. Sister Mary Muldowney in *Sermons on the Liturgical Seasons* (New York: Fathers of the Church, 1959), 362.
60 'Sermon 243,' in Ibid., 278.

And, like many of his Church contemporaries, he appears to have been content to explain away the Old Testament references to musical instruments in the service as having been only metaphors. He says, for example, that the famous 'Praise the Lord with cymbals,' in Psalm 150, is really talking about good neighbors.

> Cymbals touch each other in order to play and therefore some people compare them to our lips. But I think it better to think of God as being praised on the cymbals when someone is honored by his neighbor rather than by himself.[61]

In this regard, we should mention that Augustine refers to the passage, Ephesians 5:19,

> Be filled with the Spirit, addressing one another in psalms and hymns and spiritual songs, singing and making melody to the Lord with all your heart.

Augustine mistranslates[62] this as 'making melody *in* your hearts,' thus eliminating any possibility that the sentence implies an addition of instrumental music.

> But, not everyone who sings with his lips sings a new canticle, but only one who sings in the way advised by the Apostle, when he says: 'singing and making melody in your hearts to the Lord.' For this joy is within, where the voice of praise sings …[63]

Considering the fact that Augustine has discussed music itself at such length, it is surprising that we have relative few comments by him regarding Church music. This is explained in part by the fact that many of his writings are lost, in particular an entire book on Church music entitled, 'Against Hilary.' This was an answer against a layman who had attacked the Church fathers for a recently introduced custom in Carthage of singing hymns at the altar.[64]

---

[61] Translated by James W. McKinnon, 'Musical Instruments in Medieval Psalm Commentaries and Psalters,' *Journal of the American Musicological Society* 21 (1968): 7.

[62] In 'Letter Nr. 100,' trans. Sister Wilfrid Parsons in *Letters of Saint Augustine* (New York: Fathers of the Church, 1953), Augustine confesses he neither understands the Hebrew language nor anything of the meters of which the Psalms are composed.

[63] 'Letter to Honoratus,' Nr. 140.

[64] This lost book is mentioned by Augustine in *The Retractions*, trans. Sister Mary Bogan (Washington, D.C.: The Catholic University of America Press), XXXVII, 'At the urging of my brethren, I answered him; the book is called Against Hilary.'

Ancient Views on Roman Church Music During the Dark Ages

Both in private and in public there was grief and dejection…
and all laughter had gone out of life.

Justinian, emperor, sixth century

WHAT DO WE MEAN BY THE 'DARK AGES?' The Dark Ages, which are dated from the sixth century, take this name primarily from the general disappearance in Western Europe of secular letters, in particular philosophy, history and science. It is reflective of the period when Gregory of Tours, in his *History of the Franks*, wrote,

> In fact in the towns of Gaul the writing of literature has declined to the point where it has virtually disappeared altogether. Many people have complained about this, not once but time and time again. 'What a poor period this is!' they have been heard to say. 'If among all our people there is not one man to be found who can write a book about what is happening today, the pursuit of letters really is dead in us!'[1]

Cassiodorus, at the beginning of the sixth century, makes a similar observation:

> Arithmetic, Theoretical Geometry, Astronomy, and Music are discoursed upon to listless audiences, sometimes to empty benches.[2]

In another place, Cassiodorus mentions that teachers' salaries were being cut back and argues that instead they should be increased.

> I have referred [to] disputes involving sons to the senators, that they may take thought for the careers of those affected by the advancement of education at Rome. For it is incredible that you should lack concern for something which brings honors to your offspring, and gives your assembly the counsel that comes from constant reading. Now recently I came to know by discreet reports from various people, that the teachers of eloquence at Rome are not receiving the constituted rewards for their labors, and that the trafficking of certain men has caused the sums assigned to the masters of the schools to be diminished.
>
> Therefore, since it is clear that rewards feed the arts, I have judged it abominable that anything should be stolen from the teachers of youth; they should instead be incited to their noble studies by an increase in their fees.

---

[1] Gregory of Tours, *The History of the Franks*, trans. Lewis Thorpe (Harmondsworth: Penguin Books, 1974), 63.

[2] Letter to 'the Illustrious Consularis,' III, lii, in *Variae*, trans. Thomas Hodgkin (London: Frowde, 1886).

> For the school of grammar has primacy: it is the fairest foundation of learning, the glorious mother of eloquence, which has learnt to aim at praise, to speak without fault. As good morals view an alien crime, so it views a dissonant error in the course of declamation. For, as the musician creates the sweetest song from a choir in harmony, so, by well ordered modulations of sound, the grammarian can recite in meter.
>
> Grammar is the mistress of words, the embellisher of the human race; through the practice of the noble reading of ancient authors, she helps us, we know, by her counsels.[3]

Edward Gibbon, in his classic study of the fall of Rome, also pictures this long period economic decline and an environment which was hardly conducive to art.

> It is almost unnecessary to remark that the civil distractions of the empire, the license of the soldiers, the inroads of the barbarians, and the progress of despotism, had proved very unfavorable to genius, and even to learning. The succession of Illyrian princes restored the empire without restoring the sciences. Their military education was not calculated to inspire them with the love of letters; and even the mind of Diocletian, however active and capacious in business, was totally uninformed by study or speculation. The professions of law and [medicine] are of such common use and certain profit that they will always secure a sufficient number of practitioners endowed with a reasonable degree of abilities and knowledge; but it does not appear that the students in those two faculties appeal to any celebrated masters who have flourished within that period. The voice of poetry was silent. History was reduced to dry and confused abridgments, alike destitute of amusement and instruction. A languid and affected eloquence was still retained in the pay and service of the emperors, who encouraged not any arts except those which contributed to the gratification of their pride or the defense of their power.[4]

In another place, Gibbon cites a dramatic symbol of the decline of the arts by the early fourth century.

> The triumphal arch of Constantine still remains a melancholy proof of the decline of the arts ... as it was not possible to find in the capital of the empire a sculptor who was capable of adorning that public monument, the arch of Trajan.[5]

In the older cities, such as Athens, Alexandria and Rome the ancient pagan religious-cults continued until the end of the fourth century, with more than seven hundred pagan temples still standing in Rome alone by the end of that century.[6] But by the fifth century there are very few remaining descriptions of these ceremonies, although we read of various attempts to revive them, which in itself suggests their general decline.

The Emperor Julian (361–363 AD) desired to reestablish these cults, especially that of Cybele and the worship of the Sun, for which he composed a hymn. Gibbon also discusses a brief revival of the festival of the Lupercalia, a festival of arts and agriculture, but there is no men-

---

3   Letter to the Senate in Rome, in Ibid., IX, xxi.

4   Edward Gibbon, *The History of the Decline and Fall of the Roman Empire* (Philadelphia: Coates), I, 455.

5   Ibid., 488.

6   Will Durant, *The Age of Faith* (New York: Simon and Schuster, 1950), 33.

tion of music.⁷ The failure of Julian in his attempt to restore the old pagan religion, together with the conversion to Christianity by Constantine (306–337 AD), effectively handed the victory to the Church.

Meanwhile, Christianity, which probably represented no more than five percent of the Roman population at the beginning of the fourth century, was exerting extraordinary influence everywhere. This was due in part to the fact that the Church addressed itself to everyone, while the empire was focused on the single person of the emperor. Some early writers suggest that the Church appealed to the poor and uneducated, but it might be more to the point to say that the Church addressed itself to the *majority*, who were poor and uneducated.

But there were also more concrete reasons for the success of the Church. Gibbon presents five of these:

1. The inflexible, and, if we may use the expression, intolerant zeal of the Christians, derived, it is true, from the Jewish religion, but purified from the narrow and unsocial spirit which, instead of inviting, had deterred the Gentiles from embracing the law of Moses.
2. The doctrine of a future life, improved by every additional circumstance which could give weight and efficacy to that important truth.
3. The miraculous powers ascribed to the primitive church.
4. The pure and austere morals of the Christians.
5. The union and discipline of the Christian republic, which gradually formed an independent and increasing state in the heart of the Roman empire.⁸

It should be noted that the Church also had to fight itself, not just Rome. There were many competing sects, which sometimes engaged in bloody battles. It has been said that in the years 342–343, more Christians were killed by other Christians than by all the Roman persecutions taken together.⁹ Even the popes themselves were not protected from all the chaos of the Dark Ages. Between 872 and 1012 AD, one-third of all elected popes were killed by strangulation, suffocation, mutilation or other violent acts.¹⁰

However great was the eventual victory of the Church, it cast at the same time a long shadow over education and the arts, for in the eyes of the early Church these were associated with the pagans. Again, Gibbon summarizes the view of the early Church:

> The acquisition of knowledge, the exercise of our reason or fancy, and the cheerful flow of unguarded conversation, may employ the leisure of a liberal mind. Such amusements, however, were rejected with abhorrence, or admitted with the utmost caution, by the severity of the [Church] fathers, who despised all knowledge that was not useful to salvation, and who considered all levity of discourse as a criminal abuse of the gift of speech … The first sensation of pleasure was marked as

---

7   Gibbon, *The History of the Decline and Fall of the Roman Empire*, III, 239ff.
8   Ibid., I, 508.
9   Will Durant, *The Age of Faith*, 8.
10 Stuart Isacoff, *Temperament* (New York: Vintage, 2001), 48.

the first moment of their abuse. The unfeeling candidate for heaven was instructed, not only to resist the grosser allurements of the taste or smell, but even to shut his ears against the profane harmony of sounds, and to view with indifference the most finished productions of human art. Gay apparel, magnificent houses, and elegant furniture, were supposed to unite the double guilt of pride and sensuality; a simple and mortified appearance was more suitable to the Christian who was certain of his sins and doubtful of his salvation. In their censures of luxury the [Church] fathers are extremely minute and circumstantial; and among the various articles which excite their pious indignation we may enumerate false hair, garments of any color except white, instruments of music, vases of gold or silver, downy pillows, white bread, foreign wines, public salutations, warm baths, shaving the beard ...[11]

In spite of five centuries of admonitions, the Christians themselves were still enjoying public entertainments. The Church father who wrote most extensively about the evils of public entertainment at this time was Salvian, in his book, *On the Government of God*. Here one finds that even in the fifth century the worst examples of the 'games' still continued.

There is almost no crime or vice that does not accompany the games. In these the greatest pleasure is to have men die, or, what is worse and more cruel than death, to have them torn in pieces, to have the bellies of wild beasts gorged with human flesh; to have men eaten, to the great joy of the bystanders and the delight of onlookers, so that the victims seem devoured almost as much by the eyes of the audience as by the teeth of beasts.[12]

Salvian was astonished that the faithful were attending public games in greater numbers than those who could be found in church.

Whenever it happens, as it does only too often, that on the same day we are celebrating a feast of the church and the public games, I ask it of everyone's conscience, which is it that collects greater crowds of Christians, the rows of seats at the public games or the court of God?[13]

Finally, it is interesting that Salvian notes that these kinds of entertainments are no longer given with the frequency of earlier times. The reason for this he cites is that the cities outside Rome have been destroyed, whereas in Rome it is because of the worsening economy.

I shall even go so far as to say that they are not now being done in all places where they have been hitherto. For instance, no shows are given now in Mayence, but this is because the city has been destroyed and blotted out; nor at Cologne, for it is overrun by the enemy. They are not being performed in the most noble city of Treves, which has been laid low by a destruction four times repeated, nor finally in many other cities of Gaul or Spain ...

Moreover, the only reason for the cessation of the games themselves [in Rome] is that they cannot be given at the present time because of the misery and poverty in which we live ... For the collapse of the imperial fiscus and the beggary of the Roman treasury do not permit money to be lavished on trifling matters that make no return.[14]

---

11 Ibid., I, 546.

12 Salvian, *On the Government of God*, trans. Eva Sanford (New York: Columbia University Press, 1930), 160.

13 Ibid., 169.

14 Ibid., 170ff.

The destruction which Salvian mentions above deserves some elaboration. With the fall of Rome and the pulling back of Roman soldiers, who had functioned as the police force of Western Europe, towns of all sizes were now left exposed to slaughter by tribes from the North and East. Consider, for example, that Paris was pillaged in 856, 861, and burned in 865. Tours was pillaged in 853, 856, 862, 872, 886, 903, and 919. How could there be culture? Culture requires peace, as Cassiodorus points out, 'Peace is the fair mother of all liberal arts, the softener of manners.'[15]

What else, but the 'Dark Ages,' can we call the Europe which one writer described in 909 AD.

> The cities are depopulated ... the country reduced to solitude ... As the first men lived without law ... so now every man does what seems good in his own eyes, despising laws human and divine ... The strong oppress the weak; the world is full of violence against the poor ... Men devour one another like the fishes in the sea.[16]

Rome, itself, was in total decay by 700, its great institutions forgotten (the Forum was used as a cow pasture already in the seventh century) and the great public buildings and temples were dismembered to provide building material for Christian churches and palaces.

We have an eye-witness description of the city during the period of the first emperor of the sixth century, Justinian, who was certainly one of the strangest of all Roman emperors. He lived and dressed like a monk, fasting, praying, and discussing philosophy. As he wanted to become a musician and poet, we must assume his neglect of the educational institutions reported here was due more to his inclination to hoard money (he once increased his income by putting ashes in the peasant's bread).

> [Justinian] caused doctors and teachers of gentlemen's sons to go short of the elementary necessities of life. For the free rations which earlier emperors ordered to be issued to members of these professions Justinian took away altogether. Moreover, the whole of the revenues which all the municipalities had raised locally for communal purposes and for entertainments he took over and shamelessly pooled with the revenues of the central government. From then on doctors and teachers counted for nothing: no one was now in a position to plan any public building projects; no lamps were lit in the streets of the cities; and there was nothing else to make life pleasant for the citizens. Theaters, hippodromes, and circuses were almost all shut ... Both in private and in public there was grief and dejection, as if yet another visitation from heaven had struck them, and all laughter had gone out of life.[17]

Gibbon adds,

> Justinian suppressed the schools of Athens and the consulship of Rome, which had given so many sages and heroes to mankind ...

---

[15] Letter to Emperor Anastasius, in *Variae*, I, i.
[16] H. W. C. Davis, *Medieval England* (Oxford, 1928), 266.
[17] Procopius, *The Secret History* (Harmondsworth: Penguin Books, 1981), 169.

> The Gothic arms were less fatal to the schools of Athens than the establishment of a new religion, whose ministers superseded the exercise of reason, resolved every question by an article of faith, and condemned the infidel or skeptic to eternal flames.[18]

Once the schools had been closed, the clergy remained the principal portion of the population who were literate and they served as the official scribes attending to the needs of the nobles. This became a self-perpetuating problem, for why should a noble learn to write, for example, when an inexpensive scribe was available to do the work. Consequently, for centuries most lay persons in Western Europe, including kings and emperors, could neither read nor write.[19]

Because the Church, after the fall of Rome, was now effectively uncontested, it has been tempting for historians to lay the blame for the Dark Ages on that institution itself. Contributing to this viewpoint is the fact that the foundation of the Church was faith, and not knowledge. Even the study of grammar was considered unnecessary by some Church leaders, as we can see in the example of Pope Gregory the Great's letter criticizing Desiderius, the Bishop of Vienne.

> A report has reached us which we cannot mention without a blush, that thou expoundest grammar to certain friends; whereat we are so offended and filled with scorn that our former opinion of thee is turned to mourning and sorrow.[20]

The entire Church rested on a foundation of Faith and this is why one can find a number of examples by various Church fathers during the first five centuries who said, in effect, 'Just accept what we say, and look no further.' In the sixth century we still find pronouncements which reflect this narrow perspective. Cassiodorus, for example, writes,

> The most holy Fathers, moreover, not tolerating harm to upright faith, have preferred to establish ecclesiastical rules at [church] councils and have destroyed the stubborn contrivers of new heresies with the divine sword, decreeing that no one ought to trouble them with new questions, but that, content with the authority of the excellent men of old, they ought to obey the wholesome decrees without evasion and treachery.[21]

And, in another place,

> … if anything happens to be found out of harmony and inconsistent with the rules of the Fathers, let us decide that it should be avoided.[22]

---

[18] Edward Gibbon, *The History of the Decline and Fall of the Roman Empire* (Philadelphia: Coates), III, 466ff.

[19] Kenneth Clark, *Civilisation* (New York: Harper & Row, 1969), 17.

[20] Quoted in Nan Cooke Carpenter, *Music in the Medieval and Renaissance Universities* (Norman: University of Oklahoma Press, 1958), 15.

[21] 'Divine Letters,' trans. Leslie W. Jones (New York: Octagon Books, 1966), XI, 1.

[22] Ibid., XXIV, 1.

As these quotations suggest, the struggle of the Church leaders was now *within* the Church, it no longer having (for the moment!) a strong pagan adversary to argue against.

In spite of the general environment of the 'Dark Ages,' there were some more cultured and forward thinking church leaders who argued on behalf of the liberal arts, including music. Cassiodorus was one of several important Church philosophers who understood the importance of preserving the liberal arts. Indeed, one modern writer states that were it not for Cassiodorus, no Latin Classics except the works of Virgil would have come down to us in complete form.[23] For Church men such as Cassiodorus, the great value of the liberal arts, including music, was to produce in the Christian the intelligence necessary to understanding the Scriptures.

> Beyond any doubt knowledge of [the liberal arts], as it seemed to our Fathers, is useful and not to be avoided, since one finds this knowledge diffused everywhere in sacred literature, as it were in the origin of universal and perfect wisdom. When these matters have been restored to sacred literature and taught in connection with it, our capacity for understanding will be helped in every way.[24]

The Venerable Bede, another enlightened Churchman, presents this same argument for the contribution of the liberal arts to Christian understanding.

> We are to be initiated in *grammatica*, then in *dialectia*, afterward in *rhetorica*. Equipped with these arms, we should approach the study of philosophy. Here the order is first the quadrivium, and in this first *arithmetica*, second *musica*, third *geometria*, fourth *astronomia*, then holy writ, so that through knowledge of what is created we arrive at knowledge of the Creator.[25]

On the question of the Church's culpability, then, we get a more accurate picture if we remember that the Church was also composed of individuals. In the spirit of the Church's attacks against the pagan writers, there were some, such as Theophilus, Archbishop of Alexandria, who destroyed all the ancient manuscripts he could find.[26] But there were other individuals who saved ancient manuscripts and their Church buildings offered the manuscripts some chance of survival during centuries of turmoil. And we must not forget the lowly monks, the scribes, who expended a good part of their lives making copies, thereby increasing the odds for survival of individual works of literature. Perhaps it was they who really transmitted these works across the gulf of the Dark Ages. Their tired backs and cramped hands were driven by superiors who told them God would forgive one of their sins for each line they copied. One monk, his superior reported, escaped Hell by the margin of a single alphabet letter! It is no wonder that we find a scribe has written at the end of one of his completed manuscripts,

---

[23] M. R. James, quoted in William Harris Stahl, *Martianus Capella and the Seven Liberal Arts* (New York: Columbia University Press), I, 7, fn. 12.

[24] Cassiodorus, *Divine Letters*, XXVII, 1.

[25] *De elementis philosophiae*, quoted in Carpenter, *Music in the Medieval and Renaissance Universities*, 20, fn. 12.

[26] For this and the following two quotations, see Will Durant, *The Age of Faith* (New York: Simon and Schuster, 1950), 907.

> This completes the whole;
> For Christ's sake give me a drink!

And another,

> For the work of the pen,
> Let the writer receive a beautiful girl.

For the earliest centuries of the Christian Era, 'to sing the praises of God' meant the hymns and psalms which we have mentioned in a previous chapter on music of the early Christians. From the sixth century we begin to read of a much broader use of hymns and psalms outside the Church by the faithful. Gregory of Tours mentions the singing of hymns during meals, replacing the traditional entertainment music.[27] He also recalls that after a great flood, Gregory the Great ordered the faithful to sing psalms for three days, including in the streets, as a means of asking the forgiveness of God.[28] A seventh-century writer, Adomnan, also describes singing hymns and praises as they led a visitor through the streets.[29]

There are several references during this period to the singing of hymns throughout the night. Once, for example, during a vigil accompanying the placing of the relics of St. Julian on an altar, 'They passed the night by singing the sacred hymns and the celestial melodies.'[30] On the death of King Chilperic, we are told Mallulf, Bishop of Senlis, 'passed the night singing hymns.'[31]

There are several references to the singing of hymns as part of the funeral service. Adomnan recalls the service for St. Columba in Ireland:

> After the departure of the holy soul, when the matin hymns were ended, the sacred body was carried back from the church, with the brothers' tuneful psalmody, to the lodging from which alive, he had come a little while before.[32]

Gregory the Great writes of the brothers' singing psalms as one of their own was actually dying, recalling the ancient Greek myth of the importance of departing to music.[33]

One of the factors which helped establish the new Church during the first centuries was the retelling of the miracles of Jesus, stories such as the restoring of life to persons, accomplishments which no pagan god could claim. Thus, perhaps to keep the momentum continuing,

---

[27] Gregory of Tours, *The History of the Franks*, VIII, iii, trans. Lewis Thorpe (Harmonsworth: Penguin Books, 1974).

[28] Ibid., X, i.

[29] Adomnan, *Life of Columba*, trans. Alan Anderson and Marjorie Anderson (London: Nelson, 1961), 14a.

[30] Gregory of Tours, 'The Suffering and Miracles of the Martyr St. Julian,' V, xxxvi, trans. Raymond Van Dam, in *Saints and their Miracles in late Antique Gaul* (Princeton: Princeton University Press, 1993).

[31] Gregory of Tours, *The History of the Franks*, VI, xlvi.

[32] Adomnan, *Life of Columba*, 133a.

[33] Gregory the Great, 'Dialogue Four,' trans. Odo Zimmerman (New York: Fathers of the Church, 1959).

one encounters numerous new stories of miracles during the subsequent years. By the period of which we speak these tales of miracles begin to include music. Adomnan, for example, tells of an occasion when the singers were spared, but the non-singers were killed.

> This also seems to be a thing that should not be passed unnoticed: that certain lay people of the same blessed man [Columba], though they were guilty men and blood-stained, were through certain songs of his praises in the Irish tongue, and the commemoration of his name, delivered, on the night in which they had sung those songs, from the hands of their enemies who had surrounded the house of the singers; and they escaped unhurt, through flames, and swords, and spears. A few of them had refused to sing, as if valuing little the singing of the holy man's commemoration, and miraculously those few alone had perished in the enemies' assault.[34]

This same writer tells of another miracle by which St. Columba, a man with a normal speaking voice, could, when he sang a hymn, be heard more than a mile away, 'so clearly that they could distinguish every syllable in the verses that he sang.'[35]

The Venerable Bede tells of a miracle upon an occasion when St. Cuthbert spent the entire night standing up to his neck in the sea, singing hymns, and was saved by two otters which came to his rescue.

> When daybreak was at hand, he went up on to the land and began to pray once more, kneeling on the shore. While he was doing this, there came forth from the depths of the sea two four-footed creatures which are commonly called otters. These, prostrate before him on the sand, began to warm his feet with their breath and sought to dry him with their fur.[36]

In the Venerable Bede's famous *Ecclesiastical History of England*, he reports that the introduction of Church music occurred in England, in Kent, in approximately 635 AD.[37] He tells of one singer sent by the pope in Rome, in 680 AD, to instruct the congregations on the 'method of singing throughout the year, as it was practiced at St. Peter's at Rome.' Bede writes that many Church men came to hear him sing and many others invited him to their towns.[38] Similarly, another singer came in 710 AD.

> He in like manner invited to him a celebrated singer, called Maban, who had been taught to sing by the successors of the disciples of the blessed Gregory in Kent, for him to instruct himself and his clergy, and kept him twelve years, to teach such ecclesiastical songs as were not known, and to restore those to their former state which were corrupted either by want of use, or through neglect.[39]

---

34   Adomnan, *Life of Columba*, 10a.

35   Ibid., 40a.

36   Bede, 'Life of St. Cuthbert,' in *Two Lives of Saint Cuthbert*, trans. Bertram Colgrave (New York: Greenwood Press, 1969), 191.

37   Bede, *Ecclesiastical History of England*, trans. J. A. Giles (London: Bohn, 1849), II, xx.

38   Ibid., IV, xviii.

39   Ibid., V, xx.

Bede, himself, sometimes betrays a lack of personal enthusiasm for congregational singing, once using the expression, 'the tediousness of psalm singing.'[40] On another occasion, he attributes to St. Cuthbert the admonition that one should lift up 'the heart rather than the voice, sighing rather than singing.'[41]

Bede's reference above, of a singer sent by the Pope in Rome, in 680 AD, to instruct the congregations on the method of singing throughout the year, reflects the fact that there was as yet no notational system for this music. He meant, in other words, that a man was sent to teach by rote. The second part of this phrase, 'the method of singing throughout the year,' may well be a reference to pope Gregory I (ca. 590–604 AD) who organized the Church's annual cycle of liturgical readings. The mention of Pope Gregory brings us to the misnomer, 'Gregorian chant.'

The oldest chant of Rome was probably a mixture of local traditions, Ambrosian (still used in Milano), Galliean and Mozarabic chants. The old story that Gregory, in response to complaints, formed a committee to study church music and that this committee produced the body of chant as we know it today, called, 'Gregorian chant,' is not possible for the reason that the notation used in this repertoire did not then exist.

Even two centuries later notation did not exist, for the emperor Charlemagne sent a request to Rome for authentic liturgical books and chants and he found there were none. Once again, singers were sent from Rome to teach this repertoire by ear. On this occasion something strange happened for an early biography claims the singers 'deviously instructed each congregation in a separate style.'[42] When Charlemagne discovered this he sent them back to Rome, where they were punished with life imprisonment. Thereupon, the Pope wrote Charlemagne,

> If I send you some more they will be just as blind with envy as the first ones, and they will cheat you in their turn ... Send me two of the most intelligent monks whom you have in your own entourage ... With God's help they will acquire the proficiency in this art which you are looking for.[43]

In any case, the Franks made changes of their own and it was their form of this repertoire that was passed down. It should be called, 'Carolingian chant,' and not 'Gregorian chant.'

But all this is not to diminish Pope Gregory's genuine interest in church music. He established a school, called *schola cantorum*, to teach boys to sing[44] and he honored one of these singers, upon his death, with a poem from his own hand.

---

40 Bede, *Life of St. Cuthbert*, 211.

41 Ibid., 213.

42 Einhard and Notker the Stammerer, *Two Lives of Charlemagne*, trans. Lewis Thorpe (Harmondsworth: Penguin Books, 1981), 103ff.

43 Ibid., 103ff.

44 According to his biographer, John the Deacon, in ca. 872 AD, 'we find preserved ... the rod with which he disciplined the boys.'

> O founts of ears, O knees, O hands of Carterius, that appeased Christ by most pure sacrifices. How like all mortals has he ceased to be. The choir there in heaven required a hymn singer.[45]

He was also apparently a keen observer of the remaining religious cults and their music, as we have an account of his discussing the 'barbarians' of Germany.

> It was during this same period that the Lombards, holding as prisoners some 400 other persons, were performing their customary rite of sacrificing the head of a goat to the Devil, dedicating to him by running around, singing sacrilegious songs.[46]

Following St. Augustine, the next extensive commentary on music is by the sixth-century writers, Boethius (475–524 AD) and Cassiodorus (480–573 AD). They wrote essentially theoretical books on music and thus we find little mention of church music. However, the existence of their works in manuscript copies made possible the education of musicians for centuries, not to mention helping to preserve the liberal arts through the Dark Ages. The book by Boethius, in particular, was the most influential music treatise of the Middle Ages. This work was still a commonly studied text in the fourteenth century, though yet unpublished.

The great work by Boethius, *De institutione musica*, is almost entirely devoted to seeing music through the lenses of Reason. Thus one finds passages which are most extraordinary to the modern reader, such as the following:

> Now one should bear in mind that every art and also every discipline considers reason inherently more honorable than a skill which is practiced by the hand and the labor of an artisan. For it is much better and nobler to know about what someone else fashions than to execute that about which someone else knows; in fact, physical skill serves as a slave, while reason, rules like a mistress. Unless the hand acts according to the will of reason, it acts in vain. How much nobler, then, is the study of music as a rational discipline than as composition and performance![47]

He presents his famous three categories of music, with Cosmic Music coming first in importance.[48] He classifies music as mathematics, but with a very interesting observation.

> There happen to be four mathematical disciplines [arithmetic, music, geometry, and astronomy], the other three share with music the task of searching for truth; but music is associated not only with speculation but with morality as well.
>
> ......
>
> Indeed no path to the mind is as open for instruction as the sense of hearing. Thus, when rhythms and modes reach an intellect through the ears, they doubtless affect and reshape that mind according to their particular character.[49]

---

45 Ibid., II, viii, 144. A poem by Gregory, in Ibid., 22, speaks of the panpipe in a metaphorical sense.

46 Gregory the Great, 'Dialogue Three,' 28, trans. Odo Zimmerman (New York: Fathers of the Church, 1959).

47 Boethius, *Fundamentals of Music*, trans. Calvin Bower (New Haven: Yale University Press), I, xxxiv.

48 The Music of the Spheres, representing God directly. The other two are 'Human Music' (vocal) and Instrumental Music.

49 Boethius, *Fundamentals of Music*, I, i. Recent clinical research demonstrates that the brain actually changes physically according to the music it listens to.

We wish he were more specific when he writes of the following contemporary music, which surely must have been secular.

> Since the human race has become lascivious and impressionable, it is taken up totally by representational and theatrical modes. Music was indeed chaste and modest when it was performed on simpler instruments. But since it has been squandered in various, promiscuous ways, it has lost its measure of dignity and virtue; and, having almost fallen into a state of disgrace, it preserves nothing of its ancient splendor.

Perhaps we owe to this 'promiscuous' music the one important passage in which Boethius leaves his fortress of Reason. In spite of all his discussion of, and argument in support of, Reason and music, here he reveals that he has taken notice of the power of the emotions in music. In this regard, he admits, the power is so strong that we 'cannot be free from it even if we so desired.' He also returns here to the idea that music is genetic, observing that even someone who 'cannot sing' nevertheless expresses his emotions in song.

> Why is it that mourners, even though in tears, turn their very lamentations into music? This is most characteristic of women, as though the cause for weeping might be made sweeter through song …
>
> Someone who cannot sing well will nevertheless sing something to himself, not because the song that he sings affects him with particular satisfaction, but because those who express a kind of inborn sweetness from the soul—regardless of how it is expressed—find pleasure. Is it not equally evident that the passions of those fighting in battle are roused by the call of trumpets? If it is true that fury and wrath can be brought forth out of a peaceful state of mind, there is no doubt that a more temperate mode can calm the wrath or excessive desire of a troubled mind. How does it come about that when someone voluntarily listens to a song with ears and mind, he is also involuntarily turned toward it in such a way that his body responds with motions somehow similar to the song heard? How does it happen that the mind itself, solely by means of memory, picks out some melody previously heard?
>
> From all these accounts it appears beyond doubt that music is so naturally united with us that we cannot be free from it even if we so desired.[50]

It makes one wonder why he did not write more about church music.[51]

Cassiodorus, like Boethius, was born to a wealthy Roman family, well-educated and active in politics. At the age of sixty or so he retired from politics and founded a monastery where for the next thirty years he directed the copying of manuscripts by his monks. Thus many scholars consider Cassiodorus the individual most responsible for saving the classics of Greek literature for posterity. His *Institutiones divinarum et humanarum lectionum* was a very influential book which includes chapters on all the seven liberal arts, including music. The chapter on music is rather brief, but because the book traveled everywhere in Europe his remarks were well-known.

---

[50] Cassiodorus, 'On Dialectic,' in *An Introduction to Divine and Human Readings*, trans. Leslie Jones (New York, Octagon Books, 1966).

[51] The Pope had him murdered because he wrote a little story in which a Christian, a Jew and a Muslim have a debate on the merits of their respective religions. Boethius made the unfortunate error, in the Pope's view, of ending the story without having the Christian win the debate.

Cassiodorus divides philosophy into two main branches, Speculative Philosophy and Practical Philosophy. Speculative Philosophy 'is that by means of which we surmount visible things and in some degree contemplate things divine and heavenly, surveying them with the mind alone, inasmuch as they rise above corporeal eyes.' This main branch of philosophy is made up of three sub-branches, Natural, Theoretical, and the Divine. Music is found under 'Theoretical,' together with Arithmetic, Geometry, and Astronomy.

> *Arithmetic* is the science of numerable quantity considered in itself. *Music* is the science which treats measure in relation to sound.

He does not write of church music as a separate topic, which would have been interesting as his concept of music theory is all bound up in the synthesis of nature and religion.

> Musical science, then, is diffused through all the acts of our life if we before all else obey the commands of the Creator and observe with pure hearts the rules which he has established. For whatever we say or whatever inward effect is caused by the beating of our pulse is joined by musical rhythms to the power of harmony. Music is indeed the science of proper modulation; and if we observe the good way of life we are always associated with this excellent science. When we sin, however, we no longer have music [we are not in 'harmony']. The sky and the earth and everything which is accomplished in them by the supernal stewardship are not without the science of music; for Pythagoras is witness to the fact that this world was founded through the instrumentality of music and can be governed by it.
>
> Music also freely permeates religion itself: witness the ten-stringed instrument of the Decalogue, the reverberations of the harp, timbrels, the melody of the organ, the sound of cymbals. There is no doubt, moreover, that the Psalter itself was named after a musical instrument because it contains the exceedingly pleasant and agreeable modulation of the heavenly virtues.[52]

It was the greatest of medieval kings, Charlemagne (768–814 AD), who must be credited with being the first to lift a small corner of the curtain of the Dark Ages. A naturally brilliant man, Charlemagne, observing the appalling illiteracy of his age, learned to read but never quite mastered writing and called leading scholars to his court for the purpose of restoring the schools of France. In 787 he issued an historic document, *Capitulare de litteris colendis*, urging the Church to establish schools. In another document of 789, he urged these schools to,

> take care to make no difference between the sons of serfs and of freemen, so that they might come and sit on the same benches to study grammar, music, and arithmetic.[53]

The result of his efforts saw the founding of numerous schools in France and Western Germany.[54] Among these were the first examples in history of free public education.[55]

---

[52] 'On Music,' in Ibid, 1.
[53] Quoted in Durant, *The Age of Faith*, 466.
[54] Carpenter, *Music in the Medieval and Renaissance Universities*, 17ff.
[55] Einhard and Notker the Stammerer, *Two Lives of Charlemagne*, trans. Lewis Thorpe (Harmondsworth: Penguin Books, 1981), 95.

As a consequence of Charlemagne attracting so many scholars to his court, we are fortunate to have historical portraits of this man and the music of his immediate circle which are unique for this period. One of these scholars, Einhard, writes of Charlemagne's personal interest in the liberal arts.

> He paid the greatest attention to the liberal arts; and he had great respect for men who taught them, bestowing high honors upon them. When he was learning the rules of grammar he studied with Peter the Deacon of Pisa ... but for all other subjects he was taught by Alcuin ... a man of the Saxon race who came from Britain and was the most learned man anywhere to be found.[56]

Another member of the court tells of Greek envoys who came to visit the court and brought a number of musical instruments. His account includes some of the most interesting details extant regarding the early organ.

> These Greek envoys brought with them every kind of organ, as well as all sorts of other instruments. These were all examined by the craftsmen of the most sagacious Charlemagne to see just what was new about them. Then the craftsmen reproduced them with the greatest possible accuracy. The chief of these was that most remarkable of organs ever possessed by musicians which, when its bronze wind chests were filled and its bellows of ox-hide blew through its pipes of bronze, equaled with its deep note the roar of thunder, and yet which, for very sweetness, could resemble the soft tinkle of a lyre or a cymbal.[57]

A description of music heard at a banquet suggests that even on such occasions this court heard a high level of aesthetic music.

> The bishop ordered skilled choristers to advance: they were accompanied by every musical instrument one could think of, and by the sound of their singing they could have softened the hardest hearts or turned to ice the limpid waters of the Rhine.[58]

Charlemagne also took an interest in jongleurs, the first of the wandering minstrels, and even rewarded them with gifts of land in Provence. One scholar points to this court as the birth of what would become the *chansons de geste*.[59] An attractive anecdote tells of a jongleur who guided Charlemagne over Mt. Cenis in 773 and was then given as a reward all the land over which his *tuba* [trumpet] could be heard when played from a hill.[60]

According to another source, Charlemagne even had prepared a collection of his hunting signals, called, *Frohliche Jagd*.[61] While this music is not extant, iconographic clues suggest it was performed by various animal horns, trumpet-types, flute-types, drums and bells.

---

[56] Ibid., 79.

[57] Ibid., 143.

[58] Ibid., 112.

[59] E.K. Chambers, *The Mediaeval Stage* (Oxford, 1903), I, 37, who quotes Philippe Mouskes, *de Poetis Provincialibus*.

[60] Chambers, Ibid., I, 37, fn. 2.

[61] Gottfried Veit, *Die Blasmusik* (Innsbruck, 1972), 20.

Charlemagne also took an active interest in Church music. Einhard describes his actual singing.

> He made careful reforms in the way in which the psalms were chanted and the lessons read. He was himself quite an expert at both of these exercises, but he never read the lesson in public and he would sing only with the rest of the congregation and then in a low voice.[62]

There are two interesting anecdotes regarding Charlemagne and his Church music. In the first,[63] a choir member appeared at an important feast somewhat drunk and intoned the final response instead of the first. This monk was fired on the spot. The monk in the second anecdote was considerably more fortunate.

> One day when Charlemagne was on a journey he came to a great cathedral. A certain wandering monk, who was unaware of the Emperor's attention to small detail, came into the choir and, since he had never learned to do anything of the sort himself, stood silent and confused in the middle of those who were chanting. Thereupon the choir-master raised his baton and threatened to hit him, if he did not sing. The monk, not knowing what to do or where to turn, and not daring to go out, twisted and contorted his throat, opened his mouth wide, moved his bottom jaw up and down, and did all that he could to imitate the appearance of someone singing. The others present had not the self-control to stop laughing. Our valiant Emperor, who was not to be moved from his serenity by even the greatest events, sat solemnly waiting until the end of the Mass, just as if he had not noticed this pretense at singing. When it was all over, he called the poor wretch to him and, taking pity on his struggles and the strain he had gone through, consoled with these words: 'My good monk, thank you very much for your singing and your efforts.' Then he ordered him to be given a pound of silver to relieve his poverty.[64]

Thanks to the enlightenment of Charlemagne, the Church began to engage in a broader educational role in the ninth century. These monastic schools, particularly in France, joining together with the Church's need to teach the new official body of Church music, developed into the first real schools of music of modern Europe. Because of the great flourishing of monasteries famous for the cultivation of music during the ninth through eleventh centuries, one can say that music education emerged out of the Dark Ages before almost any other discipline.[65] In the *Enchiridion musices*, by Odo of Cluny, when the teacher promises an effective new system of learning sight-singing, the student replies with relief,

> ... he will never [again] torment me with blows or abuse when provoked by the slowness of my sense.[66]

---

[62] Einhard and Notker, *Two Lives of Charlemagne*, 80.

[63] Ibid., 98ff.

[64] Ibid., 100ff.

[65] The growth of these monastic schools is summarized in Nan Cooke Carpenter, *Music in the Medieval and Renaissance Universities* (Norman: University of Oklahoma Press, 1954), 13–31.

[66] Quoted in Oliver Strunk, *Source Readings in Music History* (New York: Norton, 1950), 109.

Similarly, Guido, in *Prologus antiphonarii sui*, remarking on the success of his new method of teaching music reading, challenges the reader,

> Should anyone doubt that I am telling the truth, let him come, make a trial, and see what small boys can do under our direction, boys who until now have been beaten for their gross ignorance of the psalms.[67]

We get another glimpse of the rigid discipline of these monastic schools when we see the unvarying daily schedule which these young music students had to observe. Here is the schedule of one of these schools.[68]

23:30	Waken
24:00–2:00	Sing Matin Service
2:00	Sleep
4:30	Waken
5:00–6:30	Sing Laudes and First Mass
7:00–9:00	School Studies
9:00–10:00	Sing Mass
11:00–15:00	Sing *Hora sexta* Service
	Lunch
	Rest Period
15:00–18:00	Sing *Hora nona* Service
	School Studies
	Dinner
18:00–19:00	Sing Vesper Service
19:30	Sleep

We believe these young music students would have applauded the phrase by which Gibbon described their Church superiors:

> The vices of the clergy are far less dangerous than their virtues.[69]

Some of the graduates of such a school became monks who were, in effect, professional singers. Now the ritual of the professional singer replaced the enthusiastic congregational singing of the first Christians. In many small monasteries the love of singing must have nearly been extinguished. Peter Damian, the leader of such a group of hermits, complains about monks who hurry the singing of their psalms at night in order to get to bed sooner and worries that evil thoughts will creep into the minds of monks who may daydream while singing.[70] Time and time again, Damian warns his monks against the sins of pleasure, with such exhor-

---

[67] Quoted in Ibid., 118.

[68] Given in Joseph Smits van Waesberghe, *Musikerziehung, Lehre und Theorie der Musik in Mittelalter* (Leipzig: VEB Deutscher Verlag fur Musik), III, Lfg. 3, 28.

[69] Gibbon, *The History of the Decline and Fall of the Roman Empire*, IV, 301.

[70] *Letters of Damian*, II, Letter 50.

tations as, 'In every struggle with titillating pleasure try always to evoke the memory of the grave.'[71] He even went so far as to prescribe exercises in crying, in order that the monks could develop suitably somber demeanors.

Regarding specific performance practices, in one place he recommends the practice of a monk, named Dominic, of singing twelve psalms twenty-four times with ones hands extended above the head in the form of a cross. This, he says, would compensate for one year of penance.[72] In another place, he mentions instrumental music in an interesting distinction between canticles and psalms.

> That a canticle is daily added to the psalms in the office of Lauds, seems to be redolent with mystery, namely, the mystery of both the contemplative and the active life. For the psaltery, an instrument made in the shape of a delta, vibrates through its ten strings when struck by the plectrum; a song, however, is produced only by the voice. Wherefore, the former, because it needs the use of the hands, denotes work and hence the active life, while the latter, because it related to a song of joy, indicated the contemplative life. And because we are able to experience contemplation only briefly and interruptedly, and that, scarcely for a moment, but are always engaged in the business of the active life, it is proper that we employ several psalms but only one canticle.[73]

The Church literature of this period remains filled with tales of new miracles and other extraordinary stories to support the faith. Music is almost never mentioned in such literature, although we find in the 'Life of Mary Magdalene,' by the ninth-century writer, Rabanus Maurus, the assertion that Mary, Martha and Lazarus were in their youth highly educated, not only in Hebrew, but 'the gifts of arts.'[74] In this romantic biography, by the way, Martha, after the death of Christ, goes to France and fights a dragon![75]

A more significant work, the play, *Paphnutius*, by the tenth-century nun, Hrotswitha, contains an extensive dialog on the subject of music.[76] The passage begins with a Disciple asking, 'What *is* music?' Paphnutius answers with a brief description of the place held by music among the liberal arts. The Disciples beg for more information and Paphnutius hesitates, 'since it is knowledge which monks don't have.'

Paphnutius, following the definition by Boethius, begins by telling the students that music is divided into three species: the celestial, the human, and that made with instruments.

> DISCIPLES. What does celestial music consist of?
> PAPHNUTIUS. Of the seven planets and the celestial sphere.
> DISCIPLES. How do you mean that?

---

[71] Ibid.

[72] Ibid., Letter 53.

[73] Ibid., I, Letter 17.

[74] *The Life of Saint Mary Magdalene and of her Sister Saint Martha*, trans. David Mycoff (Kalamazoo: Cistercian Publications, 1989), I, 29.

[75] Ibid., XL, 2365.

[76] *The Plays of Hrotswitha of Gandersheim*, trans. Larissa Bonfante (New York: New York University Press, 1979), 108ff.

PAPHNUTIUS. Because, you see, they produce the same harmonious music as the strings of stringed instruments; For just as in the case of instruments, we find the same concordances and intervals of like number and length.
DISCIPLES. And what are these 'intervals' you speak of?
PAPHNUTIUS. They are the distances which exist between the planets, as between the notes of strings.

Upon further questions about the 'notes' just mentioned, Paphnutius begins to speak in the complex mathematical language of Boethius. The students object to this conceptual language and respond, 'What has this got to do with *music*?,' implying, we presume, their instinctive realization that music has instead to do with feelings and emotions, not mathematics. The teacher's answer, like that of so many theory teachers today, is, 'But that is how you *talk* about music!' The reader will notice that he introduces here the word 'symphonia,' which represents our term 'harmony.'

PAPHNUTIUS. A tone is formed of two sounds, of which the proportion is that of an *epothos* number, a sesquioctave: that is of nine to eight.
DISCIPLES. (Discouraged.) The faster we try to keep up with you and follow the basic notions you give us, and technical terms of this discussion, the more you go on adding more difficult concepts for us to take in.
PAPHNUTIUS. But that is how this kind of discussion is carried on.
DISCIPLES. Well at least tell us something—but only the simplest account—about what they mean by concordances, just so we will know what the word means.
PAPHNUTIUS. A concordance or 'symphonia' is a proper combination of sounds.

The students now ask the difficult question, 'Why can't we hear the music of the spheres?' Of all early philosophers, Paphnutius now gives the most complete answer, indeed four possible explanations.

DISCIPLES. Well, why can't we hear them, then?
PAPHNUTIUS. Many different reasons are given to explain why we can't hear the music of the heavenly spheres. Some assert it can't be heard because the music never stops, and we become accustomed to its sound. Others say it is the density of the air, while there are some who claim that a sound of such grand volume cannot physically be taken in by the narrow passages of our human ears. And there are some who say that the spheres give forth a sound so sweet, of such great joy, that if men ever heard it, they would all join together, of one common accord, forget about themselves and any other interest, and be intent only on following this sound as it led them from the East to the Western regions.

Well, say the students, we have heard enough of the music of the spheres. Now tell us about 'human' music, and how it is produced.

PAPHNUTIUS. Not only, as I said before, in the harmonious connection between body and soul, and in the deep bass or high pitched soprano voices, but even in the rhythmic throbbing of our veins, and in the measure and proportion of each of our limbs, as for example in the joints of our fingers, for which we find the same proportions when we measure off their sections. These are the same proportions, if you remember, which we talked of in our discussion of the meaning of 'symphonias,' because music is in fact an agreeable combination not only of voices, but of other unlike elements as well.

DISCIPLES. (They have been looking at the joints of their fingers. They are quite frankly lost.) If we had only known before we asked, how knotty all these problems were for laymen like us, and how difficult to follow or resolve, we would have preferred never to have known about the 'lesser world' than try to learn such difficult lessons.

PAPHNUTIUS. It did you no harm to try, for now you have learned things you did not know before.

DISCIPLES. That's true. But we are exhausted from this philosophical lecture, since we are not able to understand the details of your explanation.

Perhaps because of the student's professed exhaustion, this discussion never continues on to the subject of instrumental music. The teacher brings the topic to a close by reminding the students of the true purpose of the acquisition of knowledge—to understand God.

PAPHNUTIUS. For to whose praise does knowledge of all the arts redound more worthily and justly, if not to His, since He is the One who created all things knowable and gave us knowledge of them?

Information on the church music of the Eastern Church is rather hard to find, but there is one extraordinary anecdote regarding the Emperor Leo V who was actually murdered during a church festival service. The signal for the perpetrators of this deed was when the emperor began to sing.

> On the great festivals, a chosen band of priests and singers was admitted into the palace by a private gate to sing matins in the chapel; and Leo, who regulated with the same strictness the discipline of the choir and of the camp, was seldom absent from these early devotions. In the ecclesiastical habit, but with swords under their robes, the conspirators mingled with the procession, lurked in the angles of the chapel, and expected, as the signal of murder, the intonation of the first psalm by the emperor himself. The imperfect light, and the uniformity of dress, might have favored his escape, whilst their assault was pointed against a harmless priest; but they soon discovered their mistake, and encompassed on all sides the royal victim. Without a weapon and without a friend, he grasped a weighty cross, and stood at bay against the hunters of his life; but as he asked for mercy, 'This is the hour, not of mercy, but of vengeance,' was the inexorable reply. The stroke of a well-aimed sword separated from his body the right arm and the cross, and Leo the Armenian was slain at the foot of the altar.[77]

The ninth through the eleventh centuries are certainly among the most interesting in music history, with respect to the development of the theory and notation of Western European music. There are a number of music treatises which are extant from this period, but they are still being written by mathematicians and not musicians[78] and therefore tell us relatively little of the church music.

---

[77] Gibbon, *The History of the Decline and Fall of the Roman Empire*, IV, 201.

[78] Aurelian of Reome, *The Discipline of Music*, trans. Joseph Ponte (Colorado Springs: Colorado College Music Press, 1968), X, observes, if one wishes to become more versed in music,

> let him turn his eyes to the harmony of proportions, to the contemplation of intervals, and to the exactitude of mathematics.

Aurelian of Reome, *Musica Disciplina* [ca. 843 AD]

It is significant that this first music treatise of the centuries which initiate the emergence from the Dark Ages reflects the fact that the 'lost' works of the ancient Greek philosophers, which the early Church tried to destroy, were now being rediscovered and were coming slowly into circulation.[79]

> There is much authority both in the ancient books, that is, those of the heathen, and in the holy books, affirming that the discipline of music should not be disdained, since there are to be found, both among the heathen and our own people, innumerable acts of efficacious through its power.[80]

Among Aurelian's comments on Church music, he finds the foundation for church music both in the Old Testament and in the Church's belief of the existence of choirs of angels. There are a few observations by Aurelian about the performance of chant, including a curious maxim which demonstrates that the spirit of the myth had not completely died.

> We pray the singer to begin concluding all the verses of the nocturnal responses from the fifth syllable before the end; and this is according to the musicians who have maintained that not more than five waves of the sea also remove all storms from the same.[81]

Aurelian finds the one moment of true contemplation for the listener of church music to be the music of Communion.

> So long as the faithful people receive heavenly benediction, their minds may be drawn by the sweet melody and suspended in sublime contemplation.[82]

Hucbald, *De harmonica institutione* [ca. 895 AD]

Hucbald, born ca. 840 AD, taught at several monastic schools and it seems clear that this treatise is intended for instruction in such a school. The functional premise of treatises such as this was to produce a church singer who understood music on a conceptual level and could read music, as opposed to what seems to have become a traditional singer who learned only by ear. In this case, Hucbald promises such a singer that if he will just study the exercises in this treatise, he,

> may at length be granted entry to the inner regions of this discipline, the darkness being gradually withdrawn from his dull eyes.[83]

---

[79] We will discuss this rediscovery in the next essay.
[80] Aurelian of Reome, *The Discipline of Music*, I.
[81] Ibid., XIX.
[82] Ibid., XX.
[83] Hucbald, 'Melodic Instruction' in *Hucbald, Guido, and John on Music*, trans. Warren Babb (New Haven: Yale University Press, 1978), 104a/16.

Anonymous, *Scholia enchiriadis* [ca. 900 AD]

This treatise, formerly ascribed to Hucbald, is the earliest which deals with the improvisation of a simple counterpoint to a given chant. This author is still thinking of the old liberal arts definition of Mathematics consisting of Arithmetic, Geometry, Music, and Astronomy. Indeed, he says 'Music is the daughter of Arithmetic' and for him the 'delight' of music is not that of the listener, but that of the responding mathematician!

> Whatever is delightful in song is brought about by number through the proportioned dimensions of sounds; whatever is excellent in rhythms, or in songs, or in any rhythmic movements you will, is effected wholly by number. Sounds pass quickly away, but numbers, which are obscured by the corporeal element in sounds and movements, remain.[84]

Odo of Cluny, *Enchiridion musices* [ca. 935 AD]

This treatise, the first in which letters are used as symbols for pitch in the modern sense, was also written for the purpose of perfecting the ability of church singers to read. With his system Odo says he has taught boys in a few days to read 'without fault anything written in music,' something which he states that until now ordinary singers could not do even after fifty years' experience.[85]

Given the purpose of this treatise, we are not surprised to find, when the Disciple asks, 'What is music?,' the Master answers, 'The science of singing correctly.' This, of course, means following the rules of music in so far as it was understood as a science. Singing something because it pleases the ear was no justification for Odo.

> Ordinary singers often fall into the greatest error because they scarcely consider the force of tone and semitone and of the other consonances. Each of them chooses what first pleases his ear.[86]

Guido of Arezzo, *Micrologus* [ca. 1026–1028 AD]

This is a treatise famous for the introduction of a staff of lines and spaces for the notation of music, but it is also one which comments on a broad range of other subjects. This treatise is another educational one, directed at the training of church singers. He begins his discussion with a little anagram which refers to the disappearance of music in the schools during the Dark Ages.

> Gone from school are the Muses; there may I hope to induce them,
> Unknown yet to adults, to unveil their light to the young ones!
> Ill will's indiscriminate rage let charity frustrate;

---

[84] Ibid., 137.
[85] Odo, 'Enchiridion musices,' in Strunk, *Source Readings*, 104.
[86] Ibid., 110.

> Dire indeed are the blights that else will ravage our planet,
> Opening letters of these five lines will spell you the author.[87]

In his Prologue, Guido immediately centers on the importance of the ability to sing at sight. If the singer cannot do this, he says, 'I do not know with what face he can venture to call himself a musician or a singer.'[88] He declares that he will discuss here only those things important to singing and then adds a comment we can only wish he had elaborated on. He says he will omit those 'things which are said but cannot be understood.'[89] We suspect that what he really means is, 'things which are understood but cannot be said!' For he is apparently speaking of those insights which musicians arrive at through experience, rather than through instruction. This same point he makes in another place, where he observes,

> In our times, of all men, singers are the most foolish. For in any art those things which we know of ourselves are much more numerous than those which we learn from a master.[90]

Again reflecting the rediscovery of the texts of the ancient Greek philosophers, Guido devotes some attention to the subject of the influence of music on character.

Guido of Arezzo, *Epistola de ignoto cantu* [ca. 1030–1032 AD]

In this treatise Guido again promises a system which will rapidly produce accurate sight-singers. Here he observes that previously singers learned by rote, after hearing the pitch on a monochord. This he calls, 'childish.'[91]

He refers to the previous treatise, which he says he has simplified for the sake of the young. He makes an implicit reference to the 'practical' versus the 'theoretical' division in music when he points out that he has not followed the model of Boethius, 'whose treatise is useful to philosophers, but not to singers.'[92]

John, *On Music* [ca. 1100 AD]

This author, formerly known as 'John Cotton,' has also written a treatise intended for a choir school. His viewpoint is again primarily a conceptual one and he clearly states that it is knowledge, the ability to judge music, which is the highest accomplishment—not that pleasing music played by uneducated jongleurs! Indeed, he says, it is knowledge which distinguishes a musician from a mere singer.

---

87   Guido of Arezzo, 'Micrologus,' 80, in *Hucbald, Guido, and John on Music*, trans. Babb.
88   Ibid., 85.
89   Ibid., 86.
90   Quoted in Strunck, *Source Readings*, 117.
91   Guido, 'Epistola de ignoto cantu,' in Strunck, *Source Readings*, 123.
92   Ibid., 125.

Nor, it seems, should we omit that the musician and the singer differ not a little from one another. Whereas the musician always proceeds correctly and by calculation, the singer holds the right road intermittently, merely through habit. To whom then should I better compare the singer than to a drunken man who does indeed get home but does not in the least know by what path he returns.[93]

He attempts to strengthen this viewpoint by quoting from Guido, that a musician who does not know what he is doing is a 'beast!'

> From the musician to the singer how immense the distance is;
> The latter's voice, the former's mind will show what music's nature is;
> But he who does, he knows not what, a beast by definition is.[94]

In his reflection on some church performances which he has heard, in which he has objected to the singers making decisions by ear (*musica ficta*) rather than by the rules of notation, he makes a statement which is remarkably similar to Mahler's famous definition of 'tradition' being 'the last bad performance.'

> We do know most assuredly that a chant is often distorted by the ignorance of men, so that we could now enumerate many corrupted ones. These were really not produced by the composers originally in the way that they are now sung in churches, but wrong pitches, by men who followed the promptings of their own minds, have distorted what was composed correctly and perpetuated what was distorted in an incorrigible tradition, so that by now the worst usage is clung to as authentic.[95]

He also has observed that the physical status of the singer can affect the performance, pointing to 'singers weighed down by weariness' singing flat and those of 'high spirits' singing sharp.[96]

John argues in favor of two ideas which were contrary to the traditional teachings of the Church. He was in favor of instrumental music and he saw no reason to restrict chant to the Gregorian repertoire.[97]

John also addresses the subject of the composition of chant and begins by listing some specific goals. What is interesting, and new, about these goals is the first faint evidence of feeling creeping back into Church music. Humanism is knocking at the door of the Church. First, he writes, the composer must fit the music to the meaning of the words, as well as to the occasion which may range from frivolity to grief.[98] As an example of the latter, he recommends the Hypolydian for lamentations because of its 'doleful sound.'

---

[93] John, 'On Music,' 51, in *Hucbald, Guido, and John on Music*, trans. Warren Babb (New Haven: Yale University Press, 1978), 52.
[94] John gives the source as the 'Micrologus,' but it actually comes from the beginning of Guido's 'Regulae rhythmicae.'
[95] Ibid., 104.
[96] Ibid.
[97] Ibid., 115.
[98] Ibid., 117ff.

Ancient Views on Roman Church Music During the Pre-Renaissance

UNDERGRADUATES IN MUSIC may see a professor draw a vertical chalk line on a blackboard under a title for the year '1300.' This line, with its accompanying labels of *ars antiqua* and *ars nova*, written before and after the chalk line, may lead the student to imagine a rather sudden and dramatic transformation from the Middle Ages to the Renaissance. While, of course, no one alive saw a chalk line moving across the sky on the morning of 1 January 1300, nevertheless extraordinary events had been taking place in the two centuries before this date and it was these movements in society which made possible the new style we now call the Renaissance. One only has to reflect that it was during this 'Pre-Renaissance' that the first crusades occurred, introducing the West to an Eastern culture which was in many ways far more advanced. The importance of this can be seen in the testimony of a priest named Theophilus, writing in 1190 from a small monastery near Paderborn, Germany.

> Here you shall find all that Greece possesses in the way of diverse colors and mixtures; all that Tuscany knows of the working of enamels ... all that Arabia has to show of works ductile, fusible, or chased; all the many vases and sculptured gems and ivory that Italy adorns with gold; all that France prizes in costly variety of windows; all that is extolled in gold, silver, copper, or iron, or in subtle working of wood or stone.[1]

The dark clouds were giving way to a new sense of optimism. The great cathedrals were begun. Why would a village build a cathedral with a seating capacity ten or twenty times the population of the village?

The wandering jongleurs and minstrels, after 1,000 years of unifying the musical culture of Western Europe, had advanced musically to a point that cities and courts were beginning to hire the better musicians they encountered. In part this reflected a new sense of civic identity and the city was now in competition with the Church for the hearts of the citizens. The civic musicians began to found guilds, which are a reflection of their sense of identity. These musicians, and especially their aristocratic cousins, the troubadours, were redefining music as a language of the emotions, in a direct challenge to the Church, and its universities, who for several more centuries would pretend that music was a branch of mathematics. The musical impact of the troubadours had apparently reached into the very cloisters of the Church, for already in 1132 we find a statue of the Cistercian Order warning its men that they should 'cease singing in a womanish manner ... as if imitating the wantonness of minstrels.'[2] It was the dawn of what we call 'Humanism' in music.

---

[1] Theophilus, 'Schedule diversarum artium,' in E. Dillon, *Glass* (New York, 1907), 126.

[2] Quoted in Stuart Isacoff, *Temperament* (New York: Vintage, 2001), 50.

Some academic studies had been kept barely alive under the justification that this information was necessary to prepare the Christian to understand the Scriptures. But now universities were beginning to appear and Matthew Paris, writing in 1254, found the students were more interested in jobs than Scripture.

> It occurred to the pope, who still remained at Rome, that the liberal arts were almost entirely converted into mechanical arts for the sake of gain, and that it might with justice be said of philosophy: 'She prostitutes herself and sits as a harlot awaiting her hire;' and he also discovered that nearly all scholars neglected the rudiments of grammar, and, deserting the study of authors and philosophers, were hurrying to study the laws, which, it is clear, are not included in the number of liberal arts; for liberal arts are sought after and acquired for their own sake; but the laws are studied for the sake of acquiring salaries.[3]

One can imagine the Church was getting nervous; it was clearly losing control. Paris quotes a rather alarmed Pope, who sent a papal letter to all the countries under his spiritual guidance, observing,

> We observe with grief how much the formerly pious and holy seminary of clerks, forgetful of its original well-doing, has fallen from the highest sanctity to the lowest depths of vice. Since a shocking report has reached and continually assailed our ears by frequent repetitions, that philosophical studies are abandoned, aye, and long ago cast aside, that all the multitude of the clerks are endeavoring to get a knowledge of secular laws, and what is still more worthy of cognizance of the divine judgment, in the greater number of the countries of the world, no one is elected by the prelates to ecclesiastical dignities, honors, or prebendaries, unless he is either a professor of secular science or a lawyer, although such men ought rather to be rejected by them, unless other things plead for them. Most of all we grieve that the students of philosophy, educated so tenderly in her bosom, so diligently taught, so excellently trained and instructed, are obliged, through want of food and clothing, to avoid the presence of men, hiding here and there like the owls, while these lawyers, or rather devils, clothed in purple and mounted on richly-caparisoned horses, reflecting the dazzle of the sun with the glare of gold, the brilliancy of silver, the sparkling of gems, with their whole raiments of silk, show themselves not the servants of Him who was crucified, but the heirs of Lucifer, making themselves a spectacle wherever they go, stirring up and incurring the indignation and odium of the laity against themselves, and what is much more grievous, against the whole Church of God.[4]

But the greatest change in society was now moving toward the surface. Like a fault under the surface which generates increasing tension until it erupts, there was an undercurrent at work which would shake the very foundations of the Church. Reason was about to challenge Faith for the minds of the faithful.

With the decline of the Roman Empire, the Roman Christian Church was positioned to step forward to take control of Rome. In doing so, they had set out to create a new Christian Roman which, among other things, led to closing schools[5] and burning books. Among the

---

3   Matthew Paris, *English History*, trans. J. A. Giles (London: Bohn, 1852), III, 65ff.

4   Ibid., III, 440ff.

5   In 529, for example, Justinian closed the Platonic Academy in Athens.

books burned were those of the 'pagan' philosophers, whom we know as not only Plato and Aristotle, but Ptolemy, Galen, Euclid and Archimedes. The Church would be the adjudicators of Faith for its members and it needed no help from earlier philosophers, as the early Church father, Tertullian, made clear already in the second century.

> Away with all projects for a 'Stoic,' a 'Platonic' or a 'dialectic' [Aristotelian] Christianity! After Christ Jesus we desire no subtle theories, no acute inquiries after the gospel.[6]

The Church's victory is called, 'The Dark Ages.' By the twelfth century, the Church had managed, for the most part, to create its own empire based on Faith and was philosophically little changed in the eight centuries since St. Augustine. But ignorance cannot be enforced forever. As it turned out, the peoples of the East had preserved the works which the Western Church had tried to suppress.[7] Here could be found in Arabic translations works which men in the West had long thought to have been lost. By the twelfth century scholars from many countries were beginning to travel to Toledo, Lisbon, Segovia and Cordoba to help with the exciting opportunity of translating these works into the languages of the West.

The most important discoveries, intellectually, were the unknown books of Aristotle, who spoke of a world of Reason, not a world of Faith. In terms of the challenge to the Roman Church, the first great agitator was the famous Peter Abelard (ca. 1079–1144). Inspired by the rational process of Aristotle, Abelard wrote a book called, *Yes and No*. In his prologue to this book, Abelard threw down the gauntlet which began the battle of Reason versus Faith for the hearts of the Christians.

> The most brilliant of all philosophers, Aristotle, encouraged his students to undertake this task with every ounce of their curiosity … For by doubting we come to inquire, and by inquiring we perceive the truth.

One can imagine the excitement of the students, especially in Paris, who heard Abelard asking questions the Church had not permitted to be asked for a thousand years. In response the Church enlisted the equally famous Bernard of Clairvaux, who denounced Abelard as a heretic, saying,

> Faith believes, it does not dispute. But this man [Abelard], apparently holding God suspect, will not believe anything until he has first examined it with his reason.[8]

---

[6] *De praescriptione haereticorum*, vii, quoted in *Documents of the Christian Church*, 2nd ed., ed. Henry Brettenson (Oxford: Oxford University Press, 1963), 6.

[7] For a wonderful study of the disappearance of these works, as well as their rediscovery and subsequent impact on the Church, see Richard Rubenstein, *Aristotle's Children* (Orlando: Harcourt, 2003).

[8] Letter of Bernard of Clairvaux to Cardinal Haimeric, in *The Letters of St. Bernard of Clairvaux*, trans. Bruno James (Chicago: Regnery, 1953), 328.

Bernard eventually persuaded the Pope, Innocent II, to order Abelard's books to be burned in St. Peter's Square, ordered Abelard to retire to a monastery where he must observe perpetual silence and excommunicated his followers. But even this heavy sentence on poor Abelard was too little and too late. The Church's own scholars soon realized that they too must master Aristotle in order to debate with those who followed Abelard. But we need not follow here the next thousand years of this debate within the Church between Reason and Faith, as interesting as it is.[9] Let us instead return to our topic and consider some of the associated developments regarding church music during this 'Pre-Renaissance.'

One of the questions the twelfth- and thirteenth-century Churchmen must have often discussed was the position they should take on the use of instrumental music in the church. Although the Church had tried to ban instrumental music for a thousand years, it was never completely successful and now she must have sensed the tide was moving against her. In particular the Church no doubt had to contend with the jongleur and minstrel whose increasing proficiency must have resulted in greater interest among the town's people. But these musicians were homeless people, with questionable reputations, and one gets the impression that it was more difficult for the Church to accept the players than their music.

By the twelfth century there were new pressures undermining the older conservative views of the Church. First, with the great progress in secular music, the citizens were regularly hearing music which was more interesting than that heard in the church. We assume it would only be consistent with human nature that some of this new music was beginning to creep from outside to inside the church. We find evidence of this in a reform of the Antiphonary used by the Cistercians under the leadership of Bernard of Clairvaux. When he states his purpose for the revision was, 'the removal of the defiling impurity of errors, and by the rejection of the illicit liberties taken by unskilled hands,' we read this to mean it was his contemporaries who had been making changes in the music.[10] This seems confirmed by his warning to the monks not to oppose the rules of Church music[11] and in his firm order, 'we forbid that [the music] be changed in any respect by any person,'[12] which in itself suggests he feared changes would continued to be made.

In an enlightening final statement, one which would have been characteristic of many Churchmen of the twelfth century, Bernard just could not understand why those 'illicit liberties' made in the ancient Gregorian Chant were so popular!

> Not even two provinces sing the same Antiphonary. It must, therefore, seem remarkable just why they have had such … widespread fame, since they are false rather than true, defective rather than sound.[13]

---

9   Really, the debate has never ended, as one can see today in the debates in some school boards relative to how to teach the evolution of man.

10 'De Revisione Cantus Cistercienis,' trans. Francisco Guentner (American Institute of Musicology, 1974), 43.

11 Ibid.

12 Ibid., 42.

13 Ibid., 59.

We cannot help but wonder what the 'illicit' music was like! Much of it must have been improvised, for Bernhard characterized it as being governed by 'chance,'[14] and not by Reason, as was his now ancient music. In any case, it must have been good, for he solemnly announces that he has replaced it all with 'sober and sensible music.'[15]

Another source of pressure on the Church was local folk traditions. In 1237 a group of the faithful in Eichstadt rebelled against an interdict by Bishop Friedrich III which forbad them to continue to bury their dead with the accompaniment of instruments.[16] Popular enthusiasm for dancing became at this time a particular problem for the Church. On the eve of important religious festivals in 1209, the Council of Avignon declared,

> There should not be, in the churches, any of this theatrical dancing, these immodest rejoicings, these meetings of singers with their worldly songs, which incite the souls of those who hear them to sin.[17]

Similarly, in 1212 the Council of Paris ruled,

> Gatherings of women for the purpose of dancing and singing shall not be granted permission to enter cemeteries or to tread on consecrated ground ... Nuns will not set themselves at the head of processions which sing and dance on the grounds of churches and their chapels ... for according to St. Gregory it is better to plough and dig on the Sabbath than to conduct these dances.[18]

A thirteenth-century interdiction by the Council of Bayeux is even stronger.

> Priests will forbid gatherings for dancing and singing in churches and cemeteries, on pain of excommunication.[19]

Clearly attitudes toward instrumental music were destined to change with the appearance of the modern organ, beginning in the tenth century. Even its acceptance was slow and by the twelfth century some still saw a basic distinction between the organ and other wind instruments.

> And of the organ alone the church has made use of in various kinds of singing ... other instruments being commonly rejected because of the abuses of the jongleurs.[20]

But the organ was only the surrogate for a real wind band, the sound being that of a wind band and its pipes being named for wind instruments. The real thing could not be far off.

---

[14] Ibid.

[15] Ibid., 45.

[16] George Grove, *The New Grove Dictionary of Music and Musicians*, ed. Stanley Sadie (London: Macmillan, 1980), VII, 810.

[17] Quoted in Romain Goldron, *Minstrels and Masters* (H. S. Stuttman), 19.

[18] Ibid.

[19] Ibid.

[20] Gilles de Zamore, 'Ars Musica,' in Martin Gerbert, *Scriptores ecclesiastici de musica sacra* (Saint Blaise, 1784), II, 388.

The monks also needed entertainment and by the thirteenth century one begins to see frequent payment, or food and shelter, to jongleurs for performance in individual monasteries and priories, particularly in those of the Augustinian and Benedictine orders.[21] An attractive story says that in 1224 a Benedictine house in England received with joy two visitors assumed by their dress to be jongleurs. When it was discovered the two visitors were only visiting friars, they threw them out!

Gradually the Church itself began to take advantage of the interest the instrumental musicians could bring to their festivities. Even the popes began to include instrumental music in their coronations during the thirteenth century. A report of the coronation of Gregory IX, in 1227, says, 'the crowds were taken by the sound of the trumpets.'[22] We begin to hear of church princes enjoying the prerogatives of their secular brothers, as in an example given by Ramon Lull.

> It happened one day that, while a certain Cardinal was dining, there came to his court a jongleur who was very well arrayed and adorned; he was a man of pleasing speech and personable, and he sang and played upon instruments very skillfully.[23]

And we even find in England wind instruments accompanied the singers in a Te Deum *inside* the church for the installation of a new abbot for St. Albans.[24] A charming reference to the use of string instruments in the service in the thirteenth century is found in the works of Gautier de Coinci (ca. 1218–1236).

> When the mouth is working hard the heart should so strive, and so press upon the strings of its viele, and so tune them up, that with the first word the bright sound ascends without delay to Paradise. Then their singing is pleasing to God. But there are many [church singers] who have such a viele that will go out of tune all the time unless it is tuned up with strong wine.[25]

This reminds us of another thirteenth-century perspective which we like very music. The Spanish kabbalist, Rabbi Isaac ben Jacob ha-Kohen, made a comparison between musicians who properly direct their fingers over the holes and strings of their instruments with the high priest who awakens the Holy Spirit through prayer.[26]

---

21 E. K. Chambers, *The Mediaeval Stage* (Oxford, 1903), I, 56.

22 Alessandro Vessella, *La Banda* (Milan, 1935), 35.

23 *Libre d'Evast e d'Aloma e de Banquerna*, quoted in Christopher Page, *Voices and Instruments of the Middle Ages* (London: Dent, 1987), 181.

24 Richard Rastall, 'Some English Consort-Groupings of the late Middle Ages,' *Music & Letters* 55, no. 2 (April 1974): 193.

25 V. R. Koenig, ed., *Les Miracles de Nostre Dame par Gautier de Coinci* (Geneva, 1955–1970), IV, 184.

26 Quoted in Stuart Isacoff, *Temperament* (New York: Random House, 2003), 112.

Bernard of Clairvaux made an effort to distinguish between the nature of spiritual music literature and the music of the public. He, for example, gave an entire sermon on the 'Song of Songs' (Song of Solomon) in which he attempts to explain how the wedding music described in this book differs from the usual wedding music. This, he says, is music divinely inspired and can be understood only by those whose mind is disciplined by serious study.

> For it is not a melody that resounds abroad but the very music of the heart, not a trilling on the lips but an inward pulsing of delight, a harmony not of voices but of wills. It is a tune you will not hear in the streets, these notes do not sound where crowds assemble.[27]

There must have been some who were still in favor of no instrumental music at all. Among them we are astonished to find Peter Abelard, who was not only a forward thinking monk in many ways, but had been a talented composer and singer.[28] Of all people, we find him maintaining the Church's ancient deception that the references to musical instruments in the Old Testament were merely metaphors and not descriptions of real performances. He suggests, for example, that the passage, 'Praise him with the timbrel and dance,'[29] is actually a metaphor in which the timbrel stands for 'the mortification of the flesh,' and the dance represents, 'that concord of charity'![30] In another place Abelard makes a prejudicial comment about instrumental music, specifically the aulos, an instrument not used in church music, distinguishing it from music with a higher purpose. The aulos, he says, 'emits a sound for the delectation of the sense, not for the understanding of the mind.'[31]

Unfortunately, 'for the understanding of the mind,' refers not to musical understanding, but simply to the understanding of the *words* of the music. This had long been the central point of church music in the eyes of many Churchmen. Bernard makes this point quite clearly in one of his letters.

> If there is to be singing, the melody should be grave and not flippant or uncouth. It should be sweet but not frivolous; it should both enchant the ears and move the heart; it should lighten sad hearts and soften angry passions; and it should never obscure but enhance the sense of the words. Not a little spiritual profit is lost when minds are distracted from the sense of the words by the frivolity of the melody, when more is conveyed by the modulations of the voice than by the variations of the meaning.[32]

---

[27] 'On the Song of Songs,' trans. Kilian Walsh, in *The Works of Bernard of Clairvux* (Spencer, MA: Cistercian Publications, 1971), II, 4ff.

[28] In a letter to Heloise, in *The Letters of Abelard and Heloise*, trans. C. K. Scott Moncrieff (New York: Knopf, 1933), 210, Abelard indicates no prejudice toward vocal music, saying of the woman in charge of music in a convent, 'it is most fitting that she be lettered, and especially that she be not ignorant of music.'

[29] Psalms 149:1.

[30] Letter to Heloise, in *The Letters of Abelard and Heloise*, 144.

[31] Letter to Heloise, in Ibid., 254.

[32] Letter to Abbot Guy, quoted in *The Letters of St. Bernard of Clairvaux*, 502. This is the most extended comment on Church music by Bernard. In this same letter he mentions that he had composed a Hymn, 'but I kept the sense clear at the expense of the meter.'

We must point out a rather humorous exception which Bernard makes to his testimonial on the importance of the words. By this date the books of the Old Testament known today as the Apocrypha, which although long accepted by the Church, were apparently beginning to be considered doubtful by Bernard. In this case of unapproved Scripture, he says, the words put you to sleep!

> We found the text of the old Antiphonary very loosely put together and carelessly constructed; interspersed with numerous falsehoods and with the trifling ditties of the Apocrypha, it aroused in those reading it not only boredom but also contempt—and this to such an extent that novices, who had been educated under ecclesiastical discipline, grew inattentive and weary of both text and melody of the Antiphonary, and became quite sluggish and drowsy during the divine praises.[33]

In addition to the elements listed above which distract from the listener concentrating on the words, the very precision of the performance was probably thought important for this reason. Bernhard actually defines music in these terms, 'Music is the science of singing correctly.'[34] Vitalis, in his description of a monk, uses language which seems to make the same point relative to precision.

> He was thoroughly versed in reading and singing, and after he grew up taught these freely to others with meticulous accuracy.[35]

John of Salisbury, in giving advise to rulers, focuses on the precision of string players to create an analogy on government.

> For if a cithern player and other performers on stringed instruments can by diligence find a way to correct the fault of a string which is out of tune and bring it again into accord with the other strings, and so out of discord make the sweetest harmony, not by breaking the strings but by making them tense or slack in due proportions; with how much care should the prince moderate his acts, now with the strictness of justice, and now with the leniency of mercy, to the end that he may make his subjects all be of one mind.[36]

As in the above quotation, the word, 'sweet,' is often found in this literature as an apparent primary virtue of music. Vitalis mentions a monk named Guitmund, whom he calls 'highly skilled in composition,' who had produced 'some of the sweetest melodies in our troper.'[37] In another place he refers to a German abbot, Ainard, whom he describes as,

---

[33] 'De Revisione Cantus Cistercienis,' 45.
[34] Ibid., 44.
[35] *The Ecclesiastical History*, II, 127.
[36] *Policraticus*, 39.
[37] *The Ecclesiastical History*, II, 109.

well versed in the twin sciences of poetry and music, and a most skilled writer of melodious songs. This is plain to all from the ... many other sweet songs which he composed to the glory of his Creator.[38]

An interesting passage in a letter of Heloise to Abelard mentions his skill in both composition and singing. Here she remembers those songs, written to relieve the tedium of study, had a sweetness which achieved universality.

> Wherewith as with a game, refreshing the labor of philosophic exercise, thou has left many songs composed in amatory measure or rhythm, which for the suavity both of words and of tune being oft repeated, have kept thy name without ceasing on the lips of all; since even illiterates the sweetness of thy melodies did not allow to forget thee.[39]

Certainly in secular music this 'sweetness' must have referred in part to harmony, which was based on the third long before it was the case in church music. This, indeed, was Lull's definition of music.

> Music is the art devised to arrange many voices so they may be concordant in a single song.[40]

There are a few more descriptions of music by these Churchmen which should be mentioned. Bernard of Clairvaux (1090–1153), in the notes to his Antiphonary, makes three interesting observations which he unfortunately does not explain. Unlike everyone else, he says, his purpose in selecting music is to follow 'Nature, rather than [common] usage.'[41] He equates *authentic* with joyfulness and *plagal* with gravity.[42] Finally, 'neumas,' he says, were invented by the Greeks in order that their 'modes could be perceived at the same time by ear and mind.'[43]

One of the most interesting Church persons of this period, and one who made some of the most enlightening observations on music, was Hildegard of Bingen. The purpose of music, says Hildegard, is to soften hard hearts.[44] In another, and more important, definition of the purpose of music, Hildegard concentrates on the listener, the critical element in aesthetics in music. Following the Aristotelian definition of aesthetics, she says that what the listener hears affects the inner person. Her frame of reference here is, of course, a religious one, which follows her mention of the numerous references to the performance of music in the Old Testament.

---

[38] Ibid., II, 353ff.

[39] Letter of Heloise to Abelard, quoted in *The Letters of Abelard and Heloise*, trans. Moncrieff, 59.

[40] 'Ars Brevis,' X, 85, in *Doctor Illuminatis*, ed. Anthony Bonner, I, 623. The editor adds this note: 'Possibly the only common medieval subject on which Lull wrote almost nothing was music.'

[41] 'De Revisione Cantus Cistercienis,' 59.

[42] Ibid., 56.

[43] Ibid., 57. On page 46ff he seems to argue against any creativity in the addition of the Bb and on page 53 he suggests the correct limit of range in church music is a tenth—corresponding to the 10-string psaltery.

[44] Quoted in *Hildegard of Bingen*, eds. Fiona Bowie and Oliver Daview (New York: Crossroad, 1993), 83.

> In these words outer realities [performance] teach us about inner ones—namely how, in accordance with the material composition and quality of instruments, we can best transform and shape the performance of our inner being towards praises of the Creator.[45]

In another place she again speaks of music reaching the heart of the listener, here mentioning the old Roman tradition of orators having a musician stand behind them to 'tune' the emotions and pace of their speaking.

> But persons who carry out their tasks in life by teaching others according to the command of almighty God resound, so to speak, on flutes of sanctity. For by the voice of reason they chant justice right into the hearts of men and women ... The Word is heard by means of sound, and it is also disseminated so that it can be heard. Just as a flute can strengthen the human voice, the teacher's voice can be strengthened among other human beings through the fear and love of God.[46]

And in one more place she mentions the impact of music on the listener, observing, 'at times, when hearing some melody, a human being often sighs and moans.'[47]

In 1178, Hildegard, in allowing the burial of a nobleman who had been excommunicated and subsequently reconciled to the Church, came in conflict with the prelates of Mainz. As a result, they placed Hildegard and her sisters under an interdict, which among other things ordered her to cease singing the divine Service. Her letter of response includes a very interesting condensed history of Church music. She begins by citing the use of music in the Old Testament and then gives the following explanation for the invention of musical instruments,[48] which again focuses on the impact of music on the listener.

> They invented musical instruments of diverse kinds ... by which the songs could be expressed in multitudinous sounds, so that listeners, aroused and made adept outwardly, might be nurtured within by the forms and qualities of the instruments, as by the meaning of the words performed with them.[49]

Next, she says, men invented organum, 'so that they could sing in the delight of their soul.' Her following comment is very important and requires some introduction. We are familiar with the 'chironomist' seen in the tomb paintings of the ancient Egyptians, a figure who was clearly a kind of conductor although in his frozen postures we cannot see how he functioned. When new systems of musical notation begin to appear, after the Dark Ages, we see notation by neume symbols, with curves and swirls looking very much like lines tracing gestures. It is our hypothesis that these neume symbols are in fact a kind of record of what the chironomist

---

45 Letter to the Mainz prelates, in Ibid., 150.

46 'Vision Seven: 10,' in *The Book of Divine Works*, ed. Matthew Fox (Santa Fe: Bear & Company, 1987), 194.

47 *Hildegard of Bingen*, 151.

48 In the Divine Words, 'Vision Seven: 10,' Hildegard suggests a slight preference for string instruments, which she says have 'look up to God ... with the simplicity of a dove.' Players of wind instruments, on the other hand, 'serve humbly upon the Earth.'

49 Ibid., 150.

did, that is, that there was an unbroken tradition. We are therefore struck by Hildegard's next comment, which seems to confirm this kind of hand-symbol conducting was still known in the twelfth century!

> ... and they adapted their singing to the bending of the finger-joints.[50]

Finally, the imagery of angels singing was a familiar one among early Church writers, due to their performance at the birth of Jesus. Hildegard mentions angel choirs frequently, sometimes 'immeasurably large choirs of angels,'[51] and has left us with a very poetic description of her vision of these singers.

> For most of the good angels look up to God. They acknowledge God with all the melodious sound of their hymns of praise, and laud in wonderful harmony the mysteries that have always been with God and are still with God today. The angels can never stop praising God because they are unencumbered by earthly bodies. They bear witness to the Godhead through the living resonance of their splendid voices, which are more numerous than the sands of the sea and which outnumber all the fruits that the Earth might ever produce. Their voices have a richer harmony than all the sounds living creatures have ever produced, and their voices are brighter than all the splendor of the sun, moon, and stars sparkling in the waters. More wonderful is this sound than the music of the spheres that arises from the blowing of the winds that sustain the four elements and are well adjusted to them.[52]

At this point, chronologically, the reader might anticipate reading commentary about Roman Church music by the most important Church writer of the late middle ages, Thomas Aquinas (1224–1274), but he left very little commentary on music. Even in a treatise on prophesy and a complete book on the ceremonial aspects of the Jewish religion,[53] Aquinas never once mentions music. The omission seems deliberate and may reflect the fact that his great model, Aristotle, also wrote little about music, although in his case there appear to be lost books on the subject. We will look at Thomas Aquinas in more detail in the following essay.

On the Music of the Crusades

Only a period which had the courage to imagine constructing the enormous arches and pillars of the great cathedrals and which had such enthusiasm for the German and French Romances could have seriously considered the incredible idea of driving the Moslems out of Jerusalem and making that city the center of the Christian world.

The First Crusade (1095–1099), urged on by Urban II, was largely a grand adventure led by French nobles. Some 30,000 troops set out and after two years of battles the surviving 12,000 conquered Jerusalem. The Latin chronicles describe the Western armies as using three types of trumpets, 'tubae, buccinae, and lituui,' as well as 'corni.' One would suppose that some of

---

[50] Ibid., 151.

[51] 'Vision One: 8,' in *Book of Divine Works*, 14.

[52] 'Vision Six: 4,' in Ibid., 181ff.

[53] Ibid., XXIX.

these instruments were used only in battle, as the historian, Fulcher of Chartres (d. 1130), who was present, mentions the English musician, Evrardus Venator, who played 'tuba' during the crusade, but was a horn player at court.[54]

After slaughtering the remaining 70,000 Moslems in the city, burning alive the remaining Jews in their synagogue, throwing babies over the walls and killing their mothers, the Christians paused to sing hymns to God.

> The Christians, having obtained with the wished-for victory … blessed God with due praises … raising to heaven hymns of thanksgiving.[55]

Upon establishing the new Latin kingdom of Jerusalem, the victorious leaders soon divided up the major cities into private principalities and began to feud among themselves. Eventually most of the Crusaders returned to Europe, leaving a small number of Christians prey to Moslems eager to avenge their losses. In the report of a speech by King Baldwin of Jerusalem intended to inspire his troops, we know that among those who remained were jongleurs.

> Remember the ten-year siege of Troy, call to mind the marvelous deeds of the heroic lords which your jongleurs chant every day and restore your strength and renew your courage from these.[56]

The Second Crusade (1146–1148) was organized at the insistence of Bernard of Clairvaux ('St. Bernard') and was led by Louis VII of France and Conrad of Germany. The Western troops were virtually annihilated en route leaving Louis and Conrad to arrive in Jerusalem without little more than the numerous ladies who had also joined the adventure. Europe was shocked by the total failure of this Crusade, Bernard was widely criticized for his role and Christians wondered how God had permitted so complete a defeat.

The Third Crusade (1189–1192) followed a period of relative peace between Christians and Saracens in the Holy Land which was primarily upset by Reginald of Chatillon who threatened to destroy Mecca. The result of Reginald's adventure was the fall of the Holy City again to the 'infidels.' Ambrose, a jongleur in the service of Richard I of the Lion Heart writing in 1196, relates that this news was such that the common people of Western Europe were very disheartened, 'forgotten were the dances, the singing of lays and of ballads, sweet converse, and every earthly joy' until they took the cross on another crusade.[57]

---

54 Henry G. Farmer, 'Crusading Martial Music,' in *Music & Letters* (1949), 244.

55 Ordericus Vitalis, *The Ecclesiastical History of England*, IX, x, trans. Thomas Forester (London: Henry G. Bohn, 1854), III, 141.

56 Ordericus Vitalis, *The Ecclesiastical History of England*, Book XI, trans. Marjorie Chibnall (Oxford: Clarendon Press, 1978), VI, 121.

57 'L'Estoire de la Guerre Sainte' (1196), quoted in E. N. Stone, *Three Old French Chronicles of the Crusades* (1939), 11.

As the respective leaders were the famous Saladin, a man of superior character, and the legendary Richard I of the Lion Heart,[58] this Crusade became the most romantic and best-known. Richard's jongleur, Ambrose, records the king's reception when he arrived in Acre in 1191.

> Great was the joyance … Nor do I think that ever was any mother's son hath seen or could describe so great a rejoicing as was made in the host over the king. There was heard the sound of timbrels, of trumpets, of horns and pipes and flutes. Then might ye see joy unrestrained, of folk of divers sort—the singing of goodly songs and lays, cupbearers bearing wine through the streets in goodly cups, both to the great folk and to the lowly.[59]

Another chronicle also contains an interesting description of Richard's arrival at Acre. The reference to 'soothing symphonies heard like blended voices' suggests that instrumental jongleurs also traveled with Richard.

> The people testified their joy by shouts of welcome and the clang of trumpets; the day was kept as a jubilee, and universal gladness reigned around, on account of the arrival of the king, long wished for by all nations … No pen can sufficiently describe the joy of the people on the king's arrival, nor tongue detail it; the very calmness of the night was thought to smile upon them with a purer air; the trumpets clanged, horns sounded, and the shrill intonations of the pipe, and the deeper notes of the timbrel and harp, struck upon the ear; and soothing symphonies were heard like various voices blended in one; and there was not a man who did not, after his own fashion, indulge in joy and praise; either singing popular ballads to testify the gladness of his heart, or reciting the deeds of the ancients.[60]

From the writings of scribes who accompanied Richard I on this Crusade we know that his army's musical instruments consisted primarily of primitive trumpet-types. Indeed Richard himself is quoted as saying, upon his arrival at Messina, 'at the third day, at the sound of the buccina, let them follow me.'[61] A few days later a scribe mentions another trumpet-type.

> In front came the terrible dragon standard unfurled. Then rode the King. Behind him the clangor of the tuba exited the army.[62]

---

[58] Geoffrey de Vinsauf, in 'Itinerary of Richard I to the Holy Land,' quoted in *Chronicles of the Crusades* (London: Bell and Sons, 1914), 155, a contemporary, describes Richard:

> He was tall of stature, graceful in figure; his hair between red and auburn; his limbs were straight and flexible; his arms rather long, and not to be matched for wielding the sword or for striking with it; and his long legs suited the rest of his frame; while his appearance was commanding, and his manners and habits suitable; and he gained the greatest celebrity, not more from his high birth than from the virtues that adorned him.

[59] Ibid., 41.

[60] Ibid., 200ff.

[61] Richard Devizes, 'The Crusade of Richard Coeur de Lion,' Section 24, in *Chronicles of the Crusades* (London: Bell and Sons, 1914), 17.

[62] Ibid., Section 26.

Another eyewitness describing this same arrival at Messina gives us a much more colorful view of the scene. Of particular interest is the phrase, 'harmoniously blended,' which suggests the possibility of multi-part trumpet music.

> And lo! they beheld the sea in the distance covered with innumerable galleys; and the sound of trumpets and clarions, loud and shrill, strike upon the ear! … You might behold the sea boiling from the number of oarsmen who plied it, and the ears of the spectators rang with the peals of the instruments commonly called trumpets … Meanwhile the trumpets blew, and their sounds being harmoniously blended, there arose a kind of discordant concord of notes, whilst the sameness of the sounds being continued, the one followed the other in mutual succession, and the notes which had been lowered were again resounded.[63]

One contemporary chronicle provides a rare glimpse of the use of Richard's trumpets in controlling the movement of his ships. For the purpose of hearing these trumpet signals, the ships sailed in the formation of a pyramid, with three ships in the first row, thirteen in the second, fourteen in the third, twenty in the fourth, thirty in the fifth, forty in the sixth, and sixty in the seventh.

> Between the ships and their ranks there was such care in the spacing of the fleet that from one rank to another the sound of a trumpet could be heard, and from one ship to another [in the same rank] the voice of a man.[64]

An account of the battle of Arsul, in 1191, gives more detail of the use of these trumpets in performing military signals in combat.

> It had been resolved by common consent that the sounding of six trumpets in three different parts of the army should be a signal for a charge, viz. two in front, two in the rear and two in the middle, to distinguish the sounds from those of the Saracens, and to mark the distance of each. If these orders had been attended to, the Turks would have been utterly discomfited; but from the too great haste of the aforesaid knights, the success of the affair was marred.[65]

In the midst of this Crusade, we have an extraordinary anecdote of a battle of music! While the Western troops were trying to take Jerusalem, some Western leaders apparently became impatient with Richard's hesitation. The jongleur, Ambrose, tells what happened next.

> And Hugo, the Duke of Burgundy, who did much to make the matter worse, with great and exceeding arrogance made a song about the king, and a right villainous song it was—yea, full of villainy; and this song spread throughout the host. What could the king do, save in his turn to make another song concerning them that through envy thus assailed and mocked him?[66]

---

[63] Vinsauf, *Chronicles of the Crusades*, 164.
[64] John T. Appleby, ed., *The Chronicle of Richard of Devizes* (London, 1963), 35.
[65] Vinsauf, *Chronicles of the Crusades*, 238.
[66] Stone, *Three Old French Chronicles of the Crusades*, 141.

Musically, the most historically significant aspect of the Crusades was the encounter by Western persons of the more sophisticated military bands of the East with much broader types of instruments, most of which rapidly became part of the Western musical scene. Arabic historians identify the instruments of the Saracens at this time as trumpets (*anafir*[67]), horns (*bugat*), shawms (*zumur*), timpani (*kusat*), drums (*tubul*) and cymbals (*kasat*).[68]

An eyewitness describes for us what it must have been like for the Western troops to face their Eastern adversaries with their frightening music.

> They came on with irresistible charge, on horses swifter than eagles, and urged on like lightening to attack our men; and as they advanced, they raised a cloud of dust, so that the sky was darkened. In front came certain of their admirals, as it was their duty, with clarions and trumpets; some had horns, others had pipes and timbrels, gongs, cymbals, and other instruments, producing a horrible noise and clamor. The earth vibrated from the loud and discordant sounds, so that the crash of thunder could not be heard amidst the tumultuous noise of horns and trumpets. They did this to excite their spirit and courage, for the more violent the clamor became, the more bold were they for the fray.[69]

Another chronicle describes the percussion signals of Saladin's troops as resembling 'the crash in the air caused by thunder and lightning.'[70] Victory and defeat alternated until a three-year peace was signed in 1192.

The Fourth Crusade (1202–1204) is remembered for the involvement of the Venetians, whose investment was repaid in the rape of Constantinople. The incredible loss of art treasures, which a contemporary said represented two-thirds of all the wealth of the world,[71] included the only copies of many plays by Sophocles and Euripides. This reprehensible Crusade led some Europeans to imagine that only the pure of heart would be supported by God in the next attempt. Thus two efforts were attempted by children, resulting in thousands of them being drowned, eaten by wolves, dying of hunger or being sold as slaves.

The pope, Innocent III, called for the Fifth Crusade, which began in 1217 with the goal of attacking through Egypt. The failure of this Crusade was blamed on the young Frederick II, Emperor of Germany and Italy, who did not participate.

Frederick II, however, led the Sixth Crusade in 1228. Frederick, one of the most literate and cultured of early nobles was personally attractive to the Saracens.[72] The peace they organized might have been the basis for a permanent one had it not been for the refusal of then Pope Gregory IX to ratify it. Therefore Jerusalem once again fell to Islam.

---

[67] From which comes the word, 'fanfare.'

[68] Farmer, 'Crusading Martial Music,' *Music & Letters* 30, no. 3 (July 1949): 243. A contemporary, quoted in Ibid., 244, describes the trumpet-types of the Saracens as 'trumpae, tubae, tibiae,' which is the earliest known mention of the cognate form of the trumpet.

[69] Goeffrey de Vinsauf, *Chronicle of Richard the First's Crusade* [1191] (London, 1914), 234–235.

[70] Ibid., 203.

[71] Stone, *Three Old French Chronicles of the Crusades*, 226.

[72] Frederick spoke nine languages and wrote in seven, wrote a definitive treatise on falconry, studied mathematics and anatomy and founded the University of Naples in 1224.

The Seventh Crusade was organized by Louis IX ('St. Louis') of France in 1248. This Crusade, memorialized by the chronicler, Jean de Joinville, after four years in the Holy Land, basically ran out of health, courage and money.

Joinville describes Louis arriving at the Egyptian port of Damietta to the welcome of 'noisy nacaires and cors sarrazinnois.' He also discusses the Sultan's band, which he calls *Haulequa*, from the Arabic, *Halqa*, 'circle.' This band consisted of 'cors sarrazinnois, tabours and nacaires.'

> And with these they made such a noise at the point of day and at nightfall, that those who were near could not hear one another speak; and clearly were they heard throughout the camp.
> Nor would the musicians have been rash enough to sound their instruments during the day, save by order of the master of the Halca; whence it happened that if the sultan wished to give an order, he sent for the master of the Halca, and gave the order through him; and then the master caused the soldan's instruments to be sounded, and all the host assembled to hear the order of the soldan.[73]

Joinville also mentions the extraordinary impression the sound of the Eastern military bands made on the Western soldiers in battle.

> The noise they made with their cymbals and horns was fearful to listen to.[74]

Meager efforts by Louis in 1267 and by Edward of England in 1268 represented the final efforts of the thirteenth century to establish European control of Jerusalem.

The last of such efforts come in the fifteenth century. One of the most interesting came in 1454 when Philip the Good of Burgundy organized a great banquet and instituted a new aristocratic order, the Order of the Golden Fleece, all for the purpose of gaining the support of his fellow nobles for a crusade to rescue Constantinople, which had fallen to the Turks the previous year. After the most discussed banquet in early European history, and sufficient drink to cloud the judgment of the fellow nobles, finally the grand chivalric moment arrived, with the entrance of two knights of the Order of the Golden Fleece and a pheasant, which had a gold collar around its neck decorated with rubies and large pearls. Then Philip handed to the Golden Fleece king-of-arms a vow to read. It announced his intention to make the crusade, even going so far as to say that if challenged, he would accept single combat with the Turk! Everyone was amazed by this and one by one the other knights took the vow, although the crusade never took place.

The final attempt at a large-scale crusade was organized by Charles VIII (1483–1498) of France. After much organization and gathering together of the soldiers, he marched west toward one of the Italian ports where he intended to board ships for Jerusalem. However, by the time they reached Milan they were all tired and stopped for several months to rest. Several

---

73 'Joinville's Chronicle of the Crusade of St. Lewis,' in *Memoirs of the Crusades*, trans. Frank Marzials (London: J. M. Dent, 1926), 205ff.

74 Ibid., 172.

months of the good life in Milan caused them all to lose their enthusiasm for going to Jerusalem to fight the Infidels, so they turned around and returned to Paris, bringing with them back to France the Renaissance and the *moribis gallicus*, a new strain of venereal disease.

St. Thomas Aquinas on Music

WITH THOMAS AQUINAS (1224–1274) we come to the most prolific Church writer of the late Middle Ages. With all the rapid developments in civic and court music and a growing dissatisfaction with style of the older church music, the *musica antiqua*, we would have anticipated significant commentary by Aquinas on music. But it is a topic he rarely mentions, the reason for which we can only begin to find by first reviewing his personification of the state of Church dogma at this time.

Born to a noble family, Aquinas spent five years at the University of Naples where he came under the influence of the recently rediscovered works of the ancient Greek philosophers. As a result, Aquinas' admiration for Aristotle is apparent on nearly every page of his many books (a number of them based directly on Aristotle) and in his emphasis on Reason. His purpose was to demonstrate that the uncompromising logic of Aristotle could be reconciled to a religion based on unquestioned faith. His 'intellectualism' was not well received by the followers of St. Francis, who sought God by Augustine's mystic road of love.[1] John Peckham, who followed Bonaventura in the chair of Philosophy in Paris criticized Aquinas for involving himself in the philosophy of a pagan.

From our perspective, his unrelenting dependence on Aristotle prevented him from developing original thought and when he does launch off on his own, it is so much centered in angels and in the soul as to be difficult in modern application. Before considering Aquinas' comments on music, it seems to us necessary to give the reader some insight into his related philosophical ideas.

First, regarding pleasure, Acquinas took the Church position that the pleasures of Reason and the intellect are far more preferred than those of the senses.

> A person gets far more pleasure from knowing something by understanding it than by feeling it ... Intellectual knowledge is more highly prized: a man would rather lose his sight than his sanity ...
> People will forgo even the greatest pleasures of the body rather than suffer loss of honor; and honor is a good appreciated only by the intellect.[2]

On the whole, this solemn Churchman saw little to recommend in pleasure for its own sake. Some of his strongest arguments against the dangers of pleasure are found in a treatise, 'On the Governance of Rulers,' written for the king of Cyprus. Here, he warns,

---

[1] Will Durant, *The Age of Faith* (New York: Simon and Schuster, 1950), 977.

[2] *Summa Theologiae* (London: Blackfriars, 1971), XX. 17. For the sixty volumes of the *Summa Theologiae*, we will cite the volume and page number of this complete edition.

> Indulgence in superfluous pleasure leads from the path of virtue, for nothing conduces more easily to immoderate increase which upsets the mean of virtue, than pleasure. Pleasure is, by its very nature, greedy, and thus on a slight occasion one is precipitated into the seductions of shameful pleasures just as a little spark is sufficient to kindle dry wood ...
>
> Also, they who give themselves up to pleasures grow soft in spirit and become weak-minded when it is a question of tackling some difficult enterprise, enduring toil, and facing dangers ...
>
> Finally, men who have become dissolute through pleasures usually grow lazy and, neglecting necessary matters and all the pursuits that duty lays upon them, devote themselves wholly to the quest of pleasure, on which they squander all that others had so carefully amassed.[3]

Looking at Pleasure relative to the life of the Christian, Aquinas, in his *Summa Contra Gentiles*, considers happiness from the perspective of the end of man. This includes a series of chapters, the titles of which outline his case.

> That Human Happiness does not Consist in Carnal Pleasures
> That Happiness does not Consist in Honors
> That Man's Happiness Consists not in Glory
> That Man's Happiness does not Consist in Wealth
> That Happiness Consists not in Worldly Power
> That Happiness Consists not in Goods of the Body
> That Human Happiness is not Seated in the Senses
> That Man's Ultimate Happiness does not Consist in Acts of Moral Virtue
> That Ultimate Happiness does not Consist in the Act of Prudence
> That Happiness does not Consist in the Practice of Art

This extensive pessimism finally reaches the conclusion, 'Therefore it is not possible for man to be happy in this life.'[4]

The overall understanding of the emotions by Aquinas is summarized in the following statement:

> All the emotions issue from certain initial ones, namely love and hatred, and finish in certain others, namely pleasure and sorrow. In like manner, all the operations that are the matter of moral virtue are related to one another, and even to the emotions.[5]

He then arranges, under these categories, all the remaining emotions as he recognized them.

> We are now in a position to arrange all of the emotions in the order of their actual occurrence. First come love and hatred; second, desire and aversion; third, hope and despair; fourth, fear and courage; fifth, anger; sixth and last, joy or sadness, which come after all the emotions. From what we have said it is clear that, within these pairs, love has precedence over hatred, desire over aversion, fear over courage, and joy over sadness.[6]

---

[3] 'On Kingship to the King of Cyprus,' trans. Gerald Phelan (Toronto: The Pontifical Institute of Mediaeval Studies, 1949), 79.

[4] *Summa Contra Gentiles* (London, Burns Oates & Washbourne, 1923), XLVIII.

[5] *Summa Theologiae*, XXIII, 183. See also, Ibid., XIX, 49, 51, 57.

[6] Ibid., XIX, 55.

At this point, however, Aquinas begins to get into trouble. He is contradictory in his statements on where exactly in man the emotions are located, encountering all the difficulties of early philosophers who failed to have our modern knowledge of the bicameral mind. He also made the mistake of associating emotions with the object, not within the person himself. All of his arguments following this line of thought make no sense today.

Because Aquinas focused on the object, rather than the person, he also failed to realize that the emotions are universal, indeed as we know today, genetic. Interestingly enough, Aquinas acknowledged that Aristotle had maintained that the emotions are universal, then goes on to say this view was now controversial, supplies a contemporary false explanation and, finally, his own incorrect analysis of what Aristotle *really* meant!

> There are some who object to Aristotle's position that passions of the soul, which vocal sounds signify, are the same for all men. Their argument against it is as follows: different men have different opinions about things; therefore, passions of the soul do not seem to be the same among all men ...
>
> Aristotle's statement should be referred to the simple conceptions of the intellect—that are signified by the incomplex vocal sounds—which are the same among all men.[7]

Aquinas also follows the Church position that it is Reason which must control the emotions. It is this alone, he says, which separates man from the animals.

> There are two ways of looking at the emotions: intrinsically, or as subject to the control of reason and will. Now intrinsically of course the emotions are simply movements of the non-rational; one cannot therefore ascribe to them moral, good or evil, which we have shown to involve the reason.
>
> But in so far as the emotions are subject to the control of reason and will, moral judgments do apply to them.[8]
>
> ......
>
> Emotion leads one towards sin in so far as it is uncontrolled by reason; but in so far as it is rationally controlled, it is part of the virtuous life.[9]

Having stressed the importance of the emotions being under the control of Reason, Aquinas nevertheless warns that strong emotions have the capacity of blinding Reason.

> There are degrees in being transformed by passion. It may go so far as to blind the reason completely, as happens when vehement rage of concupiscence makes a man beside himself or out of his mind; this may come also from some physical disorder. Passion, remember, goes with physiological change. In this condition men become like the beasts, driven of necessity by passion; they are without the motion of reason, and, consequently, of will.[10]

---

7 *Commentary on Peri Hermeneias*, trans. Jean Oesterle (Milwaukee: Marquette University Press, 1962), 27ff.
8 *Summa Theologiae*, XIX, 33.
9 Ibid., 37.
10 Ibid., XVII, 91.

In general this is a difficult topic for a Church philosopher who must explain in left hemisphere of the brain language something which is not located there at all. Being consequently unable to explain the Church logic on this subject, Aquinas engages in a bit of 'weird science,' in attributing an influence on the emotions to the planets.

> We have already noted that emotional feeling is an act of a bodily organ. Consequently there is nothing to prevent us holding that impressions from heavenly bodies render some people more prompt to anger than others, or to concupiscence, or to some such emotion. Indeed they are such by temperamental constitution. Most men follow their passions; only the wise resist. And therefore in the majority of cases astrological predications may well be verified.[11]
>
> ......
>
> [The heavenly bodies] may make impressions on our own body, and when the body is affected movements of the passions arise; either because such impressions make us liable to certain passions; for instance the bilious are prone to anger; or because they produce in us a bodily disposition that occasions a particular choice, thus when we are ill, we choose to take medicine. Sometimes too, the heavenly bodies are a cause of human acts, when through an indisposition of the body a person goes out of his mind, and loses the use of reason.[12]

With regard to the general subject of art, we find in Aquinas some principles which have some correspondence with music as well. For example, he writes that for beauty three things are required: a) integrity or perfection, b) right proportion or consonance, c) splendor of form.[13]

In another place where Aquinas contrasts Beauty and the Good, he adds the very interesting comment that of all the senses, only sight and hearing also contribute to knowledge in their association with Beauty.

> Those senses are therefore chiefly associated with beauty which contribute most to our knowledge, viz. sight and hearing when ministering to reason; thus we speak of beautiful sights and beautiful sounds, but not of beautiful tastes and smells: we do not speak of beauty in reference to the other three senses.[14]

A final observation on Beauty is very Aristotelian in character, in that the emphasis is on the observer. Aquinas makes a significant point in associating the perception of Beauty with the inherent quality of the observer himself.

> We have pointed out that a thing is called valuable in itself because of its beauty shaped by intelligence. To this shapeliness we respond because of what we are by our nature: each and everything delights in what matches it.[15]

---

[11] Ibid., 79.

[12] *Summa Contra Gentiles*, LXXXV.

[13] Quoted in James F. Anderson, *An Introduction to the Metaphysics of St. Thomas Aquinas* (Chicago: Henry Regnery, 1953), 88.

[14] *Summa Theologiae*, XIX, 77.

[15] Ibid., XLIII, 39, 77.

There are some more of his views on art which have a relationship with how he perceived music. He places great importance in this kind of knowledge, pointing out that 'men who have an art are wiser and more knowing than those who have [mere] experience.'[16] And it is in this same light that he several times stresses that the man who has ideas is more important than the man who carries them out.[17]

For the artist, Aquinas believed the next step was more important, the actual engagement of this technique. In one place he describes the process in the artist as being exactly like that of the speaker.

> An artist first intends his work of art, next shapes it in his mind and fancy, and then in his material. Similarly, a speaker first conceives the meaning he intends to convey, afterwards finds a sign for it [language], and finally pronounces it.[18]

In several places, Aquinas clearly suggests that Art is in this technique, this carrying out of the Art work, and not in the Art object itself, concluding, 'Art does not exist in the thing produced by art but in something else.'[19] Aquinas recognized that a mistake in the technique is not the same thing as deviation from the norm due to genius.

> An artist who deliberately breaks the rules of his art is reckoned a better artist, as keeping a sound judgment of what they are, than one who involuntarily breaks them, from a fault, it would seem, of judgment.[20]

For Aquinas, one characteristic of the fine artist was that the technique, important as it is, should not be apparent in the performance of the art. For illustration, he provides here one of his rare references to a musician.

> It is obvious that art does not deliberate. Nor does the artisan deliberate insofar as he has the art, but insofar as he falls short of the certitude of the art. Hence the most certain arts do not deliberate, as the writer does not deliberate how he should form letters. Moreover, those artisans who do deliberate, after they have discovered the certain principles of the art, do not deliberate in the execution. Thus one who plays the harp would seem most inexperienced if he should deliberate in playing any chord.[21]

---

[16] *Commentary on the Metaphysics of Aristotle*, trans. John Rowan (Chicago: Henry Regnery, 1961), 15 (I. L. 1: C 29).

[17] Ibid., 14 (I. L. 1:C 26), 19 (I. L. 2: C 41); *Commentary on Aristotle's Physics*, trans. Richard Blackwell (New Haven: Yale University Press, 1963), 84 (194 a 12 - b 15); and *Summa Theologiae*, I, 23.

[18] *Disputations*, IV de Veritate, 1, quoted in *Theological Texts*, trans. Thomas Gilby (London: Oxford University Press, 1955), 63.

[19] *Commentary on the Metaphysics of Aristotle*, 529 (VII. L. 6: C 1381). In *Summa Contra Gentiles*, LXXV, Aquinas explains why the nature of the technique of the teacher to be more comparable to the physician than the builder of a house.

[20] *Summa Theologiae*, XXXVI, 29.

[21] *Commentary on Aristotle's Physics*, 123 (199 a 34 - b 33). An exception, apparently, is the case of the dancer,

> For men who do not have the art of dancing can move about but not in the way in which those men do who have this art. [*Commentary on the Metaphysics of Aristotle*, 546 (VII. L. 8: C 1439)].

He mentions the harpist again in observing that it is by experience that the artist acquires his technique.

> For it seems impossible that anyone should become a builder who has not first built something; or that anyone should become a harpist who has not first played the harp.[22]

On the other hand, in other places Aquinas suggests a more modern view, that the purpose of Art to be simply itself—Art for Art's sake.

> The worth of things produced by art, however, does not consist in their being good for human appetite, but in the good of the products of art themselves.[23]

Aquinas rarely speaks of music as an independent topic and why this is so is a mystery, although it may have some relationship to the fact that Aristotle also wrote relatively little about music. But, when writing lengthy treatises on subjects like the emotions, or pleasure, why does Aquinas never associate these topics with music? Likewise, in a treatise on prophesy and a complete book on the ceremonial aspects of the Jewish religion[24] Aquinas never once mentions music. In this case, since music is closely associated with both prophesy and religious ceremony in the Old Testament, his omission seems deliberate.

There are almost no direct references in the writings of Aquinas to music performances he actually heard and the indirect references offer a mixed view of his sophistication as a listener. In one place it would appear he appreciated fine players, for in a discussion of the soul he mentions the body might be 'lissome and agile … like an instrument in the hands of a skilled player.'[25] But in another place we would have to question his ear, if not his disinterest, for he says it is no great sin, 'when someone brags about his singing, when in fact he was out of tune.'[26]

All in all, it seems apparent that Aquinas was not enthusiastic about music in general, but why? Was it the competition for the attention of the faithful from the rapidly developing secular music of the civic domain? Was it disgust for the Church music he heard while teaching in Paris—especially in the example of the callous deception of the Church perpetrated by the thirteenth-century motet? One cannot say.

In his most lengthy discussion of music,[27] a discussion of Church music, it is very clear that on the balance Aquinas found little to recommend in it. In this discussion he presents four rather negative perspectives on Church music.

---

[22] *Commentary on the Metaphysics of Aristotle*, 684–685 (IX.L.7:C 1850).

[23] *Summa Theologiae*, XXIII, 51.

[24] Ibid., XXIX.

[25] *Compendium Theologiae*, 168, quoted in *Theological Texts*, 409.

[26] *Disputations*, IX de Malo, 2, c. & ad 8, quoted in Ibid., 137.

[27] *Compendium Theologiae*, XXXIX, 249ff.

1. St. Jerome does not condemn singing absolutely, but he corrects those who sing theatrically, or who sing not in order to arouse devotion but to show off or to provoke pleasure.
2. Arousing men to devotion through preaching and teaching is a more excellent way than through singing.[28]
3. Musical instruments usually move the soul to pleasure rather than create a good disposition to it.
4. The soul is distracted from the meaning of a song when it is sung merely to arouse pleasure.

It is in this discussion as well that Aquinas makes his only reference to the rich tradition of music in the Old Testament. It is a comment anti-Semitic throughout.

> Old Testament [musical] instruments were used both because the people were more coarse and carnal, so that they needed to be aroused by such instruments as well as with promises of temporal wealth, and because these instruments presaged the future.

In fact, the only enthusiastic vote of confidence Aquinas can make for Church music in this discussion is that it might help the fainthearted!

> Vocal praise is necessary to arouse man's devotion for God, and whatever is useful for this purpose is fittingly used in divine praise. Clearly, the human soul is moved in various ways by different sounds of music, as Aristotle and Boethius recognized. Wisely, therefore, song has been used in praising God so that the minds of the fainthearted may be incited to devotion.

Aside from this discussion there is only one significant reference to music used in the Service, but it is an interesting one. Here,[29] he not only clearly associates singing with the 'mystery' of the Mass, but mentions that there is one reference in the New Testament to Jesus singing![30] He elaborates on neither.

His views on Church music notwithstanding, Aquinas gives evidence of familiarity of the history of early Christian music. In one interesting passage he mentions that the earliest period, when services were held in secret, included only silent recitation, but that singing began 'at a time when the faith had come out in the open.'[31]

Other than on the subject of Church music, Aquinas continued the view held by the writers who commented on the liberal arts during earlier centuries that music 'takes its principles from arithmetic.'[32]

---

[28] Aquinas wrote a few hymn texts which are extant and are given in *Selected Writings of St. Thomas Aquinas*, ed. M. C. D'Arcy (New York: Dutton, 1950). Perhaps he found his preaching more successful than his composing.
[29] *Summa Theologiae*, LIX, 159.
[30] Matthew 26:30.
[31] *Summa Theologiae*, XXXI, 53.
[32] Ibid., I, 11. See also *Commentary on Aristotle's Physics*, 12 (184 b 15–185 a 19), 'Music is subalternated to arithmetic,' and 80 (193 b 22–194 a 11).

Aquinas rarely mentions hearing when discussing the senses, and never with respect to music, but in the following passage it is clear that he trusted the eye more than the ear. The exception which he offers here seems little more than a disguised warning to the Christian not to question the Church.

> All things being equal, seeing is more certain than hearing. But if one from whom something is heard far excels the sight of one who sees, then hearing is more certain than seeing. An example: a person with scant learning is far surer of something he hears from an expert than he is of any insight of his own. Thus anyone is far surer of what he hears from the infallible God than of what he sees with his own fallible reason.[33]

In only one place does Aquinas hit upon the essence of aesthetics in music, which, of course, is the nature of the perception of the listener. In this passage he is talking about the emotions, and not about music, but the point is an important one.

> The intensity of a given passion varies, not only with the active power of the agent, but also with the passive capacity of the patient.[34]

Thomas Aquinas, as a philosopher, was a thirteenth-century regression to the schools of Greek philosophy which trusted only Reason. As a teacher he was no doubt outstanding in his ability to explain this older material, but nowhere in Aquinas is there the slightest evidence that he was aware of the tremendous cultural explosion going on all around him in music and literature, of the rebirth of philosophy or the blossoming of commerce, trade, travel and politics.[35] His vision was firmly fixed on the past, while the Renaissance was beginning all around him! He must have seen it all, but, for a man who loved Aristotle almost as much as he loved the Church, to acknowledge it was probably a price too high.

---

[33] Ibid., XXXIX, 145ff.

[34] Ibid., XIX, 15.

[35] Durant, *The Age of Faith*, 963, without giving a source, explains,

> He became so absorbed in the religious and intellectual life that he hardly noticed what happened about him. In the refectory his plate could be removed and replaced without his being aware of it.

Ancient Views on Roman Church Music of the Fourteenth Century

The term 'Renaissance' was first coined in 1840, by Jules Michelet, to mean 'discovery of the world and man.'[1] Perhaps a better definition would be the '*rediscovery of the world of* man,' for it is the rediscovery of the values of the human and his secular life, in contrast to a galaxy of Christian spirits, angels and the sacred dogma of the Church. One might go further and call it the rediscovery of man as a *human*, which is why this new spirit is called 'Humanism.' This change is clearly seen in the paintings of Giotto (d. 1337), where, instead of the cartoon-like figures of medieval art, now we feel we are seeing real people. The English critic, John Ruskin, made this same point in 1874 while studying Giotto's frescoes.

> He painted the Madonna and St. Joseph and the Christ—yes, by all means, if you choose to call them so—but essentially, Mamma, Papa, and the baby.[2]

Some, such as Petrarch, were concerned with this new vivid humanism in the art of Giotto. He complained of,

> images bursting from their frames, and the lineaments of breathing faces, so that you expect shortly to hear the sound of their voices. It is here in that the danger lies, for great minds are greatly taken with this.[3]

Whatever Petrarch's concern, the power of this new style in Giotto was such that in the following century Leonardo da Vinci declared that after Giotto, art declined.[4]

Important societal developments also contributed to the new environment. In Italy, in particular, the growth of trade and industry produced the wealth by which more enlightened princes could imitate the fostering of the arts they had learned from the East through the crusades. The rediscovery of the ancient literature, again through the East, went hand in hand with the developing sophistication of the vernacular languages. Finally, all of these developments joined to provide the courage and freedom of thought necessary to break the long domination of thought by the Church. Man at long last could freely begin to think independently, and to ask questions—something the early Church had specifically discouraged.

There is no better symbol of this new self-confidence than an incident which occurred during the trial of Galileo. Though he was forced, prostrate on the floor before a commission of cardinals, to retract his view that the earth moves in an orbit and is not the center of the universe, when he rose from the floor he quietly whispered 'Nevertheless, it moves!'

---

[1] John Addington Symonds, *Renaissance in Italy* (New York: Holt, 1881), I, 15n.
[2] Quoted in Stuart Isacoff, *Temperament* (New York: Vintage, 2001), 53.
[3] Ibid., 53.
[4] Ibid.

With the new ability of man to think of himself apart from the Church came a great sense of self-confidence, which was a necessary prerequisite for many of the advances in science and the arts. These new attitudes, which were all essential parts of humanism, rapidly repaid society with accomplishments which the Church had been unable to achieve in 1,200 years. In a relatively short period of time come the achievements of da Vinci, Michelangelo, Isaac Newton, Galileo, Copernicus and Gutenberg.

In Italian literature, it was Petrarch and Boccaccio who carried this new banner of humanism at the dawn of the Renaissance. The nineteenth-century scholar, Francesco de Sanctis, writing in defense of Boccaccio's *The Decameron*, has written a passage which we believe goes right to the heart of the essential difference between the philosophy of life in the Middle Ages and the Renaissance.

> Many people blame Boccaccio, saying that he spoiled and corrupted the Italian spirit. He himself, in his old age, was overcome by remorse, became a religious clerk, and condemned his book. But his book would not have been possible if the Italian spirit had not been well on its way to being spoiled—if spoiled is the correct word for it. If the things Boccaccio laughed about had been venerated, his contemporaries would have felt indignation. But the opposite proved to be true. The book seemed to respond to something in people's souls which had been wanting to come out for a long time. It seemed to proclaim what everyone had been saying secretly, in the depths of their souls, and it was received with so much applause and success that the good Passavanti became frightened and set against it his *Specchio di penitenza* as an antidote. Boccaccio was, then, the literary voice of a world about which men, in their consciousness, were already confusedly aware. A secret existed: Boccaccio guessed it and everyone applauded him. This fact, instead of being damned, deserves to be studied.
>
> The essential quality of the Middle Ages was transcendence: a sort of ultrahuman and ultranatural 'beyond' outside of nature and man, the genus and the species outside the individual, matter and form outside their unity, the intellect outside the soul, perfection and virtue outside life, the law outside consciousness, the spirit outside the body, and the purpose of life outside the world …
>
> The natural product of this exaggerated, theocratic world was asceticism. Life here on earth was losing its seriousness and value, so that while man continued to dwell here, his spirit was in the next life …
>
> Feeling, as the product of human or natural propensity, was always considered a sin. Passions were banned and poetry was considered the mother of lies. The theater was the food of the Devil and stories and romances were regarded as profane types of literature. All these things were called by one name: 'the senses' …
>
> But a state of tension and imbalance like this cannot last. Art and culture, the knowledge and experience of life, work to modify it and transform it. Thus art, by seizing this world, had begun to humanize it, bring it closer to man and nature.[5]

From the perspective of the musician, the beginning of the Renaissance appears clearly and almost suddenly defined. The changes desired in Church music by the composers of the early fourteenth century were sufficiently different as to give birth to the terms *ars nova* and *ars anti-*

---

[5] Francesco de Sanctis, 'Boccaccio and the Human Comedy,' quoted in *The Decameron*, trans. Mark Musa and Peter Bondanella (New York: Norton, 1977), 216ff.

qua to distinguish these composers from their teachers. Outside the Church the explosion of thirteenth-century troubadour repertoire was no less dramatic in its new emphasis, indeed this music was the harbinger of humanism.

Our view of music performance in the Renaissance has been clouded in several ways as the result of directions taken by nineteenth-century musicology. The subsequent traditional view has been, basically, that to study music, you have to study extant music. The problem is that relatively little music in the fourteenth century was notated, and that which has survived has been mostly the Church music of the Northern countries. No where in music history texts can one find extensive discussion of the broad early Renaissance musical practice which is documented in the literature of that period. Indeed, in reading some of the most revered music history texts you might get the impression that music somehow disappeared from Italy after 1350. But Pirrotta, one of the really knowledgeable persons in this field, knows better.

> It is not surprising to me that no attempt to solve the case of the missing Quattrocento music has led to a satisfactory answer. It has been my contention that the secret, if there is one, is in the island, not in the gap that divides it from the continent. For the island is largely a mirage of our historical perspective, a tiny object magnified by our faith in the written tradition, at best a floating island, not only surrounded but also supported by the waves of a sea now opaque to our eye, once full of light, of life, and of sound—the sound of unwritten music.[6]

What he means is that written music, namely Church music, was really just one kind of music performance. Pirrotta hastens to add that we must not assume that the 'unwritten' music of the fourteenth century was only monophonic.[7]

Among the 'unwritten' music of the fourteenth century which we wish we could hear was the organ improvisation of Landini. The Florentine chronicler, Filippo Villani, heard this great *blind* organist and reported he played,

> as readily as though he had the use of his eyes, with a touch of such rapidity (yet always observing the measure), with such skill and sweetness that beyond all doubt he excelled beyond comparison all organists who can possibly be remembered.[8]

There is a scene in Giovanni da Prato's *Pradiso degli Alberti* in which Landini appears and is asked to perform outdoors and in doing so all the birds, we are assured, stopped to listen.

Because traditional musicology has for so long focused almost exclusively on the study of surviving music, the study of the page, it has failed to see the importance of what Humanism was all about. A traditional textbook attempting to find the Renaissance in a church work of Machaut will generally describe the conceptual parts, the components of that work, things like the major chords passing unobtrusively by. But these things are not what make

---

[6] Nino Pirrotta, 'Ars Nova and Stil Novo,' in *Music and Culture in Italy from the Middle Ages to the Baroque* (Cambridge: Harvard University Press, 1984), 28, where he devotes a more lengthy argument to this contention.

[7] Nino Pirrotta and Elena Povoledo, *Music and Theatre from Poliziano to Monteverdi* (Cambridge: Cambridge University Press, 1982), 26.

[8] Isacoff, *Temperament*, 59.

Machaut sound different, they are only the *result* of what makes Machaut sound different. A new emphasis on the importance of expressing *feeling* is what prompted Machaut to make the choices he made. Most music texts which look for early humanists speak primarily of the renewed interest in ancient Greek writings. But for us *feeling* is the key, not scholarly retrospection. It was not their interest in Greek treatises, but what they found in them which distinguish the humanistic point of view. In our view, it was the intellectual freedom to think about and value his own feelings which most distinguishes the Renaissance man from Medieval man.

The Church included some humanists and those monks who had embraced humanism suddenly found themselves under attack by a conservative backlash. The old battle fought one thousand years earlier in the Church reemerged among some who said the reading of pagan [the ancient Greeks] authors was impious. A leading spokesman for the Church humanists, Coluccio Salutati (1331–1406), argued that Virgil should be read allegorically and that those who knew how to thus understand Virgil would find in his poetry the mysteries of the Christian faith. He also pointed out that the early Church fathers, such as Jerome and Augustine, had read these Greek classics.

> Is it possible that anyone can be considered so foolish and senile, so deceived by false opinion as to condemn the poets with whose words Jerome overflows, Augustine glistens, and Ambrose blossoms? Gregory and Bernard are not devoid of them.[9]

This philosophical dispute was enlivened in 1397 when Carlo Malatesa, a captain of the guard of the Florentine League, ordered a statue of Virgil in Mantua destroyed. At this time Salutati extended his defense of the humanists by noting that the Scriptures were themselves written with the figural and allegorical language of the poets. It is ironic, he said, that the Scholastic theologians who did not study classical literature must run to schoolboys to learn what they could not understand in the teachings of the Fathers. Thus he makes the argument made one thousand years earlier, that study of the Liberal Arts was fundamental to the understanding of the Scriptures.

There were some Church representatives who still believed they could defeat Humanism by reminding the faithful that the Church would do their thinking for them. John Gower (1330–1408), of England, for example, reaches back one thousand years to say, in effect, 'don't think, you don't need education, just believe what we tell you (Faith).'

> Submit your mind to faith, for a mortal creature cannot understand the mysteries of eternal judgment …
>
> Since it is certainly not for us to understand the circumstances of the world, to what purpose does man labor to understand creation? For us to experience faith tested by reason—that task is not for human powers. It is not a human task to mount up to the stars; mortal man does not grasp that by

---

9 Charles Stinger, *Humanism and the Church Fathers* (Albany: State University of New York Press, 1977), 8ff.

Ancient Views on Roman Church Music of the Fourteenth Century

his reason … It is helpful for man to be in ignorance about a great deal; most facts offend the senses. Therefore, a man should acquire knowledge prudently. Let him entrust to faith what he would not have been able to trust to reason.[10]

It is no surprise, of course, that in this same book Gower complained that the young were not paying attention to his teaching.

> Knowing very little used to be a great disgrace for an old man … But nowadays if old age is wise in any way or teaches what it has learned earlier, its voice hardly receives the welcome of a youth's. Even if they are fervent in their zeal, the words which old men write are, as a rule, acceptable to young men only quite rarely. Yet no matter how much the voices of the dogs may bark in objection, I shall not run away, but instead I shall sing out my words. Imbibe oil from the rocks and honey from the stones for yourself, and single out the sweet notes from my harsh song.[11]

This same writer, in his *The Voice of One Crying*, is especially critical of the clergy he knew at the end of the fourteenth century for their apparent interest in the newly available translations of Aristotle. He finds the clergy being satisfied with 'natural knowledge,' rather than sacred theology.[12]

His conservative writings also retain the medieval Church's curious negative characterization of women:

> Neither learning nor understanding, neither constancy nor virtue such as men have flourishes in woman.[13]

His view of Art also reflects the old Church position that we must respect not the art work, but the artist (who was made by God).

> Was not all the world first founded for you, and its treasures laid out for your enjoyment? The world was not made for adoration but for use; it was made to be your servant, not your god. Therefore, does reason urge you that what the artisan melts in the fire or carves on smooth wood is a god? … This insanity of worshiping mute gods while they themselves know nothing is worse than all vices … The sculptor is worthier than his sculpture; it is therefore conclusive that the worker who worships his own work is all too foolish.[14]

At the very beginning of the fourteenth century (actually, ca. 1300!) we find a treatise, *De Musica*, by Johannes de Grocheo, that for the first time begins to move away from the Church and university's position that music should be thought of as a part of mathematics. Grocheo presents the old mathematical descriptions, of course, but he also seems aware that there is

---

[10] John Gower, *The Voice of One Crying*, trans. Eric Stockton in *The Major Latin Works of John Gower* (Seattle: University of Washington Press, 1962), II, ix.

[11] Ibid., II, Prologue.

[12] *The Voice of One Crying*, III, xvii.

[13] Ibid., IV, xiii.

[14] Ibid., II, x.

something more to music. In particular is his recognition of the importance of live performance. When he says, yes, numbers may define the form of music, but it is of the nature of music to be performed, he has left Boethius far behind.

> Certain people, considering its form and material, describe music by saying that it is a science of number related to sound. Others, looking at its performance, say that it is an art devoted to singing. We, however, intend to take it in both ways, just as it is made known as a tool and ought to be made known as an art. Just as natural warmth is a first tool through which the soul exercises its functions, so as an art [music] is a principal tool or rule through which the practical intellect explains and exposes its functions. We may say, therefore, that music is an art or science concerning numbered sound taken harmonically, designed for singing easily. I say also a *science*, insofar as it treats of the knowledge of principles, an *art*, insofar as it rules the practical intellect in performing, concerning *harmonic sound*, since it is this basic material around which it is performed. By *number* its form is defined. But by *singing* performance is touched upon, to which it is properly *designated*.[15]

Turning now to the classification of music, Grocheo mentions the three genre of Boethius: Music of the Spheres, Human Music, and Instrumental Music. Although music theorists had accepted this classification without comment for half a millennium, Grocheo now blasts Boethius into oblivion. He courageously attacks the faulty logic, the pseudo-science, the beliefs of the Church and, let us admit it, the nonsense which Boethius had put forth.

> Those who make this kind of division either invent their opinion or they wish to obey the Pythagoreans or others more than the truth, or they are ignorant of nature and logic. First of all, they say universally that music is a science concerning numbered sound. Nevertheless, celestial bodies in movement do not make a sound, although our ancestors believed this, nor do they divide their rotation as does Aristotle, whose idea and hypothesis in his book concerning the theory of the planets should be proposed. Nor is sound properly to be found in the human constitution. Who has heard a constitution sounding?[16] The third type which is called *musica instrumentalis* is distributed in three parts, that is, in the diatonic, chromatic and enharmonic, according to which they say the three concords of the monochord come. They call that diatonic which proceeds by tone, tone and semitone, according to the manner which most melodies use; chromatic which proceeds by diesis, diesis and three semitones. And they say the planets use such a song. They also call that enharmonic which proceeds by diesis, diesis and ditone. They say this is the sweetest, since angels use it. We do not understand this division, since they distinguish here only *musica instrumentalis*, leaving out the other categories. Nor is it pertinent for a musician to treat of the song of angels, unless he has been at the same time a theologian and a prophet; no one can have any experience of such song except by divine inspiration. When they say the planets sing, they seem to be ignorant of what is a sound.[17]

Grocheo proposes to bring music down from the spheres and instead will use the practical classifications practiced by 'the men in Paris,' for it is there that the principles of all liberal arts are 'sought out diligently.' Therefore, to replace the three classifications of Boethius, Grocheo presents three new ones:

---

[15] Johannes de Grocheo, *De Musica*, trans. Albert Seay (Colorado Springs: Colorado College Music Press, 1967), 9.

[16] Physicists of the late twentieth century! Every organ of the body produces a pitch.

[17] Ibid., 10.

1. Civic or simple music, which they call vulgar [*vulgus*: of the masses] music.
2. Composed or regular music by rule, which they call measured music.
3. Ecclesiastic music, designed for praising the Creator, made from the first two and to which these two are best adapted.[18]

His brief descriptions of the various forms used in church music are interesting to us primarily because they seem to witness a new recognition of *feeling* in church music. It tells us that some in the Church as well heard the message of the Humanists.

Organum is ecclesiastical music, sung for the praise of God. Music in the same style which is sung at 'parties and feasts given by the learned and the rich,' is called *conductus*. Commonly, he says, both are called *organum*. University text books sometimes identify *organum* as two part vocal music, but two important early sources, Isidore of Seville (560–636 AD), and Robert Grosseteste, call *organum* the generic name for all musical instruments.

The *Hymn* is 'an ornate song, having many verses,' sung for the faithful, that 'it may excite their hearts and souls to devotion,' before the readings and psalms. It is sung again afterward to 'reawake them and reinvigorate them' for the reading of the evangelical psalms.[19]

The *Kyrie Eleyson* is intended to 'move the hearts of those hearing it to devout praying and to listening devoutly to the Oration.' He adds to this description a curious further sentence.

> It is performed in the Greek language, either because the Latins seem to have gotten the foundations of all the arts from the Greeks, or because Greek words are more weighty than others or more exact in designation, or because of some mystery which we do not wish to express at the present time.[20]

The *Responsory* and *Alleluia* are sung 'in the manner of *stantipes* or *coronate cantus*, so that they may impose devotion and humility in the hearts of their audience.' But the *Sequence* is sung,

> in the manner of *ductia*, so that it may make them joyful and lead them to receive correctly the words of the New Testament.[21]

The *Preface*, he calls a simple song intended to make the faithful devout and prepared for the *Sanctus*. The latter he calls 'a sign of the earthly and militant Church,'[22] and is sung 'ornately and slowly, to move Christians to fervent charity and delight in God.'[23]

---

[18] Ibid., 11.

[19] Ibid., 35.

[20] Ibid., 38.

[21] Ibid., 40.

[22] Here he seems to be thinking of the Jesus of the book of Matthew, rather than the Jesus of the book of Luke. Luke describes Jesus as the gentle shepherd who says, 'turn the other cheek,' while Matthew pictures a Jesus who says, 'Do not think that I have come to bring peace on earth; I have not come to bring peace, but a sword!'

[23] Ibid., 41.

The *Agnus Dei*, Grocheo suggests, is to create in the listener a feeling of 'peace and concord.'²⁴

It is also very interesting that when he reflects back on the extraordinary thirteenth-century motet, that brief experiment in using indigenous languages together with Latin, and which led to the use of bawdy songs (the high church officials understood little French), he tries to gloss over this by making it a kind of exclusive music, but not for the public.

> This kind of song ought not to be propagated among the vulgar, since they do not understand its subtlety nor do they delight in its hearing, but it should be performed for the learned and those who seek after the subtleties of the arts.²⁵

Another very interesting treatise on music is the *Speculum Musicae* of 1313 by Jacques de Liege of Paris. He was one of the *ars antiqua*, the 'old guys,' and he resents that the old scholastic-mathematics structure is being ignored by the 'new guys,' the *ars nova* composers.

> Now in our day have come new and more recent composers, writing on mensurable music, little revering their ancestors, the ancient doctors; nay, rather changing their sound doctrine in many respects, corrupting, reproving, annulling it, they protest against it in word and deed …
>
> ……
>
> Should the men who composed and used these [older] sorts of music, or those who know and use them, be called rude, idiotic, and ignorant of the art of singing?
>
> ……
>
> I do not deny that the moderns have composed much good and beautiful music, but this is no reason why the ancients should be maligned and banished from the fellowship of singers.²⁶

Especially interesting is his choice of language in describing the new music.

> What profit can there be in adding to a sound old doctrine a wanton and curious new one.²⁷

'Wanton?' What kind of church music is he talking about? He was hearing a new expression of feeling and he probably associated it with popular music, but it was only the advance guard of Humanism.

At this time the Church was fully engaged in fighting off the newly discovered Aristotelian world of Reason's assault against the Church's fortress of Faith. It is interesting, therefore, that de Liege uses the argument of 'Reason' to advocate the old system of music based on mathematics. Certainly everyone could understand that mathematics is based on Reason!

---

24 Ibid.

25 Ibid., 25.

26 Quoted in Oliver Strunk, *Source Readings in Music History* (New York: Norton, 1950), 181, 185, 189.

27 Strunk, Ibid., 181, 183.

ANCIENT VIEWS ON ROMAN CHURCH MUSIC OF THE FOURTEENTH CENTURY   147

> There must be a place for what accords with Reason and with Art, since this lives by Art and Reason in every man. Reason follows the law of nature which God has implanted in rational creatures.[28]

Another member of the old conservative school was Pope John XXII, who in 1324–1325 issued an attack against the *ars nova* in his bull, *Docta Sanctorum*. This document is very interesting because the catalog of things he objects to gives us an insight into just how different the 'new' church music was. He objects to the faster note values, which, according to scholarly tradition, were first advanced by Philippe de Vitry in his *Ars Nova*. When he complains that the new composers 'must be losing sight of the fundamental sources of our melodies,' we would venture to guess he means that secular tunes were still creeping into the service. Or perhaps this was a reference to his hearing improvisation over the chant tunes, a practice which had been going on for some time. He too uses the term 'wanton' and objects that the singers are even using body language to express the feelings of the music. He therefore hastens to ban all these practices, but again it is too late. The return of the role of feeling in music could not be denied.

> Certain disciples of the new school, much concerned with measured rhythms, write in new notes, preferring to devise methods of their own rather than to continue singing in the old way. The music therefore of the divine offices is now performed with semibreves and minims, and with these notes of small value every composition is pestered. Moreover, they truncate the melodies with hoquets, they lubricate them with counterpoints [*discantibus*], and sometimes they even stuff them with upper parts [*triplis et motetis*] made out of secular songs. So that often they must be losing sight of the fundamental sources of our melodies in the Antiphoner and Gradual, and may thus forget what that is upon which their superstructure is raised. They may become entirely ignorant concerning the ecclesiastical Tones, which they already no longer distinguish, and the limits of which they even confound, since, in the multitude of their notes, the modest risings and temperate descents of the plainsong, by which the scales themselves are to be known one from another, must be entirely obscured. Their voices are incessantly running to and fro, intoxicating the ear, not soothing it, while the men themselves endeavor to convey by their gestures the emotions of the music which they utter. As a consequence of all this, devotion, the true end of worship, is little thought of, and wantonness, which ought to be eschewed, increases. Thus, it was not without good reason that Boethius said: 'A person who is intrinsically sensuous will delight in hearing these indecent melodies, and one who listens to them frequently will be weakened thereby and lose his virility of soul.'
>
> This state of things, hitherto the common one, we and our brethren have regarded as standing in need of correction; and we now hasten therefore to banish those methods, nay rather to cast them entirely away, and to put them to flight more effectually than heretofore, far from the house of God. Wherefore, having taken counsel with our brethren, we straightly command that no one henceforward shall think himself at liberty to attempt those methods, or methods like them, in the aforesaid Offices, and especially in the canonical Hours, or in the solemn celebrations of the Mass.[29]

---

[28] Ibid., 182.

[29] Quoted in H. E. Wooldridge, *The Oxford History of Music*, 2nd edition (London, 1929), 294ff.

We have mentioned in a previous essay the practice in the ancient Roman religious cults of using music to cover up the cries of the victims. We thought of this when we first read of a later fourteenth-century Pope, Urban VI, residing in a castle in Nocernia in 1385. He ordered a new motet composed to console him and reports are that 'he listened contentedly while the cries of his tortured prisoners reverberated throughout the castle's corridors.'[30]

Philippe de Vitry's famous treatise is disappointing for us. He is concerned mostly with notation and reveals little about the important changes taking place in performance practice. Aside from the changes in notation, the only real indication that he is thinking of more contemporary music practice is his comment on *musica ficta*. While earlier Church fathers were very hesitant to allow any changes in the music of the Church, de Vitry clearly seems to be judging by the ear and not by the rule.

> Clearly, the question arises of what occasions the necessity in regular music of musica falsa, or of false mutation, when nothing governed by rule ought to accept that which is false, but rather the true. To this it is to be answered that false mutation or musica falsa is not useless; indeed it is necessary in order that good sounds may be achieved, and bad ones avoided.[31]

The fourteenth-century church composer whom all music history texts assign great importance to, Guillaume de Machaut, doesn't discuss church music much at all in his philosophic poetry.[32] There is one interesting passage, however, where he describes a group of flagellants and their music, a bizarre form of religious piety stemming from the thirteenth century.

> At this time a company arose
> At the urging of Hypocrisy, their lady,
> Who beat themselves with whips
> And crucified themselves flat on the ground,
> While singing to an instrument
> Some new song or other,
> And according to them, they were worth more
> Than any saint in Paradise.
> But the Church attended to them,
> Forbidding them to beat themselves,
> And likewise condemned their song,
> Which little children were singing,
> And excommunicated all of them
> By the power God had granted it,
> Because their self-abuse
> And their song were heresy.[33]

---

[30] Quoted in Isacoff, *Temperament*, 54.

[31] Wooldridge, *The Oxford History of Music*, 212. Nicholas Oresme, a very important scientist, dedicated his treatise, 'Algorismus proportionum,' to de Vitry,

> whom I would call Pythagoras if it were possible to believe in the opinion about the return of souls. [Quoted in Issacoff, *Temperament*, 52]

[32] His pride was his secular love songs.

[33] 'The Judgment of the King of Navarre,' Guillaume de Machaut, *Oeuvres*, ed. Ernest Hoepffner (Paris, 1908–21), lines 241ff.

Information on performance practice in fourteenth-century Italy is rather scant, other than the deductions one might make from the objections of the popes. There are some interesting hints to be found in literature never mentioned in music history texts, such as in the *Decameron* by Boccaccio. Two very interesting such references are found in the the seventh day of *The Decameron*, where Boccaccio mentions the 'Laudsingers of Santa Maria Novella,' an order centered in Florence. They were particularly active during Lent, when their *laude* were even set to popular melodies. In this same story there is a reference to a hymn attributed to St. Ambrose, the 'Te lucis,' sung at the end of the day to protect one from evil dreams.[34]

We find in literature no evidence that instruments were being used as yet in the mass, but the rich use of instruments in religious iconography makes one wonder. For example, the fourteenth-century fresco in the apse of the church of San Leonardo al Lago near Siena pictures an extraordinarily large ensemble accompanying angelic singers, including a large number of string and wind instruments (even an aulos) and a percussion section which includes not one, but two timpani players.[35]

In fourteenth-century England it is the *quality* of the church singing that writers object to. William Langland criticizes those clerics who take money on the side for the private masses they sing[36] and another who after thirty years still can't sing!

> I've been a priest and parson passing thirty years now,
> Yet I can't either sing or chant *sol-fa*.[37]

Similarly, Chaucer complained about a prioress who sang the divine service 'intoned full seemly in her nose.'[38]

Another charming description by Chaucer regards the use of music to learn the Latin prayers of the Church.[39] A child in the church school hears the older students singing the *Alma redemptoris* daily. After repeatedly hearing this, the child himself soon knows the music and the first verse by heart, but, of course, he has no idea what it means. When he asks an older child, one of the singers, what the words mean, the older child says he has heard that it is a salute to 'our blessed Lady and pray her to be our help and succor when we die.' But, he brings into question the effectiveness of using music to teach Latin by observing that he really can't say more about it, for 'I learn singing, but know little grammar.'

> I kan namoore expounde in this mateere;
> I lerne song, I kan but smal grammeere.

---

34 *The Decameron*, trans. Mark Musa and Peter Bondanella (New York: Norton, 1977), II, 489, 491; see also, III, 881, 882.

35 A discussion of the fresco, together with reproductions of the pictures, can be found in Federico Ghisi, 'An Angel Concert in a Trecento Sienese Fresco,' in Jan LaRue, ed., *Aspects of Medieval and Renaissance Music* (New York: Norton, 1966), 308ff.

36 William Langland, 'Piers Plowman,' trans. E. Talbot Donaldson (New York: Norton, 1990), III, 253.

37 Ibid., V, 415.

38 'Prologue, The Canterbury Tales.'

39 'The Prioress's Tale.'

The woes of the church singer trying to learn his skills is pictured in an exceptional extant poem which also contains interesting hints of the performance expectations of these singers, including perfect intonation, knowledge of *musica ficta* and accuracy in the reading of rhythmic and melodic notation.

Unfit for the cloister I cower full of concern;
I look like an idiot and, well listen to my tale.
The song of the *si-sol-fa* makes me sick and sore
And I sit stuttering over a song a month and more.

I go wailing about as does a cuckoo.
There is many a sorrowful song I sing in my book;
I am held so hard at it, I scarcely dare look up.
All the mirth of this world I gave up for God.

I wail over my gradual and rore like a rook;
Little I knew when singing I undertook!
Some notes are short and some are long,
Some bend a-wayward like a meat-hook.

When I can sing my lesson, I go to my master
He hears my performance and doubts I have done well.
'What have you been doing, Master Walter, since Saturday noon?
You don't hold a single note, by God, in tune!

'Oh my dear Walter, your performance is a shame,
You start and stumble as though you were lame!
Your tones are not the tones which are named;
You bite asunder the B natural, for a B flat you are blamed.

'Oh my dear Walter, your work leaves much to wonder!
Like an old cauldron you begin to rumble!
You don't hit the notes, you sing under them.
Hold up, for shame! you sing flat.'

Then is Walter so woeful his heart nearly bleeds,
And he goes to visit William and wishes him luck.
'God knows,' says William, 'that I need it!'
Now I know how *judicare* was set in the Credo!

'I am as woeful as a bee that flounders in the water:
I work on the Psalms until my tongue tires.
I have not performed since Palm Sunday.
Are all songs as miserable as the psalms?'

'Yes, by God! You've said it, and it is worse.
I practice solfege, and sing afterwards, but I'm never better;
I hurl at the notes and heave them out of here!
Everyone who hears me knows that I error.

'Of B flat and B natural I knew nothing
When I left the secular world and, well listen to my tale—
Of *ef-fa-ut* and *e-la-mi* I knew nothing before;
I fail strongly in the *fa*, in it my fortune fails more.

'And there are other notes, *sol* and *ut* and *la*,
And that troublesome wretch men call *fa*:
Often it makes me ill and makes me full of woe;
I can never get it in tune when it is *ta*.[40]

'And there is a held note with two long tails;
For it our master has often knocked down my skittles.
How little you know what sorrow ails me:
It is but child's play what you do with the psalms!

'When one note leaps to another and causes riot,
That we call motion in high *ge-sol-re-ut*.
You were better not born if a mistake you would;
For then our master says "You're no good."'[41]

The discipline demanded of choral singers may have made it difficult to recruit for the Chapel Royal during the reign of Richard II. Therefore an order went out to one, John Melynek, to kidnap ('Impress') boys for this purpose.

> ... to take and seize for the king all such singing-men expert in the science of music as he could find and think able to do the king's service, within all places of the realm.[42]

---

[40] A rule of *musica ficta* is that *ti* is sung like *fa* (*ta*, as our singer says), or B natural becomes B flat, when it is the top of a phrase forming an arch.

[41] 'Choristers Training,' in our modern English from the original quoted in Celia and Kenneth Sisam, ed., *The Oxford Book of Medieval English Verse* (Oxford: Clarendon Press, 1970), 184ff.

[42] Quoted in Edmonstoune Duncan, *The Story of Minstrelsy* (Detroit, 1968), 85.

Ancient Views on Roman Church Music of the Fifteenth Century

NOTHING SO MARKS THE PROGRESS OF HUMANISM IN ITALY, not to mention the distance traveled by the Church since the Middle Ages, than a pronouncement made by Pope Nicholas V (1447–1455) shortly before his death. He urged Church officials to follow his example in supporting the arts and learning for the good of the Church. He even went so far as to proclaim the humanities as an essential part of the education of the clergy.[1] This pope, in fact, not only provided large stipends to leading scholars to make translations of ancient Greek literature, and to scribes to make copies, but he himself had personally made discoveries of important manuscripts.[2]

One of the most interesting aspects we find in accounts of fifteenth-century Church music in Italy is a suggestion that the *joy* of Church music had returned—the joy so often described in the early years of the Church, but so rarely mentioned during the Middle Ages. It is this new attitude, influenced by the humanists and amplified by the return of instruments to the mass during the fifteenth century, which would make possible in the following century the extraordinary church music of Giovanni Gabrieli. One senses this new joy and enthusiasm in an eyewitness report of the first performance of Dufay's motet, 'Nuper rosarum flores':

> It was as though the symphonies and songs of the angels and of divine paradise had been sent forth from Heaven to whisper in our ears an unbelievable celestial sweetness. Wherefore in that moment I was so possessed by ecstasy that I seemed to enjoy the life of the blessed here on earth.[3]

This new spirit even results in a new type of vernacular sacred music, as we see in one of the important Church humanists of the fifteenth century, Ambrogio Traversari (b. 1386). As a monk he was of course trained to sing the necessary services, but in his correspondence with the Venetian humanist and composer, Leonardo Giustiniani (1388–1446), we learn he also delighted in singing vernacular songs in honor of God. Giustiniani had written such songs, with instrumental accompaniment, which were popular and when Traversari requested copies, the composer posed the question whether a humanist should be devoted to vernacular music. Yes, wrote Traversari, for,

---

[1] John D'Amico, *Renaissance Humanism in Papal Rome* (Baltimore: Johns Hopkins University Press, 1983), 122. The late fifteenth-century cleric-philosopher, Gaffurio, agreed, 'For the belief that [the study of music] is preeminently suitable to clerics has long been accepted.' See Irwin Young, trans., *The Practica musicae of Franchinus Gafurius* (Madison: University of Wisconsin Press, 1969), 5.

[2] Charles Stinger, *The Renaissance in Rome* (Bloomington: Indiana University Press, 1985), 283ff. Not all Church officials were so enlightened. The important philosopher, Giovanni Pico della Mirandola, was charged with heresy and had to flee to France in 1486 after he invited fellow scholars to Rome to debate his 'Nine Hundred Theses,' which he had deduced from his study of ancient and medieval philosophy. [Ibid., 301]

[3] Quoted in Stuart Isacoff, *Temperament* (New York: Vintage, 2001), 74.

> those ancients, whom we admire, hardly despised this as uncultured. As is well-known, Socrates as an old man sang, accompanying himself with a lyre, a skill he had not cultivated before.[4]

Traversari also mentions the joy of Church singing in a letter to Agostino da Portico, a monk at S. Maria degli Angeli.

> I cannot help but mourn being deprived of such joy, and the rich consolation which I experienced ... when I celebrated with you the delightful Sabbath, when we sang to the Lord a new song and intoned psalms of joy.[5]

If there were a new sense of joy in the Church, accompanied by a relaxation of the rules to the extent that popular music could find praise, one is tempted to almost take seriously the description of chaos in the German church services by Sebastian Brant, certainly an environment not conducive to contemplative listening.

> One must not ask who they may be
> Whose dogs in church bark furiously
> While people pray at mass or sing,
> Who bring a hawk that flaps its wing
> And rings its bell with tinkling gay,
> That one can neither sing nor pray.
> The hood is lowered o'er the hawk,
> There's pattering and many a squawk,
> Affairs are aired and tongues are loose,
> There's clattering with wooden shoes,
> That brings disturbance, great ado;
> He peers to Lady Kriemhild's pew
> To mark if she will turn and gape
> And make the cuckoo-bird an ape.
> If men would leave their dogs at home
> To watch for thieves that prowl and roam,
> While men would worship there in church,
> If birds were left upon the perch,
> And wooden shoes were worn for street
> To pick up dirt or mud or peat,
> And other people's ears be spared—
> But when have fools for others cared?[6]

It is difficult to believe that church services were so noisy in general. It was in this regard that we noticed a statement by the Florentine philosopher, Leon Battista Alberti (b. 1404) in which he seems to praise church music in particular for its ability to sooth his rattled nerves.

---

4   Stinger, *The Renaissance in Rome*, 3. Part of Traversari's effectiveness as a humanist was that he had not studied in the university and was thus free of medieval scholasticism.

5   Stinger, *The Renaissance in Rome*, 4.

6   Sebastian Brant, *The Ship of Fools*, trans. Edwin Zeydel (New York: Columbia University Press, 1944), 44.

> All other modes and kinds of singing weary with reiteration; only religious music never palls. I know not how others are affected; but for myself, those hymns and psalms of the Church produce on me the very effect for which they were designed, soothing all disturbance of the soul, and inspiring a certain ineffable languor full of reverence towards God. What heart of man is so rude as not to be softened when he hears the rhythmic rise and fall of those voices, complete and true, in cadences so sweet and flexible? I assure you that I never listen in these mysteries and funeral ceremonies to the Greek words which call on God for aid against our human wretchedness, without weeping. Then, too, I ponder what power music brings with it to soften us and soothe.[7]

This new atmosphere of joy, together with the rapid improvement in court and civic instrumental music, surely must have contributed to the growing disinterest on the part of the public for the old scholastic-mathematical polyphonic style of church music. Of course it would take a long time for the Church to fully realize how unpopular their music had become (and it would require even longer for most authors of music history to realize it). By the sixteenth century one can find numerous hostile comments about polyphony, not to mention reference to the addition of non-notated instruments in the performance of polyphonic music, neither of which will the reader find discussed in detail in music history texts. We can see this change in taste beginning to change in fifteenth-century Italy. One fifteenth-century writer, Paolo Cortese, criticized the Northern polyphony, in particular the music of Isaac, Brumel, Compere and others, for being 'so florid that it more than satiates the ordinary capacity of the ear.'[8] The severe preacher, Savonarola, made the same objection late in the century.

> These princes have their cappelle of singers which are a great confusion, because there stands one singer with a big voice who sounds like a calf, and the others howl around him like dogs, and no one understands what they are saying. So let these *canti figurati* go and sing instead the *canti fermi* ordered by the church.[9]

In spite of Savanarola's description, there were fine singers to be found. Indeed, we begin to find, at this time, accounts of individual Church singers who were independently recognized as artists. When Matteo of Perugia was hired in 1402 by the cathedral in Milan, it was noted that he was recognized 'for his sweet and mellifluous songs and measures.' His successor in 1411, Ambrosio da Pessano, was hired 'that the church might be honored with mellifluous voices and sweet and beauteous songs.'[10]

These singers were no doubt influenced by an improving quality in secular singers. In a letter of 1429 by Ambrogio Traversari he praises a solo art song singer, Leonardo Giustinian, for his ability in singing 'sweet songs.'[11] Pirrotta adds that Giustinian was only one of,

---

7 John Addington Symonds, *Renaissance in Italy* (New York: Capricorn Books, 1964), I, 188.

8 Paolo Cortese, 'De cardinalatu libri tres,' quoted in Nino Pirrotta, in *Music and Culture in Italy from the Middle Ages to the Baroque* (Cambridge: Harvard University Press, 1984), 104.

9 Quoted in Lewis Lockwood, 'Strategies of Music Patronage in the Fifteenth Century: the Cappella of Ercole I d'Este,' in Iain Fenlon, ed., *Music in Medieval and Early Modern Europe* (Cambridge: Cambridge University Press, 1981), 243.

10 John Larner, *Culture and Society in Italy, 1290–1420* (New York: Scribner's, 1971), 169.

11 Nino Pirrotta, *Music and Culture in Italy from the Middle Ages to the Baroque*, 145.

> a series of musicians whose names were better known to the fifteenth-century than those of Dufay, Ockeghem, or Josquin ... In the daily life of the fifteenth century they, not written music, were the elements of a resounding open-air stream, which gave pleasure ... to every layer of society.[12]

In another place, Pirrotta elaborates further on the importance of the 'unwritten' music. This music, he says, was,

> much more widely influential amongst the common people as well as amongst the wealthy. However, either because they were wholly or partially based on improvisation, or because they were transmitted without the use of written notation, much less evidence about these forms has survived. We cannot afford to overlook this unwritten ... tradition ... however elusive it might prove. Indeed, it becomes especially important to consider it carefully when one is studying the different manifestations of humanist culture, for though we are better acquainted with the written tradition, the humanists themselves were almost suspicious of it, associating it as they did with scholasticism.
>
> Poliziano and his contemporaries were quite right in seeing the works of musical theory on which polyphony was based as one of the most typical examples of that convoluted scholastic thought against which they were reacting.[13]

Along with the sense of joy in the church, the expanding thoughts about the nature of the music of the church and the presence of some church singers who could be called 'artists,' there must have also been increasing attention given to those singers whose quality left something to be desired. Craig Wright has found among the documents for even a large cathedral such as that of Cambrai evidence of the employment of adult singers who could not read music. In one case in 1491 a man was hired as a vicar who not only could not read music, but was even married—which must surely suggest a difficulty in finding good voices.[14]

Perhaps another clue to the quality of some of these singers may be inferred from documents which refer to disciplinary actions taken against them for various offenses committed during the actual church service. The most surprising of these is one of 1493 when the singers were admonished for,

> throwing meat and bones from one side of the choir to the other during the divine service.[15]

The most important document we have from this period which concentrates on the quality of church singing is the treatise, *De modo bene cantandi* (1474) by Conrad von Zabern, who was associated with Heidelberg University.[16] His first observations have to do primarily with the more technical aspects of appropriate Church singing, including the maintenance of perfect

---

[12] Ibid., 167ff.

[13] Nino Pirrotta and Elena Povoledo, *Music and Theatre from Poliziano to Monteverdi* (Cambridge: Cambridge University Press, 1982), 22.

[14] Craig Wright, 'Performance Practices at the Cathedral of Cambrai 1475–1550,' *The Musical Quarterly* 64, no. 3 (July 1978): 313.

[15] Ibid., 297.

[16] The amazing Leonardo da Vinci, who wrote on every topic imaginable, also wrote a book, now lost, entitled, 'On Voice.' When he last saw it, he says, it was 'in the hands of Messer Battista dell' Aquila, steward-in-waiting to the pope.'

ensemble in unison singing, consistent tempi from each side of the choir and using the middle register of the voice, rather than the high register.[17] He equates tempi with the nature of the service, recommending the use of slower tempi for more solemn feast days. He expects strict observance of the appropriate modes and allows no improvisation (which, of course, suggests he was hearing improvisation).

The most interesting discussion, in terms of the quality of singing, is found in Conrad's sixth major topic, 'Singing with Proper Refinement,' which he says he finds many clerics to have overlooked, to the extent of becoming 'a vicious habit.' He begins this discussion with a general definition of proper refinement.

> Singing with proper refinement means avoiding all that reprehensible coarseness (of which we will speak below) which is commonly and frequently practiced in singing even by those with a certain reputation and by those who observe the five marks of good singing discussed previously. This fact we cannot pass over in silence. First of all, let us explain what we mean in this context by 'proper refinement.' *Urbs* is the word for city, and in the cities men are generally more discriminating than they are in the country or in villages, thus in this instance 'refined' means 'discriminating' or 'skillful.' Hence the adverb *urbaniter*. Singing with proper refinement is thus singing with discrimination and without coarseness ... There are so many of these crudities that I despair of enumerating all of them. Still I would like to enumerate and explain in sufficient detail the most important, obvious and frequently committed ones, so that if they become better known they can in the future be more easily avoided. An evil unrecognized is avoided only with difficulty.

He begins with basic vocal production such as singing through the nose and adding an 'h' before vowel sounds. The latter he says reminds him of the sounds butchers make in driving sheep to pasture.

> This is not elegant singing, and we can say without fear of contradiction that it is very coarse.

In this regard he stresses the importance of correct Latin, in the syllables and vowels. Some clerics, he has observed, sound as if they had food in their mouths.

> Indeed, from Frankfurt to Koblenz and as far as Trier I have noticed this very often, especially in students. They all distort the chant, inclined as they are to pronounce the vowels *e* and *i* poorly and without sufficient differentiation—a situation which has not infrequently caused me much displeasure. Their masters ought to restrain them from this error forthwith, lest they perpetuate it into old age.

He criticizes inaccurate intonation, especially in ascending and descending pitches. This may have been caused in part by his next objection, forcing the voice.

> Truly I know people better instructed than others in chant who nevertheless render all their singing unworthy of praise by this very defect. Though it appears to them that they are singing well, this is just because no one has suggested to them how offensive this fault really is, and how much to be avoided.

---

[17] This discussion is based on Joseph Dyer, trans., 'Singing with Proper Refinement,' *Early Music* 6, no. 2 (April, 1978): 207ff.

We find his next topic the most interesting of all. Modern clinical research has proven that the brain automatically increases the perception of high tones, beginning at the third space C of the treble clef. The most evident cause of this, now genetic, brain function is undoubtedly due to the need for the species to discern speech clearly, beginning with animal speech (the tiger outside the cave). While most modern choral and ensemble conductors are unfamiliar with the physical aspects, many have learned from experience that a more beautiful sound is achieved by creating more volume in the lower pitches, and less in the upper, to accommodate for this automatic brain function. This knowledge of this practical adjustment is not new. It is discussed, for example, by Praetorius in Volume III of his *Syntagma Musicum* of 1619. The following discussion by Conrad, on the subject of singing too loud in the upper register, is the earliest we know to offer the correct accommodation for this problem.

> Another fault which is more obvious than the others is singing high notes with an unstintingly full and powerful voice. This is even more careless than what we have cited above, as will soon become evident. When this shouting is done by individuals with resonant and trumpet-like voices it disturbs and confuses the singing of the entire choir, just as if the voices of cattle were heard among the singers. In a certain eminent collegiate establishment I once heard singers with these trumpet-like voices singing with all their strength in the highest register as if they wished to break the windows of the choir, or at least to shake them. As I marveled not a little at their coarseness, I was moved to make up this rhyme:
>
> *In choir you bellow*
> *Like cows in the meadow!*
>
> I use this jingle in an informal fashion in my efforts and teaching regarding the art of good singing in order to ridicule all those presuming to sing loudly in the high register, to the end that they might recognize their careless crudeness and, after recognizing, zealously desist from it.
>
> In order to recognize this error completely it must be realized that whoever wishes to sing well and clearly must employ his voice in three ways: resonantly and trumpet-like for low notes, moderately in the middle range and more delicately for the high notes—the more so the higher the chant ascends …
>
> Therefore, let him who wishes to sing flawlessly never again presume to sing with a full and strong voice in the upper register, for this disfigures the chant, pointlessly weighs down and fatigues the singer, makes him hoarse and consequently useless for singing. The human throat is delicate and easily injured when it is abused, as it is by loud singing in the upper register. The harm having been done, hoarseness soon ensues. Everyone has experienced this personally.

Conrad carefully explains that connected portions of chant must correspond in their tonal relationships. He has been so disturbed by this as to think, 'or even say: "What clods these monks are!"'

His next objection involves a demand for enthusiastic singing from the heart. Here, again, are two more instances of the use of the word, 'joy,' used in association with church music of the fifteenth century.

> Another error is singing sleepily and lifelessly and without emotion, like a poor old woman on the brink of the grave. This deprives the chant of the joy appropriate to it, and as it is less well heard it seems to be more of a moan than a chant ... Behold how animatedly, affectively and with what great joy singing should be done, lest we fall into yet another extreme: some shouting loudly, while others can scarcely be heard. The old proverb rings true: 'Either too little or too much ruins the game.' Happy those who hew to the golden mean!

If his concern above was that the singer inspire, his final concern is that he not detract.

> The last error to be mentioned at this time is singing with inappropriate deportment: not standing straight but moving back and forth, holding the head up too high or noticeably to one side, resting the head on the hand and either distorting the mouth or opening it too widely. It would be tedious to enumerate all the other kinds of inappropriate behavior which are to be avoided for the simple reason that they provoke laughter in the beholder, who ought rather to be moved to devotion by the chant.

The most important development in Roman Church music of the fifteenth century was the reintroduction of instruments in the service, ending a ban of fifteen centuries. As the reader will see in a later chapter, this practice of adding instruments to polyphonic church music becomes fairly standard in the sixteenth century. It is most curious that traditional music history texts ignore this fact. When the music of Palestrina was being sung in the Sistine Chapel, for instance, there was not, and still is not, an organ in the room, but the pay records exist for a number of papal wind players being paid to perform. In so far as traditional music history is concerned, these full-time papal wind players simply do not exist. But for anyone who has heard a polyphonic work, such as those by Palestrina, performed with winds doubling, the effect is like going from a black and white world to one of color.

There were several factors which contributed to this historic change in Church policy. First, the growing sense of identity of the cities and towns, and their developing use of music, created a competition with the Church for the minds and souls of the townspeople. Thus, following the festive celebrations organized by the town governments, special celebrations of the Church begin to make more use of music. In Rome, in 1462, a great Church celebration was held to honor the arrival of the relic, the head of Andrew, brother of St. Peter. On this occasion one heard the singing of children dressed as angels and the sounds of winds and trumpets.[18] For some of the faithful, apparently, it was important as well for their funerals to reflect this expanding sense of ceremony. The 1412 will of Ludovico Cortusi, a professor of canon law at the University of Padua, stipulated that his funeral procession should include fifty musicians, performing on trumpets, string instruments and organs, together with twelve virgins singing and rejoicing.[19]

Clearly, an even greater contribution to ending the ban on instrumental music in the church came from the local nobles. By the fifteenth century every noble of any pretension whatsoever now had a five- or six-member wind band in his employment. They traveled with him and

---

[18] Stinger, *The Renaissance in Rome*, 177.

[19] Nan Cooke Carpenter, *Music in the Medieval and Renaissance Universities* (Norman: University of Oklahoma Press, 1958), 38.

represented him aurally as much as his coat-of-arms did visually. Therefore, when the local duke had the occasion to use the church for weddings, christenings or funerals, there was no local Church official who would presume to prevent him from bringing his wind band into the building to participate in the service in question. Once instruments were allowed to enter the church building for private services, it would require only a short step to using these same instruments in the mass.

We can trace this transformation of Church policy clearly in the records of the dukes of Burgundy. Even as early as 1385, we notice the mass for the marriage of Philip the Bold (1363–1404) in 1385 was sung by 'many singers and musical *flusteurs.*'[20] Then we have brief references to the performances of Philip the Good's (1419–1457) singers in the masses associated with the meetings of his Order of the Golden Fleece. In one in particular, a reference to the 'Mass of St. Andrew,' a phrase seems to point to the addition (*cum*) of instruments performing with the choir, '*cum una superba e suavissima musica.*'[21] And, finally, during the reign of Charles the Bold, the accounts of his marriage to Margaret of England in 1468 relate that the wind band of Charles performed for the actual wedding service, which included a motet and a chanson performed by an ensemble of shawms, trombones and bombards, with 'excellent effect.'[22]

The great Burgundian mathematician and music theorist, Johannes Tinctoris (1435–1511), even mentions the use of string instruments in the church, in particular the viol and rebec.

> I am similarly pleased by the rebec, my predilection for which I will not conceal, provided that it is played by a skillful artist, since its strains are very much like those of the viol. Accordingly, the viol and the rebec are my two instruments; I repeat, my chosen instruments, those that induce piety and stir my heart most ardently to the contemplation of heavenly joys. For these reasons I would rather reserve them solely for sacred music and the secret consolations of the soul, than have them sometimes used for profane occasions and public festivities.[23]

In a rare instance of a music historian mentioning the use of instruments in the church service, Gustave Reese points to this very reference by Tinctoris as valuable 'supplementary evidence that instruments were used' in the performance of Church music.[24]

We must digress here briefly to point out that Tinctoris also is a witness to the existence of improvisation in music of the Church, a topic few music history texts will admit and none, to our knowledge, has discussed at length. Tinctoris uses the term, *super librum*, to mean improvi-

---

[20] Keith Polk, 'Ensemble Instrumental Music in Flanders: 1450–1550' [Unpublished], 18. Flusteurs was a term often used to mean 'winds' in general.

[21] William Prizer, 'Music and Ceremonial in the Low Countries,' in *Early Music History* 5 (1985): 124.

[22] Wangerme, *Flemish Music* (New York, 1968), 213; Eric Simons, *The Reign of Edward IV* (London, 1966), 155; Olivier de La Marche, Mémoires d'Olivier de La Marche (Paris, 1785), III, 152ff; E. Dahnk, 'Musikausubung an den Hofen von Burgund und Orleans wahrend des 15. Jahrhunderts,' in *Archiv fur Kulturgeschichte* (1934–1936), 210; and G. Thibault, 'Le Concert Instrumental au XVe Siecle,' in Jean Jacquot, *La Musique Instrumentale de la Renaissance* (Paris, 1955), 31, which suggests several chansons which may have been used.

[23] Anthony Baines, 'Fifteenth-century Instruments in Tinctoris's *De Inventine et Usu Musicae,*' *The Galpin Society Journal* 3 (March 1950): 24ff.

[24] Gustave Reese, *Music in the Renaissance* (New York: Norton, 1959), 148.

sation in general. But in his treatise, *De Inventione et Usu Musicae*, he suggests the existence of a tradition for improvisation over plain chant, a tradition so distinct that he recognizes a specific name for it, *cantus regalis*.[25]

In Milan, when Giangaleazzo Sforza was married in 1488 to Isabella of Aragon, an ensemble of fifty woodwind and brass participated.[26] In Paris, an early fifteenth-century treatise, *Tractatus de Canticis*, by the chancellor of the University of Paris, Jean de Gerson, appears to assume that the addition of the organ is now considered as standard practice, to which are being joined a variety of other instruments.

> Ecclesiastical custom has retained only or especially this same musical instrument, to which, as we have seen, the tuba may be occasionally joined, but very rarely bombardae, chalemiae, cornemusae or other instruments which we will not name here, of which the Book of Daniel includes in the adoration of the statue with all kinds of instruments.[27]

Like their brothers the secular nobles, the Church bishops of fifteenth-century Germany also employed personal wind bands. These can be documented in numerous town beginning about 1430.[28] When gathering for a church conference, these bishops brought their musicians with them. The most extensively documented such event in the fifteenth century was the great Council of Constance (1414–1418). Here assembled no fewer than three popes (John XXIII of Rome, Gregory XII, the Avignon pretender, and Benedict XIII, who was a creation of Ludwig of Bavaria), five patriarchs, thirty-three cardinals, forty-seven archbishops, five thousand three hudred priests, three hundred noblemen and one thousand five hundred knights in an attempt to deal with the problem of the three popes and also with the growing Hussite movement in Bohemia.

In all, during the course of the four years, some sixty-three thousand visitors came to this town of seven thousand! One report said that it was so crowded that five hundred accidental drownings occurred in the lake.[29] And apparently everyone brought his personal musicians, for

---

[25] Also admitted by Reese, *Music in the Renaissance*, 147.

[26] O. Kinkeldey, *Orgel und Klavier in der Musik des 16. Jahrhunderts* (Leipzig, 1910), 165ff., and Grove, *The New Grove Dictionary of Music and Musicians* (London: Macmillan, 1980), XIV, 568.

[27] Jean de Gerson, 'Tractatus de Canticis,' trans. Christopher Page, in 'Early 15th-century instruments in Jean de Gerson's *Tractatus de Canticis*,' *Early Music* 6, no. 3 (1978): 348.

[28] Walter Salmen, *Musikleben im 16. Jahrhundert* (Leipzig: Deurscher Verlag für Musik VEB, 1976), 163, 176; H. Federhofer, 'Beitrage zur altern Musikgeschichte Karntens,' in *Carinthia* (1955), CXLV, 377; and J. H. Wylie, *History of England under Henry the Fourth* (London, 1884), IV, 236.

[29] Ernest Henderson, *A Short History of Germany* (New York, 1916), I, 208.

one account speaks of 346 'pfifer, prussuner und spillut,'[30] another 426 minstrels, actors and wind players and still another 500 winds and singers.[31] One official reported 1,700 musicians, which must have included the entire period of the Council.[32]

Among the individual ensembles mentioned was one with the Pope from Rome, consisting of shawms and trombones, but they may have been hired for the occasion as one observer who heard them said they played in 'wild discord.'

> … prosuner und pfiffer, die ymer me dar prosonten und pfiffen zu wilderstrit.[33]

One who certainly had to hire temporary musicians for the occasion was the emperor Sigismund, who was not well supported financially by the other German princes and constantly complained of needing money. A miniature published by one of the eyewitness to this gathering pictures the ensemble of Sigismund, consisting of four trumpets and three shawms. As they appear not being in identical dress, it is assumed they were not permanent employees.[34]

Musically, the most interesting reference is to the arrival of the ensemble of the English prelates.

> The trombonists played together in three parts as one is otherwise accustomed to sing.[35]

---

[30] M. Schuler, 'Die Musik in Konstanz wehrend des Konzils 1414–1418,' in *Acta Musicologica* (1966), 163 and J. Riegel, *Die Teilnuhmerlisten Konstanzer Konzils* (Freiburg, 1916), 74ff.

[31] R. Fester, 'Die Fortsetzung der Flores temporum von Reinbold Slecht,' in *Zeitschrift fur die Geschichte des Oberrheins* (1894), 132; A. Henne, *Die Klingenberger Chronik* (Gotha, 1861), 193 and O. Nedden, *Quellen und Studien zur oberrheinischen Musikgeschichte im 15. und 16 Jahrhundert* (Kassel, 1931), 53.

[32] M.R. Buck, ed., *Ulrichs von Richental Chronik des Constanzer Conzils* (Tublingen, 1882), 215.

[33] Ulrichs von Richental, *Das Konzil zu Konstanz* (Konstanz, 1964), 252.

[34] Copies in Prag, Universitn' knihova (Ms. XVI A 17, fol. 70) and the New York Public Library (Spencer Collection, Ms. 32, fol. 86).

[35] Gerald Hayes, 'Musical Instruments,' in *New Oxford History of Music* (London, 1960), III, 425ff.

> Die pusauner pusaunoten uber einnander mit dreyen stymmen, als man sunst gerwonlichen singet.

Ancient Views on Church Music of the Sixteenth Century

> *I most heartily desire that music, that divine and most precious gift, be praised and extolled before all people.*
>
> Martin Luther, 1538

> *[Music] pierces the heart much more strongly [than words] and enters within ... so venom and corruption are distilled to the very depths of the heart by melody.*
>
> Jean Calvin, 1538

THIS EXTRAORDINARY DISAGREEMENT regarding the value of music by two famous preachers, writing at the same time, reflects a continuing struggle in the Church between the forces of Humanism and those of strict New Testament orthodoxy. The paths represented by Luther and Calvin would continue to divide, resulting in the following century (the Baroque) in, on one hand, immortal music written for the Church and, on the other hand, official orders by the Puritans to destroy all the organs in England (and they did).

Music was caught up in this struggle in part because it had become too important; music could no longer be ignored by the Church. Certainly, from the perspective of the listeners in the congregation, one factor which contributed to the growing importance of Church music was the return of instruments, joining with the voices. After a ban of some fifteen centuries, the faithful could now enjoy those instruments so praised in the Old Testament.

While the reintroduction of instruments into the service began in earnest in the fifteenth century, as we have discussed in the previous chapter, in the sixteenth century one not only finds innumerable references to their appearances in the church, but now also in the mass itself. Even at the beginning of the century (1 March 1500) we find a pleased listener at the court of Johann of Saxony who heard a mass with instruments conducted by Adam von Fulda.

> On the Tuesday after Quinquagesima ... the singers belonging to my Most Gracious and Noble Lord sang two masses with the help of the organ, 3 sackbuts and a cornett, and also 4 crumhorns with the positive organ which were almost joyful to hear.[1]

---

[1] A. Aber, *Die Pflege der Musik unter den Wettinern und Wettinischen Ernestinern Von den Anfangen bis zur Auflosung der Weimarer Hofkapelle 1662* (Buckeburg, 1921), 82.

Another notable early example was heard during the meeting of François I and Henry VIII, in 1520, when one eyewitness reported a Mass, composed by Perino, performed with voices, organ, sackbutts and cornetts,[2] and declared 'it was heavenlie hearing.'[3] One notes the Zwichau civic wind band was paid in 1559–1560 to perform the mass in church ('*in der Kirchen in die Messe geblase*n').[4]

On the basis of the evidence we have seen it appears that instruments were used in particular in polyphonic church compositions. Why have music historians kept this secret for so long a time? Have they thought that the addition of instruments not mentioned in the score would somehow diminish Palestrina, and his contemporaries? We even remember a time when historians called the sixteenth century 'the a cappella era.' Well, the evidence suggests the contrary. In the Lutheran areas one can also find many civic contracts which specify that the civic instrumentalist were to help out with the polyphony. A Stadtpfeifer contract in 1569 in Zwickau assigns the player to help out in the church with his instrument when polyphonic music is performed and an almost identical contract is found for Delitzsch in 1580.[5] Jakob Gallus wrote in his *Opus Musicum* (1587) that where there were small numbers of singers the winds *must* help out.[6] A report by a trumpeter in the service of the Lutheran bishop of Halle a. d. Saale says that winds were used all the time for this kind of church music.[7] A civic contract of 1572 in Dresden demands the civic musicians 'strengthen and enhance' the Kreuzchor, 'on feast days, Sundays and at weddings and other occasions when polyphony is performed.'[8]

In the Catholic areas, as in the Lutheran, civic contracts specify that the civic wind bands will perform in church with the singers in polyphonic music. Such a contract is found for Munich in 1580[9] and a civic ordinance of 1571 in Ulm calls for the cornetts and trombones to play in Munster Cathedral.[10] We find this same kind of evidence in Italy as well, as for example in a civic contract of 1556 for Udine which seems to refer to the regular Sunday mass.

> To the shawm and crumhorn players in the service of the city, 5 in number, serving in the choir of the aforementioned church of Udine …[11]

---

[2] Joycelyne Russell, *The Field of Cloth of Gold* (New York, 1938), 175. The celebrant on this occasion was Cardinal Wolsey, even though he had not personally conducted a mass in years. But, this was a special occasion, with three kings, three queens, twenty-one bishops and three cardinals present.

[3] Ibid., 174.

[4] Arno Werner, *Vier Jahrhunderte im Dienste der Kirchenmusik* (Leipzig: Merseburger), 204.

[5] Ehmann, *Tibilustrium* (Kassel, 1950), 149.

[6] In Part Three, 'Instructio ad musicos.'

[7] Ehmann, *Tibilustrium*, 149.

[8] Grove, *The New Grove Dictionary of Music and Musicians* (London: Macmillan, 1980), V, 615.

[9] Walter Salmen, *Musikleben im 16. Jahrhundert* (Leipzig, 1976), 18; also Grove, *Dictionary*, XII, 781.

[10] Salmen, Ibid., 18.

[11] Quoted in G. Vale, 'La Capella Musicale dl Duomo di udine dal Secolo XIII al XIX,' in *Note d'Archivio* (1930), VII, 106.
    Tibicinibus et aduncorum cornum inflatoribus …

In addition to these kinds of civic contracts which required the civic musicians to also perform with the choir on Sundays, we begin to see during the sixteenth century instrumental musicians hired by private noblemen specifically to play with their choirs. The emperor Maximilian I had trumpets, shawms and organists in his private church music, '*des kunigs cantarei*.'[12] His son, Philip, followed his example and one eyewitness describes hearing a mass in Philip's chapel, during which the trombones joined in playing the 'Deo gratias' and the 'Ite messa est.'[13] The elector Moritz of Saxony hired six cornett and sackbut players in 1549 for his church music. One of those hired was the composer Antonio Scandello (1517–1580), who was also a cornettist of such fame that cornett students came from great distances to study with him.[14] The elector Ottheinrich of Heidelberg, in his will, expressed the hope that his chapel musicians would be maintained, especially his famous '*Organisten, pusauner, ... zincKhenbleser vnd Trumpetter*.'[15] This was, of course, only a logical extension of the duties of the court musicians. For some of them, however, such as the aristocratic trumpet players, this expanded duty may have been unwelcome. A document, dated 1 May 1572, by Archduke Ferdinand II of Innsbruck refers to the regular use of trumpets in church and this regulation seems to suggest he had been having some discipline problems with his trumpet corps for which he threatens to transfer them to another court. In addition, he orders,

> [The trumpet corps] must have diligent attention and must also appear for services on Sundays and holidays. Unless one has a better reason not to appear, he or they will receive serious punishment.[16]

If these trumpeters thought this was serving beyond the call of duty, one wonders what the private trumpets who belonged to the bishop of Munster thought. Like many nobles in Germany, he suffered from common drunkenness.[17] In his case, he used to keep an ensemble of trumpets and drums at hand just to wake him when he passed out from drink.[18]

In the same manner in which the court or civic winds doubled the voices in larger polyphonic works, this practice was on occasion no doubt often carried out in smaller works such as motets. We find an account from St. Anne's Church in Dresden, for 1578, which gives the

---

[12] Wolfgang Suppan, *Lexikon des Blasmusikwesens* (Freiburg, 1976), 23.

[13] M. Brenet, 'Notes sur l'introduction des instruments dans les eglises de France,' in *Riemann-Festschrift* (Leipzig, 1909), 281.

[14] Grove, *Dictionary*, XVI, 547.

[15] Quoted in Suppan, *Lexikon des Blasmusikwesens*, 24.

[16] Walter Senn, *Musik und Theater am Hof zu Innsbruck* (Innsbruck, 1954), 135. It could be worse: for the marriage of Christian I of Saxony in 1582 some of his musicians were required to perform while swimming in a reservoir, disguised as 'nymph-musicians.' See, Johannes Janssen, *History of the German People After the Close of the Middle Ages*, trans. A. Christie (New York, 1966), XV, 265.

[17] Janssen, *History of the German People*, XV, 249. One duke quoted his pastor as saying, 'after the holy days you are free to drink well and to let the heavenly sackbuts ring on.' [Ibid., 239] This, we take it, is not what Brahms had in mind in his Begräbnisgesang, Op. 13, for band and chorus, when he speaks of 'God's trombones.'

[18] Ibid., 243.

actual repertoire in which the Dresden civic wind band joined the choir. On this occasion they performed a six-part motet, 'Jubilato Deo,' by Clemens non Papa and a six-part motet, 'Te Deum Patrem,' by Lassus.[19]

An actual Seville cathedral document of 1586, appears to specify a certain variety in instrumental sound for aesthetic purposes.

> At greater feasts there shall always be a verse played on recorders. At Salves, one of the three verses that are played shall be on shawms, one on cornetts and the other on recorders; because always hearing the same instrument annoys the listener.[20]

And, of course, Spain was responsible for the introduction of these instruments into the New World. Writing of Mexico, Geronimo de Mendieta's *Historia Eclesiastica Indiana* (ca. 1571–1596) observes that,

> nowhere in all of Christendom are there so many recorders, shawms, sackbuts, orlas, trumpets and drums as in the Kingdom of New Spain.[21]

In the case of special occasions, such as the marriages of the nobility, one finds records of newly composed church works which were performed by voices and instruments. For the wedding of Duke Ludwig of Württemberg in 1575, an eyewitness describes an eight-part work for singers and trombones which was 'so lovely and noble that the heart was refreshed.' Later, this same person, in a descriptive poem, makes reference to the duke's wind band as,

> Zinks and five shawms,
> Held with flying fingers,
> Faster than an eye-blink,
> They played the best pieces.[22]

An eyewitness speaks of the combination of singers and wind players during a performance for Ludwig III of Württemburg's wedding to Ursula, Duchess of Bavaria, in 1585.[23] Similarly, an eyewitness of the wedding of Margrave Casimir of Brandenburg (d. 1527) and Dorothea Pfalzgrafin bei Rhein in 1518 reports of the music performed in the church, that it was solemn and elegant, 'especially through the triumphant performance of the Margrave's singers, organ-

---

[19] Ehmann, *Tibilustrium*, 149.

[20] Robert Stevenson, *Spanish Cathedral Music in the Golden Age* (Berkeley, 1961), 152ff. See also Walter Salmen, *Musikleben im 16. Jahrhundert* (Leipzig, 1976), 182, and Grove, *Dictionary* (1980), VII, 627, 789.

[21] Quoted in J. A. Guzman, 'Mexico, Home of the First Musical Instrument Workshops in America,' *Early Music* 6, no. 3 (1978): 355.

[22] Nicodemus Frischlin, quoted in Josef Sittard, *Geschichte der Musik und des Theaters am Württembergischen hofe* (Stuttgart, 1890), I, 18ff. Another connection between the Württemberg court and the Church can be seen in the fact that the rector of Bempflingen served as the purchasing agent for instruments used by the court musicians. [G. Bossert, 'Die Hofkantorei unter Herzog Christof,' in *Württembergische Vierteljahresheftes für Landesgeschichte* (1898), Neue Folge, VII, 153]

[23] G. Pietzsch, 'Beschreibungen deutscher Fürstenhochzeiten von der Mitte des 15. bis zum Beginn des 17. Jahrhunderts als musikgeschichtliche quellen,' in *Anuario Musical* (1960), XV, 53.

ists and trombone and cornett players.'²⁴ The practice of composing original Church music for voices and instruments reaches a great level by the end of the century in those works by Gabrieli and others which are known as 'ecclesiastical concerti.'²⁵

Finally, extant music for instruments alone is also a witness to the practice of the use of instruments in the church. One need only mention the *26 Fugen* (1542) by Johann Walter, Luther's musical advisor, composed 'especially for cornetts,'²⁶ or the huge canzoni repertoire published in Venice. Canzoni were used as an instrumental alternative to the organ in the Italian Church services and we can see this practice very clearly in a catalog kept by the organist, Carlo Milanuzzi, of Venezia, which included such items as,

> Canzon a 5 detta la Zorzi per l'Epistola
> Concerto a 5 per l'Offertorio
> Canzon a 5 detta la Riatelli per li Post Communio²⁷

And then, there are accounts of outdoor church ceremonies which employ instruments. A passage in Machiavelli's short story, *Belfagor*, perhaps provides us with a glimpse of the use of instruments to add to the ceremony of outdoor Church functions.

> So arrange to have set up in the square of Notre Dame a platform big enough to hold all your barons and all the clergy of this city [Florence]; have the platform decorated with cloth of silk and of gold; set up in the middle of it an altar, and Sunday morning I want you and the clergy and all your princes and barons, with regal splendor, with gorgeous and rich costumes, to assemble there; after celebrating a solemn mass ... Besides this, I need to have ready on one side of the square at least 20 persons with drums, horns, kettledrums, bagpipes, shawms, cymbals and noise-makers of every sort; these men, when I lift my hat, will strike up on their instruments and as they play will come toward the platform.²⁸

In this same spirit of contributing to the ceremonial, the Church also called upon instruments to help celebrate her murders. An account during the religious strife under Catherine de Medici indicates that even the execution of Huguenots, known as the 'St. Bartholomew massacre,' was accompanied by 'drums and fifes playing gay airs during the executions.'²⁹ In Spain, also, good Catholics joyously celebrated this same infamous massacre of Protestants in Paris, as an eyewitness tells us.

---

24 Th. Garzoni, *Allgemeiner Schauplatz aller Kunst, Professionen und Handwerker* (1659).

25 In the following period there will be both large and small ecclesiastical concerti forms as well as large and small concerti da camera. Music history texts always speak of the sinfonia da camera, but only rarely mention the concerto da camera (even though the libraries of Europe are filled with manuscripts with this title].

26 The manuscript is in DDR:LEu (MS. Cod. Mus. 50, 'Thomaskirche').

27 Quoted in Denis Arnold, 'Brass Instruments in the Italian Church Music of the Sixteenth and Early Seventeenth Centuries,' *Brass Quarterly* (1957), 89.

28 *Machiavelli, the Chief Works*, trans. Allan Gilbert (Durham: Duke University Press, 1965), II, 876.

29 Paul Van Dyke, *Catherine de Medicis* (New York, 1922), II, 14.

> With anthems in Saint Gudule, with bonfires, festive illuminations, roaring artillery, with trumpets also, and with shawms, was the glorious holiday celebrated in court and camp, in honor of the vast murder committed by the Most Christian King upon his Christian subjects.[30]

We trust these representative examples of the use of instruments by the church during the sixteenth century will provoke in the reader the same astonishment that we continue to feel in finding this topic being virtually unmentioned in the music history texts.

Another topic seemingly forbidden of discussion by music history officialdom is the evidence that improvisation was occurring in church music, as the reader saw documented in the previous chapter by Tinctoris. Thomas Morley recognized and accepted improvisation in church music[31] and Craig Wright has documented the improvisation over chant in the cathedral at Cambrai over some years.[32]

Some derogatory commentary from the Italians only serves to suggest that they were hearing some extraordinary attempts at improvisation. Zarlino, the great Italian theorist, in Part Three of his *Le Istitutioni Harmoniche* discusses this question. When one reflects on the extraordinary harmonies found in Rore, Gesualdo, Monteverdi and Purcell, all efforts to communicate strong feelings before the 'rules' of modern harmony were worked out, one cannot help but wonder if what Zarlino called 'errors' might have in fact been some very expressive music.

> Matters for the singer to observe are these: First of all he must aim diligently to perform what the composer has written. He must not be like those who, wishing to be thought worthier and wiser than their colleagues, indulge in certain improvisation [*diminutioni*] that is so savage and so inappropriate that they not only annoy the listener but are ridden with thousands of errors, such as many dissonances, consecutive unisons, octaves, fifths, and other similar progressions absolutely intolerable in composition. Then there are singers who substitute higher or lower tones for those intended by the composer, singing for instance a whole tone instead of a semitone, or vice versa, leading to countless errors as well as offense to the ear. Singers should aim to render faithfully what is written to express the composer's intent, intoning the correct steps in the right places. They should seek to adjust to the consonances and to sing in accord with the nature of the words of the composition; happy words will be sung happily and at a lively pace whereas sad texts call for the opposite.[33]

Later in this work he mentions in passing that he had heard performances in which twelve improvised parts were added to a composition in two written parts![34]

Another Italian, Bottrigari, gives us more description of the apparent freedom in improvisation in church music.

---

30   John Motley, *The Rise of the Dutch Republic* (New York, 1864), II, 393.

31   *A Plain and Easy Introduction to Practical Music* (1597).

32   Craig Wright, 'Performance Practices at the Cathedral of Cambrai 1475–1550,' *The Musical Quarterly* 64, no. 3 (July 1978): 297.

33   Gioseffo Zarlino, *The Art of Counterpoint*, trans. Guy Marco and Claude Palisca (New Haven: Yale University Press, 1968), 110ff.

34   Ibid., 221.

> Because of the presumptuous audacity of performers who try to invent improvisation [*passaggi*], I will not say sometimes, but almost continuously, all trying to move at the same time as if in a contest, and sometimes showing their own virtuosity so far from the counterpoint of the musical composition they have before them that they become entangled in their dissonances—it is inevitable that an insupportable confusion should occur. This increases so greatly as they continue, that even those (and you see clearly how far this caprice and mania has gone) who play the low part, and the Bass, do not remember—not to say are ignorant of the fact—that it is the base and the foundation upon which the *cantilena* was built. And not standing firm beneath it, as the fabric requires, they go on up, they add nonsensical passages and allow themselves, because they enjoy it, to go so far as not only to pass into the Tenor part but even into that of the Contralto. Even this not sufficing, they go almost to that of the Sopranos, climbing in such a way to the top of the tree that they can't come down without breaking their necks.[35]

If this extraordinary description can be taken as in any way representative of ordinary improvisation in church music, then we can understand how the great composer, Josquin, would cry in exasperation,

> You ass! If you wish to improve on finished compositions, make your own, but leave mine unimproved.[36]

A German theorist, Coclico, in a book written for the training of church singers, seems to reflect an improvisation tradition so common that certain pedagogical ideas had been developed. After a brief discussion of intervals, Coclico briefly mentions improvisation, which he recommends should first be studied in note to note practice of the intervals, followed by more 'florid counterpoint.'[37] This art, he advises, requires constant practice. Later, he gives ability in improvisation even more weight.

> The first requirement of a good singer is that he should know how to sing counterpoint by improvisation. Without this he will be nothing.[38]

Another German writer, Glarean, mentions the practice of improvisation over chant, but complains, on the basis of his experience, that this is rarely done well.

> For how often do you find, I should like to know, three or even two who will [improvise] polyphony with you? I speak from experience, for something is always intervening at these times, some weariness or trouble is always at hand. Those who are skilled in this matter want to be asked, but one who does not understand it stands by, somewhat downcast, while the others are singing, either because he wished he were also able to sing or because he was ashamed that he had not learned this skill, or because he disdains what he neither understands nor attains; those who have progressed in this skill

---

[35] Hercole Bottrigari, *Il Desiderio*, trans. Carol MacClintock (American Institute of Musicology, 1962), 61ff.

[36] Quoted in Stuart Isacoff, *Temperament* (New York: Vintage, 2001), 120.

[37] Ibid., 23.

[38] Adrian Coclico, *Musical Compendium*, trans. Albert Seay (Colorado Springs: Colorado College Music Press, 1973), 24. He also mentions all too briefly singing contests in Belgium where no music is ever written down and the fact that his own teacher, the great Josquin, taught without the use of written materials.

to some extent but are not sure of themselves, and their number is great, repeatedly make errors in singing, which produces great disgust among the skilled. Thus it is rare that even three can harmonize together in this manner.[39]

We should mention that in another place Glarean objects to another tradition of improvisation, where singers improvise at the end of a chant, purposely cadencing on the wrong tone. Which, he says, 'certain singers plainly do for pleasure … and to turn up their noses at the listener.' Then he adds,

> But someone will say that nobody is so stupid not to understand that a song is corrupted in this way. Well, why then does the corruption generally occur in the Nicene Creed, also in the Lord's Prayer, and has no one at all observed this? Is the ear really more discerning in our time than formerly?[40]

Another apparent reference to improvisation at cadences is found in a comment by Erasmus:

> The Creed is shortened, the Lord's Prayer is not heard, and the singing of the prosa detains the congregation a full half hour. Added to this song are melismas [*caudae vocum*] which are just as long or even longer.[41]

An interesting reference to improvisation is found in a treatise of Giustiniani written ca. 1628. In this work he is objecting to church composers who are now abandoning the church styles of the past and are writing in a style influenced by the new opera movement. But, notice that as he introduces his objection he seems to imply that improvisation was rather common in sixteenth-century church music.

> For having left the old style, which was somewhat unpolished, and also the excessive [improvisation] with which they embellished it …[42]

Praetorius, in discussing the various 'arts' of performing large church concerti in the Italian sixteenth-century tradition, mentions, under the 'Third Art,' that one possibility is to have two choirs of singers with the 'discant parts improvising.'[43]

The existence of improvisation in church music is actually no surprise to those readers who understand that improvisation in secular music was very common in the sixteenth century. Indeed, so common that Galilei suggests in one place that it was playing *from music* which was not expected.

---

39 Glarean, *Dodecachordon*, trans. Clement Miller (American Institute of Musicology, 1965), I, 209.

40 Ibid., I, 196.

41 Erasmus, *Opera omnia*, ed. J. Clericus (Leiden, 1703–1706), VI, 731C–732C, quoted in Clement A. Miller, 'Erasmus on Music,' *The Musical Quarterly* 52, no. 3 (July, 1966): 336.

42 Vicenzo Giustiniani, *Discorso sopra la Musica* (ca. 1628), trans. Carol MacClintock (American Institute of Musicology, 1962), 77.

43 *Syntagma Musicum*, III.

> And let it not come into your mind to try to defend yourself with the silly excuse of some who say they did not feel called upon to do more than that which they found written or printed ...[44]

Another topic which music history texts will never discuss in depth is the influence of popular music on sixteenth-century church music. One contemporary observer, Agrippa, found considerable popular influence already in the first decade of the sixteenth century.

> But now days the unlawful liberty of music is so much used in churches, that together with the Canon of the Mass, very filthy songs have like tunes in the organs, and the Divine Service is sung by lascivious musicians hired for a great stipend, not for the understanding of the listeners, but for the stirring up of the mind. But for dishonest lasciviousness, not with manly voices, but with beastly [effects],[45] while the children bray the Discant, some bellow the Tenor, some bark the Counterpoint, some howl the Treble, some grunt the Bass, and cause many sounds to be heard, and no words or sentences to be understood.[46]

With regard to the reference here to 'very filthy songs' sung in church and 'lascivious musicians' hired for church music, we are reminded that Erasmus at this time warned women to keep away from the 'brawny, swill-bellied monks. Chastity is more endangered in the cloister than out of it.'[47]

It would certainly be interesting if we had access to more contemporary discussion such as that by the Spanish writer, Pietro Cerone, where he objects to elements of secular music which he finds forcing their way into Church music, in particular syncopation.

> In all the varieties of composition thus far explained, the syncopated minim and quaver are out of place, equally so the semiminim rest, for these ... are opposed to the gravity, majesty, and devout character required by ecclesiastical music, for all that many do the opposite today, either because they lack the knowledge necessary to the finished composer and excellent musician, or because, having it, they use it only to delight the sensual and to attract with their *firinfinfin* the vulgar throng.[48]

By the way, it is interesting to find that religious dancing was still practiced in Spain in the sixteenth century, in particular in Seville by the boys of the choir known as the *seises*. These boys danced to percussion instruments and the dances were performed just before the Blessed Sacrament.[49] Regarding this subject, dance in the service, we recall that Cervantes once wrote of the singing of 'sarabandes in the sacred mode, which leave the Portuguese themselves amazed.'[50]

---

44 Vincenzo Galilei, *Fronimo* (1584), trans. Carol MacClintock (Neuhasen-Stuttgart: Hanssler-Verlag, 1985), 83.

45 Agrippa gives 'skeekinge,' the meaning of which, in old English, is no longer understood.

46 Henry Cornelius Agrippa, *Of the Vanitie and Uncertaintie of Arts and Sciences*, ed. Catherine Dunn (Northridge: California State University, Northridge Press, 1974), 68.

47 Quoted in Isacoff, *Temperament*, 122. In the same place he recalls the fourteenth-century comment by Boccaccio,
   Christianity must be divine or it could never have survived the immorality of its clergy.

48 Pietro Cerone, *El melopeo y maestro*, quoted in Oliver Strunk, *Source Readings in Music History* (New York: Norton, 1950), 273.

49 Reese, *Music in the Renaissance*, 597.

50 Miguel de Cervantes, *The Jealous Hidalgo*, trans. Harriet de On's, in *Six Exemplary Novels* (Great Neck: Barron's Educational Series, 1961), 212.

We find additional evidence regarding the intrusion of popular idioms into the church primarily in the objections voiced against this trend. Erasmus, for example, observes in one place,

> We have brought into sacred edifices a certain elaborate and theatrical music, a confused interplay of diverse sounds, such as I do not believe was ever heard in Greek or Roman theaters. Straight trumpets, curved trumpets, pipes and sambucas resound everywhere, and vie with human voices. Amorous and shameful songs are heard, the kind to which harlots and mimes dance. People flock to church as to a theater for aural delight[51]

He also objected to the use of the music of the church service to celebrate secular occasions.

> Likewise ... song now used in some churches for peace or against pestilence, or for a successful harvest, can be omitted without detriment to religious devotion.[52]

Some of the things Erasmus objected to seem to have continued for we find specific condemnation of these popular elements by the Council of Trent (1545–1563).

> In the case of those Masses which are celebrated with singing and with organ, let nothing profane be intermingled, but only hymns and divine praises ... They shall also banish from church all music that contains, whether in the singing or in the organ playing, things that are lascivious or impure.[53]

We hope these representative illustrations will cause the reader to begin to wonder if perhaps the music heard in sixteenth-century churches was a much more diverse experience than is suggested in music history texts—typically a solemn world where only unaccompanied polyphony was sung.

In view of the two quotations which open this essay, we must now consider the question of how this church music, with instruments now added, with improvisation and with secular influences, was heard by the listeners of the sixteenth century. That is to say, what was their reaction from an aesthetic perspective? First, however, we must acknowledge that the environment in which church music was heard in the sixteenth century was one of unusual intellectual turmoil. In Northern Europe Luther had not only launched a new institution for the practice of religion but had released entire peoples from the control of Rome, which led to civic uprisings and riots as society struggled to reorganize itself.

Even without the challenge of Luther, the Roman Church was having its own internal problems, including the discipline of its clergy. Already in 1503, Christopher, Bishop of Basel, had addressed the synod of his diocese on the subject of the immorality of the clergy as follows:

---

[51] Erasmus, *Opera omnia*, ed. J. Clericus, 338ff.

[52] Ibid., 336.

[53] Quoted in Reese, *Music in the Renaissance*, 449.

> Since we have learned with the greatest chagrin that the greater part of the priests of our city and diocese when they are called to conduct the funeral services of nobles and other persons, give themselves up to gaming and drunkenness, so that many of them at times sit the whole night at play; others exhaust themselves with swilling and drunkenness and sleep the whole night on the benches, and by other extraordinary excesses bring scandal, disgrace, and derision upon the clerical profession: Therefore, we command that all clergymen who are so invited, and all others, shall not give up themselves to dicing and card-playing, nor to other irregular and disgraceful actions at any time whatever, and especially in taverns ...
>
> The clergy shall see to it that during the worship in the church they do not walk up and down with laymen ... nor shall they go out upon the market in choir dress during worship to buy eggs, cheese, or anything else.[54]

In the Roman sphere liberal thinking soon came under attack by the Counter-Reformation, which might as well be called 'Counter-Renaissance,' in so far as humanism was concerned. The Church, faced with the challenge of Luther, retreated to its strong point—medieval dogma. Some of these retrenchments, such as abolishing the right of the individual to act on his own conscience or judgment,[55] remain with us still today. We can see the impact of this primarily in Rome, where the Humanist School of painting begins to disappear, to be replaced by a style called Mannerist.[56] In addition, the Renaissance itself suffered a significant setback in Italy due to invasions. Between 1512 and 1530, Brescia, Genoa, Pavia, Naples and Florence were sacked. In the famous 'Sack of Rome,' in 1527, looters even entered the Sancta Sanctorum of the Lateran and played ball with the relic heads of St. Peter and St. Paul![57] Rome did not become a center of the arts again until 1600. Stinger finds in Michelangelo's 'Last Judgment' an expression of the somber mood in Rome following the sack and believes it was ordered to reflect 'a forceful reassertion of theology over philosophy, of faith over reason, of divine grace over human free will.'[58] And speaking of Michelangelo, the Counter-Reformation made an attempt to insert Puritanism into art. In a famous letter to Michelangelo on the subject of the artist's 'Last Judgment,' Pietro Aretino wrote,

> As a baptized Christian, I am ashamed of the license so flagrant, which you have taken ... Even the Gentiles, depicting the naked Venus, caused her to cover with her hands those parts that should be covered.[59]

This intellectual retreat, as the Roman Church sought refuge in old dogma while it attempted to come to grips with its role in the new post-Luther world, resulted in much negative commentary by her philosophers. Especially representative is one who is associated with

---

54 Samuel Jackson, *Huldreich Zwingli* (New York: Putham, 1901), 26.

55 Anthony Blunt, *Artistic Theory in Italy, 1450–1600* (Oxford: Clarendon Press, 1959), 105.

56 Ibid., 106.

57 Charles Stinger, *The Renaissance in Rome* (Bloomington: Indiana University Press, 1985), 322.

58 Ibid., 325.

59 Quoted in Frank Chambers, *The History of Taste* (New York: Columbia University Press, 1932), 48.

the spirit of the Counter-Revolution, Giordano Bruno. Born in Nola, near Naples, in 1548, he entered the Order of Dominic at age fifteen, became a priest at age twenty-four and traveled in university circles in a number of countries, including England and Germany. From our perspective, his philosophic views were very conservative, indeed some call him the last medieval philosopher, but ironically the Church considered him a free-thinker and the Inquisition had him put in prison and then burned.

Bruno was often critical of traditional philosophy, once observing that to call someone a philosopher 'is tantamount to insulting him as a quack, a good-for-nothing, a howling pedant, a charlatan, a mountebank …'[60]

> To tell you the truth, the race of philosophers is rated by the general run of men as more despicable than [the clergy]. The latter, raised up out of every sort of riffraff, have brought the priesthood into contempt; the former, designated out of all sorts of brutes, have dragged philosophy down into disrepute.[61]

He is remembered today as perhaps the most important philosopher of his time to be opposed to the writings of Aristotle, whom he accused of 'impurities, blots, with certain empty conclusions and theories'[62] and 'uncultured … offensive and pretentious.'[63] Speaking of philosophers, monks and courtiers, he says that each appears a fool to someone else,[64] and like many Church writers, he was not kind in his writings about women.

> Women are a chaos of irrationality, a wood [*hyle*] of wickedness, a forest of ribaldry, a mass of uncleanliness, an aptitude for every perdition …
>
> [Quoting Secundus], Woman is an obstacle to quiet, a continual damage, a daily war, a life-prison, a storm in the house, the shipwreck of man.[65]

The German writer, Agrippa, was also reflecting a distrust of philosophy.

> Philosophy disputes and judges all things, yet is certain of nothing. Wherefore I know not whether I should include philosophers among beasts, or among men: they seem to exceed brutish beasts because they have reason and understanding: but how shall they be considered men, when their reason can persuade no constant and certain thing, but always waivers in mutable opinions, whose understanding is doubtful of every matter.[66]

---

[60] Giordano Bruno, *Cause, Principle and Unity*, trans. Jack Lindsay (New York: International Publishers, 1962), 63.

[61] Ibid., 64.

[62] Ibid., 69.

[63] Ibid., 110.

[64] Ibid., 73.

[65] Ibid., 118, 120.

[66] Agrippa, *Of the Vanitie and Uncertaintie of Arts and Sciences*, 143.

It is against this environment of intellectual and civic turmoil, then, that one must imagine the impact on sixteenth-century listeners of completely new and free church music, music now accompanied with instruments, music crowned with improvisation and music attempting to capture interesting elements of popular music. All things considered, it appears that it was all too much for many persons. This was music which called attention to itself, instead of playing the old role of servant to the ritual.

The ever conservative Erasmus objected to the popularity of music itself, to the new styles he was hearing and even to the cost of this new music.

> In some countries the whole day is now spent in endless singing, yet one worthwhile sermon exciting true piety is hardly heard in six months ... not to mention the kind of music that has been brought into divine worship, in which not a single word can be clearly understood. Nor is there a free moment for singers to contemplate what they are singing.
>
> ......
>
> To this end organists are maintained at large salaries, and crowds of children spend every summer in practicing such warblings, meanwhile studying nothing of value. The dregs of humanity, the vile and the unreliable (as a great many are drunken revelers), are kept on salary, and because of this pernicious custom the church is burdened with heavy expenses. I ask you to consider, how many paupers, dying in want, could be supported on the salaries of singers?[67]

Erasmus is quoted in a passage by the German theorist, Ornithoparchus, who heard all this new enthusiasm as just being too loud.

> Let a singer take heed, least he begin too loud, braying like an ass, or when he has begun at an unusual height, disgracing the song. For God is not pleased with loud cries, but with lovely sounds. As Erasmus says, it is not the noise of the lips, but the ardent desire of the heart, which most impresses God's ears ... But why the Saxons, and those that dwell on the Baltic coast, should so delight in such clamoring I know of no reason, unless they have a deaf God or they think he has gone to the South side of heaven and therefore cannot so easily hear the singers from the East.[68]

In yet another attack on contemporary polyphonic church music, again an example of information not found in traditional music history texts, Erasmus mentions in passing,

> I was not speaking as much about any kind of ecclesiastical song as about unseemly music and alluring songs which the whims of naive women or simple men have added to religious services.
>
> Clamorers are so named because presently in many churches and monasteries, by thundering forth in a raucous bellowing, they so fill up the church that all sounds are obscured and nothing can be understood ...
>
> I call booming the nearly warlike sound of organs, straight trumpets, curved trumpets, horns, and also bombards, since these too are accepted in religious services ...
>
> But my judgment differs very much from those who condemn proper church song. I do not dispute about current polyphonic music if it is used with moderation and discretion.[69]

---

[67] Erasmus, *Opera omnia*, ed. J. Clericus (Leiden, 1703–1706), VI, 731C-732C, quoted in Clement A. Miller, 'Erasmus on Music,' 338ff.

[68] Ornithoparchus, *Musicae active mirologus* and Dowland, *Introduction: Containing the Art of Singing* (New York: Dover, 1973).

[69] Erasmus, *Opera omnia*, 340.

What does he mean, 'those who condemn proper church song'? And why does he say he is not one who disputes the current polyphonic style? You will not find the controversy he refers to in the traditional music histories of sixteenth-century music, constructed as they usually are as edifices on the foundation of the polyphonic music of Josquin, Palestrina, et. al. But the evidence suggests perhaps that people who actually lived in the sixteenth century did not appreciate this music. They heard it as 'scholastic,' meaning the old mathematics-based kind of music. It would appear that to those actually attending church in the sixteenth century, polyphonic music sounded very old-fashioned compared to all the other sixteenth-century music they were hearing.

Thus we have a fine irony. The nineteenth- and twentieth-century music historians have built an entire history of the sixteenth century based on music they find interesting, not the music found interesting by the people who actually lived in the sixteenth century. But let us allow some of these people to give testimony for us, and we hasten to point out to the reader that similar objections to the polyphonic style exist in a surprising number.

The great Italian theorist of the middle of the sixteenth century, Zarlino, refers to the most common objection to polyphony, the difficulty in understanding the words when one hears four or more different words at any given moment.

> Although many singing together stir the soul, there is no doubt that songs in which the singers pronounce the words together are generally heard with greater pleasure than the learned compositions in which the words are interrupted by many voices.[70]

Bardi, making the same point to the composers of his day, pleas,

> to endeavor not to spoil the verse, not imitating the [polyphonic] musicians of today, who think nothing of spoiling it to pursue their ideas or of cutting it to bits to make nonsense of the words …
>
> In composing, then, you will make it your chief aim to arrange the verse well and to declaim the words as intelligibly as you can, not letting yourself be led astray to the counterpoint like a bad swimmer who lets himself be carried out of the course by the current and comes to shore beyond the mark that he had set, for you will consider it self-evident that, just as the soul is nobler than the body, so the words are nobler than the counterpoint. Would it not seem ridiculous if, walking in the public square, you saw a servant followed by his master and commanding him?[71]

It was this same problem that was, as all music historians know, a subject of concern by the Council of Trent.

---

[70] 'Istitutioni,' II, 9, p. 75, quoted in Claude V. Palisca, *Humanism in Italian Renaissance Musical Thought* (New Haven: Yale University Press, 1985), 371ff.

[71] Giovanni de' Bardi, 'Discourse on Ancient Music and Good Singing,' in Oliver Strunk, *Source Readings in Music History* (New York: Norton, 1950), 294ff. Bardi (b. 1534) was a gentleman vitally interested in the arts. It was in his home, in Florence, where the male 'salon' known as the 'Camerata' met to discuss Greek tragedy. Their discussions were an important step toward opera.

Another objection to polyphony, by those sixteenth-century listeners who were becoming enthralled by the emotional emphasis which Humanism had restored to music, was the lack of emotions in the old mathematics-based polyphonic style. Galilei, writing in 1581, and thinking, as a humanist, of the accounts of the power of the emotions in music on the listeners in the ancient world, makes this criticism of polyphony.

> For all the height of excellence of the practical music of the moderns, there is not heard or seen today the slightest sign of its accomplishing what ancient music accomplished, nor do we read that it accomplished it fifty or a hundred years ago ... Thus neither its novelty nor its excellence has ever had the power, with our modern musicians, of producing any of the virtuous, infinitely beneficial and comforting effects that ancient music produced.[72]

He finds the reason for this in the elements of music itself, reasons which the polyphonic composers ignore.

> [It is clear] that the rules observed by the modern contrapuntists as inviolable laws, as well as those they often use from choice and to show their learning, [are] directly opposed to the perfection of the true and best harmonies and melodies.

The explanation which Galilei finds for the failure of the sixteenth-century polyphonic composers to understand the importance of the communication of the emotions is that they simply concentrated on pleasing the ear through sound itself, without consideration of emotion.

> Consider each rule of the modern contrapuntists by itself, or, if you wish, consider them all together. They aim at nothing but the delight of the ear, if it can truly be called delight ... And in truth the last thing the moderns think of is the expression of the words with the passion that these require ... And if it were permitted me, I should like to show you, with several examples of authority, that among the most famous contrapuntists of this century there are some who do not even know how to read, let alone understand. Their ignorance and lack of consideration is one of the most potent reasons why the music of today does not cause in the listeners any of those virtuous and wonderful effects that ancient music caused.[73]

Mattheson, reflecting back on this very problem in the seventeenth century, observed that if the sixteenth-century composers could have only figured this out and found a way to add emotions to their polyphony, then there would be nothing which could compare with it.[74] And by 1607, Agostino Agazzari, declares the polyphonic era is dead.

> That kind of music is no longer in use, both because of the confusion and babel of the words, arising from the long and intricate imitations, and because it has no grace, for, with all the voices singing, one hears neither period nor sense, these being interfered with and covered up by imitations; indeed,

---

72 Galilei, in Strunk, *Source Readings*, 306ff.

73 Galilei, in Ibid., 312ff.

74 Johann Mattheson, *Der vollkommene Capellmeister* (1739), trans. Ernest Harriss (Ann Arbor: UMI Research Press, 1981), I, x, 50.

at every moment, each voice has different words, a thing displeasing to men of competence and judgment … Such compositions are good according to the rules of counterpoint, but they are at the same time faulty according to the rules of music that is true and good.[75]

Reading some of the contemporary descriptions above, one can understand how some sixteenth-century listeners felt that church music had lost its sense of purpose. Ornithoparchus warned singers in 1517 to remember their purpose:

> Above all things, let the singer study to please God and not men. There are foolish singers who condemn the devotion they should seek and affect the wantonness which they should shun, because they intend their singing for men, not God; seeking for a little worldly fame, so that they may lose eternal glory; pleasing men while they may displease God …; and seeking the favor of the creature, condemning the love of the Creator.[76]

The theorist, Listenius, writes in 1537 that music is a serious art which moves souls to virtue.

> With all peoples at all periods of music, [music] has been used in sacred observances, not as a useless voluptuousness, to play some kind of game, but in song, as souls are made more tranquil and are aroused to understand the harmony of divine guidance and are attuned to the correct movement of heavenly teaching; hence its doctrines will more efficiently move souls when song arises.[77]

There were some among those worrying about church music having lost its purpose who argued for a return to the simple music of the early Christians. Glarean (who believed the original Christians' music was in the Aeolian mode) was one who held this view.

> But now it is worthwhile to observe … with how much simplicity, also with how much seriousness the songs of the first church musicians were undertaken, with all ostentation completely removed, with all shallowness excluded, in a word, with such grace that everyone must approve them unless he does not possess any hearing. How justly we ought to be ashamed to have degenerated in such a degree from this![78]

One of the philosophers who supported the new church music, Richard Hooker, answered those who called for a return to the style of the early Christians by suggesting that the simple chant was appropriate for the early simple Christians, but for the 'grosser and heavier minds' of sixteenth-century men, 'the sweetness of melody might make some entrance for good

---

75 Agostino Agazzari, *On Playing upon a Bass in … Consort*, quoted in Oliver Strunk, *Source Readings*, 430.

76 Ornithoparchus, *Musicae active mirologus* and Dowland, *Introduction: Containing the Art of Singing* (New York: Dover, 1973), 210,

77 Nicolaus Listenius, *Musica*, trans. Albert Seay (Colorado Springs: Colorado College Music Press, 1975), 1.

78 Glarean, *Dodecachordon*, trans. Clement Miller (American Institute of Musicology, 1965), I, 143.

things.'[79] This reminds us that there were even some philosophers who believed that the purpose of church music was to reach the less capable minds of the lower classes. Giustiniani, for example, wrote,

> Many preachers are heard who in order to move the ignorant and low classes make use more of songs than of ideas, particularly in the sermons for Good Friday.[80]

A similar view is found in Agrippa, who maintained the Church singing, together with organs, bells, etc., exists for ignorant people, who have no respect for anything but what they see before them.[81]

One can see that many of such objections to the new church music of the sixteenth century offered convenient ammunition for the rising Puritan movement, which in the next century would attempt to ban all instrumental music. But, on the other hand, there were philosophers who spoke strongly in favor of music in general and of the new church music. One of these was Luther, whom we will discuss in the following chapter. Another was Richard Hooker (1553–1600), one of the important rational voices which tried to counter the arguments of the radical Puritans. Hooker wrote of the value of church music as being almost like Aristotle's concept of catharsis, an empathy which has a positive influence on the soul.

> Touching musical harmony whether by instrument or by voice, it being but of high and low in sounds a due proportionable disposition, such notwithstanding is the force thereof, and so pleasing effects it hath in that very part of man which is most divine, that some have been thereby induced to think that the soul itself by nature is or hath in it harmony … The reason hereof is an admirable facility which music hath to express and represent to the mind, more inwardly than any other sensible means, the very standing, rising, and falling, the very steps and inflections every way, the turns and varieties of all passions whereunto the mind is subject; yea so to imitate them, that whether it resemble unto us the same state wherein our minds already are, or a clean contrary, we are not more contentedly by the one confirmed, than changed and led away by the other. In [music] the very image and character even of virtue and vice is perceived, the mind delighted with their resemblances, and brought by having them often iterated into a love of the things themselves. For which cause there is nothing more contagious and pestilent than some kinds of [music]; then some nothing more strong and potent unto good. And that there is such a difference of one kind from another we need no proof but our own experience, inasmuch as we are at the hearing of some more inclined unto sorrow and heaviness; of some, more mollified and softened in mind; one kind more apt to stay and settle us, another to move and stir our affections; there is that draweth to a marvelous grave and sober mediocrity, there is also that carrieth as it were into ecstasies, filling the mind with an heavenly joy and for the time in a manner severing it from the body. So that although we lay altogether aside the consideration of the text of a [song] and substance, the very harmony of sounds being framed in due sort and carried from the ear to the spiritual faculties of our souls, is by a native puissance and efficacy greatly

---

79 Richard Hooker, *On the Laws of Ecclesiastical Polity*, V, xxxviii, in *The Works of Mr. Richard Hooker* (Oxford: Clarendon Press, 1888), II, 161ff.

80 Vicenzo Giustiniani, *Discorso sopra la Musica* (ca. 1628), trans. Carol MacClintock (American Institute of Musicology, 1962).

81 Agrippa, *Of the Vanitie and Uncertaintie of Arts and Sciences*, 187.

available to bring to a perfect temper whatsoever is there troubled, apt as well to quicken the spirits as to allay that which is too eager, sovereign against melancholy and despair, forcible to draw forth tears of devotion if the mind be such as can yield them, able both to move and to moderate all affections.[82]

Melanchthon, when after the death of Frederick the Wise in 1525 his successor dissolved the choir of the Castle Church of Wittenberg in order to put the money to use for 'better purposes,' came to the defense of church music by arguing that it was pleasing to God.

> We have need of such people, not only in order that the good music that has been used might not be buried, but also that new and better music be written. I consider retaining the services of such people a good work from which God derives pleasure. Thus far many people in many places maintained music groups for unnecessary pomp and other unbecoming purposes. Why should the noble art of music not remain active now for God's sake?[83]

And, finally, there were some aristocrats who supported church music for secular reasons, as for example to demonstrate the completeness or wealth of their court. A notable example was Elizabeth I of England. Even at home in more private circumstances, accounts speak of a surprising number of instruments participating in her services. A secretary of the visiting Duke of Württemberg, who attended a service in 1592, records,

> This Castle stands upon a knoll; in the outer or first court there is a very beautiful and immensely large church, with a flat even roof, covered with lead, as is common with all churches in this kingdom. In this church his[84] Highness listened for more than an hour to the beautiful music, the usual ceremonies, and the English sermon. The music, especially the organ, was exquisitely played; for at times you could hear the sound of cornetts, flutes, then fifes and other instruments ... After the music, which lasted a long time, had ended ...[85]

A similar account of services at Whitehall in 1597 speaks of 'voices, organs, cornetts, and sackbutts, with other ceremonies and music.'[86]

Beyond this, it is clear that Elizabeth used Church music for political purposes, in particular to impress foreign diplomats that religion had not ended in England with Henry VIII. We can see this clearly in the report of a visiting Italian diplomat in 1589.

> ... seeing him [the archbishop] upon the next Sabbath day after in the Cathedral Church of Canterbury, attended upon by his Gentlemen, and servants ... also by the Deane, Prebendaries, and Preachers in their Surplesses, and scarlet Hoods, and heard the solemne Musicke with the voyces, and Organs, Cornets, and Sagbutts, hee was overtaken with admiration, and tolde an English Gentleman of very good qualitie, That they were led in great blindness at Rome, by our own Nation, who made

---

82 Richard Hooker, *The Works of Mr. Richard Hooker*, II, 159.
83 Quoted in Walter Buszin, 'Luther on Music,' *The Musical Quarterly* 32, no. 1 (January, 1946): 86.
84 Such was the prejudice at the time that female rulers were nevertheless referred to in the masculine.
85 Jacob Rathgeb, *A True and Faithful Narrative ...* (Tubingen, 1602), quoted in William Rye, ed., *England as seen by Foreigners* (New York: Blom), l15ff.
86 G. Harrison, ed., *The Elizabethan Journals* (New York: MacMillian), 184.

the people there believe, that there was not in England, either Archbishop, or Bishop, or Cathedral, or any Church or Ecclesiastical government; but that all was pulled down to the ground, and that the people heard their Ministers in the Woods, and Fields, amongst Trees, and brute beasts; but, for his own part, he protested, that (unless it were in the Popes Chappell) he had never saw a more solemne sight, nor heard a more heavenly sound.[87]

Another eyewitness account by a visitor at this time makes a similar comparison with Rome.

> ... the altar was furnished with rich plate, with two gilt candlesticks, with lighted candles, and a massy crucifix in the midst; and that the service was sung not only with organs, but with the [artful] music of cornets, sacbuts, etc., on solemn festivals ... That, in short, the service performed in the queen's Chapel, and in sundry cathedrals, was so splendid and showy, that foreigners could not distinguish it from the Roman, except that it was performed in English.[88]

Before concluding these thoughts on 16th century church music, we pass on the following information in the event there is a reader out there with an 'Indiana Jones' inclination. Ornithoparchus informs us (according to his reading of the Old Testament) that the inventor of music was Tubal and that Tubal engraved the rules of music on two tablets, one of slate and one of marble. Ornithoparchus reports having heard that the marble tablet survived the flood and could be found in Syria.[89]

---

[87] G. Paule, *The Life of the most reverend and religious prelate John Whitgift Lord Archbishop of Canterbury* (London, 1612), 79.

[88] Quoted in Edmondstoune Duncan, *The Story of Minstrelsy* (London, 1968), 177.

[89] Ornithoparchus, *Musicae active micrologus*, 125.

Martin Luther on Music

THE GREAT DRAMA OF THE EARLY ROMAN CHURCH was its struggle to preserve its great fortress built on Faith in the face of the widespread intellectual doubt which followed the rediscovery of the books devoted to Reason by the ancient Greek philosophers. This struggle is no better personified than in Thomas Acquinas, who was so dedicated to finding an intellectual marriage between Faith and Reason that he was blind to the beginning of the Renaissance going on all around him. Martin Luther was quite a different story. He began as the most dedicated and humble of Catholic priests but when his natural intellect came into battle with the Church dogma the result was a strengthened intellect leading to a really modern (Renaissance) man. The values he attributed to music, in particular, represented the present and not the past and reflected the great progress of music in the sixtenth century. The Church was itself responsible for the conversion of this man to Humanism.

Ten years before Luther posted his famous ninety-five theses on the door of the Castle Church in Wittenberg he was a model Catholic priest preparing, at age twenty-four, to conduct his first mass. In a letter inviting a friend to attend, Luther describes himself in these words.

> God, who is glorious and holy in all his works, has deigned to exalt me magnificently—a miserable and totally unworthy sinner—by calling me into his supreme ministry, solely on the basis of his bounteous mercy.[1]

By 1517, Luther was serving as a lecturer at the university in Wittenberg, in addition to his duties as a priest. Now age thirty-four, nothing remarkable had happened in his life when one day a papal representative appeared selling indulgences to help raise money for the rebuilding of St. Peter's in Rome. When members of Luther's flock showed him the documents they had purchased which, among other things, obtained the entry into Heaven for their long dead ancestors who were never even believers, Luther refused to play the game. His 'Theses' were in effect statements in opposition which he offered to discuss or debate with whomsoever. This was the last chance the Church had either to deal with him rationally or, as Erasmus volunteered, to burn him at the stake. Instead, he was told to recant his views.

They picked the wrong man, for Luther, aside from being a strong and rather earthy German, happened to be a thorough scholar of the Scriptures. He could quote Scriptural support for everything he said and in his 'trials' he drove the authorities mad by simply saying, 'I will recant if you can prove I'm wrong.'

---

[1] Letter to John Braun [1507], in *Luther's Works* (St. Louis: Concordia, 1961), XLVIII, 3.

Within three years Luther was clearly planting his feet and taking his stand. In an 'Open Letter' to Pope Leo X, in 1520, Luther seems to want to honor the pope, although he is quick to admit that he will fight back if attacked.

> I have never alienated myself from Your Blessedness to such an extent that I should not with all my heart wish you and your see every blessing, for which I have besought God with earnest prayers to the best of my ability. It is true that I have been so bold as to despise and look down upon those who have tried to frighten me with the majesty of your name and authority.[2]

But Luther was growing in confidence and after another three years he could call the Pope 'a miserable bag of maggot-fodder'[3] and by 1541 a 'stupid ass.'[4]

In addition to his debates with the Church, Luther's publications after 1517 are also characterized by strong attacks against the universities, which with their long Scholastic tradition had been one of the pillars of support for the Church. When one reads these statements, one cannot help but wonder if a bright younger Luther had had some bad personal experience as a university student. By 1524, in the process of pleading for the foundation of public schools, Luther's language in attacking the universities is extraordinary.

> We have today the finest and most learned group of men, adorned with languages and all the arts, who could also render real service if only we would make use of them as instructors of the young people. Is it not evident that we are now able to prepare a boy in three years, so that at the age of fifteen or eighteen he will know more than all the universities and monasteries have known before? Indeed, what have men been learning till now in the universities and monasteries except to become asses, blockheads, and numskulls? For twenty, even forty, years they pored over their books, and still failed to master either Latin or German, to say nothing of the scandalous and immoral life there in which many a fine young fellow was shameful corrupted.
>
> ......
>
> We have taken upon ourselves the support of a host of doctors, preaching friars, masters, priests, and monks; that is to say, great, coarse, fat asses decked out in red and brown birettas, looking like a sow bedecked with a gold chain and jewels. They taught us nothing good, but only made us all the more blind and stupid. In return, they devoured all our goods and filled every monastery, indeed every nook and cranny, with the filth and dung of their foul and poisonous books, until it is appalling to think of it.[5]

Luther believed the first step in reforming university education was to return to original sources, rather than studying the Church's commentary on those sources.

---

[2] Quoted in, 'The Freedom of a Christian' [1520], in Ibid., XXXI, 334.

[3] 'Exhortation to the Knights of the Teutonic Order' [1523], in Ibid., XLV, 144.

[4] 'Against Hanswurst' [1541], in Ibid., XLI, 221.

[5] 'To the Councilmen of All Cities in Germany That They Establish and Maintain Christian Schools' [1524], in Ibid., XLV, 351, 375.

In this way the subtle hair-splitting finally may perish altogether, and genuine philosophy, theology, and all the arts may be drawn from their true sources.[6]

But he was also aware that this was difficult in view of all the literature which had been destroyed by the Church during the Dark Ages, as he observed in one place,

> This situation lasted until, as we have experienced and observed, the languages and the arts were laboriously recovered—although imperfectly—from bits and fragments of old books hidden among dust and worms. Men are still painfully searching for them every day, just as people poke through the ashes of a ruined city seeking the treasures and jewels.[7]

In a treatise of 1525, Luther again turns to education, saying 'The preachers are to exhort the people to send their children to school so that persons are educated for competent service both in church and state.'[8] He now presents more specific details on how this public education should be organized and makes music a core subject. He proposes dividing the children into three age groups.

The first group, or Division, are children just beginning to read. These children are to learn Latin a phrase or two at a time and are to be taught to write.

> These children shall also be taught music and shall sing with the others.

The second division includes those children able to read and now ready for grammar, which he says should only be taught in the hours before noon. While discussing this group Luther specifies,

> All the children, large and small, should practice music daily, in the first hour in the afternoon.

The Third Division, consisting of children well trained in grammar, are now given substantial literature, including Virgil, Ovid and Cicero. And once again,

> Along with the others these shall rehearse music the hour after noon.

Luther, on several occasions, suggested that he found something of the divine in music. In part this reflects his awe of it and his inability to explain its effects. His longest discussion which reflects this feeling is found in his preface to Georg Rhau's *Symphoniae iucundae* of 1538.

> I would certainly like to praise music with all my heart as the excellent gift of God which it is and to commend it to everyone. But I am so overwhelmed by the diversity and magnitude of its virtue and benefits that I can find neither beginning nor end or method for my discourse. As much as I want to commend it, my praise is bound to be wanting and inadequate. For who can comprehend it all? And even if you wanted to encompass all of it, you would appear to have grasped nothing at

---

6 Letter to George Spalatin [1518], in Ibid., XLVIII, 96.
7 'To the Councilmen,' 374.
8 'Instructions for the Visitors of Parish Pastors in Electoral Saxony' [1525], in Ibid., XL, 314ff.

all. First then, looking at music itself, you will find that from the beginning of the world it has been instilled and implanted in all creatures, individually and collectively. For nothing is without sound or harmony. Even the air, which of itself is invisible and imperceptible to all our senses, and which, since it lacks both voice and speech, is the least musical of all things, becomes sonorous, audible, and comprehensible when it is set in motion …

Philosophers have labored to explain the marvelous instrument of the human voice: how can the air projected by a light movement of the tongue and an even lighter movement of the throat produce such an infinite variety and articulation of the voice and of words? And how can the voice, at the direction of the will, sound forth so powerfully and vehemently that it cannot only be heard by everyone over a wide area, but also be understood? Philosophers for all their labor cannot find the explanation; and baffled they end in perplexity; for none of them has yet been able to define or demonstrate the original components of the human voice, its sibilation and (as it were) its alphabet, e.g., in the case of laughter—to say nothing of weeping. They marvel, but they do not understand.[9]

In a conversation with Anthony Lauterbach, in a period in which music was still spoken of as being either theoretical or practical, Luther observed,

It's so in all fields that activity and practice make men better informed than mere knowledge.[10]

Luther himself apparently had an ear for music sufficient to distinguish between the theory of music and that which was pleasing. When one, Lukas Edemberger, gave him some songs, Luther did not like them, responding,

He has sufficient art and skill, but lacks sweetness.[11]

Having been educated in a choir school himself, he enjoyed participating in singing in his home, as one recollection by Johann Walter indicates.

I spent many a pleasant hour singing music with him and often experienced that he seemingly could not weary of singing or even get enough of it; in addition, he was able to discuss music eloquently.[12]

And, as is generally known, Luther had sufficient skill to engage in some composition of his own, including at least one extant motet.[13] While he is commonly credited with the composition of *Ein feste Burg*, this cannot be documented. But, there is no reason to believe

---

[9] Ibid., LIII, 321ff.

[10] In a conversation of 1538 reported by Anthony Lauterbach, in Ibid., 274.

[11] 'Artis sat habet, sed caret suavitate,' quoted in Walter Buszin, 'Luther on Music,' *The Musical Quarterly* 32, no. 1 (January, 1946): 90.

[12] Mentioned in the *Syntagma Musicum* of Praetorius, quoted in Buszin, Ibid., 96.

[13] The music is reproduced in Ibid., LIII, 339ff.

he did not participate in writing some of the early hymn tunes.[14] At least two hymns exist in his manuscript,[15] while in other cases he was careful to point out in print examples which had been attributed to him but were not his.[16]

Luther left a number of commentaries on the subject of the purpose of music. In a remarkable letter to the great composer of the court in Munich, Ludwig Senfl, Luther speaks not only of the power of music to soothe but also the virtues of music in general and of his own love for music.

> Even though my name is detested, so much that I am forced to fear that this letter I am sending may not be safely received and read by you, excellent Ludwig, yet the love for music, with which I see you adorned and gifted by God, has conquered this fear. This love also has given me hope that my letter will not bring danger to you. For who, even among the Turks, would censure him who loves art and praises the artist? Because they encourage and honor music so much, I, at least, nevertheless very much praise and respect above all others your dukes of Bavaria, much as they are unfavorably inclined toward me.
>
> There is no doubt that there are many seeds of good qualities in the minds of those who are moved by music. Those, however, who are not moved by music I believe are definitely like stumps and blocks of stone. For we know that music, too, is odious and unbearable to the demons. Indeed I plainly judge, and do not hesitate to affirm, that except for theology there is no art that could be put on the same level with music, since except for theology, music alone produces what otherwise only theology can do, namely, a calm and joyful disposition … This is the reason why the prophets did not make use of any art except music; when setting forth their theology they did it not as geometry, not as arithmetic, not as astronomy, but as music, so that they held theology and music most tightly connected, and proclaimed truth through Psalms and songs. But why do I now praise music and attempt to portray...such an important subject on such a little piece of paper? Yet my love for music, which often has quickened me and liberated me from great vexations, is abundant and overflowing.[17]

In a conversation held with Luther during dinner in his home, one present recalled a similar praise of music's ability to soothe.

> One of the most beautiful and most precious gifts of God is music. Satan is very hostile to it, since it casts out many scruples and evil thoughts. The devil does not remain near it, for music is one of the finest of all arts. Its notes instill life into its texts. Music drives away the spirit of sadness, as may be seen from the life of King Saul …
>
> For a person beset by grief music is the most effective balm, for through it the heart is made content, is inspired and refreshed.[18]

---

[14] Ibid., LIII, 191ff, documents his involvement in the early hymns at some length.

[15] Ibid., 295.

[16] Ibid., 333ff.

[17] Letter to Ludwig Senfl [1530], in Ibid., XLIX, 427ff.

[18] Quoted in Buszin, 'Luther on Music,' 91ff.

An extraordinary testimonial to the ability of music to soothe and comfort the listener is found in a poem by Luther, found in his publication of 1538 called *A Preface for All Good Hymnals*, in which Music speaks as follows:

> Of all the joys upon this earth
> None has for men a greater worth
> Than what I give with my ringing
> And with voices sweetly singing.
> There cannot be an evil mood
> Where there are singing fellows good,
> There is no envy, hate, nor ire,
> Gone are through me all sorrows dire;
> Greed, care, and lonely heaviness
> No more do they the heart oppress.
> Each man can in his mirth be free
> Since such a joy no sin can be.
> But God in me more pleasure finds
> Than in all joys of earthly minds.
> Through my bright power the devil shirks
> His sinful, murderous, evil works …
> The best time of the year is mine
> When all the birds are singing fine.
> Heaven and earth their voices fill
> With right good song and tuneful trill.
> And, queen of all, the nightingale
> Men's hears will merrily regale
> With music so charmingly gay;
> For which be thanks to her for aye.
> But thanks be first to God, our Lord,
> Who created her by his Word
> To be his own beloved songstress
> And of *musica* a mistress.
> For our dear Lord she sings her song
> In praise of him the whole day long;
> To him I give my melody
> And thanks in all eternity.[19]

And in an unfinished treatise, 'Concerning Music,' Luther observed,

> Music drives away the devil and makes people happy; it induces one to forget all wrath, unchastity, arrogance, and other vices.[20]

---

[19] Ibid., LIII, 319ff.

[20] Quoted in Buszin, 'Luther on Music,' 88.

In 1538 Luther wrote the preface for a collection of part-songs based on the suffering and death of Jesus. In addition to mentioning the emphasis on music in the Old Testament, together with his own awe of the art, Luther touches on the most fundamental purpose of music, to express feelings.

> I most heartily desire that music, that divine and most precious gift, be praised and extolled before all people. However, I am so completely overwhelmed by the quantity and greatness of its excellence and virtues, that I can find neither beginning nor end, nor adequate words and expressions to say what I ought; as a result, though I am full of the highest praise, I remain nothing more than a jejune and miserable eulogist.
>
> Here ought one to speak of the use one might make of so great a thing, but even this use is so infinitely manifold that it is beyond the reach of the greatest eloquence of the greatest orators. We are able to adduce only this one point at present, namely, that experience proves that, next to the Word of God, only music deserves being extolled as the mistress and governess of the feelings of the human heart.[21]

Luther makes an extended testimonial to music's ability to express feeling in his preface to Rhau's *Symphoniae iucundae*, published in the same year. He could not be more correct when he says 'music is a language [of feelings] without words.'

> Here it must suffice to discuss the benefit of this great art. But even that transcends the greatest eloquence of the most eloquent, because of the infinite variety of its forms and benefits. We can mention only one point (which experience confirms), namely, that next to the Word of God, music deserves the highest praise. She is a mistress and governess of those human emotions which as masters govern men or more often overwhelm them. No greater commendation than this can be found—at least not by us. For whether you wish to comfort the sad, to terrify the happy, to encourage the despairing, to humble the proud, to calm the passionate, or to appease those full of hate—and who could number all these masters of the human heart, namely, the emotions, inclinations, and affections that impel men to evil or good?—what more effective means than music could you find? …
>
> Thus it was not without reason that the fathers and prophets wanted nothing else to be associated as closely with the Word of God as music. Therefore, we have so many hymns and Psalms where message and music join to move the listener's soul, while in other living beings and [sounding] bodies music remains a language without words.[22]

In several places, Luther also comments on the purpose of music so often mentioned by the ancient Greeks, the power of music to affect the character of the listener. He seems to have noticed this first in the quality of people he knew who were also musicians. We may presume that it was his recognition of this purpose of music which fostered his frequent recommendation that music be part of the school curriculum.

---

[21] Ibid., 81

[22] *Luther's Works*, LIII, 323.

> I have always loved music. Those who have mastered this art are made of good stuff, they are fit for any task. It is necessary indeed that music be taught in the schools. A teacher must be able to sing; otherwise I will not as much as look at him. Also, we should not ordain young men into the ministry unless they have become well acquainted with music in the schools.
>
> Music is a beautiful and glorious gift of God and close to theology. I would not give up what little I know about music for something else which I might have in greater abundance. We should always make it a point to habituate youth to enjoy the art of music, for it produces fine and skillful people.[23]

In 1524 Luther returned to this idea when he wrote the preface to his and Walter's *Geistliches Gesangbuchlein*.

> That it is good and God pleasing to sing hymns is, I think, known to every Christian; for everyone is aware not only of the example of the prophets and kings in the Old Testament who praised God with song and sound, with poetry and psaltery, but also of the common and ancient custom of the Christian church to sing Psalms …
>
> And these songs were arranged in four parts to give the young—who should at any rate be trained in music and other fine arts—something to wean them away from love ballads and carnal songs and to teach them something of value in their place, thus combining the good with the pleasing, as is proper for youth. Nor am I of the opinion that the gospel should destroy and blight all the arts, as some of the pseudo-religious claim. But I would like to see all the arts, especially music, used in the service of Him who gave and made them … As it is, the world is too lax and indifferent about teaching and training the young for us to abet this trend.[24]

Luther is reported to have mentioned this purpose in another dinner conversation.

> Music is a semi-discipline and taskmistress, which makes people milder and more gentle, more civil and more sensible.[25]

Luther seemed to have two central objections to the practice of music in the Catholic Church as he knew it in the sixteenth century. First, he was bothered by the use of money purely for the 'extras' of ceremony, although he suggests in one place that 'singing, churches, decorations, organs' are needed to coax the most childish of men to know the teachings of faith.[26] In any case, he complained in a publication of 1524 that instead of people giving money to the poor they give it to the Church for designated purposes, such as 'chapels, alters, towers, bells, organs, paintings, images, [and] singing.'[27] In this regard he also objected to a tradition of endowed masses, the paying for masses for particular private purposes.

---

[23] Quoted in Buszin, 'Luther on Music,' 85.

[24] *Luther's Works*, LIII, 315ff.

[25] Quoted in Buszin, 'Luther on Music,' 92.

[26] 'Treatise on Good Works' [1520], in *Luther's Works*, XLIV, 35.

[27] 'Trade and Usury' [1524], in Ibid., XLV, 284.

> That is to say, they have been reduced to anthem singers, organ wheezers, and reciting decadent, indifferent masses to get and consume the income from the endowments.[28]

In an early treatise dealing with prayer, Luther suggests that the proper role for church music is not ceremonial, but to move the listener to devotional thought. In making the point that although one can pray silently nevertheless hearing the words stimulates thought, he uses the analogy of music.

> The spoken words have no other purpose than that of a trumpet, a drum, or an organ, or any other sound which will move the heart and lift it upward to God.[29]

It must perhaps be viewed from the perspective that Luther was an experienced singer and musician, that he wrote complaining that it was a waste of time to try to teach monks to sing.

> If now some unbeliever were to enter into the midst of these men and heard them braying, mumbling, and bellowing, and saw that they were neither preaching nor praying, but rather, as their custom is, were sounding forth like those pipe organs (with which they have so brilliantly associated themselves, each one set in a row just like his neighbor), would this unbeliever not be perfectly justified in asking, 'Have you gone mad?' What else are these monks but the tubes and pipes Paul referred to as giving no distinct note but rather blasting out into the air? Is it any different from a man who seeking to lecture mounts the platform and talks for a whole hour in a language which is foreign to the people and which nobody understands? ... Would we not think this man mad? I grant that divine worship of this kind suits sacrilegious and blasphemous enemies of Christ, since they are not one whit better than those dumb, wooden pipes, sounding forth with much effort, teaching nothing, learning nothing, and praying nothing. And yet they boast that this senseless work is the highest worship, and draw to themselves the world's wealth on the merits of this work ...
>
> In this way audacious and blasphemous men adapt the divine oracles of Christ to fit in with this childish, ridiculous, and foolish performance, in which they actually stand in rows to worship God like rows of tubes, pipes, and trumpets, mute and insensate ... Do you think God wants a lot of dumb pipes to assemble themselves and delight him by blowing off into thin air?[30]

It is clear in his writings that he wanted to preserve some of the older musical traditions. A case in point was the burial hymns. While he pointed out that the new church should not sing 'dirges or doleful songs,' but rather 'comforting hymns of the forgiveness of sins,' he nevertheless retained some of the older melodies in a collection of *Burial Hymns* of 1542, although he changed the text.

> This is why we have collected the fine music and songs which under the papacy were used at vigils, masses for the dead, and burials ... But we have adapted other texts to the music so that it may adorn our article of the resurrection, instead of purgatory with its torment and satisfaction which lets their dead neither sleep nor rest. The melodies and notes are precious. It would be a pity to let them perish. But the texts and words are non-Christian and absurd. They deserve to perish ...

---

[28] 'To the Christian Nobility' [1520], in Ibid., XLIV, 192.

[29] 'An Exposition of the Lord's Prayer for Simple Laymen' [1519], in Ibid., XLII, 25.

[30] 'The Judgment of Martin Luther on Monastic Vows' [1521], in Ibid., XLIV, 324ff.

> And indeed, they also possess a lot of splendid, beautiful songs and music, especially in the cathedral and parish churches. But these are used to adorn all sorts of impure and idolatrous texts. Therefore, we have unclothed these idolatrous, lifeless, and foolish texts, and divest them of their beautiful music …
>
> But we do not hold that the notes need to be sung the same in all the churches. Let every church follow the music according to their own book and custom. For I myself do not like to hear the notes in a responsory or other song changed from what I was accustomed to in my youth. We are concerned with changing the text, not the music.[31]

Earlier, in 1525, he had recommended the German hymn, *Mitten in dem Leben*, for use in burial services.[32]

It appears that at one point, at least, Luther was thinking of retaining some of the old Catholic music for the purpose of promoting the Latin language.

> At vespers it would be excellent to sing three evening hymns in Latin, not German, on account of the school youth, to accustom them to the Latin. Then follow the simple antiphons, hymns, and responses, and a lesson in German … Then one might sing the Magnificat or a Te Deum Laudamus or Benedictus … so that the youth remain close to the Scriptures. Thereupon the whole congregation may sing a German hymn …
>
> Since it is not fitting that singing should be uniform at all festivals, it would be well on high festivals to sing the Latin Introits, the Gloria in Excelsis, the Hallelujah, the simple sequences, the Sanctus, and Agnus Dei.[33]

The following year, in a publication dealing with the new order of the service, Luther mentions this again.

> For in no wise would I want to discontinue the service in the Latin language, because the young are my chief concern. And if I could bring it to pass, and Greek and Hebrew were as familiar to us as the Latin and had as many fine melodies and songs, we would hold mass, sing, and read on successive Sundays in all four languages, German, Latin, Greek, and Hebrew. I do not at all agree with those who cling to one language and despise all others.[34]

On beginning to think about a new kind of church service, Luther recognizes the importance of keeping some traditions.

> Let the chants in the Sunday masses and Vespers be retained; they are quite good and are taken from Scripture.[35]

---

[31] Ibid., LIII, 326ff.

[32] 'Instructions for the Visitors of Parish Pastors in Electoral Saxony' [1525], in Ibid., XL, 310.

[33] Ibid., 307ff.

[34] 'The German Mass and Order of Service' [1526], in Ibid., LIII, 63.

[35] 'Concerning the Order of Public Worship' [1523], in Ibid., LIII, 13ff.

But in general he seemed in favor of cutting back the amount of choral participation.

> The Quadragesima graduals and others like them that exceed two verses may be sung at home by whoever wants them. In church we do not want to quench the spirit of the faithful with tedium.

By 1523 he was beginning to think of creating new music with German words.

> Our plan is to follow the example of the prophets and the ancient fathers of the church, and to compose psalms for the people in the vernacular, that is, spiritual songs, so that the Word of God may be among the people also in the form of music. Therefore we are searching everywhere for poets ... But I would like you to avoid any new words or the language used at court. In order to be understood by the people, only the simplest and most common words should be used for singing; at the same time, however, they should be pure and apt; and further, the sense should be clear and as close as possible to the psalm. You need a free hand here: maintain the sense, but don't cling to the words ... I myself do not have so great a gift that I can do what I would like to see done here.[36]

One reason for favoring German was his preference for having the congregation participate in singing. In the same year, he wrote,

> I also wish that we had as many songs as possible in the vernacular which the people could sing during mass, immediately after the gradual and also after the Sanctus and Agnus Dei. For who doubts that originally all the people sang these which now only the choir sings or responds to while the bishop is consecrating?[37]

He mentions this again in 1525, in his 'Against the Heavenly Prophets.'

> Although I am willing to permit the translating of Latin texts of choral and vocal music into the vernacular with the retention of the original notes and musical settings, I am nevertheless of the opinion that the result sounds neither proper nor correct; the text, the notes, the accents, the tune, and likewise the entire outward expression must be genuine outgrowths of the original text and its spirit.[38]

By 1524 he was beginning to think of a complete German Mass.

> I desire a German mass more than I can promise. I am not qualified for this task, which requires both a talent in music and the gift of the Spirit.[39]

The earliest church music which Luther published looked very much like chant, expect for German words. By 1538 he had apparently heard some new examples of polyphony, which he endorses in his preface to a collection of part-songs.

---

[36] Letter to George Spalatin [1523], in Ibid., XLIX, 68.
[37] 'An Order of Mass and Communion' [1523], in Ibid., LIII, 36.
[38] Quoted in Buszin, 'Luther on Music,' 95.
[39] Letter to Nicholas Hausmann [1524], in *Luther's Works*, XLIX, 90.

But when learning is added to all this and artistic music which corrects, develops, and refines the natural music, then at last it is possible to taste with wonder (yet not to comprehend) God's absolute and perfect wisdom in his wondrous work of music. Here it is most remarkable that one single voice continues to sing the tenor, while at the same time many other voices play around it, exulting and adorning it in exuberant strains and, as it were, leading it forth in a divine roundelay, so that those who are the least bit moved know nothing more amazing in this world. But any who remain unaffected are unmusical indeed and deserve to hear a certain dunghill poet or the music of the pigs.[40]

---

[40] Ibid., LIII, 324.

Praetorius on Sixteenth-Century Performance Practice

*Music has reached such a high level that
any further advance would seem inconceivable.*

Michael Praetorius, 1619

IN 1975 WE HEARD A MUSIC PROFESSOR at the University of California, Berkeley declare in public, 'The study of the clarinet is to music, as the study of the typewriter is to English literature.'

He meant that music and English literature were important as subjects belonging to the mind, whereas the clarinet and the typewriter were mere instruments of utility and of no importance in themselves. This fundamental prejudice in the field of music was already more than a thousand years old when this Berkeley professor made his pronouncement.

This Scholastic prejudice toward performance began when Cassiodorus (480–573) made the basic philosophical division of the 'Speculative,' which are subjects appropriate to the mind, and the 'Practical,' the domain of how to do things. While Cassiodorus did not include music in his discussion, following writers quickly adopted this division to justify the academic teaching of 'Speculative Music,' meaning composition, theory, music physics, etc., while any teaching in 'Practical Music' was left to the musicians out in the street. Any reader familiar with higher music education today will immediately recognize that the echoes of these two basic definitions are strongly felt in many university music departments today. There are major universities in the United States where still today conductors of university bands and orchestras are not members of the regular faculty.

This distinction between 'Speculative Music' and 'Practical Music' was strongly held in Western European Church music as long as the Church banned instrumental music. But once the instruments began to return in the fifteenth and sixteenth centuries the pendulum very quickly began to swing in the direction of the study of performance practice. But we speak here of composers and performers for whom the old prejudice against 'Practical Music' remained very noticeable well into the twentieth century. It was this long held view which has, for example, for so long delayed scholarly publication in the field of performance practice. And it is this view, we presume, which can only explain why the third volume of Praetorius' *Syntagma Musicum*, the single greatest contemporary discussion of performance practice of 16th century music, was *never* published in entirety in *any* modern language by the time we first wrote this essay in the 1970s.[1] Music historians have long been interested in, and have

---

[1] A facsimile of the original German publication has been printed by Barenreiter Kassel, 1958. The page numbers we cite, therefore, are from the original print. We understand a modern edition as now been printed, but we do not have a copy of it and therefore cannot comment on the quality of its translation.

translated and published in modern editions, the first two volumes, which deal basically with theory and physical descriptions of instruments, but not the third volume, which deals with how music functioned in society.[2]

Although not published until 1619, the third volume is a description of late Renaissance style as practiced in Italy and Germany. It is particularly valuable as Praetorius gives us a first hand look at a critical moment in performance history, just when the use of Italian words for tempi were being introduced, when the slur designation was first introduced, when written dynamic markings were first being used, when thorough-bass was being introduced and, most important, an eyewitness account of the new form, the church concerto form, known to most musicians today in the music of Gabrieli. But beyond this one finds an astonishing freedom in performance of the basic form of the music found on paper. The freedom which Pretorius describes in the performance of the large Church Concerto, in particular, goes far beyond what most conductors in our far more conservative world today would dare to even think about.

Starting with the category of works with text, Praetorius begins with the concerto,[3] which he seems to have understood both as a style and a form. Here he presents the meaning of the term as a style, whereas below we shall see his extensive remarks on the practical application of this style. Before presenting Praetorius' comments on the concerto style, we should remind the reader that between the late Renaissance and the late Baroque, this term went through three distinct transformations in meaning. The term first meant the name of a group, as we might use the term 'ensemble' today, such as 'Concerto di Milano.' Then it became a style word and only later a form.

To Praetorius, 'concerto' as a style, was 'a dialog in which different voices or instruments are combined.'[4] In an apparent reference to Church polychoral form, he adds that the pleasure comes not from the craft involved, but from the variety.

He associates the style of a concerto with a multi-voice composition in which separate choirs alternate. This follows from the term itself, which he says derives from *concertare*, 'to compete with one another.'

> Let us imagine several of the best and most competent musicians singing or playing on various instruments—such as cornetts, trombones, recorders or transverse flutes, cromornes, bassoons or dulcians, rackets, viols, large and small violins, lutes, harpsichords, regals, positives, or organs—alternating in the manner of choirs and striving, as it were, to outdo one another.[5]

---

[2] Praetorius speaks of a fourth volume, which apparently he never actually wrote. Praetorius (1571–1621), whose real name was Schultheiss, studied in the Latin school at Torgau and worked in the court of the Duke of Brunswick and later as Kapellmeister in Wolfenbüttel.

[3] In this essay we focus on Praetorius' discussion of church music.

[4] Ibid., 4. For 'concerto' he gives *concertatio* in Latin and *ein Concert* in German. He also adds that *Cantio*, *concentus* and *symphonia* all mean at this time, 'a composition for several voices.'

[5] Ibid., 5.

When he adds, 'more properly a composition is called a concerto if a high and a low choir are heard in alternation and together,' we can see the root of the late Baroque *concertato* style.

Curiously, when Praetorius speaks of the English practice, he reverts to an older use of this term, meaning simply a group of players.

> The English call this a Consort, from *consortium*, as when several people with various instruments such as harpsichord, large lyra, double harp, lute, theorbo, pandora, *penorcon*, cither, viol, small violin, transverse flute or recorder, sometimes also a soft trombone or rackett, play together quietly and softly, forming a pleasant and harmonious relationship with one another.[6]

In the case of the motet, Praetorius seems at a loss to fulfill his earlier promise of explaining 'Italian terms which are so puzzling to many musicians.' It strikes the reader as odd that he, not to mention several Italian treatises he cites, did not recognize this as a French word. 'Opinions vary regarding the origin of the word *motet*,'[7] he says as he proceeds to give some possibilities which are incorrect. Philip de Monte, he maintains, thought it derived from *mutare*, 'to alter,' as in changing verses. Others believed it came from *modo tecta*, 'obscure as to mode' or even from *moda* in Italian for 'fashion.' We never read the correct answer, but in the process Praetorius does provide more accurate descriptions of the style of the motet, in particular 'elegance' and a work which 'moves one most profoundly by its seriousness and artfulness.'

Praetorius also points out that this form is sometimes confused with concerto, but he recognizes a distinction in style.

> The concerti should be set for several choirs and composed quite plainly, without particular elaboration and imitative passages; the motet, however, should be written with greater artfulness and care and for not more than eight voices.[8]

Other church forms which Praetorius mentions include dialogues and canzoni. The Dialogue he does not define, because 'everyone knows what dialogues are.' It is also interesting that he includes echo songs in this category.[9] The canzoni he understands first as 'rather worldly' songs with varying orders of verses. He is also familiar with the Italian instrumental form and he recognizes that many beautiful canzoni are being composed there, particularly by Gabrieli.[10] Shorter songs carry the diminutive, canzonette, and usually have secular texts. It is also interesting that he identifies this form with the German *Mestergesange*.

---

[6] Ibid.

[7] Ibid., 6ff. 'Motet,' of course, comes from Mot, French for 'word.'

[8] Ibid., 8ff. He points out that Gabrieli has composed works for up to sixteen voices which are 'motets' in style, but organized into choirs as concerti.

[9] Ibid., 16.

[10] Ibid., 17.

Praetorius' second large division of forms, those without text (or instrumental music), also include forms associated with the church. Praetorius was under the impression that ricercar was merely the Italian name for fugue. He devotes little space to these forms, although he notes that the composer who can write them suited to particular modes and construct them correctly will be held in the highest esteem.[11]

Sinfonia means, to the Italians, he says, an instrumental work in four or more voices in the manner of a toccata, pavan, galliard or similar 'Harmony.' His most interesting observation is that while the sinfonia may be used at the beginning, it is often used inserted in the middle of a polychoral concerto![12] This apparently corresponds to the practice of having instrumental canzoni or other works performed between movements of the Mass.

Praetorius' brief discussion of the sonata is quite interesting. He finds the word itself is derived from *sonare* [Latin, 'to sound'], which he says simply refers to the fact that it is an instrumental work. He seems, moreover, to have associated the word with *style*, for he adds that beautiful examples of sonatas can be found *in* the canzoni and sinfonias of Gabrieli and other composers. He elaborates on the style association as follows:

> In my opinion there is this difference: the sonatas are composed in a stately and splendid manner like motets, but the canzoni have many black notes and move along crisply, gaily and fast.[13]

As an after thought, Praetorius adds that the word 'sonata' is often used in reference to the music performed by trumpet corps for banquets and dances.

Book Two, of his third volume, is devoted to 'Necessary Precepts' of music. Much of this is theoretical in nature, dealing with the modes, harmony and notation and we shall mention only a few very interesting passages which offer insight to performance.

We find it quite striking that he begins by suggesting that complex ligatures should be replaced with the slur indication.[14] Ligatures are usually presented in early notation literature as a kind of shorthand and we know of no place where there is a suggestion that there was a phrase association, such as would be indicated by a slur. The slur mark itself, of course, was new to notation at this time.

In discussing the necessity of *musica ficta*, the necessary alterations when changing modes, or to avoid the tritone, Praetorius advises the composer that this should *not* be left to the performers.

---

[11] Ibid., 21ff. In the original publication, page numbers 22 and 23, but not the text, were mistakenly omitted.

[12] Ibid., 24.

[13] Ibid.

[14] Ibid., 29.

Composers would do well, as an excellent precaution, to indicate clearly the two chromatic signs, the *cancellatum* [sharp sign] and *rotundum* [flat sign] whenever they are to be employed, in order to prevent hesitation or doubt. This is useful, convenient, and also most necessary to keep singers from becoming confused, as well as for the benefit of ignorant town musicians and organists who cannot read music, let alone sing correctly.[15]

Some of Praetorius' recommendations are of a very practical nature, such as advising that everyone should start expressing in *numbers* the number of rests in the various parts. He observes that he has learned from experience, 'not without some embarrassment,' that this is necessary as musicians are inclined not to pay strict attention or are sometimes caught up in listening to the music.[16]

He also offers a system he devised for numbering the separate parts of large concerti, to avoid confusion, since in a polychoral works there will be several parts named 'tenor,' etc. He also mentions that he made it a habit to count the number of breves in a composition and notate it at the end of his score. Then, when planning the music for a service, by glancing at a chart he had worked out, he could immediately determine how long it would take to perform the composition.[17] This, he observes, is important so as not to delay the remaining church ceremonies. Similarly, he describes a system of marking cuts,[18]

> in case the latter does not work, which enables the musicians to stop in a hurry,
> in case the conductor finds the composition before or after the sermon threatens to last too long—
> since a musician is likely to overdo things.

Another instance of practical advice, which Praetorius has learned from his own experience, has to do with his recommended seating plan for singers.

> I have always put the sopranos together with the tenors and the altos with the bass … The reason is that I have not only seen most other composers do the same, but that it is because of the harmony and the intervals. If the singers stand close to each other and have to read and sing from one part, sopranos and tenors will produce pleasant sixths and the alto and basses fifths and octaves. Otherwise a singer would fill the other's ears with unpleasant fourths, the usual progressions between soprano and alto, or tenor and alto, spoiling the music and making singing distasteful, particularly if the performers carrying the other two parts are not placed near enough to complete and round out the harmony.
>
> Nevertheless I do not want to dictate to anyone in this or other matters, but merely to give my own modest ideas and to tell what I have found to be good from my own experience; for everyone will have his own ideas and will act accordingly.[19]

---

[15] Ibid., 31.
[16] Ibid., 33ff.
[17] Ibid., 88. He had found, for example, that a composition of 640 breves required one hour to perform.
[18] Ibid., 35.
[19] Ibid., 90.

When discussing various signatures at the beginning of compositions, Praetorius finds a general lack of agreement. He suggests that the slower common time signature is used in madrigals and the faster *alle-breve* sign is used in motets.[20] However, he has noticed that in *all* the compositions of Gabrieli, he uses only the *alle-breve* sign. In the works of Viadana, he finds the *alle-breve* sign in compositions with text and the common time sign in instrumental works. His own opinion, agreeing with what he has found in the works of Lassus and Marenzio, was that the common time sign should be used,

> for those motets and other sacred compositions which have many black notes, in order to show that the beat is to be taken more slowly … Anyone, however, may reflect upon such matters himself and decide, on the basis of text and music, where the beat has to be slow and where fast.

In concerti, where madrigal and motets *styles* are found, it is necessary to change tempo. Here, instead of using the common time and *alle-breve* signs, Praetorius suggests it might be better to employ the new practice of using Italian words, such as *adagio*, *presto*, etc.[21]

Praetorius also treats proportional signs and their meaning here, as a topic which he obviously related to the speed of a given beat. Here he feared the conductor might end up beating so fast that,

> we make the spectators laugh and offend the listeners with incessant hand and arm movements and give the crowd an opportunity for raillery and mockery.[22]

That tempo in the sixteenth century was a decision made by the performer, and not the composer, may surprise some readers. Praetorius clearly recommends[23] a level of rubato never mentioned in other treatises. First he makes two general rules, that a performance must not be hurried and that all note values must be observed. Then he adds,

> But to use, by turns, now a slower, now a faster beat, in accordance with the text, lends dignity and grace to a performance and makes it admirable … Some do not want such mixture of [tempi] in any one composition. But I cannot accept their opinion, especially since it makes motets and concerti particularly delightful, when after some slow and expressive measures at the beginning several quick phrases follow, succeeded in turn by slow and stately ones, which again change off with faster ones.

The purpose of this he says is to avoid monotony and he adds the same advice relative to dynamics.

---

[20] Ibid., 48ff.

[21] Ibid., 51.

[22] Ibid., 74.

[23] Ibid., 79ff.

> Besides, it adds much charm to harmony and melody, if the dynamic level in the vocal and instrumental parts is varied now and then.[24]

Later Praetorius returns to dynamics, mentioning that the Italians are beginning to use *forte*, *piano*, etc., to mark changes within a concerto. It is interesting that, in this case at least, he seems to suggest the two, dynamics and tempo, go together.

> I rather like this practice. There are some who believe that this is not very appropriate, especially in churches. I feel, however, that such variety [in dynamics] and change [in tempo] are not only agreeable and proper, if applied with moderation and designed to express the feelings of the music, and affect the ear and the spirit of the listener much more and give the concerto a unique quality and grace. Often the composition itself, as well as the text and the meaning of the words, requires that one [change] at times—but not too frequently or excessively—beating now fast, now slowly, also that one lets the choir by turns sing quietly and softly, and loudly and briskly. To be sure, in churches there will be more need of restraint in such changes than at banquets.[25]

It is particularly interesting here, that Praetorius gives one Latin term, *lento gradu*, which he says was understood to mean that the voice became both softer and slower.

Now Praetorius makes two quite extraordinary suggestions regarding performance, and both have to do with the performance of cadences.[26] Moreover, he switches his text from German into Latin for this discussion, making us wonder if this were exclusive information allowed only to those who were formally educated. In any case, the importance of these two observations cannot be stressed enough, in our view.

Traditional teaching today has always given the understanding that a modern *ritardando* is usually inappropriate for Renaissance music, especially as the composer so often accomplishes this effect through a gradual lengthening of note values at the final cadence. But one will perhaps be surprised to read, for this early date, his recommending of making a fermata on the next-to-last harmony, which he suggests was common practice by fine musicians!

> It is not very commendable and pleasant when singers, organists, and other instrumentalists from habit hasten directly from the penultimate note of a composition into the last note without any hesitation. Therefore I believe I should here admonish those who have hitherto not observed this as it is done at princely courts and by other well-constituted musical organizations, to linger somewhat on the penultimate note, whatever its time value—whether they have [already] held it for four, five, or six *tactus*—and only then proceed to the last note.

His second 'secret' regarding the performance of cadences is based on a principle which can be found in earlier literature, having to do with acoustics. Most musicians know that music sounds better if balanced in such a way that the lower tones are performed louder than higher tones. What is surprising here is the extent to which Praetorius carries this.

---

[24] Later he mentions, with regard to concerti, that a softer dynamic level can also be achieved by simply not having as many instruments doubling in a particular choir. [Ibid., 128 (108)].

[25] Ibid., 132 (112).

[26] Ibid., 80.

> As a piece is brought to a close, all the remaining voices should stop simultaneously at the sign of the conductor or choir master. The tenors should not prolong their tone, a fifth above the bass or lowest voice ... after the bass has stopped. But if the bass continues to sound a little longer, for another two or four *tactus*, it lends charm and beauty to the music [*Cantilenae*], which no one can deny.

Praetorius was probably recalling here of hearing music in a large cathedral where, as one can easily imagine, it would indeed be moving to hear that final bass tone circulating around through the vast empty space of the building.

One of the chapters in this volume Praetorius calls, 'The Method of Teaching Choir Boys who Love and Enjoy Singing, According to the new Italian Style.'[27] Praetorius begins this discussion by presenting his primary aesthetic purpose in music. As the orator must, through his style of speaking, arouse the emotions of the listeners, so,

> Similarly a musician must not only sing, but he must sing artfully and expressively in order to move the hearts of the listeners, to arouse their emotions and to allow the music to accomplish its ultimate purpose.

In order to accomplish this, Praetorius says the singer must have a naturally fine voice, a good mind and a thorough knowledge of music. But he must also understand what makes good taste in music, in particular the art of improvisation.

> He must know ... where to introduce runs or coloraturas (called *passaggi* by the Italians), that is, not anywhere in a composition, but appropriately, at the right time and in a certain way, in order that the listener may not only be aware of the loveliness of the voice, but also be able to enjoy the art of singing.

The singer who has been gifted with a fine voice, but does not know how to do these things correctly will 'provide little joy for the listeners, particularly those who have some knowledge of the art; on the contrary, it makes them sullen and sleepy.'

Learning the art of beautiful singing, says Praetorius, as in all the other arts, is a matter of Nature, Doctrine and Practice. Regarding Nature, Praetorius says again that the singer must have a beautiful, pleasantly vibrating voice ('not, however, in the manner to which some singers in schools are accustomed, but with moderation'), a smooth round throat (which apparently was thought to aid diminutions), be able to sustain a long tone and find some range in which he can produce a full sound without falsetto. The undesirable qualities in a voice are taking too many breaths, singing through one's nose and keeping the voice in the throat and singing with the teeth closed.

Praetorius mentions two specific sixteenth-century vocal techniques which are quite interesting. The first, *Intonatio*,

---

[27] Ibid., 229ff.

refers to the manner in which a vocal piece is started. Opinions vary about this, some wanting to start the tone on the proper written pitch, some a second below, but in a way that the pitch is gradually raised. Some prefer to begin on the third, some on the fourth, some with a delicate and soft voice. All these methods, for the most part, are designated by the term *accentus*.

The second vocal technique, *Exclamatio*,

is the proper means of moving the emotions and must be achieved by increasing the voice. It can be employed with all dotted minims and semiminims in descending motion. Especially the following note which moves somewhat fast, arouses the emotions more than the semibreve, which is more frequently used and more effective with a raising and lowering of the voice, and without *exclamatio*.

By Doctrine, Praetorius seems to mean the proper art of embellishment and improvisation. He provides considerable discussion, including musical examples, but we shall only quote his basic definitions. He begins with diminution.

One speaks of diminution when a longer note is broken up into many other faster and smaller notes. There are different kinds of them [including] accent, tremulo, groppi and tirata.

His examples of 'accent' appear to be single and multiple passing tones, in a variety of rhythmic configurations.

Tremulo 'is nothing but a quiver of the voice over one note; organists call it a mordent.'

Gruppi 'are used in cadences and have to be executed more sharply than the tremuli.' His examples appear as main-note trills.

Tirate 'are long, fast, diatonic runs up or down the keyboard.' The examples, in each case, fill an octave diatonically.

Trills, although he provides numerous configurations in which a trill may be found, he finds more difficult to explain.

These can only be learned through live demonstration and the efforts of a teacher. Then one may learn from the other just as one bird learns by watching another.

Passaggi 'are fast runs which are employed over longer notes, both diatonically and in skips of any size, ascending as well as descending.' In other words, a form of improvisation.

Regarding the third essential, Practice, Praetorius says it would take too long to discuss—better to just study everything he has provided in this volume!

An idea new to the sixteenth century, but one which would of course become a fixture of the Baroque, was the thorough-bass. The discussion of this new idea by Praetorius[28] is interesting not only because it permits us to observe an early contemporary reaction, but for how he discusses its use in actual practice. It is clear that the chief value, in so far as Praetorius was concerned, was that the organ part of a larger work, often called 'General Bass,' was in effect transformed into a kind of miniature score. Previously organists would attempt to fill in har-

---

[28] Ibid., 144 (124) ff.

monies above this single-line general bass part, without, of course, having any real idea what the composer wrote. As a working organist himself, Praetorius is quick to accept this new idea for its help in preventing the organist from being embarrassed in public.

> To be sure, the thorough-bass was not invented for the benefit of negligent or unwilling organists who dislike preparing their scores …
>
> In my humble opinion the greatest advantage of the thorough-bass lies in the fact that it furnishes a fine summary for the benefit of a Kapellmeister or other music director. When several copies are made of such a thorough-bass, especially in concerti for several choirs, these can then be distributed among the organists and lutenists of each choir … marking in red ink the passages they are to play. The conductor should keep one copy for himself, in order to have the entire composition before him, not only because of changes in the *tactus*, to *tripla* and other kinds of time, but also in order to be able to cue the individual choirs.

Before continuing his discussion of thorough-bass, Praetorius digresses to discuss the player who will most use this new form of notation, the organist.[29] The organist, he says, must have three qualifications:

1. He must know counterpoint or at least be able to sing reliably, recognize proportions and the tactus or mensuration correctly, know how to resolve dissonances into consonances on any degree …
2. He has to have a good grasp of the score and be well practiced in handling the keys, keyboards, or stops on the neck of his instrument, be it organ, regal, lute, theorbo or a similar fundamental instrument, so that he does not have to grope for the intervals.… For he knows that the eye has to be turned toward the score, and the motet, concerto, madrigal, or canzona before him at all times and therefore he can divert little attention to the keyboard …

Here he adds, in passing, that since most German organists are accustomed to playing from tablature, they should first write out the score to see how thorough-bass works.

3. He has to have a good ear and be able to follow the singers.

Since we are seeing the thorough-bass practice at its birth, at least so far as Praetorius knows, it is interesting to find that the Italian composers were as yet only sporadically using the numeric symbols. Praetorius is quick to say that if this system is going to work, the numbers must be used all the time. To illustrate the potential problem, Praetorius quotes from a new score he has just received by Bernardo Strozzi:

> Therefore I must not fail to demonstrate clearly and conclusively that such figures are absolutely necessary, no matter what others may say, especially since no organist can know or guess the intentions of the composer. For when the organist would assume the composer had put a fifth in a certain place, it might well have been a sixth … Anyone with a discriminating ear can reflect how pleasant a performance will sound when the organist decides to play a fifth while the singer sings a sixth …

---

[29] Ibid., 145 (125) ff.

> Some say indeed, that one should indulge one's ear and move one's fingers according to what one hears. To those I reply that this will bring no good results. For once the keyboard is struck, a sound is immediately produced, and though one may want to remove one's finger quickly, it has accomplished its task and the dissonance has been heard.

To this Praetorius adds,

> If he were deaf or would not hear very well and had to be constantly afraid of playing a fifth instead of a sixth ... he would with all his fear hardly be able to pay much attention to the thorough-bass. While looking for the sixths and sevenths which he hears, he would skip notes and get off the track completely.

Interestingly, he also has observed that organists, who had not yet mastered reading this new notation, and thus encountered problems in performance, would simply begin improvising to hide the problems!

> But when they heard their own mistakes, they would quickly start with diminutions and runs until finally they managed to calm down. But in this way they would often disturb the [improvisation] of the singers.

In the end, as Praetorius sees it, the real value of the thorough-bass numbers is to help the organist, to prevent errors which might embarrass him.

> Without these figures one would rather have to regard him as a fool whose lot it is, among other things, to have to guess all kinds of foolishness and stupidity. When the organist thus dares to guess and anticipate the ideas in the composer's mind, he will come to grief and appear like a clumsy idiot. Therefore one immediately says that the organist is crazy and has lost his head.

Another advantage of this new invention, especially to Praetorius, an organist himself, was that one only had to keep the thorough-bass parts themselves and not the entire scores. Why, he says, if one had to keep in books of tablature just the music played in one church in Rome during a single year, 'the organist would have to have a bigger library than a doctor at laws.'

The most extraordinary discussion of all, in Volume III of the *Syntagma Musicum*, is Praetorius' description of the new church concerto in its practical application. If one thinks of one of the Gabrieli works for one choir in four-parts for voices and one choir in four-parts for instruments, for example, it is stunning to read the suggestion by Praetorius that such a work was not intended to be played as it appears on paper, but rather what appears on paper can serve as a kind of 'source material' from which more vocal and instrumental parts are extracted to form more choirs. What he is talking about, in effect, is freedom in doubling and he suggests that this should come as no surprise since this kind of doubling of church singers by instrumentalists has been practiced for some time, a fact almost never admitted by music history texts.

> This will hardly annoy anyone who has had experience in princely and other chapels, nor town musicians, if they stop to consider that in their own church choirs they put a cornett or trombone player next to the choir boys with whom they play in unison and octaves.[30]

We see this freedom in application distinctly when he defines *capella*, or one of the choirs which make up a polychoral composition in the Italian style.

> In my opinion the Italians originally used *capella* to designate an additional separate choir, extracted from several different choirs with various kinds of instruments and voices, as they are employed at the larger imperial, Austrian or other Catholic musical establishments ... In every concerto one, two or three such *capellae* can be extracted and set up in different parts of the church, each of them consisting only of four persons, or more if available. In case there is a lack of performers, they can be left out entirely.[31]

Praetorius, an experienced Church conductor, devotes a significant portion of this volume to explaining the perimeters, possibilities and problems in such reassembling and re-orchestrating of the original music. While our purpose here will be to simply outline his major suggestions, it will soon become apparent to the reader how pale in comparison are our performances today of the works of composers such as Giovanni Gabrieli.

Praetorius begins with some observations regarding the vocal parts alone.[32] The reader must keep in mind that Praetorius is thinking here of a work, let us say, which appears on paper for *two* four-voice choirs, one of four voices of singers and one of four voices of instruments, which might be performed as *five or more* four-voice choirs, spread throughout the church. The additional, newly created choirs, consist of material taken from the original two choirs.

The soprano part, 'sung by light and delicate voices of small boys,' he recommends doubling to the extent that it can be heard by all the other choirs. We get our first indication of what Praetorius means by 'doubling' when he speaks in general of the middle vocal parts.

> The middle voices, such as alto and tenor, may similarly move in unison in all choirs. For in such a case it sounds no different than when eight, nine or ten boys—if there are enough singers available—are put on a single part next to one another, sometimes along with an instrumentalist, on trombone, cornett or violin. When one separates the various choirs and puts one here, one there, the third still further off, and so on, it is surely best if all the middle parts in each choir continue throughout a composition. This will allow the harmony to resound more fully and to be more clearly heard throughout the entire church.

The handling of the bass part was a very sensitive issue with Praetorius, for purposes of harmony and acoustics. There is what he calls a 'foundation bass' in every composition, which would be the true bass line in a modern analytical sense. But in polychoral compositions this is (on paper) found at the bottom of only one choir, the remaining or other choirs having

---

[30] Ibid., 138 (118).

[31] Ibid., 133 (113).

[32] Ibid., 91ff.

parts labeled 'bass,' but which are not in fact the true bass. These other basses, Praetorius calls middle basses. The problem is that if a given listener in the church happens to be seated near a choir which does not have the true bass, and is seated too far away to hear the true, or foundation, bass, wherever that choir is located, the listener hears harmonies in incorrect inversions, etc. There are two immediate solutions. If the church has an organ, then the organist plays 'the lowest bass for a foundation,' presumably loud enough to serve as the true bass for the listener. If there is no organ, the conductor or choir master extracts the true bass and spreads it around to the other choirs, thus,

> making the foundation bass heard everywhere and therefore doubling it in each choir is particularly necessary in schools and municipal churches, where one cannot have an organist, regal or positive with every choir as in princely and other chapels.[33]

Having made these suggestions regarding the vocal parts, Praetorius turns to the production at large. He begins by stating that from his experience in the performances he has heard, there are 'three general kinds of flaws frequently heard in concerti.' The first objection is directed toward those who perform the composition as it is written.

1. The discrimination of the performers does not always go far enough to explore and grasp the potential of the artfulness of the written composition.
2. That the instruments are not selected according to the type of concerto, or do not agree with the voices and form discords with them.
3. They put the lowest bass in one choir only.

With regard to the third 'flaw,' Praetorius again recommends that in tuttis the forces be rearranged so that *all* the basses are given the true bass in unison. He quotes an unnamed musician in this regard:

> When the choirs are far separated, the real bass or lowest voice in motets of eight, ten, twelve, sixteen, or more voices should be retained in all choirs whenever they sing together; particularly at the end it should be heard clearly above all others. Otherwise, with no foundation underneath, cacophony results, as both [score] and experience prove.[34]

Now, regarding the distribution of the music in the 'new' choirs which one might create, Praetorius offers some general rules. This discussion,[35] which includes creating new doublings several octaves higher and lower than the original music, is so enlightening we feel obligated to quote it in full.

> Unison doubling can be used throughout a composition without hesitation in high, low and middle voices as well as by instruments.

---

[33] Ibid., 92.

[34] Ibid., 94ff.

[35] Ibid., 95ff.

> Octave doubling can be permitted in all voices, provided one part is sung while the other part is played. In arranging a concerto it is quite customary in the case of a low choir, in which the soprano is to be sung by an alto with three trombones or three bassoons, to double the alto with a violin. The instrumentalist then must play the alto part an octave higher. In tuttis—also when only a few choirs join in together—one can quite fittingly have the alto part of the vocal choir transposed one octave higher and use it with the instrumental choir.
>
> The same thing may be done in all voices, and it does not offend the ear when the part of the singer in a choir is played an octave higher or lower by cornetts, violins, recorders, trombones, or bassoons. For some melody instruments, especially recorders are to be played one or two octaves higher than written. This compares with the practice of combining many different stops on an organ in unisons, octaves, super-octaves and sub-octaves and contrabasses.
>
> Provided enough players are available, quite a splendid sound is produced in tuttis if one assigns to a bass part—at the regular pitch—a common or a bass trombone, a chorist-bassoon, or pommer; in addition a double bass trombone, double bassoon, or large double pommer, and double bass, which all sound an octave lower, like the sub-basses on organs. This is particularly common in contemporary Italian concerti and can be sufficiently justified.

After giving several more examples of doubling, taken from his own experience, Praetorius addresses the principal objection which one might have to this freedom of doubling, which is that it creates parallel octaves. For Praetorius this was a question not of theory but rather a question of the ear responding to the acoustics of the specific performance.

> If someone should have a concerto with only two choirs—one high and one low, positioned at opposite ends—performed at a church or a large hall and should remain standing with the higher choir, he will scarcely hear the lower choir in tuttis when both choirs join in together. He will find then that he can hear no foundation with the higher choir; but in absence of the lower fifths—formed by the foundation bass against the bassett or tenor of the higher choir—dissonant fourths will be heard for the most part, especially if there is no fundamental instrument present, such as a positive or regal. Someone wrote me recently from Venice that,
>
>> the leading musicians in Italy make frequent use of unisons and octaves in tuttis. For they know from their own experience that in large churches, where the choirs are far apart, a much fuller sound is achieved in tuttis when the choirs move in unison or octaves with one another than when they are arranged in such a way that unisons and octaves are carefully avoided, with the result that a perfect and full harmony can no longer be heard.
>
> I could name a number of very excellent older theorists and practical musicians who would not allow me to do this at first. But later, when they had tried it themselves and further reflected upon the matter they had to approve of it and agree with me that having previously considered it very bad, almost like a deadly sin, they themselves now found that unisons as well as octaves in the basses could not be avoided if in all choirs a complete harmony were to be maintained.

Praetorius also quotes the Italian composer Viadana in this regard.

> In concerti for several choirs one can without danger of confusion extract various capellae at one's pleasure. It does no damage then if there are octaves and unisons between the choirs, since one can hardly hear them, the choirs being placed far apart from one another.[36]

---

[36] Ibid., 99.

After arguing for freedom in unisons and octaves, Praetorius adds that parallel fifths are not allowed in any circumstances. He says, however, that he sees frequent diminished fifths in Italian music as well as improvisation [*diminution*] which 'helps to excuse and cover up a great deal.'[37]

Praetorius devotes extensive discussion to the possible choirs of instruments which may be used to augment concerti. Considering that the custom of using wind instruments to double the voices in church was by 1619 now a tradition of more than a hundred years, our attention is drawn to his reference to a new consort, the pure string consort.[38]

> I have come to the conclusion that there is some need for such a capella. For some among us Germans are still unaccustomed to the new Italian invention, according to which sometimes only one, sometimes two or three *Concertat-Stimen* sing to the accompaniment of organ or regal, and do not like this style very well; they are of the opinion that it sounds too empty and is not particularly pleasing and agreeable to those who know nothing about music. Therefore I have had to think of a way to add a choir in four parts which could at all times join in with trombones or *Geigen*.
>
> Since such an ensemble, when used in church, makes for a richer sound, I soon achieved public acclaim ...
>
> It is to be noted here that this capella I have called *fidicinia* because it is better to have it made up of string instruments such as *Geigen*, lutes, harps, and especially viola da gamba, where these are available, and viols da braccio. For the sound of viols and *Geigen* has particular delicacy and is continuous, without the breathing necessary on trombones and other wind instruments.[39]

But, he admits, the idea of a string consort is a new one and not everyone will like it.

> But it is up to anyone's pleasure to use this capella, or leave it out. For, as mentioned above, I have only added it because of the approbation of certain listeners and would not otherwise have deemed it very important.
>
> But if one would wish to compose or arrange for such a *capella fidicinia* ... one would attract those listeners in Germany who still do not know what to make of the new style, and once having roused their interest one would undoubtedly succeed in giving them great pleasure and satisfaction.

Praetorius mentions the string choir again in association with the cornett choir,[40] both being recommended for high choirs. If the part is very high, he prefers the violin,[41] 'unless a good cornett player having complete control of his instrument is available.' For the lower parts he recommends a trombone or a *Tenorgiege*, since the lower cornetts sound 'as unpleasant as a cowhorn.'

He makes his recommendations on the basis of the clef seen in the original music, but also on the basis of mode. Thus for the transverse flute choir we read,

---

[37] Ibid., 100.

[38] The reader is reminded that, in general, the 'professional' player was a wind player until after the middle of the sixteenth century.

[39] Ibid., 136 (116) ff.

[40] Ibid., 154.

[41] Praetorius always uses Geigen.

> On the transverse flute one generally plays the tenth mode, Hypoaeolian, one tone lower. None of the modes are better fitted for these instruments than Dorian, Hypodorian and Hypoaeolian taken down a tone.[42]

He mentions that the lower parts of such a flute choir cannot be heard well on flute and recommends trombone or *Tenorgeige*. However, he says, such a part could be played by a flute an octave higher, 'along with all kinds of other instruments, if no other transverse flutes are involved.'

The recorder choir is of such a range that Praetorius points out such parts can be just as effective with voices or viols da gamba.[43] In the case of a vocal choir, he mentions that boys can learn to sing high A 'provided one would take the pains with them and not mind the trouble to teach them.' He adds that it is sometimes nice if a boy sings the tenor part an octave higher. If a choir of recorders is used, 'I find it better to give the bass part to a bass trombone, or even better a bassoon.' In general, he recommends,

> If one wishes to use recorders alone without any other instruments, in a canzona, motet or concerto for several choirs, one can effectively use the entire consort of recorders, particularly the five sizes beginning with the largest—because the small ones make too much noise—which produce a very pleasant, soft and delicate harmony. They are especially effective in smaller rooms; in the church, however, the large bassett and bass recorders cannot be heard very well.

Regarding the trombone and bassoon choirs, Praetorius is primarily concerned with warning the reader of their limited upper ranges.[44] No trombonist, he says, can play a high G, and bassoons and pommer should be limited to the D above middle C, although 'some players are getting to the point now where they can play four, five and more tones higher with good intonation, provided they are quite skillful and have particularly good reeds.' He concludes with a comment on modes.

> It should be noted here that for such large and low bass instruments as pommers, bassoons or dulcians, and trombones, no compositions are better fitted than those written in Hypodorian (in our usage the second mode) and Hypoionian, which we call the twelfth mode, otherwise called the fifth or sixth mode.

The crumhorn choir presented a difficulty in the fact that the instrument known to Praetorius had a very limited range.[45] For them he recommends Mixolydian transposed down a fourth or Hypomixolydian.

---

42 Ibid., 156.

43 Ibid., 157.

44 Ibid., 159ff.

45 Ibid., 165.

Although the shawm choir was a basic sixteenth-century consort, Praetorius finds them difficult to use as an optional choir in a concerto because they are constructed a fifth apart and hence exceed the ranges of the music.[46] He warns that the higher, or smaller, the shawms are, the more intonation problems there are. In particular, it is best 'to leave the squeakey discant shawm alone.'

The final consort Praetorius discusses is the lute choir, by which he means an ensemble consisting of harpsichords or spinets, theorbos, lutes, pandoras, *Orphoreon*, cithers, a large bass lyra, or 'whatever fundamental instruments of this kind one may be able to gather together,' a mixture he associates with the English.[47] In another illustration of the freedom in performance practice which he documents in his book, Praetorius offers an interesting example from his own experience.

> I once arranged to have the magnificent, immeasurably beautiful motet by de Wert, 'Egressus Jesus,' in seven voices, performed by 2 theorbos, 3 lutes, 2 cithers, 4 harpsichords and spinets, 7 viols, 2 transverse flutes, two boys and an alto singer and large bass viol. This produced a brilliant and magnificent resonance.

In addition to this discussion of the various consorts used in concerti, Praetorius also comments on the proper style of playing the fundamental organ part. This discussion is very important because it reveals, in passing, the extent to which improvisation was also a part of the performance tradition of such works as the familiar concerti of Gabrieli. He begins by quoting Viadana.[48]

> The organist should play from the thorough-bass part, or score, in a very plain style and as cleanly and correctly as possible just as the notes follow one another, without using many runs, especially in the left hand which carries the foundation. But if he wishes to employ some faster movement in the right hand, as in agreeable cadences or similar figures, he has to do this with particular moderation and restraint. Otherwise the singers are impeded and confused, and their voices covered up and drowned out.

Praetorius, in adding his own observations, reveals that the voices as well were engaging in improvisation.

> I have been told by discriminating music lovers of high and noble rank that there are outstanding organists in Italy and elsewhere who, in such concerti, use neither diminutions, nor groppi in cadences, nor mordents. They simply play one chord after another as indicated in the thorough-bass so that the motion of the hands is hardly noticeable.
>
> I rather like the idea that no black notes are used. [But] it does not seem so inappropriate to me if in some concerti the organist observes carefully where the singer makes his diminutions and passaggi and then plays in a plain style, moving stepwise from one key to the next. But as the singer, after completing many varied passaggi, beautiful diminutions, groppi, tremoletti, and trilli, becomes tired

---

[46] Ibid., 166.

[47] Ibid., 168.

[48] Ibid., 137ff.

and sings the following notes without elaboration, the organist may introduce agreeable diminutions, etc., but only in the right hand—and attempt to imitate the singer's figures, diminutions, variations, etc. Thus the two collaborate, as it were, in producing an echo, until the singer recovers and again proceeds to display his artful embellishments. In my humble opinion, one should not omit all mordents and tremoletti when no diminution or similar figures are employed; for they will not disturb the singer's voice at all, or not nearly as much as all sorts of runs and diminution.

Continuing his discussion of performance practice, Praetorius says it is not possible for the organist to perform all concerti bass parts at sight. Therefore he should look over the composition, to determine the style and to plan his progressions more perfectly. During tuttis in concerti, the organist should 'use both manual and pedal simultaneously.' However, Praetorius advises, that is enough.

> But one should not add other stops, for the delicate and soft tone of the singers would otherwise be smothered by the heavy noise of the many organ stops and then the organ would be more prominent than the singers.

Praetorius also mentions the well-known tradition of having one or more string instruments double the fundamental organ line. In his discussion of the various instruments appropriate to this function, we are most interested in his reference once again to frequency of improvisation. Here, as in all cases Praetorius has mentioned, he means by 'improvisation' what the player does with the part in front of him. In this light the following is rather extraordinary.

> He who plays the lute (which is the noblest instrument of them all) must play it nobly, with much invention and variety, not as is done by those who, because they have a ready hand, do nothing but play runs and diminution from beginning to end, especially when playing with other instruments which do the same, in all of which nothing is heard but babel and confusion, displeasing and disagreeable to the listener. Sometimes, therefore, he must use gentle strokes and repercussions, sometimes slow *passaggi*, sometimes rapid and repeated ones, sometimes something played on the bass strings, sometimes beautiful conceits, repeating and bringing out these figures at different pitches and in different places; he must, in short, so weave the voices together with long *Gruppen*, trills, and accents, each in its turn, that he gives grace to the consort and enjoyment and delight to the listeners, judiciously preventing these embellishments from conflicting with one another and allowing time for each.[49]

The new violin also appears on the scene playing in the same fashion.

> The discant Geige, known as Violono, must also play beautiful *passaggi*, distinct and long, with playful figures and little echoes and imitations repeated in several places, passionate accents, mute strokes of the bow *Gruppi*, trills, etc.[50]

---

49 Ibid., 146ff.

50 Ibid., 148.

It is necessary to pause briefly here to invite the reader to imagine the era of ensemble performance before the composer took on the responsibility of orchestration. If one attended a banquet and heard, for example, five players with crumhorns for the entire evening the sound itself would soon become tiresome to the ear. The early civic musicians eliminated this problem by erecting a long table in the banquet hall which was filled with five instruments each of a variety of families of instruments. Then the performers could perform one composition on crumhorns, the next on trombones, followed by singing a composition, etc. This alternation was the mother of the art of orchestration. Following this long tradition, Praetorius documents a similar practice in the performance of the new church concerti. Here he presents examples of this kind of tonal alternation[51] by grouping according to what he calls the 'Arts.' Again, we can only briefly outline his extensive proposals.

The First Art he calls *Tubiciniae and Tympanistriae*, in which one employs the aristocratic trumpet corps.[52] The problem here is that these trumpet corps often did not read music and performed only memorized 'concert' works, their so-called sonatas. But Praetorius found that if the trumpets were, let us say, in D, if he wrote a Church concerto in D they could simply join in, playing their memorized pieces, and it would sound OK—provided the Church choir master took their tempo!

> One thing should be remembered here: since the trumpeters are in the habit of rushing, because the trumpet requires a good deal of breath which cannot be sustained very well at a slow pace, one should accelerate the beat when the trumpeters enter, otherwise they always finish their sonatas too soon. Later the beat may be lengthened, until the trumpeters start in again.

And if, due to some greater need by the duke, the trumpeters do not show up, you can perform the composition anyway.

> But if one cannot, will not, or must not use the trumpeters and timpanists, such compositions can nevertheless be performed quite well in town churches without trumpeters.

The Second Art consists of having four boys placed in separate locations in the church, with three of the boys joined by various instruments and the fourth by the full choir. The special effect occurs with,

> each of them singing what is found in his part, cleanly and with animation, clearly and distinctly as if reciting the notes. Thereupon the entire vocal and instrumental ensemble and organ respond, in a style which the Italians call *concerti ripiani* …
>
> It is also quite delightful, and the words of the text can be heard better, if at the beginning the first verse is sung by the boys alone to the accompaniment of a soft and delicate stop on the organ, the *Geigen* and lutes being omitted entirely …

---

51 Ibid, 169ff., with reference to his own compositions.

52 At the end of this volume [Ibid., 224] Praetorius lists his books. Among these is a now lost work entitled, *Instruction in the use of trumpets and timpani with full ensemble in electoral and princely chapels, also in other churches, depending on time and place, without producing confusion or drowning out the other vocal and instrumental parts.*

> If one or two discant parts are blown on instruments and not sung, one can nevertheless easily guess the preceding texts and rhymes of the first and third discants from the parts of the second and fourth discants which respond to the former like an echo.
>
> On some organs there are *Cymbel-Glücklein* which, added to the full choir, sound quite delightful and attractive. If they are not too loud, they may sometimes be used even when the boys sing alone.

The Third Art is what we would call today a small church concerto,[53] familiar in such compositions by Schütz, for example, for one singer and three trombones. Such a choice, in the process of alternating sonorities, would represent a kind of church chamber music. Praetorius discusses this type extensively, with respect to instrumentation and placement. One may have two, three or four singers standing with or apart from an organ; or one may have choirs with solo singers and instruments; or one can alternate singers and instruments, as in the case of a psalm. Another 'manner,' as he calls it, is to have choirs with the discant parts improvising.

One may have a string choir double the organ, 'good for inexperienced organists.' The reader gains the impression here that the current string playing must have been rather robust, for Praetorius warns,

> It must be noted here that in small churches, chapels, and rooms, when one, two or a few more voices alone are singing and a regal or other fundamental instrument is available, the string choir must play quite delicately and softly or must be omitted entirely. Otherwise the voices cannot be heard properly because of the sound of the instruments. But in large churches, the string choir can be separated a little further from the voices and placed by itself. But it must not be left out; on the contrary it is highly necessary in order to provide a richer sound.

Another manner of the Third Art is to have a full chorus, with instruments, which enters in the middle or at the end of a composition. An alternative manner is to have two instrumental choirs, carrying the inner parts, but positioned in a separate location. He adds that the further away the instruments are from the singers, the better the individual voices can be heard. Another manner related to these is to have the two discants improvising, with instrumental choirs used in alternation.

The Fourth Art is a polychoral work in which an entirely different chorale is sung between the verses of the original composition, with the penultimate verse sung in unison with the congregation. Similarly, the Fifth Art is the insertion of an independent 'Hallelujah' or 'Gloria' fragment 'at the beginning, in the middle and at the end of a composition.' This, he says, may be thought of as a kind of ritornello and he mentions that he got the idea from an Italian composition, by Fattorini, in which the composer had inserted some Latin phrases in this manner. Praetorius found this style to be very pleasing[54] and he mentions that he thought of

---

53   Although music history texts do not discuss it, there were at this time four general kinds of concerti: a large and small church concerto and a large and small concerto da camera.

54   The repeating ritornello was one of the important steps toward later 'architectural forms,' which are found pleasing by the right hemisphere of the brain.

writing out a separate Hallelujah or Gloria in every mode so they could be published and made available for this purpose. But, he moans, in his previous efforts which have been published there were 'so many errors that the mere thought of it makes me break out in a cold sweat.'

The Sixth Art follows in the same manner, but with an instrumental sinfonia played as a kind of prelude at the beginning of the choral work. An alternative might be to perform a 'pavan, mascherada, or ballet in place of the sinfonia,' but one must make sure the piece has a full harmony. Here again, ritornelli may be inserted in the middle of the choral work and astonishingly he recommends,

> a galliard, saltarello, courante, volta, or similarly gay canzonette, which, however, must not be too long. I have found that quite a few people have liked this very well.

This, of course, will strike the reader as being rather extraordinary, performing light dance works in the service. But it seems to have been a practice which continued for some time. A notable example is the famous Gossec *Te Deum*, performed in 1790 for the great first celebration of the French Revolution. This very somber, slow-paced work for band and choir has within its over all design two independent instrumental dance pieces, of a faster tempo and a completely different character from the rest of the work. One wonders, in modern performance, what in the world the listener thinks of this.

In the Seventh Art,

> The chorale is sung by one voice while the other parts, be it two, three, four, five or more, play on instruments alone, producing harmony, but also fantasies and imitations against the chorale.

Four more 'Arts' follow which involve various combinations of the previous recommendations. The Twelfth Art, and final one, involves the use of echo effects.

Praetorius, at the end of this volume, lists a number of his own compositions which demonstrate these varied concerti techniques. Some of these have as many as thirty-five separate voices in nine choirs! We can only say again, how pale in comparison are our performances today of the Italian polychoral compositions.

Finally, putting everything together, Praetorius deals with an essential problem in the performance of large-scale concerti, and that is tuning. His first suggestion is that it would be nice if the organist could play a little prelude to the concerto, for then the players could simultaneously be tuning.

> In conclusion I must kindly suggest to all organists that they should generally make use of an appropriate introduction when attempting to perform a concerto with several choirs in church or at a banquet. Although it may not belong to the main work, it would serve to make the audience favorably disposed, receptive and attentive, and thus entertain them better—just as excellent orators do who intend to hold forth extensively on important matters. Using their preludes at the beginning they

should thus call the listeners and the entire ensemble of musicians together, as it were, so that they may look for their parts and tune their instruments properly and that way prepare themselves for the start of a good and well-sounding performance.[55]

That is theory; practice is something else! Praetorius suddenly remembers his own experience, when, as he was playing an organ prelude, the instruments suddenly ruined his performance by beginning to tune for the following concerto. Being an organist, he cannot understand why all those players can't tune their instruments and 'warm-up' at home, before they come to perform!

But it creates great confusion and din if the instrumentalists tune their bassoons, trombones, and cornetts during the organist's prelude and carry on loudly and noisily so that it hurts one's ears and gives one the jitters. For it sounds so dreadful and makes such a commotion that one wonders what kind of mayhem is being committed. Therefore everyone should carefully tune the cornett or trombone in his lodging before presenting himself at the church or elsewhere for performance and he should work up a good embouchure with his mouthpiece [at home] in order that he may delight the ears and hearts of the listeners rather than offend them with such cacophony.

Praetorius returns to the problem of pitch in the performance of concerti, now as it is affected by personalities of the performers, as he pleas for a more democratic spirit of unity.

This point above all must be carefully kept in mind in all concerti, by instrumentalists as well as singers. No one must cover up and outshout the other with his instrument or voice, though this happens very frequently, causing much splendid music to be spoiled and ruined. When one thus tries to outdo the other, the instrumentalists, particularly cornett players with their blaring, but also singers through their screaming, they cause the pitch to rise so much that the organist playing along is forced to stop entirely. At the end it happens then that the whole ensemble through excessive blowing and shouting has gone sharp by a half, often indeed a whole tone and more.[56]

---

[55] Ibid., 151.

[56] Ibid., 148ff.

Ancient Views on Church Music in the Baroque

Know thyself,
what a vile, horrible, abominable sinner thou art ...[1]
John Bunyan

IT HAS EVER BEEN THE MOST BASIC NATURE AND PURPOSE OF MUSIC to communicate the feelings and emotions of man. During the seventeenth century this ancient truth comes out into the open where it finally becomes a topic of discussion by all members of society, including the Church, as the reader will notice in the pages that follow.

The ability to openly discuss feelings was one of the byproducts of that seventeenth-century explosion of free thought in science and philosophy which we call the Enlightenment. While we associate the Enlightenment today with religious crises and scientific breakthroughs, its spirit reached everywhere. Consider, for example, the English language itself. Between 1580 and 1623 nearly eleven thousand new words were coined. There were so many new books coming out that Robert Burton, author of the famous *Anatomy of Melancholy*, moaned, 'We are oppressed with them, our eyes ache with reading, our fingers with turning.'[2]

The concurrent Thirty Years War had the effect not of solving religious divisions, but instead forever creating a Europe of multiple religious convictions. It follows that one begins to find more pronounced views on music, including church music.

In Rome, the Vatican still labored in its ancient dogma,[3] partly as a very human response to its fear of the Reformation. This had, of course, a negative impact on the arts, perhaps most apparent in painting, where nudes were no longer allowed and only the fervent pleas of a group of artists prevented the Pope Clement VIII from having Michelangelo's *Last Judgment* completely painted over. And let us not forget the Inquisition, which was also a product of the paranoid, conservative atmosphere in the Vatican. Monteverdi, in his letters, writes of the great lengths he had to go to to get his son (a doctor of medicine!) released after being imprisoned by the Inquisition for reading a book he did not realize was on the prohibited list. This hostile atmosphere cannot be separated from the fact that during the seventeenth century great numbers of distinguished musicians left for other countries, making Italian music important everywhere except in Italy.

---

[1] 'The Saints' Knowledge of Christ's Love,' in *The Works of John Bunyan*, ed. George Offor (London: Blackie and Son, 1853), II, 28. John Bunyan (1628–1688) is considered the greatest prose writer among the Puritans of the seventeenth century.

[2] Quoted in Stuart Isacoff, *Temperament* (New York: Vintage, 2001), 159.

[3] Isaac Newton reported he believed in a divine creator, but he was unconvinced that God abides by Church doctrine. [Quoted in Isacoff, *Temperament*, 21]

All this notwithstanding, things were changing in Rome. We have a report by Andre Maugars, a violist and secretary to Cardinal Richelieu, who was sent to Rome in 1639, in which he clearly documents a festival day performance in Rome of a work in the new church concerto style.[4] He describes this composition as requiring nine choirs, with nine conductors, and featuring much variety in instrumentation and much improvisation. Another contemporary, Vicenzo Giustiniani, also reports on this new style of Roman church music, commenting especially on the new emphasis on emotion and the use of improvisation.

By the second half of the seventeenth century, the greatest musical problem facing the Vatican was the amazing growth in popularity of Italian opera and the danger of its influence on church music. Consequently, a series of papal edicts, in 1657, 1662, 1678 and 1692 were issued in an attempt to prevent secular influences from entering the service. In the 'Edict on Music' of 1665, the pope demands that no words but the Latin in the Roman Missal be used and that the music be 'grave, ecclesiastical and devout' in character.[5] The rather dark character of this attack can be seen in the following provisions.

> Eighth, that within a period of twenty days from the publication of the present edict by the Fathers Superior and others whose duty it is, that shutters or narrow grilles be placed in the choirs, be the latter temporary or permanent, and that the said shutters be of such a height as the singers will not be seen, under pain of privation of office and other penalties at the discretion of the Holy Visitation.
>
> Ninth, that no maestro di cappella or other person entrusted with ordering the music or giving the beat contravene the aforesaid prescriptions under pain of privation of office and perpetual disqualification from the exercise of this office and the right to make music; and, moreover, that he be punished with a fine of 100 scudi, of which one quarter be given the denouncer (whose name will be held secret), three quarters to the holy places at the discretion of the Holy Visitation, and with other penalties—including corporal punishment—at the discretion of the said Holy Visitation.

Pope Urban VIII tried to divert this influence by attempting to interest composers in writing large-scale theater works focusing on the lives of the saints. These must have been as tedious as a Latin sermon, for one of them, *Il palazzo incantato*, by Luigi Rossi, lasted eight hours in performance!

In any case, the influence of opera on church music in Italy can be clearly documented, as for example, in the writings of Banchieri:

> The Masses, Psalms, Canticles, Motets and Concerti to be performed with the organ must be in the *affettuoso*, devout, attractive, and *recitativo* styles, imitating the words and employing gravity in concerting them.[6]

---

4   Andre Maugars, 'Response faite a un curieux sur le Sentiment de la Musique d'Italie, Ecrite a Rome le premier Octobre 1639,' quoted in Carol MacClintock, *Readings in the History of Music in Performance* (Bloomington: Indiana University Press, 1979), 118ff. He also reports on the extraordinary improvisation he heard performed by Frescobaldi.

5   The full text is quoted in Lorenzo Bianconi, *Music in the Seventeenth Century*, trans. David Bryant (Cambridge: Cambridge University Press, 1987), 108ff.

6   Adriano Banchieri, 'Conclusioni nel suono dell' organo,' quoted in Ibid., 129ff. Banchieri (1567–1634) was a priest at the monastery S. Michele near Bologna, as well as a composer and organist.

He particularly recommends in this regard the works of Viadana, in which 'one, two and three voices sing in *stile recitativo*.' One reference to theater style also reminds us that Italian terms such as 'allegro' had earlier conveyed a style as well as a tempo.

> The *stile allegro* should not always be used, only at certain times; and also at the Elevation of the Holy Sacrament some serious sonata that moves one to devotion should be used.[7]

Whatever was the line between the influence of theatrical styles and the inclusion of actual secular music in the service, it was a line which seems to have been repeatedly crossed. A visitor to Venice in 1709 reported,

> I do not know whether it is to cheer the Satans' days up even more and for the special satisfaction of those who only go to church as they go to the theaters, that they do scarcely ever fail in this noisy music to mingle the same that one has heard at the operas, and which have pleased more, and that with no scandal to the favor of the words which one changes and which, instead of expressing, for example, the loves of Pyramus and Thisbe, say something of the life of the saint whose feast day it is.[8]

Tosi was one who was particularly concerned with what he was hearing in the church.

> Since poor counterpoint has been condemned, in this corrupted age, to beg for a piece of bread in churches, while the ignorance of many exults on the stage, the most part of the composers have been prompted from avarice, or indigence, to abandon in such manner the true study, that one may foresee (in not succored by those few, that still gloriously sustain its dearest precepts) music, after having lost the name of science, and a companion of philosophy, will run the risk of being reputed unworthy to enter into the sacred temples, from the scandal given there, by their Jiggs, Minuets, and Furlanas; and, in fact, where the taste is so depraved, what would make the difference between the church music and the theatrical, if money were received at the church doors?[9]
>
> ......
>
> [We must condemn] the presumption of a singer who gets the words of the most wanton airs of the theater rendered into Latin, in order to sing them with applause in the Church; as if there were no manner of difference between the style of one and the other; and, as if the scraps of the stage were fit to offer to the Deity.[10]

Marcello, in his satire, 'Theater in the Modern Style' [1720] also mentions hearing disguised secular music in the church.

> The composer will have little facility in reading and still less in writing, and therefore will not understand Latin, even though he must compose church music, into which he will introduce sarabands, gigues, courantes, etc., calling them fugues, canons, double counterpoints, etc.[11]

---

[7] Ibid., 127.

[8] C. Freschot, *Nouvelle relation de Venise* (Utrecht, 1709), 318.

[9] Pier Francesco Tosi, *Opinioni de' cantori antichi, e moderni* (Bologna, 1723), VII, xxv.

[10] Ibid., IX, lxiv.

[11] Benedetto Marcello, *Il treatro alla moda*, quoted in Oliver Strunk, *Source Readings in Music History* (New York: Norton, 1950), 525.

Another change in church music was the growing interest in string instruments. This change in taste, which brought to an end centuries of domination by winds in art music, was due in part to the advance in the quality of the manufacture of string instruments during the seventeenth century and in part because of the interest of the humanists in the ancient Greek accounts of singing accompanied by strings. Of the wind instruments, Agazzari notes,

> I shall say nothing, because they are not used in good and pleasing consorts, because of their insufficient union with the stringed instruments and because of the variation produced in them by the human breath, although they are introduced in great and noisy consorts.[12]

At the same time, during the seventeenth century the winds were going through a dramatic transformation of their own, with the retirement of nearly all the renaissance instruments and their replacement by the modern instruments by 1675. Clearly a long period ensued during which makers struggled with improvements and players struggled with having to learn entirely new instruments, resulting in complaints about such things as intonation. A typical example is found in Charles Burney, who maintains he heard Alessandro Scarlatti say, 'My son, you know I hate wind instruments, they are never in tune.'[13]

Before leaving this subject, we might digress to mention that it appears that only in Spain, more conservative than the Vatican, did the wind choir continue to hold its place of preference in the church. In the cathedral in Granada during the seventeenth century one found flutes, cornetts, shawms, bassoons, horns, trumpets and trombones. In the royal chapel in Toledo, the pastoral chants were accompanied by two shawms, a small 'bassoon-serpentine' and bassoon.[14] There are also extant three Masses by Francisco Soler (1625–1688), composed for voices and wind band.[15] In Portugal, during the seventeenth century, cornetts, sackbuts and bassoons regularly accompanied the singers in the Badajoz Cathedral.[16]

If anything, there seemed to be a greater enthusiasm for church music in Spanish Mexico. Torquemada, writing in 1615, found singers proficient in polyphonic music in every town of a hundred or larger and 'competent instrumentalists are also found everywhere.'[17] An Englishman in 1625 concluded the people were drawn to the churches 'more for the delight of the music than for any delight in the service of God.'[18]

---

[12] Agostino Agazzari, *On Playing upon a Bass in … Consort*, quoted in Ibid., 425. One of his letters in 1606 speaks of the individual aesthetic characteristics of the lute, viols and violin.

[13] Quoted in Robert Donnington, *The Interpretation of Early Music* (New York, 1964), 548.

[14] Edmond Vander Straeten, *La Musique aux Pays-Bas* (New York, 1969), VIII, 194ff.

[15] Copies in E:Bc and E:G.

[16] George Grove, *The New Grove Dictionary of Music and Musicians* (London: Macmillan, 1980), IV, 817.

[17] Juan de Torquemada, Monarqu'a indiana, quoted in Steven Barwick, 'Mexico,' in *The Early Baroque Era* (Englewood Cliffs: Prentice Hall, 1994), 352.

[18] Ibid., 355.

In Puebla, the second largest city in seventeenth-century Mexico, the cathedral used recorders, shawms, cornetts, sackbuts and bassoons to double, or even replace the voices. Violins do not appear until the eighteenth century. Surviving documents indicate that one of the leading composers, Juan Gutierrez de Padilla, maintained a shop in his home in which salaried workers produced 'ecclesiastical instruments,' bassoons, shawms and recorders.[19] The most important composer of this cathedral, Antonio de Salazar (1650–1715), set to music a poem by Juana Ines de la Cruz, which speaks of the typical church ensemble as being 'clarino, trumpet, cornett, trombone, bassoon, and organ.'[20]

To return to our consideration of Italy, one cannot forget Venice, which always seemed to operate apart from the complete control of the Vatican. An Englishman, Thomas Coryat, visiting in 1608, heard one of the new strings in church, in addition to the older trombones and cornetts.

> At that time I heard much good Musicke in Saint Markes Church, but especially that of a treble violl which was so excellent, that I thinke no man could surpasse it. Also there were sagbuts and cornets as at St. Laurence feast which yeeled passing good musicke.[21]

Already in 1614 we can see in Alessandro Grandi, then working in Ferrara but soon to become *vicemaestro* to Monteverdi at St. Mark's, a desire to introduce the principles, if not the style, of the new opera into his motets. In the preface to this publication, Grandi makes both a subtle attack on the old, but official, polyphonic style and a subtle argument for something new.

> Here, the clarity of the words is not impaired by the fugues of the composer, nor [are the words] rendered any less excellent through the art of song; on the contrary, the latter is elevated and humbled, runs, rests and cries with the [words]; in whatever way the former is arranged, the latter gives rise to a more effective portrayal of the affections therein.[22]

A very large number of instrumental works, especially canzoni, were published at this time in Venice and records at the cathedral prove this music was performed during the service. In particular, between 1600 and 1620 many canzoni were published by such composers as Canale, Quagliati, Bonelli, Troilo, Bona, Merula, among many others, in addition to collections of such works. Among the latter is the collection published by Rauerij (Venice, 1608), which includes some Gabrieli works found nowhere else and the canzona for four instrumental

---

[19] Grove, *Dictionary*, XV, 441 and XIV, 76.
[20] Ibid., XVI, 412.
[21] Quoted in Egon Kenton, *Life and Works of Giovanni Gabrieli* (American Institute of Musicology, 1967), 37.
[22] Quoted in Bianconi, *Music in the Seventeenth Century*, 118.

choirs by Massaino.[23] This cathedral was also a great center for organ playing and the organists there were especially known for their improvisation. But even in Venice one could be too progressive. The officials of the cathedral in 1639 issued an edict warning that,

> in musical solemnities, the use of instruments other than those normally used in the church is not allowed; in particular, refrain from the use of warlike instruments such as trumpets, drums and the like, more suitable for armies than for the house of God … and that all the musicians, secular and ecclesiastical alike, while serving their musical functions, must come dressed in surplices; and, finally, that the transposition of words or the singing of newly-invented words not contained in the holy books [is not] permitted except at Offertory, Elevation and after the Agnus Dei.

Musically, some of the most interesting performances in Venice were heard in the educational institutions supported by the Church. There were the widely-known concerts sponsored by the *Scuole San Rocco*, for which one has been left us a recollection by an English visitor:

> This feast consisted principally of Musicke, which was both vocall and instrumental, so good, and delectable, so rare, so admirable, so super-excellent, that it did even ravish and stupifie all those strangers that never heard the like. But how others were affected with it I know not; for mine own part I can say this, that I was for the time even rapt up with Saint Paul into the third heaven. Sometimes there sung sixteen or twenty men together, having their master or moderator to keepe them in order; and when they sang, the instrumentall musitians played also. Sometimes sixteene played together upon their instruments, ten Sagbuts, foure Cornetts, and two Viol-de-gambaes of a extraordinary greatness; sometimes tenne, six Sagbuts and foure Cornets; sometimes two, a Cornet and a treble violl. Of these treble viols I heard three severall there, whereof each was so good, especially one that I observed above the rest, that I never heard the like before. Those that played upon the treble viols, sung and played together, and sometimes two singular fellowes yeelded admirable sweet musicke, but so still that they could scarce be heard but by those that were very neare them. These two Theorbists concluded that nights musicke, which continued three whole hours at the least. For they beganne about five of the clocke, and ended not before eight.[24]

The other remarkable church institutions which fostered music in Venice were the four *Ospedali*, charitable institutions and schools for female orphans, which in the case of those in Naples and Venice began to develop into early conservatories. We are fortunate to have eyewitness accounts of several of the individual *Ospedali*. In 1698 the Russian, Petr Tolstago, wrote from Venice regarding the *Incurabili*:

> In Venice there are convents where the women play the organ and other instruments and sing so wonderfully that nowhere else in the world could one find such sweet and harmonious song. Therefore people come to Venice from all parts with the wish to refresh themselves with these angelic songs.[25]

---

[23] This collection is available in a modern score from Leland Bartholomew, Music Department, Fort Hays State College, Fort Hays, Kansas.

[24] Quoted in Denis Arnold, 'Music at the Scuola de San Rocco,' *Music and Letters* 40 (July, 1959): 236ff.

[25] Quoted in W. Kolneder, *Antonio Vivaldi, his life and work* (London, 1756), 10ff.

A rather extraordinary account of another of these *Ospedali*, that of the *Mendicanti*, is found in the *Confessions* of Jean-Jacques Rousseau, dating from two years after the death of Vivaldi.

> A kind of music to my mind far superior to that of the operas, and which has not its like in Italy is that of the *scuole* ... Every Sunday at the Church of each of these schools one has during Vespers motets for full choir and orchestra composed and directed by the greatest masters in Italy, performed in balconies with grilles, entirely by girls of whom the oldest is not twenty. I can imagine nothing so voluptuous, so touching as this music ... The church [the *Mendicanti*] was always full of those who liked this sort of music; even the actors from the Opera would come and conform themselves to the true taste in singing on these excellent models. What grieved me were those accursed grilles, which only allowed the sound to pass, and hid from me the angels of beauty of which the sound was worthy.[26]

Naturally we are most interested today in the *Seminario musicale dell' Ospitale della Pieta*, for it was there that the great Vivaldi was employed between 1704 and 1740. There is a curious reference to this *Ospitale*, and its musical activities, by a traveling Englishman in 1720.

> There are in Venice four of these female hospitals ... the Incurabili, the Pieta, Ospitaletto and the Mendicanti ...
> Every Sunday and holiday there is a performance of music in the chapels of these hospitals, vocal and instrumental, performed by the young women of the place; who are set in a gallery above and are hid from any distinct view of those below by a lattice of iron-work. The organ parts, as well as those of the other instruments, are all performed by the young women. They have an eunuch [Vivaldi!?] for their master and he composes their music. Their performance is surprisingly good; and many excellent voices are among them.[27]

Another interesting account, because it hints at the amorous activities for which the Italian Catholic institutions were known, is by K. L. von Poellnitz, who visited in 1729.

> I am in some doubt whether I should reckon the music of the Venetian churches in the number of its pleasures; but on the whole, I think I should, because certainly their churches are frequented more to please the ear, than for real devotion. The church of La Pieta which belongs to the nuns who know no other father but love, is most frequented. These nuns are entered very young, and are taught music, and to play on all sorts of instruments, in which some of them are excellent performers. Apollonia actually passes for the finest singer, and Anna-Maria for the first violin in Italy. The concourse of people to this church on Sundays and holidays is extraordinary. It is the rendezvous of all the coquettes in Venice, and such as are fond of intrigues have here both their hands and hearts full. Not many days after my arrival in this city I was at this very church, where was a vast audience, and the finest of music.[28]

---

[26] J. J. Rousseau, *Confessions*, II, vii.

[27] Quoted in Marc Pincherle, 'Vivaldi and the Ospitali of Venice,' The Musical Quarterly 24 (July, 1938): 301.

[28] K. L. von Poellnitz, *Memoirs* (London, 1737), I, 414.

In 1739, just before Vivaldi retired from this service, another visitor recalled,

> The most transcendent music here is that provided by the Ospitali. There are four of these, all of them for girls—illegitimate, orphans, or those whose relatives are not able to care for them. They are being brought up at the expense of the state and are being trained most especially to excel in music. In addition they sing like angels, they play the violin, the flute, the organ, the clarinet, the violoncello, and the bassoon. In short, there is no instrument so large as to give them pause … They are the sole performers at each concert, and some forty of them take part. I swear there is nothing more pleasing to be seen than one of these pretty young sisters in her white dress with a cluster of pomegranate blossoms over one ear, conducting an orchestra and beating time with all the grace and precision imaginable.[29]

In this same year Charles de Brosses also mentions the quality of the orchestral performances.

> The one of the four *ospedali* I visit most often, and where I enjoy myself most, is the Ospedale della Pieta; it is also the first for the perfection of the symphonies. What strictness of execution! It is only there that one hears the first attack of the bow, so falsely vaunted at the Paris Opera.[30]

It is generally understood that a great deal of Vivaldi's music, in particular the concerti, was composed for these students. This seems clear by his contract for 1735.

> The same maestro will have to provide for our girls concertos and other compositions for all sorts of instruments, and he will have to come with the assiduousness necessary for instructing the girls and making them well able to perform them.[31]

Church music in Germany during the Baroque suffered greatly from the Thirty Years' War (1618–1648). This epic battle between the Protestants and Catholics not only was very destructive of the church buildings themselves, but, of course, drained the various states of available funds. There was very little left to support professional musicians who formerly made their career in the church. It is hard to imagine Heinrich Schütz having to write this plea in 1652 to the secretary of the Elector of Saxony on behalf of a court chapel singer.

> But now I can no longer conceal from you that the bass singer who some time ago had to pawn his clothes again, and ever since has been living at his house like a wild beast of the woods, has informed me through his wife that he now must and wishes to leave us.[32]

After thirty years of war it then took a number of years for the necessary economic recovery which would make possible renewed spending on large-scale musical productions. Thus even by 1661, Schütz cannot yet see any improvement in the city where he has been employed, as he writes the elector:

---

29 Quoted in Arnold, 'Music at the Scuola de San Rocco,' 301ff.
30 Charles de Brosses, *Lettres familieres sur l'Italie* (Paris, 1931), I, 238ff.
31 Archivio di Stato, Venice, Ospitali, busta 692, Notatorio Q, fol. 113r.
32 Letter to Christian Reichbrodt, May 28, 1652, quoted in Gertrude Norman and Miriam Shrifte, *Letters of Composers* (New York, Knopf, 1946), 14ff.

> In conclusion, so far as I am personally concerned, I must protest that, after promising practically everything but the blood from my veins, actually advancing a part of my means to suffering musicians, it will be altogether impossible for me to continue here in Dresden any longer. With regard to this place I am not merely announcing but stating positively that I would prefer death to living under such harassing conditions.[33]

And let us not fail to contemplate on the loss to musical literature the war caused in the case of this one single man, one of the most talented composers of the seventeenth century. What great church concerti this man, a student of Gabrieli, might have composed!

In areas not so directly in the path of the armies, the churches still profited from the availability of the civic instrumentalists, whose contracts often required their presence not only on Sundays, but also at choir rehearsals. Such a contract from Rothenburg o. T. reads,

> The Stadtpfeifer should appear with their instruments as early as Vesper prayer time, on Sundays and Festival days, but also during the week as the Kantor requires, to help rehearse the music to be used the following Sunday.[34]

These instrumentalists were, no doubt, continuing the tradition begun in the fifteenth century of doubling the voices where the old polyphony was being used or performing their own parts in church concerti. In one case, in Wittenberg in 1628, when some choir director did not make use of the available instruments, preferring *a cappella* music, he was fired.[35] In most cases, however, there was close cooperation between the civic and church authorities and Bach, as a person in charge of church music, on occasion served on a jury to select new civic instrumentalists.

Churches began to assemble their own instrument collections, although generally the new strings appear fairly late (St. Thomas in Leipzig bought its first violin in 1701). By the end of the Baroque, however, the nucleus of the modern orchestra had arrived, as we find in the cantatas of Bach. But perhaps there were more people like Mattheson, who, in 1739, looked back with nostalgia to the old Renaissance and early Baroque practice.

> Here this question occurs to me: why then do the good cornetts and trombones, which were formerly closely related and were highly esteemed as staples by the expert civic musicians as well as the composers, seem to be banished now so completely from the churches, at least from the ones here, as if they had been discovered to be incompetent? For the former instrument is still very penetrating, with all its harshness; whereas the other sounds very majestic and fills a large church beautifully. Whoever wants to may answer this question.[36]

---

33 Quoted in Hans Moser, *Heinrich Schütz* (St. Louis: Concordia, 1936), 209.

34 Quoted in Wilhelm Ehmann, *Tibilustrium* (Kassel, 1950), 41.

35 A. Werner, *Stadtische und fürstliche Musikpflege in Weissenfels* (Leipzig, 1911), 219.

36 Johann Mattheson, *Der vollkommene Capellmeister* (1739), trans. Ernest Harriss (Ann Arbor: UMI Research Press, 1981), III, xxv, 7.

In Germany as elsewhere there was now open ridicule of the old polyphonic-mathematic style of composition. Johann David Heinichen, in 1711, refers to the old Scholastic Church mathematic rules as 'lifeless manipulation of notes but not on the actual sound,' thus 'the more one sinks into the excesses of such stereotyped artifices, the more one necessarily must depart from the Ear.' Writing polyphonic counterpoint is laborious, he says, 'on the order of a farmer loading manure onto wheelbarrows.' The excessive use of counterpoint, he says, 'is the shortest path to musical pedantry, ruining many fine talents that otherwise could have been developed into something worthy … From such study, one can make a dull contrapuntist out of any dumb boy, but one cannot make a composer with good taste.'

Another German who criticized the polyphonic style was Johann Mattheson, who, in quoting the text to Bach's *Cantata* Nr. 21, provides a witty demonstration of the nonsense of this style.

> I, I, I, I had much grief, I had much grief, in my heart, in my heart. I had much grief, etc., in my heart, etc., etc., I had much grief, etc., in my heart, etc., I had much grief, etc., in my heart etc., etc., etc., etc., etc. I had much grief, etc., in my heart, etc., etc.[37]

During the seventeenth century there were some German composers who found it much more difficult to break with the past. The gifted composer, Samuel Scheidt, who wanted a funeral motet in the style of Palestrina for his own funeral, observed that he heard nothing which surpassed the old style.

> I am astonished at the foolish music written in these times. It is false and wrong and no longer does anyone pay attention to what our beloved old masters wrote about composition. It certainly must be a remarkably elevated art when a pile of consonances are thrown together any which way.[38]

The composers of both schools seemed to agree on one idea, that the church was no place for music which resembled that of the rapidly growing new medium: opera. Heinrich Schütz, warned,

> If you will forgive me, gentlemen of the music profession, there now prevails in the church an altogether new kind of song, but one that is prolix, abrupt, fragmentary, dance-like, and not at all reverential. It is better suited to the theater and the dance hall than to the church. In seeking Art, we are losing time-honored devotion to prayer and song.[39]

Another who complained of the influence of the theater was Christian Gerber, who wrote in 1732,

---

[37] Quoted in Hans T. David and Arthur Mendel, *The Bach Reader* (New York: Norton, 1966), 299.

[38] Letter to Heinrich Baryphonus, January 26, 1651, quoted in Gertrude Norman and Miriam Shrifte, *Letters of Composers* (New York, Knopf, 1946), 17.

[39] Hans Moser, *Heinrich Schütz*, 702.

> Although a moderate kind of music may remain in the church … it often sounds so secular and gay, that such music better suits a dance floor or an opera than a divine service. Least suitable of all is it, in the opinion of many pious souls, to the Passion, when the latter is sung …
>
> But gradually the Passion story, which had formerly been sung in simple plain chant, humbly and reverently, began to be sung with many kinds of instruments in the most elaborate fashion, occasionally mixing in a little setting of a Passion Chorale which the whole congregation joined in singing, and then the mass of instruments fell to again. When in a large town this Passion music was done for the first time, with twelve violins, many oboes, bassoons, and other instruments, many people were astonished and did not know what to make of it. In the pew of a noble family in church, many Ministers and Noble Ladies were present, who sang the first Passion Chorale out of their books with great devotion. But when this theatrical music began, all these people were thrown into the greatest bewilderment, looked at each other, and said: 'What will come of this?' An old widow of the nobility said: 'God save us, my children! It's just as if one were at an Opera Comedy.'[40]

And in a letter to the Leipzig town council after his appointment, Bach promised of his future composition for the church,

> that it shall not last too long, and shall be of such a nature as not to make an operatic impression, but rather incite the listeners to devotion.[41]

In Hamburg local preachers took the opportunity to attack even the cantata as being too much like opera, an influence they declared to be unchristian and the work of the Devil.[42] It was in this same town, by the way, that an incompetent organist obtained a post in competition with Bach, by bribing the audition committee.

> I remember, as will still a large number of parishioners, that some years ago a certain great virtuoso [Bach], whose merits have since earned him an important cantorate [in Leipzig], presented himself as an organist in a town of no small size [Hamburg], performed on many of the finest organs, and aroused the admiration of everyone for his mastery. But there also appeared among other incompetent journeymen, the son of a wealthy artisan [named Heitmann], who could execute preludes better with thalers than with his fingers. It was he (as might easily be guessed), who gained the post.[43]

In France the conservative clergy of Paris issued the *Ceremoniale parisiense* in 1662, a document based on the discussions of the Council of Trent, which warned against using any instrument but the organ in the church. This may have retarded somewhat the introduction of string instruments in French church music, as one does not find violins introduced at Notre Dame in Paris until the end of the seventeenth century or in the case of Chartres and Nantes,

---

[40] Quoted in Hans T. David and Arthur Mendel, *The Bach Reader*, 442, 229ff.

[41] Johann Sebastian Bach, letter to the Leipzig town council, May 5, 1723, quoted in Piero Weiss, *Letters of Composers Through Six Centuries* (Philadelphia: Chilton, 1967), 65.

[42] George J. Buelow, 'Hamburg and Lubeck,' in *The Late Baroque Era* (Englewood Cliffs: Prentice Hall, 1994), 201.

[43] Johann Mattheson, *Der musicalische Patriot*, 316.

the early years of the eighteenth century.⁴⁴ In any case, no doubt influenced by popular demand, some of the larger cathedrals of Paris also appear to have ignored the *Ceremoniale parisiense*, for one finds complaints such as that of Le Cerf de la Vieville:

> Very many people no longer go to High Mass or Vespers in the Cathedrals unless the Bishop is officiating there with additional Musical forces; nor to Tenebrae unless the lessons are set by the hand of a famous composer.⁴⁵

He complains that for the past twenty-five years even trumpets and drums have been heard in the church.

But in some churches there must have been only unaccompanied singing, which at least one listener, the Duchesse d'Orleans, Elisabeth Charlotte, found very boring. She recalled one occasion when a cough kept her from sleeping for three days:

> I remembered that I always sleep in church as soon as I hear preaching and nuns singing. Therefore I drove to a convent where there was to be a sermon. The nuns had barely begun to sing when I went to sleep, and I slept throughout the three-hour service; that made me feel much better.⁴⁶

She mentions this again a few years later.

> If your Grace were Catholic and had to go to mass, she would find it even more boring, for not only is it always exactly the same, but one never hears anything but the singing of vowels, like 'aaaa eeee oooo iiii'; it is enough to make one burst out of one's skin with sheer impatience.⁴⁷

And she holds these views even though she preferred church music with no instruments. She assures us, 'I doubt that Our Lord is all that amused by instruments.'⁴⁸

Finally, we must not pass by without reference to Voltaire, who was always a careful observer of everything going on in France. While Catholic France remained unchanged by the Reformation, Voltaire was inspired by the times to create infamous writings about religion. Although he never failed to state that he believed in God, his attacks focused on a long list of rather vulnerable topics, such as the selling of indulgences, errors and impossibilities in the accounts of the Scriptures (such as the Flood⁴⁹) and the general topic of money—the wealth

---

44   Grove, *Dictionary of Music* (1980), XIV, 194; IV, 177; XIII, 21.

45   Marcelle Benoit, in 'Paris, 1661–87: the Age of Lully,' in *The Early Baroque Era* (Englewood Cliffs: Prentice Hall, 1994), 257.

46   Letter to the duchess Sophie, March 19, 1693, quoted in Charlotte Elisabeth Orléans, *A Woman's Life in the Court of the Sun King* (Baltimore: Johns Hopkins University Press, 1997), 81.

47   Letter to the Electress Sophie, January 15, 1696, quoted in Ibid., 89.

48   Letter to the Electress Sophie, December 16, 1699, Ibid., 118.

49   Voltaire, in his *Philosophical Dictionary*, 'Universal Deluge,' in *The Works of Voltaire* (New York: St. Hubert Guild, 1901), VIII, 75, observed of the Flood,

> I do not comprehend how God created a race of men in order to drown them, and then substituted in their room a race still viler than the first.

of the Churchmen vowed to poverty then representing about a third of the wealth of France. Voltaire was particularly hard on all forms of Church-encouraged superstitions and relics, as for example the church of Puy-en-Velay which claimed to possess the foreskin of Jesus.[50]

As time went on, he became more outspoken about the Roman Church. In a letter to Catherine, Empresses of Russia, he observed,

> I confess, your Majesty, that I loathe the papal government: I find it ridiculous and abominable: it has brought stupidity and bloodshed to half of Europe for too many centuries.[51]

We have chosen a representative passage by Voltaire on music he heard in the church and it is in the spirit of the previous thought, here, specifically, on the idea of performing a Te Deum after victories on the field.

> The most wonderful part of this infernal enterprise is that each chief of the murderers causes his flags to be blessed, and solemnly invokes God before he goes to exterminate his neighbors. If a chief has only the fortune to kill two or three thousand men, he does not thank God for it; but when he has exterminated about ten thousand by fire and sword, and, to complete the work, some town has been leveled with the ground, they then sing a long song in four parts, composed in a language unknown to all who have fought, and moreover replete with barbarism.[52]

In England, the most important seventeenth-century story is that of the Puritans and their attempts to reform church music. We shall return to this subject below, but first we must wonder, since music and art is always a mirror of life, if it were not, in part, the poor state of church music which opened the door for the Puritans' attack on music.

Consider, for example, John Earle's characterization of 'The Common Singing-men in Cathedral Churches.' They are, he says,

> a bad society, and yet a company of good fellows, that roar deep in the choir, deeper in the tavern. They are the eight parts of speech, which go to the Syntax of Service, and are distinguished by their noises much like bells, for they make not a consort but a peal. Their pastime or recreation is prayers, their exercise drinking, yet herein so religiously addicted that they serve God oftenest when they are drunk … Though they never expound the scripture they handle it much, and pollute the Gospel with two things, their conversation and their thumbs. Upon work-days they behave themselves at prayers as at their pots, for they swallow them down in an instant. Their gowns are laced commonly with streamings of ale, the superfluities of a cup or throat above measure.[53]

---

[50] *Philosophical Dictionary*, 'Superstition,' in Ibid., XIV, 18. He also quotes here a letter purported to have been left by Jesus after he visited a French church in 1771.

[51] Letter to Catherine of Russia (November, 1770), in *Voltaire and Catherine the Great*, trans. A. Lentin (Cambridge: Oriental Research Partners, 1974), 93.

[52] *Philosophical Dictionary*, 'War,' in Ibid., XIV, 195ff. When Gossec was commissioned to write a large-scale work for the anniversary of the fall of the Bastille in 1790, and elected to write a Te Deum, he was much criticized in the press for this same association of this form with past military exploits.

[53] John Earle, *Microcosmography* [1628] (St. Clair Shores: Scholarly Press, 1971), 94. John Earle (1600–1665) was a chaplain to Charles II, during the king's exile, and a dean of Westminster during the Restoration.

In the view of Thomas Mace the reason for this state of affairs was the poor pay given cathedral singers, which Mace found 'very low, inconsiderable, insufficient, unbecoming and uncomfortable.' As a consequence, the singers often were forced to take other jobs. Why should we be surprised, Mace asks, that when they sing in church they 'make sour faces, and cry, or roar out aloud.' He concludes,

> Now I say, these things considered how certainly true they are, first in reference to the [singers] pitiful-poor-wages, and likewise to the general dead-heartedness, or zeal-benumbed-frozen-affections in these our time, toward the encouragement of such things; how can it be imagined that such [singers] should be fit and able performers in that duty, which necessarily depends upon education, breeding and skill in that quality of music, which is both a costly, careful and a laborious-attainment, not at all acquirable (in its excellency) by an inferior-low-capacitated men.[54]

Mace was also disturbed by the intonation of the singers and declared it better not to sing at all than to sing out of tune. This, because of the close relationship he perceived between music and the divine.

> For as I often used to say, that as concording unity in music is a lively and very significant simile of God, and Heavenly joys, and felicities, so on the contrary, jarring discords are as apt a simile of the Devil, or Hellish tortures.[55]

Another difficulty for the choir was that since the time that Henry VIII closed all the Catholic schools in England, a primary source of the training of boy singers, England, in effect, began to run out of boy singers for the churches. This is one reason why Roger North proposes that now perhaps is the time to allow women to sing.

> One might without a desperate solescisme maintain that if females were taken into the choirs instead of boys, it would be a vast improvement of choral music, because women come to a judgment as well as voice, which the boys's do not arrive at before their voices perish ... But both text[56] and morality are against it; and the Roman usage of castration is utterly unlawful, and a scandalous practice where it is used.[57]

There is one eyewitness account we know which suggests the congregation itself shared the poor discipline associated above with the singers. It is found in, of all places, Defoe's *Robinson Crusoe*, when he recalls attending a special religious service celebrating the victory of the English over the French at Ramillies.

---

54 Thomas Mace, *Musick's Monument* [1676] (Paris: Editions du Centre National de la Recherche Scientifique, 1966), 23 ff. Mace (1613–1709) was a 'clerk' at Trinity College, Cambridge.

55 Ibid., 3.

56 I Corinthians 14:34:
> As in all the churches of the saints, the women should keep silence in the churches.

57 Quoted in John Wilson, *Roger North on Music* (London: Novello, 1959).

> But I observed these grave people, in the intervals of their worshiping God, when it was not their turn to sing, or read, or pray, bestowed some of the rest of their time in taking snuff, adjusting their perukes, looking about at the fair ladies, whispering, and that not very softly neither, to one another, about this fine lady, that pretty woman, this fine duchess, and that great fortune, and not without some indecencies, as well as words as of gestures.[58]

Contrary to the almost total lack of discussion found on this subject in music history texts, improvisation had been practiced in churches for centuries. There is evidence to suggest that this practice was also found in England during the Baroque. A complaint in the famous *Spectator* for 25 October 1711, describes a visiting woman from the city who improvises during village church music.

> But what gives us the most offense is her theatrical manner of singing the psalms. She introduces above fifty Italian Airs into the Hunderdth Psalm, and whilst we begin 'All People' in the old solemn tune of our fore-fathers, she in quite a different key runs divisions on the vowels, and adorns them with the graces of Nicolini … we are certain to hear her quavering them half a minute after us to some sprightly airs of the opera.

A contemporary poem by George Herrick is especially interesting for its reference to improvisation by a singer and an instrumentalist together.

> What sweeter musick can we bring,
> Than a Carol, for to sing
> The Birth of this our heavenly King?
> Awake the voice! Awake the string!
> Heart, ear, and eye, and everything
> Awake! the while the active finger
> Runs divisions with the singer.[59]

When Charles II returned from his exile in France to begin the Restoration, he brought back much culture, including the concept of the large string ensemble, known in Paris as the 'Twenty-four Violins of the King.' Subsequently we find in the Diary of John Evelyn, for 21 December 1662, a record of the first introduction of strings in the royal chapel.

> One of his Majesty's chaplains preached; after which, instead of the ancient, grave, and solemn wind music accompanying the organ, was introduced a concert of twenty-four violins between every pause, after the French fantastical light way, better suiting a tavern, or a playhouse, than a church. This was the first time of change, and now we no more heard the cornett which gave life to the organ; that instrument quite left off in which the English were so skillful.

---

[58] Daniel Defoe, *Robinson Crusoe*, (Garden City: Doubleday, n.d.), III, 151ff.

[59] L. C. Martin, *The Poetical Works of Robert Herrick* (Oxford: Clarendon Press, 1963), 364. Herrick (1591–1674) is considered one of the most gifted of the so-called Cavalier Poets.

For the uninformed reader we might explain that for centuries wind players had been the professional musicians and string players the amateurs, often called 'beer fiddlers.' Beyond this tradition, at least one writer explained that besides only the winds are always in tune and for this reason should be maintained in the church.

> [String instruments] ar often out of tun; (Which soomtime happeneth in the mids of the Musik, when it is neither good to continue, nor to correct the fault) therefore, to avoid all offence (where the least shoolde not bee givn) in our Chyrch-solemnities onely the Winde-instruments (whose Notes ar constant) bee in use.[60]

Although the arrival of the string ensemble concept initiated a new chapter of both church and court music in England, so wonderfully represented in the music of Purcell, there was an ill-wind beginning to blow which would have dramatically harmful political consequences in England and on all later music of the English-speaking world. A radical, fundamentalist religious movement had begun during the sixteenth century and within it there began to appear voices who wanted to sever the connection of music and the church. We read this, for example, in Spinoza, who knows only a God who recognizes no emotion.

> God is without passions, neither is he affected by any emotion of pleasure or pain.[61]

Why, he says, 'there are men lunatic enough to believe that even God himself takes pleasure in [hearing] harmony.'[62]

More harmful were the Puritans, who returned to the fourth-century world of the New Testament as a model for their faith. As there are no descriptions of instrumental music used in the service in the New Testament, instruments must go—and so, in England, they destroyed all church organs. The actual order (Lords and Commons Ordinance of 1644) called for,

> the speedy demolishing of all organs, images and all matters of superstitious monuments in all Cathedrals ... throughout the kingdom of England and the Cominion of Wales, the better to accomplish the blessed reformation so happily begun and to remove offences and things illegal in the worship of God.

In the spirit of this ordinance, we have an account from Exeter, for example, that records that soldiers,

---

60 Charles Butler, *Principles of Musick* (1636).
61 Spinoza, *The Ethics*, 'Of the Power of the Understanding, or of Human Freedom,' Proposition XVII.
62 Ibid., 'Concerning God,' Appendix .

brake down the organs, and taking two or three hundred pipes with them in a most scorneful and contemptuous manner, went up and down the streets piping with them; and meeting with some of the Choristers of the Church, whose surplices they had stolne before, and imployed them to base servile offices, scoffingly told them, 'Boyes, we have spoyled your trade, you most goe and sing hot pudding pyes.'[63]

In addition, the Puritans wished to remove from the service all the elaborate trappings of the Catholic tradition. We find this point, and music again, condemned in a typical sermon given in 1628.

> This makes me call to remembrance, a strange speech little better than blasphemy, uttered lately by a young man, in the presence of his Lord, and many learned men: 'I had rather goe forty miles to a good service, then two miles to a Sermon.' And what meant he by a good service? His meaning was manifest; where goodly Babylonish robes were worn, imbroydered with images. Where he might heare [an ensemble] of singers, with Shakebuts, and Cornets, and Organs, and if it were possible, all kinde of Musicke, used at the dedication of Nabuchodonosors golden Image ... For if religion consist in Alter-ducking, Cape-wearing, Organ-playing, piping and singing ... if I say religion consist in these and such like superstitious vanities, ceremoniall fooleries, apish toyes, and popish trinckets, we had never more Religion then now.[64]

A few men who considered themselves strong Puritans nevertheless argued for the value in the use of music in religion. One was the famous John Milton (1608–1674). In his treatise on 'Church-Government,' Milton, after pointing to the numerous instances of songs and lyric poetry in the Old Testament, defines the purpose of church music. Music, he says, should be a,

> power beside the office of a pulpit, to inbreed and cherish in a great people the seeds of virtue, and public civility, to allay the perturbations of the mind, and set the affections in right tune.[65]

One of his poems, 'Il Penseroso,' is a testimonial to his being moved by the emotional power of music.

> But let my due feet never fail,
> To walk the studious Cloisters pale,
> And love the high embowed Roof,
> With antique Pillars massy proof,
> And storied Windows richly dight,
> Casting a dim religious light.
> There let the pealing Organ blow,
> To the full voiced Choir below,
> In Service high, and Anthems clear,
> As may with sweetness, through mine ear,

---

[63] Peter Holman, in 'London: Commonwealth and Restoration,' in *The Early Baroque Era* (Englewood Cliffs: Prentice Hall, 1994), 307.

[64] Peter Smart, *A Sermon Preached in the Cathedrall Church of Durham, July 7, 1628* (London, 1640), 22ff.

[65] 'Church-Government,' in *The Works of John Milton*, ed. Frank Patterson (New York: Columbia University Press, 1931–1938), III, 238.

> Dissolve me into extasies,
> And bring all Heaven before mine eyes.[66]

Another religious theme, under which Milton discusses music at length, is the creation of the world. All musicians must take pleasure in the discovery in Milton's 'Paradise Lost' that on the seventh day God rested, as we are told in the Old Testament, but, says Milton, he did not rest in silence—he listened to a concert!

> But not in silence holy kept; the Harp
> Had work and rested not, the solemn Pipe,
> And Dulcimer, all Organs of sweet stop,
> All sounds on Fret by String or Golden Wire
> Tempered soft Tunings, intermixt with Voice
> Choral or Unison …
> Creation and the six Days acts they sung.[67]

Adam, in this same poem, also has the opportunity to hear an advance performance of the 'Carol' which the angels would sing in the future when they announce the birth of Jesus.[68]

An English Puritan of the following generation was William Penn (1633–1718), one of the most strict and fervent of the Quaker preachers. His preaching led to a famous trial in 1669 in which the jury acquitted him and the judge imprisoned the jury for doing so! In 1677 he traveled to America to help bring Quakerism to the new continent and one of the American states still carries his name.

In the few references to music in his sermons, Penn's view is invariably negative. In a typical passage, which he based on Amos 6:4–5, Penn warns,

> Woe unto you Protestants … that chant to the sound of music of the viol, and invent to yourselves instruments of music.[69]

He includes music again in a list of luxuries not appropriate to a Christian, and he considers all of them 'an excessive indulgence of self in ease and pleasure … A disease as epidemical as killing: it creeps into all stations and ranks of men.'[70]

---

[66] 'Il Penseroso,' in Ibid., I, 45.

[67] Ibid., VII, 594ff.

[68] Ibid., XII, 365.

[69] 'Truth Exalted,' in *The Select Works of William Penn* (London: William Phillips, 1825), I, 122. Amos 6: 4, 5 reads,

> Woe to those who lie upon beds of ivory …
> who sing idle songs to the sound of the harp,
> and like David invent for themselves instruments of music.

[70] 'No Cross, no Crown,' in Ibid., I, 454ff.

> Sumptuous apparel, rich unguents, delicate washes, stately furniture, costly cookery, and such diversions as balls, masques, music-meetings [concerts], plays, romances, etc., which are the delight and entertainment of the times, belong not to the holy path that Jesus and his true disciples and followers trod to glory.

Later in this sermon, Penn promises condemnation for those who attend such diversions.

Needless to say, Penn never described in his publications any specific musical performance he may have heard in England. In fact, the only such description is found in a publication describing his impressions of the New World. Penn includes a brief description of the music of the Indians, as part of what he calls their worship service.

> The other part is their cantico, performed by round dances, sometimes words, sometimes songs, then shouts, two being in the middle that begin, and by singing and drumming on a board, direct the chorus: their postures in the dance are very antic, and differing, but all keep measure. This is done with equal earnestness and labor, but great appearance of joy.[71]

The poison spread by the Puritans has not yet been eradicated. There are pockets of Christians even today who will not permit instrumental music in their religious services solely because the practice is not found in the New Testament.

But the Puritans changed society in another way, it was they who removed music from the practice of the cultured class in England. Even after a century during which two great leaders, Henry VIII and Elizabeth I, were performing musicians, by the end of the sixteenth century the Puritans had managed to completely reverse the cultural role of music. No longer a characteristic of the definition of the gentleman, it was now to be avoided by gentlemen. Music was to be played by the lower class, by slaves. One could listen, but not participate, as in the famous analogy by Chesterfield which held that it was OK to eat beef, but a gentleman should not be his own butcher. It is difficult for the modern reader to believe that society could change so dramatically, to go so quickly from a society in which music had a noble and appreciated position to one in which Chesterfield could write, in one of his famous letters to his son in Italy,

> As you are now in the musical country, where singing, fiddling and piping are not only the common topics of conversation, but almost the principal objects of attention; I cannot help cautioning against giving into those (I will call them illiberal) pleasures (though music is commonly reckoned one of the liberal arts), to the degree that most of your countrymen do when they travel in Italy. If you love music, hear it; go to operas, concerts, and pay fiddlers to play to you; but I insist upon your neither piping nor fiddling yourself. It puts a gentleman in a very frivolous, contemptible light; brings him into a great deal of bad company; and takes up a great deal of time, which might be better employed. Few things would mortify me more, than to see you bearing a part in a concert, with a fiddle under your chin, or [an instrument] in your mouth.[72]

---

[71] 'A General Description of Pennsilvania,' in Ibid., III, 230.

[72] Earl of Chesterfield, letter to his son, April 19, 1749.

It must be acknowledged that music in the English-speaking world has never recovered from the impact of these radical, fundamentalist Puritans. We musicians are still slaves and every musician has had some experience where he has felt this prejudice directed toward him by the 'upper class.' The major orchestras of the United States may consist of very talented and highly educated musicians, who are very highly paid, but they remain slaves of their local aristocracy—their job is to do what they are told.

One of the balms of the study of the lessons of history is that the basic nature of music lying in its ability to communicate emotions, and in the universality of those emotions, leave us assured that music will eventually and inevitably outlast the angry voices of prejudice. Thank God!

Bibliography

CHAPTER ONE: ANCIENT VIEWS ON MUSIC AND RELIGION IN ANCIENT CIVILIZATIONS

Arrian. *The Campaigns of Alexander*. New York: Penguin, 1978.

Athanassakis, Apostolos N. *The Homeric Hymns*. Baltimore: Johns Hopkins University Press, 1976.

Athenaeus. *Deipnosophistae*.

Bacon, Roger. 'Causes of Error,' XIV, in *The Opus Majus of Roger Bacon*. Translated by Robert Burke. New York: Russell & Russell, 1962.

Clement of Alexandria. *The Miscellanies*. Translated by William Wilson (Edinburgh: T & T Clark, 1884.

Euripides. *Electra*, 868.

_____. *Iphigenia in Aulis*.

_____. *The Heracleidae*.

Farmer, Henry G. 'The Music of Ancient Mesopotamia,' in *The New Oxford History of Music*. London: Oxford University Press, 1966.

Gilbert Murray. *The Complete Plays of Aeschylus*. London: George Allen, 1952.

Herodotus. *The History of Herodotus*. Translated by David Grene Chicago: University of Chicago Press, 1987.

Horace. *Epistle*

_____. *Odes*.

Josephus. *Jewish Antiquities*.

Lactantius. 'The Divine Institutes,' in *The Works of Lactantius*. Translated by William Fletcher. Edinburgh: T. & T. Clark, 1886.

Manniche, Lise. *Music and Musicians in Ancient Egypt*. London: British Museum Press, 1991.

Martyr, Saint Justin. *The Monarch or The Rule of God*. Translated by Thomas B. Falls. New York: Christian Heritage, Inc.

Origen. *De Principiis*. Translated by Frederick Crombie, in *The Writings of Origen*. Edinburgh: T. & T. Clark, 1871.

Ovid. *Amores*.

_____. *Metamorphoses*.

_____. *The Art of Love*.

Plato. *Ion*

_____. *Laws*.

_____. *Meno*.

_____. *Republic*.

Propertius. *Poems*

Scotus Eriugena, Johannes. *Periphyseon on the Division of Nature*. Translated by Myra Uhlfelder. Indianapolis: Bobbs-Merrill, 1976.

Sendrey, Alfred. *Music in the Social and Religious Life of Antiquity*. Rutherford: Fairleigh Dickinson University Press, 1974.

Strabo. *The Geography of Strabo*. Translated by H. L. Jones. Cambridge: Harvard University Press, 1960.

Symonds, John. *Wine Women and Song; Mediaeval Latin Students' Songs*. New York: Cooper Square Publishers, 1966.

Tacitus. *Annals*

Tertullian. *De Anima*. Translated by Alexander Roberts in *Ante-Nicene Christian Library*. Edinburgh: T. & T. Clark, 1884.

Thucydides. *The Peloponnesian War*. New York: Modern Library, 1951.

Tibullus, *Poems*.

Tourneur, Cyril. *The Atheist's Tragedy*.

Whicher, George. *The Goliard Poets*. [self-Published], 1949.

Zeydel, Edwin H., trans. *Vagabond Verse*. Detroit: Wayne State University Press, 1966.

CHAPTER TWO: ANCIENT VIEWS ON MUSIC AND PROPHESY

Bacon, Roger. 'Causes of Error,' XIV, in *The Opus Majus of Roger Bacon*. Translated by Robert Burke. New York: Russell & Russell, 1962.

Booty, Jill, in *Lope de Vega, Five Plays* (New York: Hill and Wang, 1961)

Cicero. *De Divinatione*

Horace. *Epodes*

_____. *Odes*

Ovid. *Amores*

_____. *Letters in Exile*

_____. *Metamorphoses*

Oigen. *De Principiis*. Translated by Frederick Crombie, in *The Writings of Origen*. Edinburgh: T. & T. Clark, 1871.

Propertius. *Poems*.

Saint Justin Martyr. *The Monarchy or The Rule of God*. Translated by Thomas B. Falls. New York: Christian Heritage, Inc.

Spencer, Herbert. *Essays on Education and Kindred Subjects*. London: J. M. Dent & Sons, 1966.

Strabo. *The Geography of Strabo*. Translated by H. L. Jones. Cambridge: Harvard University Press, 1960.

Tibullus, *Poems*.

Virgil, *Aeneid*. Translated by L. R. Lind. Bloomington: Indiana University Press, 1958.

_____. *Georgics*

Chapter Three: Ancient Hebrew Views on Music and Religion

Engel, Carl. *The Music of the Most Ancient Nations*. London: Reeves, 1909.

Josephus. *Jewish Antiquities*.

Revised Standard Version (Old Testament). New York: Nelson, 1952.

Sendrey, Alfred. *Music in the Social and Religious Life of Antiquity*. Rutherford: Fairleigh Dickinson University Press, 1974.

Chapter Four: Ancient Views on Music and Religion among the Romans and Early Christians

Aquinas, Thomas. *Disputations*, XXXIX.

Caesar, Julius. *Civil Wars*

Catullus. *Poems*.

Cicero. *Pro Balbo*.

Clement of Alexandria. *The Instructor*. Translated by William Wilson. Edinburgh: T. & T. Clark, 1884.

_____. *Exhortation to the Greeks*. Translated by G. W. Butterworth. Cambridge: Harvard University Press, 1939.

_____. *The Miscellanies*. Translated by Alexander Roberts. Edinburgh: T. & T. Clark, 1869

Commodianus. *In Favor of Christian Discipline* in *The Writings of Tertullianus*.

Durant, Will. *Caesar and Christ*. New York: Simon and Schuster, 1944.

Eisenman, Robert. *James the Brother of Jesus*. New York: Viking, 1996.

Felix, Marcus Minucius. *Octavius*. Translated by G. W. Clarke. New York: Newman Press, 1974.

Lactantius. *Epitome of the Divine Institutes*. Translated by William Fletcher in *The Works of Lactantius*. Edinburgh: T. & T. Clark, 1871.

_____. *The Divine Institutes*. Translated by William Fletcher in *The Works of Lactantius*. Edinburgh: T. & T. Clark, 1886.

_____. *Epitome of the Divine Institutes*. Translated by William Fletcher in *The Works of Lactantius*. Edinburgh: T. & T. Clark, 1871

Letters of the Younger Pliny. New York: Penguin Books, 1985

Livy. *History of Rome*.

Lucretius. *The Way Things Are*.

McKinnon, James W. 'Musical Instruments in Medieval Psalm Commentaries and Psalters,' *Journal of the American Musicological Society* 21 (1968): 3–20.

Novatian. *The Spectacles*. Translated by Russell J. DeSimone, in *Fathers of the Church*. Washington, D.C.: The Catholic University of America Press.

Origen. *De Principiis*. Translated by Frederick Crombie, in *The Writings of Origen*. Edinburgh: T. & T. Clark, 1871.

Origen. *Word as Flesh* in Hans Urs von Balthasar, *Spirit and Fire*. Translated by Robert J. Daly. Washington, D.C.: The Catholic University of America Press, 1984

Ovid. *Amores*

_____. *Fasti*.

_____. *Metamorphoses*.

Philetaerus. *The Aulos Lover*, quoted in Athenaeus, *Deipnosophistae*.

Poems of St. Paulinus of Nola. Translated by P. G. Walsh. New York: Newman Press, 1975

Saint Cyprian. *On the Dress of Virgins*. Translated by Sister Angela E. Keenan. New York: Fathers of the Church, Inc., 1958.

Saint Gregory of Nazianzus. *Concerning his Own Affairs*. Translated by Denis Meehan. Washington, D.C.: The Catholic University of America Press.

Sendrey, Alfred. *Music in the Social and Religious Life of Antiquity*. Rutherford: Fairleigh Dickinson University Press, 1974.

St. Augustine. *Sermon 257*. Translated by Sister Mary Muldowney in *Sermons on the Liturgical Seasons*. New York: Fathers of the Church, 1959.

_____. *The Confessions*.

St. Basil. *The Long Rules*. Translated by Sister Monica Wagner, in *Saint Basil Ascetical Works*. New York: Fathers of the Church, Inc., 1950

_____. *Homily 14*, in *Exegetic Homilies*. Translated by Sister Agnes Way. Washington, D.C.: The Catholic University of America Press.

_____. *Letter to the Clergy of Neo-Caesarea*, in *Letters of Saint Basil*. Translated by Sister Agnes Way. New York: Fathers of the Church, 1955.

St. John Chrysostom. 'Exposition of Psalm XLI,' in Oliver Strunk, *Source Readings in Music History*. New York: Norton, 1950.

_____. *Exposition of Psalm XLI* in Oliver Strunk, *Source Readings in Music History*. New York: Norton, 1950

Tertullian, *On Prescription Against Heretics*. Translated by Alexander Roberts in *Ante-Nicene Christian Library*. Edinburgh: T. & T. Clark, 1884.

Varro, Marcus. *On the Latin Language*.

Virgil. *Aeneid*. Translated by, L. R. Lind. Bloomington: Indiana University Press, 1958

_____. *Georgics*.

CHAPTER FIVE: ANCIENT VIEWS ON MUSIC IN HEAVEN

Bunyan, John. *The Works of John Bunyan*. Edited by George Offor. London: Blackie and Son, 1853.

Crashaw, Richard. *The Complete Poetry of Richard Crashaw*. Edited by George Williams. New York: New York University Press, 1972.

Gibbon, Edward. *The History of the Decline and Fall of the Roman Empire*. Philadelphia: Henry T. Coates & Co., 1845.

Gregory of Tours. 'The Suffering and Miracles of the Martyr St. Julian.' Translated by Raymond Van Dam, in *Saints and their Miracles in late Antique Gaul*. Princeton: Princeton University Press, 1993.
Guarini, Giambattista. *The Faithful Shepherd [Il Pastor Fido]*, in *Five Italian Renaissance Comedies*. New York: Penguin Books, 1978.
Isacoff, Strart. *Temperament*. New York: Random House, 2003.
Johannes de Grocheo. *De Musica*. Translated by Albert Seay. Colorado Springs: Colorado College Music Press, 1967.
Lydgate, John. *The Life of Saint Alban and Saint Amphibal*. Edited by J. E. Van Der Westhuizen. Leiden: Brill, 1974.
Mace, Thomas. *Musick's Monument* [1676]. Paris: Editions du Centre National de la Recherche Scientifique, 1966.
Magee, Bryan. *The Philosophy of Schopenhauer*. Oxford: Clarendon Press, 1983.
Mattheson, Johann. *Behauptung der Himmlischen Musik* ... (1747).
_____. *Der vollkommene Capellmeister* (1739). Translated by Ernest Harriss. Ann Arbor: UMI Research Press, 1981.
Mills, David. *The Chester Mystery Cycle*. East Lansing: Colleagues Press, 1992.
Milton, John. *The Book of Divine Works*. Edited by Matthew Fox. Santa Fe: Bear & Company, 1987.
_____. *The Works of John Milton*. Edited by Frank Patterson. New York: Columbia University Press, 1931–1938.
Palisca, Claude V. *Humanism in Italian Renaissance Musical Thought*. New Haven: Yale University Press, 1985.
Pope, Alexander. *The Works of Alexander Pope*. New York: Gordian Press, 1967.
Purvis, J. S. *The York Cycle*. London: S.P.C.K, 1957.
Rolle, Richard. 'Of the Vertu,' in Hope Allen, ed., *English Writings of Richard Rolle*. Oxford: Clarendon Press, 1963.
_____. 'The Pricke of Conscience.' Berlin: A. Asher, 1863.
Ronsard, Pierre de. *Songs and Sonnets of Pierre de Ronsard*. Translated by Curtis Page. Westport: Hyperion Press, 1924.
Sudre, François. *The International Language of Music*. Austin: Whitwell Publications, 2012.
The Works of Voltaire. New York: St. Hubert Guild, 1901.
Thomson, James. *The Poetical Works of James Thomson*. London: Bell and Daldy, ca. 1860.
Tibullus. *Poems*.
Traherne, Thomas. *Centuries, Poems and Thanksgivings*. Oxford: Clarendon Press, 1958.
Young Edward. *Edward Young: The Complete Works*. Hildesheim: Olms, 1968.

Chapter Six: St. Augustine's Views on Music

McKinnon, James W. 'Musical Instruments in Medieval Psalm Commentaries and Psalters,' *Journal of the American Musicological Society* 21.

St. Augustine. 'Letter Nr. 100.' Translated by Sister Wilfrid Parsons in *Letters of Saint Augustine*. New York: Fathers of the Church, 1953.

____. 'Letter to Jerome,' in *Letters of Saint Augustine*. Translated by Sister Wilfrid Parsons. New York: Fathers of the Church, 1955.

____. 'Letter to Paulinus and Therasia,' in *Letters of Saint Augustine*. Translated by Sister Wilfrid Parsons. New York: Fathers of the Church, 1951.

____. 'Sermon 243.' Translated by Sister Mary Muldowney in *Sermons on the Liturgical Seasons*. New York: Fathers of the Church, 1959..

____. 'Sermon 257.' Translated by Sister Mary Muldowney in *Sermons on the Liturgical Seasons*. New York: Fathers of the Church, 1959.

____. *Against Julian*. Translated by Matthew A. Schumacher. New York: Fathers of the Church, 1957.

____. *Answer to Skeptics*. Translated by Ludwig Schopp. New York: CIMA Publishing Co.

____. *Divine Providence and the Problem of Evil*. Translated by Ludwig Schopp. New York: CIMA Publishing Co.

____. *Eighty-Three Different Questions*. Translated by David L. Mosher. Washington, D.C.: The Catholic University of America Press.

____. *On Music*. Translated by William Francis Jackson Knight. London: Orthological Institute, 1949.

____. *The City of God*. Translated by Gerald G. Walsh. New York: Fathers of the Church, 1952.

____. *The Confessions*. Translated by Edward B. Pusey. New York: Collier.

____. *The Free Choice of the Will*. Translated by Robert P. Russell. Washington, D.C.: The Catholic University of America Press.

____. *The Magnitude of the Soul*. Translated by Ludwig Schopp, in *Writings of Saint Augustine*. New York: CIMA.

____. *The Retractions*. Translated by Sister Mary Bogan. Washington, D.C.: The Catholic University of America Press.

____. *The Retractions*. Translated by Sister Mary Bogan. Washington, D.C.: The Catholic University of America Press.

____. *The Teacher*. Translated by Robert Russell. Washington, D.C.: The Catholic University of America Press.

Chapter Seven: Ancient Views on Roman Church Music During the Dark Ages

Adomnan. *Life of Columba*. Translated by Alan Anderson and Marjorie Anderson. London: Nelson.

Aurelian of Reome. *The Discipline of Music*. Translated by Joseph Ponte. Colorado Springs: Colorado College Music Press, 1968.

Bede. 'Life of St. Cuthbert,' in *Two Lives of Saint Cuthbert*. Translated by Bertram Colgrave. New York: Greenwood Press, 1969.

____. *Ecclesiastical History of England*. Translated by J. A. Giles. London: Bohn, 1849.

Boethius. *Fundamentals of Music*. Translated by Calvin Bower. New Haven: Yale University Press.

Carpenter, Nan Cooke. *Music in the Medieval and Renaissance Universities*. Norman: University of Oklahoma Press.

Cassiodorus. 'On Dialectic,' in *An Introduction to Divine and Human Readings*. Translated by Leslie Jones. New York, Octagon Books, 1966.

____. In *Variae*, Translated by Thomas Hodgkin. London: Frowde, 1886.

____. *Divine Letters*. Translated by Leslie W. Jones. New York: Octagon Books, 1966.

Chambers, E. K. *The Mediaeval Stage*. Oxford, 1903.

Clark, Kenneth. *Civilisation*. New York: Harper & Row, 1969.

Davis, H. W. C. *Medieval England*. Oxford, 1928.

Durant, Will. *The Age of Faith*. New York: Simon and Schuster, 1950.

Einhard and Notker the Stammerer. *Two Lives of Charlemagne*. Translated by Lewis Thorpe. Harmondsworth: Penguin Books, 1981.

Gibbon, Edward. *The History of the Decline and Fall of the Roman Empire*. Philadelphia: Coates.

Gregory of Tours. 'The Suffering and Miracles of the Martyr St. Julian.' Translated by Raymond Van Dam, in *Saints and their Miracles in late Antique Gaul.*. Princeton: Princeton University Press, 1993.

____. *The History of the Franks*. Translated by Lewis Thorpe. Harmondsworth: Penguin Books, 1974.

Gregory the Great. 'Dialogue Four.' Translated by Odo Zimmerman. New York: Fathers of the Church.

Hrotswitha. *The Plays of Hrotswitha of Gandersheim*. Translated by Larissa Bonfante. New York: New York University Press, 1979.

Hucbald, Guido, and John on Music. Translated by Warren Babb. New Haven: Yale University Press, 1978.

Isacoff, Stuart. *Temperament*. New York: Vintage, 2001.

Maurus, Rabanus. *The Life of Saint Mary Magdalene and of her Sister Saint Martha*. Translated by David Mycoff. Kalamazoo: Cistercian Publications, 1989.

Procopius. *The Secret History*. Harmondsworth: Penguin Books, 1981.

Salvian. *On the Government of God*. Translated by Eva Sanford. New York: Columbia University Press.

Stahl, William Harris. *Martianus Capella and the Seven Liberal Arts*. New York: Columbia University Press.
Strunk, Oliver. *Source Readings in Music History*. New York: Norton, 1950.
Veit, Gottfried. *Die Blasmusik*. Innsbruck, 1972.
Waesberghe, Joseph Smits van. *Musikerziehung, Lehre und Theorie der Musik in Mittelalter*. Leipzig: VEB Deutscher Verlag für Musik.

Chapter Eight: Ancient Views on Roman Church Music during the Pre-Renaissance

Appleby, John T., ed. *The Chronicle of Richard of Devizes*. London, 1963.
Bernard of Clairvaux. 'De Revisione Cantus Cistercienis.' Translated by Francisco Guentner. American Institute of Musicology, 1974.
Bingen, Hildegard. *The Book of Divine Works*. Edited by Matthew Fox. Santa Fe: Bear & Company, 1987.
Bowie, Fiona and Oliver Daview, eds. *Hildegard of Bingen*. New York: Crossroad, 1993.
Brettenson, Henry, ed. *Documents of the Christian Church*. Oxford: Oxford University Press, 1963.
Chambers, E. K. *The Mediaeval Stage*. Oxford, 1903.
Chronicles of the Crusades. London: Bell and Sons, 1914.
Dillon, E. *Glass*. New York, 1907.
Durant, Will. *The Age of Faith*. New York: Simon and Schuster, 1950.
Farmer, Henry G. 'Crusading Martial Music,' *Music & Letters* 30, no. 3 (July 1949): 243–249.
Goldron, Romain. *Minstrels and Masters*. H. S. Stuttman.
Grove, George. *The New Grove Dictionary of Music and Musicians*. Edited by Stanley Sadie. London: Macmillan, 1980.
Isacoff, Stuart. *Temperament*. New York: Random House, 2003.
'Joinville's Chronicle of the Crusade of St. Lewis,' in *Memoirs of the Crusades*. Translated by Frank Marzials. London: J. M. Dent, 1926.
Koenig, V. R., ed. *Les Miracles de Nostre Dame par Gautier de Coinci*. Geneva, 1955–1970.
Page, Christopher. *Voices and Instruments of the Middle Ages*. London: Dent, 1987.
Paris, Matthew. *English History*. Translated by J. A. Giles. London: Bohn, 1852.
Rastall, Richard, 'Some English Consort-Groupings of the late Middle Ages.' *Music & Letters* 55, no. 2 (April 1974): 179–202.
Rubenstein, Richard. *Aristotle's Children*. Orlando: Harcourt, 2003.
The Letters of Abelard and Heloise. Translated by C. K. Scott Moncrieff. New York: Knopf, 1933.
The Letters of St. Bernard of Clairvaux. Translated by Bruno James. Chicago: Regnery, 1953.
Vessella, Alessandro. *La Banda*. Milan, 1935.
Vinsauf, Goeffrey, de. *Chronicle of Richard the First's Crusade [1191]*. London, 1914.

Vitalis, Ordericus. *The Ecclesiastical History of England*. Translated by Thomas Forester. London: Henry G. Bohn, 1854.

____. *The Ecclesiastical History of England*. Translated by Marjorie Chibnall. Oxford: Clarendon Press, 1978.

Walsh, Kilian. *The Works of Bernard of Clairvux*. Spencer, MA: Cistercian Publications, 1971.

Zamore, Gilles de. 'Ars Musica,' in Martin Gerbert, *Scriptores ecclesiastici de musica sacra*. Saint Blaise, 1784.

CHAPTER NINE: ST. THOMAS ACQUINAS ON MUSIC

Acquinas, Thomas. 'On Kingship to the King of Cyprus. Translated by Gerald Phelan. Toronto: The Pontifical Institute of Mediaeval Studies, 1949.

____. *Commentary on Aristotle's Physics*. Translated by Richard Blackwell. New Haven: Yale University Press, 1963.

____. *Commentary on Peri Hermeneias*. Translated by Jean Oesterle. Milwaukee: Marquette University Press, 1962.

____. *Commentary on the Metaphysics of Aristotle*. Translated by John Rowan. Chicago: Henry Regnery, 1961.

____. *Disputations*, IV de Veritate, 1, quoted in *Theological Texts*. Translated by Thomas Gilby. London: Oxford University Press, 1955.

____. *Selected Writings of St. Thomas Aquinas*. Edited by M. C. D'Arcy. New York: Dutton, 1950.

____. *Summa Contra Gentiles*. London, Burns Oates & Washbourne.

____. *Summa Theologiae*. London: Blackfriars

Anderson, James F. *An Introduction to the Metaphysics of St. Thomas Aquinas*. Chicago: Henry Regnery, 1953.

Durant, Will. *The Age of Faith*. New York: Simon and Schuster, 1950.

CHAPTER TEN: ANCIENT VIEWS ON ROMAN CHURCH MUSIC OF THE 14TH CENTURY

Boccaccio. *The Decameron*. Translated by Mark Musa and Peter Bondanella. New York: Norton, 1977.

Duncan, Edmonstoune. *The Story of Minstrelsy*. Detroit, 1968.

Gower, John. *The Voice of One Crying*. Translated by Eric Stockton, in *The Major Latin Works of John Gower*. Seattle: University of Washington Press, 1962.

Grocheo, Johannes de. *De Musica*. Translated by Albert Seay. Colorado Springs: Colorado College Music Press, 1967.

Isacoff, Stuart. *Temperament*. New York: Vintage, 2001.

Langland, William. *Piers Plowman*. Translated by E. Talbot Donaldson.. New York: Norton, 1990.

LaRue, Jan, ed. *Aspects of Medieval and Renaissance Music*. New York: Norton, 1966.

Machaut, Guillaume de, *Oeuvres*. Edited by Ernest Hoepffner. Paris, 1908–21.
Pirrotta, Nino and Elena Povoledo. *Music and Theatre from Poliziano to Monteverdi*. Cambridge: Cambridge University Press, 1982.
Pirrotta, Nino. 'Ars Nova and Stil Novo,' in *Music and Culture in Italy from the Middle Ages to the Baroque*. Cambridge: Harvard University Press, 1984.
Sisam, Celia and Kenneth, eds. *The Oxford Book of Medieval English Verse*. Oxford: Clarendon Press, 1970.
Stinger, Charles. *Humanism and the Church Fathers*. Albany: State University of New York Press, 1977.
Strunk, Oliver. *Source Readings in Music History*. New York: Norton, 1950.
Symonds, John Addington. *Renaissance in Italy*. New York: Holt, 1881.
Wooldridge, H. E. *The Oxford History of Music*, 2nd edition. London, 1929.

CHAPTER ELEVEN: ANCIENT VIEWS ON ROMAN CHURCH MUSIC OF THE 15TH CENTURY

Baines, Anthony, 'Fifteenth-century Instruments in Tinctoris's *De Inventine et Usu Musicae*,' *The Galpin Society Journal* 3 (March 1950): 19–26.
Brant, Sebastian. *The Ship of Fools*. Translated by Edwin Zeydel. New York: Columbia University Press, 1944.
Buck, M.R., ed. *Ulrichs von Richental Chronik des Constanzer Conzils* (Tublingen, 1882.
Carpenter, Nan Cooke. *Music in the Medieval and Renaissance Universities*. Norman: University of Oklahoma Press, 1958.
Dahnk, E. 'Musikausubung an den Hofen von Burgund und Orleans wahrend des 15. Jahrhunderts,' in *Archiv fur Kulturgeschichte* (1934–1936).
D'Amico, John. *Renaissance Humanism in Papal Rome*. Baltimore: Johns Hopkins University Press,1983.
Federhofer, H. 'Beitrage zur altern Musikgeschichte Karntens,' in *Carinthia* (1955), CXLV.
Fenlon, Iain, ed. *Music in Medieval and Early Modern Europe*. Cambridge: Cambridge University Press, 1981.
Fester, R. 'Die Fortsetzung der Flores temporum von Reinbold Slecht,' in *Zeitschrift fur die Geschichte des Oberrheins* (1894).
Gafurius. *The Practica musicae of Franchinus Gafurius*. Translated by Irwin Young. Madison: University of Wisconsin Press, 1969).
Gerson, Jean de. 'Tractatus de Canticis.' Translated by Christopher Page, in 'Early 15th-century instruments in Jean de Gerson's *Tractatus de Canticis*,' *Early Music* 6, no. 3 (1978): 339–349.
Grove, George. *The New Grove Dictionary of Music and Musicians*. London: Macmillan, 1980.
Hayes, Gerald. 'Musical Instruments,' in *New Oxford History of Music*. London, 1960.
Henderson, Ernest. *A Short History of Germany*. New York, 1916.
Henne, A. *Die Klingenberger Chronik*. Gotha, 1861.

Isacoff, Stuart. *Temperament*. New York: Vintage, 2001.

Jacquot, Jean. *La Musique Instrumental de la Renaissance*. Paris, 1955.

Kinkeldey, O. *Orgel und Klavier in der Musik des 16. Jahrhunderts*. Leipzig, 1910.

La Marche, Olivier de. *Mémoires d'Olivier de La Marche*. Paris, 1785.

Larner, John. *Culture and Society in Italy, 1290–1420*. New York: Scribner's, 1971.

Nedden, O. *Quellen und Studien zur oberrheinischen Musikgeschichte im 15. und 16 Jahrhundert*. Kassel, 1931.

Pirrotta, Nino and Elena Povoledo. *Music and Theatre from Poliziano to Monteverdi*. Cambridge: Cambridge University Press, 1982.

Pirrotta, Nino. *Music and Culture in Italy from the Middle Ages to the Baroque*. Cambridge: Harvard University Press, 1984.

Polk, Keith. 'Ensemble Instrumental Music in Flanders: 1450–1550' [Unpublished].

Prizer, William. 'Music and Ceremonial in the Low Countries,' in *Early Music History* 5 (1985): 113–153.

Reese, Gustave. *Music in the Renaissance*. New York: Norton, 1959.

Richental, Ulrichs von. *Das Konzil zu Konstanz*. Konstanz, 1964.

Riegel, J. *Die Teilnuhmerlisten Konstanzer Konzils*. Freiburg, 1916.

Salmen, Walter. *Musikleben im 16. Jahrhundert*. Leipzig: Deurscher Verlag für Musik VEB, 1976.

Schuler, M. 'Die Musik in Konstanz wehrend des Konzils 1414–1418,' in *Acta Musicologica* (1966).

Simons, Eric. *The Reign of Edward IV*. London, 1966.

Stinger, Charles. *The Renaissance in Rome*. Bloomington: Indiana University Press, 1985.

Symonds, John Addington. *Renaissance in Italy*. New York: Capricorn Books, 1964.

Wangerme. *Flemish Music*. New York, 1968.

Wright, Craig. 'Performance Practices at the Cathedral of Cambrai 1475–1550,' *The Musical Quarterly* 64, no. 3 (July 1978): 295–328.

Wylie, J. H. *History of England under Henry the Fourth*. London, 1884.

Zabern, Conrad von. *Singing with Proper Refinement*. Translated by Joseph Dyer in *Early Music* 6, no. 2 (April, 1978): 207–229.

Chapter Twelve: Ancient Views on Church Music of the 16th Century

Aber, A. *Die Pflege der Musik unter den Wettinern und Wettinischen Ernestinern Von den Anfangen bis zur Auflosung der Weimarer Hofkapelle 1662*. Buckeburg, 1921.

Agrippa, Henry Cornelius. *Of the Vanitie and Uncertaintie of Arts and Sciences*. Edited by Catherine Dunn. Northridge: California State University, Northridge Press, 1974.

Arnold, Denis, 'Brass Instruments in the Italian Church Music of the Sixteenth and Early Seventeenth Centuries,' in *Brass Quarterly* (1957).

Blunt, Anthony. *Artistic Theory in Italy, 1450–1600*. Oxford: Clarendon Press, 1959.

Bossert, G. 'Die Hofhantorei unter Herzog Christof,' in *Württembergische Vierteljahresheftes für Landesgeschichte* (1898).

Bottrigari, Hercole. *Il Desiderio*. Translated by Carol MacClintock. American Institute of Musicology, 1962.

Brenet, M. 'Notes sur l'introduction des instruments dans les eglises de France,' in *Riemann-Festschrift*. Leipzig, 1909.

Bruno, Giordano. *Cause, Principle and Unity*. Translated by Jack Lindsay. New York: International Publishers, 1962.

Buszin, Walter. 'Luther on Music,' *The Musical Quarterly* 32, no. 1 (January, 1946): 80–97.

Cervantes, Miguel de. *The Jealous Hidalgo*. Translated by Harriet de On's, in *Six Exemplary Novels*. Great Neck: Barron's Educational Series, 1961.

Chambers, Frank. *The History of Taste*. New York: Columbia University Press, 1932.

Coclico, Adrian. *Musical Compendium*. Translated by Albert Seay. Colorado Springs: Colorado College Music Press, 1973

Duncan, Edmondstoune. *The Story of Minstrelsy*. London, 1968.

Ehmann. *Tibilustrium*. Kassel, 1950.

Galilei, Vincenzo. *Fronimo* [1584]. Translated by Carol MacClintock. Neuhasen-Stuttgart: Hanssler-Verlag, 1985.

Giustiniani, Vicenzo. *Discorso sopra la Musica* [1628]. Translated by Carol MacClintock. American Institute of Musicology, 1962.

Glarean. *Dodecachordon*. Translated by Clement Miller. American Institute of Musicology, 1965.

Grove, George. *The New Grove Dictionary of Music and Musicians*. London: Macmillan, 1980.

Guzman, J. A. 'Mexico, Home of the First Musical Instrument Workshops in America,' *Early Music* 6, no. 3 (1978): 350–355.

Harrison, G., ed. *The Elizabethan Journals*. New York: MacMillian.

Isacoff, Stuart. *Temperament*. New York: Vintage, 2001.

Jackson, Samuel. *Huldreich Zwingli*. New York: Putham, 1901.

Janssen, Johannes. *History of the German People After the Close of the Middle Ages*. Translated by A. Christie. New York, 1966.

Listenius, Nicolaus. *Musica*. Translated by Albert Seay. Colorado Springs: Colorado College Music Press, 1975.

Machiavelli, the Chief Works. Translated by Allan Gilbert. Durham: Duke University Press, 1965.

Mattheson, Johann. *Der vollkommene Capellmeister* [1739]. Translated by Ernest Harriss. Ann Arbor: UMI Research Press, 1981.

Miller, Clement A. 'Erasmus on Music,' *The Musical Quarterly* 52, no. 3 (July, 1966): 332–349.

Morley, Thomas. *A Plain and Easy Introduction to Practical Music*. 1597.

Motley, John. *The Rise of the Dutch Republic*. New York.

Ornithoparchus. *Musicae active micrologus* and Dowland, *Introduction: Containing the Art of Singing*. New York: Dover, 1973.
Paule, G. *The Life of the most reverend and religious prelate John Whitgift Lord Archbishop of Canterbury*. London, 1612.
Pietzsch, G. 'Beschreibungen deutscher Fürstenhochzeiten von der Mitte des 15. bis zum Beginn des 17. Jahrhunderts als musikgeschichtliche quellen,' in *Anuario Musical* (1960).
Russell, Joycelyne. *The Field of Cloth of Gold*. New York, 1938.
Rye, William, ed. *England as seen by Foreigners*. New York: Blom.
Salmen, Walter. *Musikleben im 16. Jahrhundert*. Leipzig, 1976.
Senn, Walter. *Musik und Theater am Hof zu Innsbruck*. Innsbruck, 1954.
Sittard, Josef. *Geschichte der Musik und des Theaters am Württembergischen hofe*. Stuttgart, 1890.
Stevenson, Robert. *Spanish Cathedral Music in the Golden Age*. Berkeley, 1961.
Stinger, Charles. *The Renaissance in Rome*. Bloomington: Indiana University Press, 1985.
Strunk, Oliver. *Source Readings in Music History*. New York: Norton, 1950.
Suppan, Wolfgang. *Lexikon des Blasmusikwesens*. Freiburg.
The Works of Mr. Richard Hooker. Oxford: Clarendon Press.
Vale, G. 'La Capella Musicale dl Duomo di udine dal Secolo XIII al XIX,' in *Note d'Archivio* (1930).
Van Dyke, Paul. *Catherine de Medicis*. New York, 1922.
Werner, Arno. *Vier Jahrhunderte im Dienste der Kirchenmusik*. Leipzig: Merseburger.
Wright, Craig. 'Performance Practices at the Cathedral of Cambrai 1475–1550,' *The Musical Quarterly* 64, no. 3 (July 1978): 295–328.
Zarlino, Gioseffo. *The Art of Counterpoint*. Translated by Guy Marco and Claude Palisca. New Haven: Yale University Press, 1968.

CHAPTER THIRTEEN: MARTIN LUTHER ON MUSIC

Buszin, Walter. 'Luther on Music,' *The Musical Quarterly* 32, no. 1 (January, 1946): 80–97.
Luther's Works. St. Louis: Concordia, 1961.

CHAPTER FOURTEEN: PRAETORIUS ON 16TH CENTURY PERFORMANCE PRACTICE

Praetorius, Michael. *Syntagma Musicum*, III. Kassel: Bärenreiter, 1958.

CHAPTER FIFTEEN: ANCIENT VIEWS ON CHURCH MUSIC IN THE BAROQUE

Archivio di Stato, Venice, Ospitali, busta 692, Notatorio Q, fol. 113r.
Arnold, Denis. 'Music at the Scuola de San Rocco,' in *Music and Letters* 40 (July, 1959): 229–241.
Barwick, Steven. 'Mexico,' in *The Early Baroque Era*. Englewood Cliffs: Prentice Hall, 1994.

Benoit, Marcelle. In 'Paris, 1661–87: the Age of Lully,' in *The Early Baroque Era*. Englewood Cliffs: Prentice Hall, 1994.

Bianconi, Lorenzo. *Music in the Seventeenth Century*. Translated by David Bryant. Cambridge: Cambridge University Press, 1987.

Brosses, Charles. *Lettres familieres sur l'Italie*. Paris, 1931.

Buelow, George J. 'Hamburg and Lubeck,' in *The Late Baroque Era*. Englewood Cliffs: Prentice Hall, 1994.

Bunyan, John. *The Works of John Bunyan*. Edited by George Offor. London: Blackie and Son, 1853.

Butler, Charles. *Principles of Musick* (1636).

David, Hans T. and Arthur Mendel. *The Bach Reader*. New York: Norton, 1966.

Defoe, Daniel. *Robinson Crusoe*. Garden City: Doubleday, n.d.

Donnington, Robert. *The Interpretation of Early Music*. New York, 1964.

Earle, John. *Microcosmography* [1628] St. Clair Shores: Scholarly Press, 1971.

Ehmann, Wilhelm. *Tibilustrium*. Kassel, 1950.

Freschot, C. *Nouvelle relation de Venise*. Utrecht, 1709.

Grove, George. *The New Grove Dictionary of Music and Musicians*. London: Macmillan, 1980.

Holman, Peter. In 'London: Commonwealth and Restoration,' in *The Early Baroque Era*. Englewood Cliffs: Prentice Hall, 1994.

Isacoff, Stuart. *Temperament*. New York: Vintage, 2001.

Kenton, Egon. *Life and Works of Giovanni Gabrieli*. American Institute of Musicology, 1967.

Kolneder, W. *Antonio Vivaldi, his life and work*. London, 1756.

MacClintock, Carol. *Readings in the History of Music in Performance*. Bloomington: Indiana University Press, 1979.

Mace, Thomas. *Musick's Monument* [1676]. Paris: Editions du Centre National de la Recherche Scientifique, 1966.

Martin, L. C. *The Poetical Works of Robert Herrick*. Oxford: Clarendon Press, 1963.

Mattheson, Johann. *Der vollkommene Capellmeister* (1739). Translated by Ernest Harriss. Ann Arbor: UMI Research Press, 1981.

_____. *Der musicalische Patriot*.

Milton, John. *The Works of John Milton*. Edited by Frank Patterson. New York: Columbia University Press, 1931–1938.

Moser, Hans. *Heinrich Schütz*. St. Louis: Concordia, 1936.

Norman, Gertrude and Miriam Shrifte. *Letters of Composers* New York, Knopf, 1946.

Orléans, Charlotte Elisabeth. *A Woman's Life in the Court of the Sun King*. Baltimore: Johns Hopkins University Press, 1997.

Penn, William. *The Select Works of William Penn*. London: William Phillips, 1825.

Pincherle, Marc. 'Vivaldi and the *Ospitali* of Venice,' *The Musical Quarterly* 24 (July, 1938): 300–312.

Poellnitz, K. L. *Memoirs*. London, 1737.

Rousseau, Jean-Jacques. *Confessions.*
Smart, Peter. *A Sermon Preached in the Cathedrall Church of Durham, July 7, 1628.* London, 1640.
Strunk, Oliver. *Source Readings in Music History.* New York: Norton, 1950.
Tosi, Pier Francesco. *Opinioni de' cantori antichi, e moderni.* Bologna, 1723.
Vander Straeten, Edmond. *La Musique aux Pays-Bas.* New York, 1969.
Voltaire. *The Works of Voltaire.* New York: St. Hubert Guild, 1901.
Weiss, Piero. *Letters of Composers Through Six Centuries.* Philadelphia: Chilton, 1967.
Werner, A. *Stadtische und fürstliche Musikpflege in Weissenfels.* Leipzig, 1911.
Wilson, John. *Roger North on Music.* London: Novello, 1959.

About the Author

Dr. David Whitwell is a graduate ('with distinction') of the University of Michigan and the Catholic University of America, Washington DC (PhD, Musicology, Distinguished Alumni Award, 2000) and has studied conducting with Eugene Ormandy and at the Akademie für Musik, Vienna. Prior to coming to Northridge, Dr. Whitwell participated in concerts throughout the United States and Asia as Associate First Horn in the USAF Band and Orchestra in Washington DC, and in recitals throughout South America in cooperation with the United States State Department.

At the California State University, Northridge, which is in Los Angeles, Dr. Whitwell developed the CSUN Wind Ensemble into an ensemble of international reputation, with international tours to Europe in 1981 and 1989 and to Japan in 1984. The CSUN Wind Ensemble has made professional studio recordings for BBC (London), the Köln Westdeutscher Rundfunk (Germany), NOS National Radio (The Netherlands), Zürich Radio (Switzerland), the Television Broadcasting System (Japan) as well as for the United States State Department for broadcast on its 'Voice of America' program. The CSUN Wind Ensemble's recording with the Mirecourt Trio in 1982 was named the 'Record of the Year' by The Village Voice. Composers who have guest conducted Whitwell's ensembles include Aaron Copland, Ernest Krenek, Alan Hovhaness, Morton Gould, Karel Husa, Frank Erickson and Vaclav Nelhybel.

Dr. Whitwell has been a guest professor in 100 different universities and conservatories throughout the United States and in 23 foreign countries (most recently in China, in an elite school housed in the Forbidden City). Guest conducting experiences have included the Philadelphia Orchestra, Seattle Symphony Orchestra, the Czech Radio Orchestras of Brno and Bratislava, The National Youth Orchestra of Israel, as well as resident wind ensembles in Russia, Israel, Austria, Switzerland, Germany, England, Wales, The Netherlands, Portugal, Peru, Korea, Japan, Taiwan, Canada and the United States.

He is a past president of the College Band Directors National Association, a member of the Prasidium of the International Society for the Promotion of Band Music, and was a member of the founding board of directors of the World Association for Symphonic Bands and Ensembles (WASBE). In 1964 he was made an honorary life member of Kappa Kappa Psi, a national professional music fraternity. In September, 2001, he was a delegate to the UNESCO Conference on Global Music in Tokyo. He has been knighted by sovereign organizations in France, Portugal and Scotland and has been awarded the gold medal of Kerkrade, The Netherlands, and the silver medal of Wangen, Germany, the highest honor given wind conductors in the United States, the medal of the Academy of Wind and Percussion Arts (National Band Association) and the highest honor given wind conductors in Austria, the gold medal of the Austrian Band Association. He is a member of the Hall of Fame of the California Music Educators Association.

Dr. Whitwell's publications include more than 127 articles on wind literature including publications in Music and Letters (London), the London Musical Times, the Mozart-Jahrbuch (Salzburg), and 47 books, among which is his 13-volume *History and Literature of the Wind Band and Wind Ensemble* and an 8-volume series on *Aesthetics in Music*. In addition to numerous modern editions of early wind band music his original compositions include 3 symphonies.

David Whitwell was named as one of six men who have determined the course of American bands during the second half of the 20th century, in the definitive history, *The Twentieth Century American Wind Band* (Meredith Music).

A doctoral dissertation by German Gonzales (2007, Arizona State University) is dedicated to the life and conducting career of David Whitwell through the year 1977. David Whitwell is one of nine men described by Paula A. Crider in *The Conductor's Legacy* (Chicago: GIA, 2010) as 'the legendary conductors' of the 20th century.

'I can't imagine the 2nd half of the 20th century—without David Whitwell and what he has given to all of the rest of us.' Frederick Fennell (1993)

About the Editor

CRAIG DABELSTEIN began studying the piano at age seven and took up the saxophone at age twelve. Mr Dabelstein has Bachelor of Arts (Music) and Bachelor of Music degrees from the Queensland Conservatorium of Music, where he majored in the performance of classical saxophone repertoire. He also has a Graduate Diploma of Learning and Teaching and a Graduate Certificate in Editing and Publishing from the University of Southern Queensland.

He has held the principal alto and tenor saxophone chairs in the Australian Wind Orchestra and has been an augmenting member of the Queensland Philharmonic Orchestra, the Queensland Symphony Orchestra, and the Queensland Pops Orchestra. For many years he was also a member of the Queensland Saxophone Quartet.

He has been a casual conductor of the Young Conservatorium Symphonic Winds, and has previously been a saxophone teacher at the Queensland Conservatorium of Music. He is a regular conductor of the Queensland Wind Orchestra, having served as their artistic director and chief conductor from 2004 to 2009.

Craig Dabelstein is a research associate for the *Teaching Music Through Performance in Band* series of books, contributing analyses to volumes 7, 8, 1 (rev. edn), and the *Solos with Wind Band Accompaniment* volume. He served as the copyeditor and layout designer of the *Australian Clarinet and Saxophone Magazine* from 2007 to 2009 and he has written many CD and book reviews for *Music Forum* magazine. He is the editor of the second editions of the books by Dr. David Whitwell including *A Concise History of the Wind Band*, *Foundations of Music Education*, *Music Education of the Future*, *The Sousa Oral History Project*, *Wagner on Bands*, *Berlioz on Bands*, *The Art of Musical Conducting*, and the *Aesthetics of Music* series (8 volumes) and *The History and Literature of the Wind Band and Wind Ensemble* series (13 volumes). From 1994 to 2012 he was a staff member at Brisbane Girls Grammar School. He now teaches woodwinds and conducts bands at St. Joseph's College, Gregory Terrace, Brisbane, Australia.

www.ingramcontent.com/pod-product-compliance
Lightning Source LLC
Chambersburg PA
CBHW081348230426
43667CB00017B/2763